ROYAL GRAMMAR SCHOOL
NEWCASTLE UPON TYNE

ROYAL GRAMMAR SCHOOL
SCHOOL

NEWCASTLE UPON TYNE

A History of the School in its Community

Edited by
BRIAN MAINS & ANTHONY TUCK

ORIEL PRESS

STOCKSFIELD

BOSTON ☆ HENLEY ☆ LONDON

© *The Royal Grammar School,*
Newcastle upon Tyne 1986

First published in 1986
by Oriel Press Limited
Stocksfield, Northumberland,
England, NE43 7NA.
14 Leicester Square,
London WC2H 7PH.
3 Park Street, Boston,
Mass. 02108, U.S.A.

Set in Times New Roman and
printed by Hindson & Co. Ltd.,
Newcastle upon Tyne

Colour separation for the jacket by
Philipson Burrill Limited
Newcastle upon Tyne

ISBN 0 85362 224 8

Contents

Page

Acknowledgements

The editors and contributors have incurred many debts of gratitude in the preparation of this volume. In particular they wish to thank the Governors of the Royal Grammar School for their support of the project and for agreeing to underwrite the costs of publication. They have received much encouragement and helpful advice from the Headmaster and from the Second Master, Mr J. C. Nichols, both of whom have read the text in its entirety and made many useful suggestions. The editors also wish to express their appreciation of the time and effort given by Mrs Margaret Heslop and Miss Elaine Dodds at Collingwood College Durham, and Miss S. Ellis and Mrs S. F. Henderson at the Royal Grammar School in typing a substantial part of the manuscript. The editors and contributors have been helped by a number of individuals who have willingly answered questions about source material, in particular Lady Margaret Sutherland, Mr Ioan Thomas, and Mr J. Gofton, formerly Clerk to the Trustees of the Hospital of St Mary the Virgin, Newcastle upon Tyne; and they have also received much help from the staff of libraries and archives on Tyneside and further afield, notably the Newcastle City Library, Tyne and Wear Archives Department, the Public Record Office, and Cambridge University Library. The editors are grateful to Mr John Farthing for transmitting the plan of the Rye Hill School and for drawing the plan of the Eskdale Terrace School; to Mr G. T. Relf for drawing the map of the School's various sites; to the City of London School for providing copies of material in their possession relating to Dr Mortimer and for granting permission to reproduce his portrait in plate X; and to the Department of Education in the University of Newcastle upon Tyne for extending facilities to Dr Mains during his sabbatical term in 1983. Finally, both editors and contibutors wish to thank Mr S. J. W. Squires for reading the proofs.

B. M.
J. A. T.
October 1985

Notes on Contributors

Alister Cox has been Headmaster of the Royal Grammar School since 1972.

Stanley Dennison has been Chairman of the Governors of the Royal Grammar School since 1969. He held the David Dale Chair of Economics at the University of Newcastle upon Tyne from 1962 until 1972, and from 1972 to 1979 was Vice-Chancellor of the University of Hull.

Roger Hennessey was a member of staff at the Royal Grammar School from 1962 to 1973 during which time he established the Economics Department. He was also the first member of the staff to organise the School archives on a systematic basis. Since 1973 he has been one of Her Majesty's Inspectors of Schools.

Gordon Hogg has been a lecturer in the School of Education, University of Newcastle upon Tyne since 1968 and has specialised in the History of Education in England.

William Lough was a pupil at the Royal Grammar School from 1922 to 1933, and returned as a member of staff from 1936 to 1939, teaching modern languages.

Brian Mains was appointed to the staff of the History Department at the Royal Grammar School in 1976. He also has responsibility for the School archives.

Donald Shipley joined the Classics Department at the Royal Grammar School in 1952 and was Head of Department from 1960 to 1983. He was General Secretary of the Old Novocastrians Association from 1978 to 1983.

Anthony Tuck was a pupil at the Royal Grammar School from 1948 to 1959. Since 1978 he has been Master of Collingwood College and lecturer in History, University of Durham.

John Tuck was a Governor of the Royal Grammar School from 1954 until 1976, and held the Chair of Education in King's College and the University of Newcastle upon Tyne from 1948 until 1976.

Richard Tuck was a pupil at the Royal Grammar School from 1956 until 1966. He is now a Fellow of Jesus College Cambridge and University lecturer in History.

Margaret Wilkinson completed a Ph.D. thesis for the University of Newcastle upon Tyne on *Educational Controversies in British Politics 1895–1914* in 1978. She is Deputy Headmistress of Durham High School for Girls.

Introduction

To entrust the history of a single institution to more than half a dozen different hands may seem not only extravagant but also destructive of the unity of theme and treatment appropriate to the history of a school which traces its origins to the sixteenth century. One of the principal justifications for a co-operative history of the kind which we have attempted is, however, to be found in the substantial discontinuities which have characterised the history of the Royal Grammar School over the four and a half centuries of its existence. As Richard Tuck shows in the opening chapter, and as the celebrations of the School's quatercentenary twice in this century, in 1925 and 1945, bear witness, the origins of the school are hard to identify with any precision or clarity. Its formal foundation was accomplished by charter of Queen Elizabeth I in 1600, and over the next fifty years it rose rapidly to a position of some national significance, particularly in curricular innovation during the Commonwealth; but in the latter half of the seventeenth century and the early eighteenth century it enjoyed a much less impressive history. In the second half of the eighteenth century the School experienced something of a renaissance under two distinguished Headmasters, one of whom was remembered with affection by some equally distinguished former pupils and both of whom played an important part in that efflorescence of cultural and scientific life in Newcastle between 1750 and 1820 which has yet to find its historian. But in the nineteenth century, as Dr Mains shows, the School faced serious difficulties over its place in the developing industrial community of Tyneside, over finance, curriculum and staffing; it suffered competition from other schools in the town, and failed to reap all the expected benefits from its move to palatial new buildings in Rye Hill. The links between the School and the Corporation of Newcastle, which had been close, if not always easy, since earliest times were broken in 1888 when the School was reconstituted with its own Governors, free of control by the city, and from that time onwards the progress of the School came to depend increasingly on its relationship with national government as government formed and implemented a national policy for secondary education. The development of a system for grant aiding secondary schools, together with the opening at much the same time of the School's new buildings in Jesmond, transformed its prospects and laid the foundations of its twentieth century success. The institutional links between the School and the city now became tenuous, and the School became part of that group of schools grant-aided by central government which from 1926 onwards may be described as direct grant schools. Thus for the twentieth century the impact of national educational policy is of greater significance for the development of the School than the policies of the local education authorities of Tyneside, though the relationship with the Newcastle Education Committee over the question of free places in the School is a subsidiary theme of some importance from the 1920s to the 1960s. The phasing out of direct grant in the late 1970s brought about another change in the status of the School and its links with central government, for the Assisted Places Scheme rests on rather different regulations from those which governed the direct grant system. It is too soon to assess the significance of this latest change in the School's constitution, but it provides one more instance of discontinuity in its history.

Even the School's present name is not securely established before the twentieth century. The charter of 1600 provides that the School should be known as Queen Elizabeth's Grammar School; for much of the seventeenth and eighteenth centuries it was known as the Newcastle Free School, or simply as the Grammar School, a name which was in familiar use in the later nineteenth century. Only with the establishment of other grammar schools in Newcastle did it become necessary to distinguish the city's ancient foundation from its more recent ones, and by the turn of the century the School was generally known as the Royal Grammar School. The gates of the building in Eskdale Terrace, which dates from 1906, carry that name, and since then Royal Grammar School has been both the formal and the familiar name of the School.

The School's history thus falls into a number of distinct phases, and in this book each of these phases is dealt with by a different historian. All contributors, however, have borne in mind the need to relate the history of the School both to the local community and, where appropriate, to the educational history of the nation. All contributors have also taken account of two themes which are relevant to the School throughout its history: the connection between the School and the medieval foundation of the Hospital of St Mary the Virgin, and the continuous physical presence of the School within the boundaries of Newcastle upon Tyne, albeit in five different homes. The presence of the School in the city, and its close links with the city's governing body until 1888, have given it a history which is different from, and in many respects more complex and less self-contained than, the history of many schools established in less populous areas as independent foundations without links to a municipality.

The history of a school, however, can be written in too abstract a manner. When its constitution, its finances, its social character and its relationship with local and national government have been analysed there remains as an important part of its history some account of the pupils and staff who have worked there and of the life of the school both inside and outside the classroom. A. R. Laws's *Schola Novocastrensis*, published in 1925, embodied a biographical approach to the School's history and it contains much valuable information not only about the early history of the School but also about the Headmasters and pupils from earliest times to the mid-nineteenth century. It is unfortunate that the third volume of his work, which would have brought the history of the school into the twentieth century, was never published. Chapter VIII of this book is intended to complement the earlier chapters by presenting impressions of the School through the eyes of some who taught there or were pupils there. Similar accounts of the School in Rye Hill days and in its early years at Jesmond have been published from time to time in the *Novo*; the intention here is to offer personal accounts of more recent times, which will still be familiar to many readers.

It should finally be noted that the source material for the history of the School is of sharply varying quantity and quality. For the late seventeenth and early eighteenth centuries the material is so sparse that a connected history of the School at that time is almost impossible to write. The archives of the School itself contain little material of any kind earlier than the last quarter of the nineteenth century, and little systematic documentation of any kind until recent decades. Even for the twentieth century there are major gaps in the evidence, the most serious being the loss of the Governors' Minutes for the years between 1922 and 1934. Very little private correspondence survives, apart from letters relating to individual pupils, which, as a deliberate policy decision, have not been used. Another difficulty facing contributors is the lack of a detailed and scholarly history of Newcastle, and several of the contributors have been breaking new ground in the history of the city as well as the history of the School. Furthermore, the Public Record Office files of correspondence relating to the school, which

Margaret Wilkinson and Anthony Tuck have exploited in their discussion of the period from 1888 to 1945, are closed from the mid-1950s onwards under the thirty year rule. It is partly for this reason, and partly because of the obvious difficulties of writing about recent events in other than an impressionistic manner, that the editors have decided not to continue the detailed history of the School beyond 1960, though Stanley Dennison describes the difficulties that the School faced in the 1970s when the direct grant system was wound up, and provides an analysis of the concluding years of that phase in the School's history.

Chapter I

CIVIL CONFLICT IN SCHOOL AND TOWN 1500–1700

Newcastle belonged to a group of East coast ports which prospered from the thirteenth century onwards on the basis of England's military and commercial activity overseas and in Scotland. Like the others (notably Hull and King's Lynn), Newcastle had as a consequence extremely inadequate ecclesiastical institutions compared with older established centres of population: none were cathedral cities, and they had few parish churches or well-endowed monasteries. Newcastle had only four churches, three of which were mere chapels-of-ease to the mother church of St Nicholas, and before the Reformation it contained only a small nunnery, a couple of hospitals (one of which after the Reformation was the wealthiest ecclesiastical institution in the city, apart from the Vicarage itself), a chapel on Tyne Bridge, and the friaries characteristic of a late-medieval trading centre.

The inadequacy of separately-endowed religious and charitable institutions in these cities meant that in all of them the burgesses themselves had in various ways to organise and pay for the charities which were even more necessary in large mercantile communities than in other kinds of town, among them, of course, education. The burgesses of Newcastle gradually took control of almost all the religious life of the city and guaranteed its finances: the curates of the three chapels seem to have been paid by the Common Council of the city from at least the late sixteenth century, while in the seventeenth century it also paid a large component of the stipend of the Vicar himself (though presentation to the living always remained in the hands of the Bishop of Carlisle).[1] In the late middle ages the mayor and burgesses had acted as trustees for many of the chantries in the four churches; the chapel on the bridge was always managed by the city, while the hospital of St Mary in the Westgate (commonly known as the Virgin Mary Hospital), the major ecclesiastical foundation, was the meeting-place for the town's guild in the fourteenth century and remained the place where the election of the mayor and Common Council took place down to 1844. The town's 'hutch' or treasury stood there, and the archives of the hospital were stored in it and wholly confused with the town's own papers. At the beginning of the sixteenth century the mayor and burgesses acquired the right to appoint its master, replacing an earlier right of election by the canons of the hospital.[2]

The city which controlled its own ecclesiastical and charitable institutions in this fashion was throughout our period the fourth or fifth largest in the kingdom, containing about 1 in 430 of the nation's inhabitants. Its population in the middle of the sixteenth century was probably about 6,500; a hundred years later it seems to have been about 12,000.[3] This last figure is about the size of Berwick upon Tweed today – a reminder that no city in early modern England (with the exception of London) was anything like a modern city in size, though they were not mere villages either. As in all European cities of the period, the crucial distinction within this population was between the freemen and the rest, for only the freemen participated in formal public life, directly constituting the Parliamentary electorate and indirectly electing the city's magistrates. The freemen in the late sixteenth and early seventeenth centuries were not the small elite they later became: indeed, in the 1630s, 1640s and 1650s almost every adult male inhabitant was likely to become free at some point in his life. It should be remembered that men were normally admitted to the freedom of their trade and therefore of the city in their maturity, and that the distinction between free and unfree was as much a matter of seniority as of birth or social status – it represented the transition from supervised work to that of a supervisor. Even in 1600 the chance for any adult male was about 1 in 3. This was by no means abnormal: in early sixteenth-century Coventry 80% of households contained a freeman, and almost half the adult males were free in sixteenth-century York.[4]

As I have said, the freemen in Newcastle directly elected their members of Parliament, but they did not directly elect the governors of the town, and many of the city's political problems in the sixteenth and seventeenth centuries sprang from this fact. Until 1604 more than half the freemen could take no part in municipal elections at all: the choice of mayor, sheriff, twelve aldermen and (from 1557) twenty-four Common Councillors was the exclusive preserve of representatives of the twelve major companies, and the members of the fourteen 'bye-trades' or lesser guilds could not take part. But most members even of the twelve major companies participated only indirectly: a complex system, in which each company separately nominated representatives who then elected members of the Council both from among themselves and from outside their number, and who had to leave the choice of civic officers to the new Council, ensured that it was relatively easy for a determined and wealthy group of senior merchants to control the day-to-day administration of the city. But alongside this structure, there were elements of more direct control: on three days in the year, all the freemen met in a Guild meeting, the powers of which relative to the Common Council were always unclear, while auditors to inspect the city's accounts annually were also directly elected by the freemen. It was also the case that dues paid by all the freemen, both on becoming free and in the course of their trading, funded the city, and that both the legal theory and the public rhetoric was that the city's government managed its affairs on behalf of all the freemen.[5]

One of their important interests, and the one that concerns us, was the free education of their sons, both in the elementary skills of literacy and in the Latin grammar which would enable them either to proceed to the universities or simply to understand most of the higher culture of their country, for Latin remained the natural language of works of scholarship, of many technical works (even on such things as mining) coming from abroad, and of much imaginative literature. Not until that ceased to be the case, in the eighteenth century, did the obvious benefits of a grammar education begin to disappear. The education was to be free, in the sense that the basic wages of the master were to be paid out of public funds or an endowment, allowing any free man of whatever wealth to send his son to the school (though there might be an entry fee and small additional payments for such things as paper and ink). A 'free school' in a sixteenth-century town was intended to be genuinely *free* for its freemen's sons.

The level of general literacy in the population of the North East in fact shifted quite dramatically during our period. In the 1560s it has been calculated that 40% of gentlemen and 80% of tradesmen and yeomen/husbandmen in the area were likely to be illiterate; labourers and women were virtually all illiterate. By the 1620s there were almost no illiterate gentlemen, and tradesmen were only 50% illiterate, though there had been very little comparable alteration among the other social groups. By the end of the century tradesmen (at least in Newcastle itself) were less than 5% illiterate; the most recent student of these changes has commented

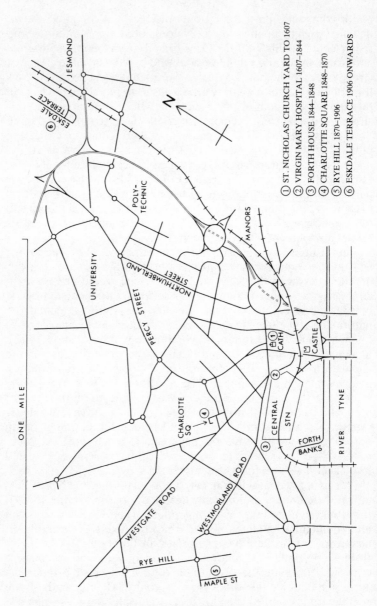

① ST. NICHOLAS' CHURCH YARD TO 1607
② VIRGIN MARY HOSPITAL 1607–1844
③ FORTH HOUSE 1844–1848
④ CHARLOTTE SQUARE 1848–1870
⑤ RYE HILL 1870–1906
⑥ ESKDALE TERRACE 1906 ONWARDS

The Sites of the Royal Grammar School

that this exceptionally low rate 'was matched elsewhere in England only by London craftsmen and tradesmen in the 1720s.'[6] This high level of literacy by 1700 was essentially an urban phenomenon, and indicates the extent to which Newcastle had been transformed since the mid-sixteenth century into a modern industrial and commercial centre. Ironically, as we shall see, this extensive urban literacy was accompanied by a falling away from traditional grammar and university education, which had been available earlier to a much higher proportion of the literate population.

As in other communities, much of the elementary education was provided on an *ad hoc*, self-help basis: in 1577 there were eleven schoolmasters in Newcastle, of whom only two (probably) taught Latin grammar and were paid by the chamberlains of the city on behalf of the freemen.[7] Most of the others must have been supported by the fees paid by parents, whether free or not. In 1557 there were probably 850 to 900 boys aged between 6 and 15 in the town, and rather fewer than half of them would be aged between 10 and 15, the usual age for a grammar education.[8] While the elementary classes under an individual master were likely to be quite small, two masters in a properly organised school could together teach up to eighty boys (or even more – in Hugh Moises's day three masters taught 133 boys): so that up to a quarter of all the boys in the city at that date *could* have been receiving a grammar education. This proportion was probably maintained throughout our period: from 1616 there was a third master or 'under-usher' at the grammar school, to take account of the steady increase in the population of the town.

What is particularly noteworthy about these figures, and characteristic of early modern England as a whole, is the high proportion of the *literate* population who received an education in Latin grammar (remembering the figures for literacy in the 1560s quoted above). A surprisingly high proportion of the literate population also went on to the universities throughout the period: from the time when proper records of university entrance become available, in the 1560s, through to the 1680s when the decline of the universities began, the proportion of the male year-group entering Oxford and Cambridge was never less than 1 in 70, and in the peak periods of the 1580s and 1630s it was 1 in 50 (this is understandably not true for the 1640s, when the proportion was much lower).[9] At a time when (nationally) more than 70% of the male population would remain illiterate, this meant that 1 in 15 of those able to read and write might proceed to higher education, approximately the same as in Britain today, and greater than the proportion going to university alone. Although figures for 1500 to 1560 are much less reliable, the best estimate is that much the same was true even then.

Again, Newcastle fitted into the national picture: between 1550 and 1660 at least one boy (on average) probably left the Newcastle school for university (almost always to Cambridge – out of the 88 pupils whose university career in those years is outlined in Laws's *Schola Novocastrensis*, 83 went to Cambridge and only 5 to Oxford). These figures, it should be said, are likely to be a substantial underestimate of the totals, for very few colleges kept accurate details of their undergraduates' schools. Both the town council and some individual companies mounted a generous programme of bursaries for boys at the university from at least the late sixteenth century;[10] even so, almost half of the Newcastle boys at Cambridge in those years whose status is known were sizars, that is, relatively poor boys working their way through college, acting (for example) as waiters in hall. A fine and very characteristic example would be Brian Walton, who went up to Cambridge as a sizar in 1616, made a career in the church through theological scholarship (among other projects, editing the Polyglot Bible), and after the Restoration became Bishop of Chester.[11] As John Selden once said with precisely such boys as Walton in mind, *a propos* the abolition of episcopacy, "Twill be a great discouragement to scholars, that bishops should be put down: For now the father can say to his son, and the tutor to his pupil, *Study hard, and you shall have vocem & sedem in parliamento*; then it must be, *Study hard, and you shall have a hundred a year if you please your parish.*'[12]

From at least the fifteenth century onwards the necessity of their sons' participation in this kind of education must have been apparent to the freemen of Newcastle, but we do not know how it was provided until the early sixteenth century. None of the chantries founded in the late middle ages in the four churches had any educational function (a commission appointed in 1548 precisely to investigate this and continue the schools if necessary reported that in Northumberland only Alnwick and Morpeth had chantry schools).[13] But boys were already proceeding regularly to university from Newcastle, both to Cambridge (where the Protestant martyr Nicholas Ridley was the most spectacular example) and, interestingly, sometimes to Louvain – a connection which continued after the Reformation, and which was a natural one for an East Coast trading port to establish.[14] Presumably they were doing so from a school run in some way by the freemen; certainly, the earliest mention of a grammar school in Newcastle suggests this. In 1525 the then mayor, Thomas Horsley, put some of his property in the town into the hands of a group of trustees with instructions that after his death they were to pay the income from it to the mayor and burgesses as part of the stipend of a grammar school master. At the same time the town agreed to pay four marks (£2 13s 4d) annually into the same estate out of its common funds after Horsley's death.[15] The fact that the estate had to be augmented in this way suggests that it did not yield very much. Horsley died in 1545; but in 1536 the Statute of Uses had decreed that anyone who benefited from such a trust in the future was to count as the legal owner of its lands.[16] Under the terms of Horsley's will the mayor and burgesses were the beneficiaries, and his estate would therefore have been swallowed up in the general property of the town, and the trustees would have ceased to have a separate existence. Horsley's will represented a legacy to the town earmarked for its school, rather than the *foundation* of a school – no body of governors or separate endowment was contemplated, and the deed between him and the mayor and burgesses (which is the only document about the arrangement to survive) does not tell us anything about the location or organisation of the school.

The next reference to a school is in 1561, when the existing Chamberlains' Accounts begin (with the exception of a fragmentary earlier series), and in that year 'the mayster of the Hygh Skull' was being paid 25s a quarter.[17] From later evidence we can deduce that his name was John Gray, a member of an extensive and prominent Newcastle family, and probably the John Gray who matriculated as sizar at Clare in 1547.[18] Laws commented, 'the pay at the rate of five pounds per annum does not seem exorbitant'[19]; he spoke more truly than he knew, for in the 1560s the daily wage of a skilled labourer such as a mason was around 10d, and he could reasonably expect to earn £7 a year (allowing for seasonal unemployment).[20] It is inconceivable that the full stipend of the Newcastle schoolmaster could have been as little as £5, even allowing for the possible extra benefits of free accommodation and admission money from the pupils, particularly as any usher whom the master chose to employ would conventionally have been paid out of the master's salary. The standard payment for the masters of comparable schools at the time was more than twice this sum.[21] Presumably in 1561 the chamberlains were merely augmenting the master's salary, as they had agreed to under Horsley's scheme, and the rest of it was coming from some other source.

What that source was, is fairly clear. In 1566 the town sold its right of presentation to the mastership of St Mary's Hospital to a couple of aldermen, Ralph Lawson and William Selby. The purchasers agreed that any master they should present 'should yearlie after his induction paie xiii li vi s viii d towards the preparinge and maintaininge of an able and sufficient schoolemaster.'[22] In 1611, when the formal reorganisation of the Hospital was in hand, it was claimed by the town that some of the recent masters of the Hospital 'in respecte the Revnewe of the said hospitall called the Westspittle is good and the charge therof not great have agreed eyther to fynde a Scholemaster for teaching the youth of the towne or else to allowe a yearlie stipend of 13 li 6s 8d p. annum for that or some other godlie use in the towne. . .'[23] Even £13 6s 8d is on the mean side, given that by 1600 a skilled labourer would normally earn 1s a day, and it may still be merely a component of the master's wages. But he will not have received much more than £20 – in the 1570s and 1580s, the vicarage of Newcastle was worth £50, the mastership of the Hospital £30, the mastership of the smaller Mary Magdalene Hospital £15 and that of the Bridge Chapel £10. (These values probably doubled during the following century.)

The town had thus, very naturally, turned to the most substantial source of charitable funds under its control in order to provide for grammar education. The Hospital, as in most English towns, had always been seen as the principal centre of charitable activity for the burgesses, and the informal use of its funds for education may have begun many years earlier. Whenever it began, it set up a connexion between Hospital and School which was to persist down to the present day, and which was of absolutely central importance to the School's history before 1844 (when the Hospital's old buildings were demolished to make way for the approach to the new railway station). Particularly after the Reformation, the charges on the Hospital's endowments were 'not great' because the medieval pattern of Hospital life had been fundamentally altered. A large medieval Hospital like St Mary's consisted originally of a group of Augustinian canons, living a communal life under a master who would normally live separately, in the manner of a prior. The master and canons were responsible

8

for the distribution of charitable funds in the community, for the care and shelter of the chronically sick, and for the housing of a number of old men (six at the time of the Reformation in St Mary's). There would also usually be some corrodians – lodgers in the Hospital performing various functions or paying suitable fees. Its activities in the town were as important a part of the Hospital's role as the life within its walls: a wide variety of causes would receive help from a Hospital, including even such things as paying the debts of Christians in debt to Jews. After the Reformation, however, the canons all disappeared (indeed, had probably done so by the early sixteenth century, when their electoral role was abandoned), and the Master was frequently non-resident, sometimes even letting his house. The 'bedesmen' were still maintained, but in a separate almshouse next to the Hospital, and its buildings were therefore very under-used.

But the Hospital's funds were not directly under the control of the town's authorities: they could get what they wanted only through the good will of the Master, or through some agreement which he might make at the time of his appointment. Fortunately, in the 1560s the town was able to put the Master under some obligation to it, for the period from 1558 to 1579 was marked by a long-running battle between the Master and the Bishop of Durham, in which the wealthiest merchants of the town seem to have supported the Master. The problem was that the pre-Reformation Master, Robert Davell (member of a great merchant family and the leading secular clergyman of the area, holding many benefices) did not die until Mary's reign, in 1558. The right to present when a benefice fell vacant was a saleable piece of property, and it had been sold by the town to a couple of leading merchants of the Swinburne family.[24] On Davell's death they duly presented their relative John Raimes, who had probably been at the Grammar School: he certainly made his career as an academic at Cambridge in the Marian years and had been elected a fellow of St John's four years earlier, under the aegis of a devoutly Catholic Master who may himself have been a Newcastle man, George Bullock.[25] The change of government and his own continued Catholicism made life difficult for Raimes, particularly as the new Bishop of Durham, James Pilkington, was also a former fellow of St John's who had been driven into exile during Bullock's mastership.[26]

In 1562 Pilkington mounted the first of a long series of inquiries and legal actions designed to unseat Raimes,[27] and in 1564 he wrote despairingly to Burleigh about the problems facing him in his diocese. He attributed many of them to 'the grete number of scholars borne heraboute, now lieing at Lovan (Louvain) without lycense. . . They be maynayned by the hospitalls of Newcastell and the welthiest of that towne and this shire . . . and be their next cousins.'[28] As well as Raimes, Pilkington must have had in mind Gilbert Lewen, Master of the Magdalene Hospital, whose father, a leading merchant of the town, had bought the advowson to the Hospital for his son before the Reformation.[29] Raimes indeed travelled to Louvain, where he matriculated in theology in 1566; but he returned to Newcastle (probably on the outbreak of the Netherlands civil war) in time to take part in the Rebellion of the Northern Earls in 1569, alongside his Swinburne relatives. He was imprisoned for a while at Durham as a consequence.[30]

The Bishop's concern about Raimes was shared by some of the lesser burgesses of the town, and he was apparently encouraged by one of them to get the Crown to assert a claim to appoint the masters of the hospitals. In 1563/4 new masters, both familiar figures at court, were appointed by letters patent to each hospital, but the Common Council of the town insisted on its own rights and the new appointments never took effect. The sale of its right to present to St Mary's in 1566 and the Magdalene in 1569 to a couple of aldermen confirmed the town's intention to proceed in the customary way. In 1567 leading figures in the town testified on Raimes's behalf, and claimed that the Bishop had no grounds to proceed against him, and even after his imprisonment there was no move in Newcastle to unseat him. Not until 1579 did the Bishop succeed in dispossessing him on the grounds of heresy and dereliction of duty.[31] In the split between wealthy and lesser burgesses, and the undisguisedly Catholic sympathies of the former, we can already see a theme which will run throughout the late sixteenth-century history of the town; while in the support given to Raimes by the town authorities we can no doubt see one explanation of the use of Hospital (which is of course to say at this time, the Master's *own*) funds to support a school.

As might have been expected, the schoolmaster during this period also shared Raimes's views: in 1569 his son was heavily involved in the Rebellion, acting as a courier to sympathisers in Scotland.[32] There is no reason to suppose that this son was not the Humphrey Gray who joined his father John in the chamberlains' payments in 1576.[33] It is worth noting that no Humphrey Gray matriculated at either Oxford or Cambridge in these years except for one who later became rector of an Ipswich church; he may have been a student in Scotland, or at Louvain (where the registers cease for some years after 1569). John and Humphrey Gray were together paid £10, which may indicate that funds from the Hospital were drying up.

If so, we can make a plausible guess as to why more money was needed from the town hutch. Originally, the Grammar School had been held in a building in St Nicholas's Churchyard referred to as 'the hally house'. 'Hally' in Northern English was 'holy', and the building was presumably some kind of pre-Reformation ecclesiastical structure. But in 1563 the accounts are full of payments for work to shore up the building, and at some point thereafter it was abandoned.[34] When a new Master arrived for the Hospital in 1585 he found 'a poore Schole Maister teaching children in the said hospitall by permission, the old Schoolehouse being decaied and not reedifyed.'[35] If the School moved into the Hospital's buildings, then this could reasonably have been seen as replacing a cash contribution; certainly in 1585 the new Master regarded free accommodation for the School as sufficient to meet his obligations towards it.

John Gray disappears from the accounts in 1581, and died three years later; Humphrey Gray continued until his death in 1594, assisted by the curate of St John's, John Murray, as usher.[36] On Humphrey's death the School was plunged into the middle of the most bitter political dispute which Newcastle experienced before the civil war – a dispute which led directly to the proper foundation of the School by royal charter in 1600, and to its formal and permanent association with the Hospital.

The background to this dispute was the realisation by the burgesses of Newcastle that vast sums of money were potentially to be made out of the coal trade. The late sixteenth century saw the creation of a coal-dominated economy in the area: it had of course been worked and sold in the region since at least the twelfth century, but the great growth of London and the exhaustion of native timber in the late sixteenth century opened up a huge new market for 'sea coal'. Newcastle became one of the apexes of a triangular trade up the East Coast, shipping coal to London and receiving grain from King's Lynn to supply its growing population of pitmen and sailors. The largest and most accessible supplies of coal in the area were on the south bank of the Tyne, in the Bishopric of Durham, and from the middle of the century Newcastle merchants sought both individually and collectively to take command of that area and to prevent Gateshead from developing as a coal-shipping centre. The idea of *collective* control was set firmly in their minds by the events of the latter part of Edward VI's reign, when Gateshead was annexed to Newcastle by Act of Parliament. Mary's accession meant the repeal of that legislation, but the future of Gateshead was now in doubt. When Pilkington was appointed to Durham in 1561 Gateshead was not included in the grant of temporalities, and was only restored in 1566. Ten years later Newcastle promoted another bill of annexation in Parliament, but it failed when Parliament was prorogued.

Two years later a different possibility emerged. In February 1578 Thomas Sutton, Master of the Ordnance in the North and a great speculative financier, negotiated a lease of Gateshead and Whickham for 79 years from the new Bishop (Barnes) to the Crown, which promptly transferred the lease to Sutton himself for a large sum.[37] Sutton (who later and as a result of similar transactions became the richest commoner in England) looked round for someone who could purchase his asset and provide the capital for investment in the mines; he first tried the Earl of Leicester, but it seems in the end to have been beyond Leicester's resources. Sutton then engineered another lease of 99 years and (again using the Crown as an intermediary) offered both leases to the mayor and burgesses of Newcastle.

At that point it was realised that, according to the most up-to-date legal advice, the town of Newcastle could not purchase such a lease, for it had never been formally incorporated.[38] Like most medieval towns, it had collectively taken over its own fee-farm from the Crown and had acquired special legal rights within its own boundaries, but its status as a legal, property-owning entity outside those boundaries was far from clear. The town had only recently begun to acquire such property, and the issue had not been raised in court. The Common Council put in motion the necessary procedures to acquire a new charter of formal incorporation, but in the meantime (and no doubt fearing that Sutton and the Crown would look for another buyer) two leading merchants of the town were provided with funds (partly out of the common treasury and partly by loans from private individuals) to buy the leases, on the understanding that when the charter was granted they would make them over to the mayor and burgesses. Thus in 1583 Henry Anderson (the mayor) and William Selby were granted the 'grand lease', as it came to be called,[39] and

12

six years later the new charter was finally granted.[40] But as early as 1585 loans for the purchase price were regarded as being secured by shares in the lease, and the shares were being traded within the town.[41] No formal undertaking had been made by Anderson and Selby to transfer the lease (it would have been illegal in 1583), and after 1589 so many other people had interests in the lease that Anderson and Selby simply retained it in their own hands and argued that all the merchants who were involved in the coal trade were already participants in the lease. These merchants were the 'hostmen', the entrepreneurs in the coal-shipping trade, who had always had the legal status merely of members of the general sea-trading company of the town, the merchant venturers.

The sums at stake in this transaction were very large. The mines of Gateshead and Whickham were reckoned to be worth £1,800 p.a., about £1,800,000 today, and the common treasury paid out £5,500 as part of the payment for the lease (about £5.5m).[42] The issues were also very clear: while the great merchants of Newcastle, who had either lent money individually or were hostmen, benefited from the lease, the lesser ones (who had partly financed it through the town's treasury) did not. Moreover, not only Newcastle was involved: the city of London saw the price of its coal rise from 6s a chaldron to 9s a chaldron during the 1580s and 1590s, and it consistently blamed the monopolistic power of the hostmen (though the hostmen equally consistently blamed increasing demand and the high cost of transport from the Tyne). In 1590 the mayor of London complained to Burleigh,[43] and in 1592 the storm broke in Newcastle itself.

In that year a guild meeting, open to all the freemen, demanded that the lease should be transferred to the mayor and burgesses.[44] The then mayor, Henry Anderson, reluctantly forwarded the demands to the Council of the North, and for the next seven years the dispute continued, with almost all the great coal merchants arrayed against the other burgesses. The lesser freemen were led by one of the hostmen themselves, Lionel Maddison, and by the surveyor of customs at Newcastle, a great supporter of London's interests there, Henry Sanderson. Both the Council of the North and the Privy Council in London were called in to settle the dispute, and Maddison and Sanderson tried to win their support by claiming that their side represented the true Protestants in the town against a gang of crypto-Catholics. The Council at York was generally disposed to give them its support, but the Privy Council were much more cautious, conscious of the financial uses of the hostmen at a time when the country's finances were being stretched to their limits to fund the war with Spain. In the end, the Privy Council decided the issue: in 1598 it sent commissioners to Newcastle to collect statements, which it handed over to a committee of expert lawyers in London. That committee decided in December that the hostmen had been 'unjustifiably charged'.[45]

But the Privy Council was determined to sort the issue out permanently, and at the same time make as much money for the war as it could. At one point during the dispute the possibility had been raised of demanding the payment from Newcastle of a lapsed tax of 1d a chaldron on coals shipped from the Tyne (a tax which had not been collected for more than a century).[46] The idea had not been officially dropped, and in 1599 the Privy Council struck a deal with the hostmen. It would arrange for them to be incorporated as a formal trading company, with the appropriate privileges, in return for two promises: the hostmen would publicly agree to pay 1s a chaldron on coal shipped to England and 5s on coal shipped overseas, and they would privately undertake not to advance the price of first-class coal at London above 10s (in order to reassure the London merchants). The hostmen would also assign the grand lease to the mayor and burgesses, since as an incorporated company they need now have no fear of other freemen competing in the trade.[47] The gross sums involved in this deal were again very large: the coal tax raised about £8,000 p.a. at the beginning of the new century, at a time when the government's ordinary revenue was only some £300,000.[48] All these provisions (with the exception of the undertaking about prices) were included in a new charter to the city, the so-called Great Charter of March 1600. The other new element in the charter was an incongruous clause founding a grammar school in the town.

Why was a school included in this final settlement of a long and bitter dispute? Humphrey Gray, whose will reveals his friendship with many of the hostmen, died in July 1594.[49] The mayor at the time, in the middle of the wrangle over the lease, was Lionel Maddison, leader of the anti-Catholic lesser burgesses: he replaced Gray with Francis Burrowes, a Staffordshire man, 'at the commendation of the late archbiship of York, the late lord president (of the Council of the North), the bishop of Durham, and the preachers of the town'.[50] The president was Henry Hastings, Earl of Huntingdon, who took a keen interest in the advance of 'godly' ministers in the North; Burrowes may indeed

14

have been related to a Leicestershire family of that name which produced a number of clergymen whose careers Hastings fostered in their – and his – home county, and it is clear that he fitted into the Newcastle Puritan circles.[51]

But at Michaelmas Maddison was replaced as mayor by Henry Anderson, and in the spring of 1595 he dismissed Burrowes – 'no other cause, in truth, can be imagined but that he is thought to be a favourite of Mr Maddison, and reformation of the town desired' wrote Sanderson, who included Burrowes as one of the eight principal opponents of the grand lessees in a letter of 1597 to Burleigh.[52] Anderson replaced Burrowes with Cuthbert Ogle, a Newcastle man, at a salary of £20 (twice what Burrowes had been receiving).[53]

For the next four years Burrowes and the mayors fought out his case, as the balance in the political struggle over the grand lease tilted in its different ways. At first, Burrowes appealed to the Council of the North, and they found in his favour. He was briefly reinstated, but in February 1597 he was dismissed again, only to be restored in May 1598 when the Privy Council sent its commissioners to the town. While Burrowes came and went, Ogle continued to be paid at his salary of £20, down to the last quarter of 1599.[54] It is not surprising that the chamberlains' clerk became so baffled by the case that in 1596 he cautiously described Ogle as 'schoolmaster of a school in the towne' and Burrowes as 'master of the hie schoole in the towne so called'.[55]

We do not know where either Burrowes or Ogle actually taught during this period. In 1585 the School, as we have seen, had been in the Hospital, but in that year Henry Ewbank was appointed Master of the Hospital by the mayor and burgesses directly (for they had abandoned their old practice of selling the right to present). Ewbank later claimed in a case before the Council of the North that he had been encouraged to take the job by the President of the Council, the same Earl of Huntingdon who was to help Burrowes, and his early career had certainly been in Leicestershire, the county which Huntingdon dominated.[56] He had moved to the church of Washington Co. Durham in 1583, and collected many preferments at Durham during the reign of Toby Matthew (who usually worked closely with Huntingdon).[57] Precisely what happened to the School during his time at the Hospital is hard to determine from the records of this case, for his alleged failure to pay the Master's salary was the principal matter in dispute, and there was good reason for all the parties to distort the facts. Ewbank admitted that having on his arrival found the 'poore Schole Maister teaching children', he had 'permitted him still so to doe as long as he would but never gave any other allowance to or any other Schole Maister.'[58] This Master must have been Humphrey Gray, and it is likely that during the wrangles which followed Gray's death Ewbank refused to allow the grand lessees' candidate, Ogle, to teach in the Hospital, while equally not being prepared to pay Burrowes a stipend out of Hospital funds to make up for his loss of income from the town. Certainly, by 1598 the School had left the Hospital buildings and returned to its old home in St Nicholas's Churchyard.[59]

But in 1599, when the hostmen knew that they had won the political battle, they decided to sort out the problems of the School through the new charter, as well as the other issues in dispute. They obtained a clause in the new charter which officially founded a grammar school in Newcastle, making it for the first time an independent legal entity, entitled to hold land in its own right (this provision was almost immediately a dead letter, a circumstance of great significance for the later history of the School, though in 1601 it still seems to have been thought that a conventional endowed school would be set up).[60] A crucial provision was that the mayor and burgesses, or a majority of them including the mayor, or the mayor and Common Council, or a similar majority, were to appoint the Master and usher, and that the appointments were to be *durante beneplacito* (at the pleasure of) the mayor and burgesses.[61] The informal arrangements of *ad hoc* payments to a Master ceased, and the absolute control of the new corporation – and in particular of the mayor, who enjoyed a veto over the appointments – was established over its school. In December 1599, knowing that this clause was to be included in the charter, the then mayor William Jenison (a prominent grand lessee) anticipated it and discontinued payments to Burrowes once again. Ogle had recently died or left the town; in his place Jenison appointed William Allanson, a 'preacher' at St Nicholas, with an usher named Cooke, and to secure Allanson's position he formally leased the schoolhouse in the churchyard to him for five years.[62]

Burrowes once again resisted, and sought to eject Allanson; Allanson countered with a legal action against Burrowes before the Exchequer of Pleas (the costs of which were borne on his behalf by the town). Eventually in October 1600 the court ruled in Allanson's favour, but at the same time the Council of the North persuaded the town to pay Burrowes £50 compensation for

16

relinquishing all further legal suits and surrendering the school.[63] Allanson was thus secured as the first master of the new 'Royal' Grammar School (though actually the charter provides that it should be called 'Queen Elizabeth's Grammar School, Newcastle', and it normally continued to be known as the Newcastle Free School). Allanson's usher from 1601 was Thomas Oxley, a recent graduate of Christ's Cambridge.[64]

But Allanson did not live very long to enjoy his position: he died in December 1602, and during the following year the politics of Newcastle were suddenly opened up again. At Michaelmas 1603 William Warmouth was elected mayor, the first mayor since the charter not to be a member of the hostmen's company. He seems to have presided over a partial reversal of the gains made by the hostmen in 1599: a decree of the Council of the North in December, ratified by a new royal charter in March 1604, ordained that henceforward the by-trades were to take a part in the election of the mayor and Council – a crucial move on behalf of the lesser burgesses. The decree also laid down that any burgess who wished to join the hostmen's company and could pay the entrance fee was entitled to do so: the company thus ceased to be the private preserve of the great coal merchants, and became merely the regulatory body for the trading by any competent burgess of the town in the coal market.[65] For the next twenty years or so the lesser burgesses had much more say in the government of the town, something the new royal government of James I seems to have favoured; and the fortunes of the School and Hospital reflect this.

The first sign of the change is that at some point before 1606 Burrowes was reappointed Schoolmaster (the accounts for this period are missing, so we cannot date it precisely). During the same period Thomas Oxley moved on to further ecclesiastical preferment, and Burrowes selected Wigham as his usher. In 1608 Wigham became curate of St John's, the post which John Murray had combined with the ushership under Humphrey Gray, and also Vicar of Hartburn, a church in the gift of the Bishop.[66] The Master and usher together at this period cost the town £40, £24 going to the Master: Wigham's total income must have been considerably more than Burrowes', who could not so easily take on other duties. Some radical improvement in the Master's finances was soon sought by the Common Council.

Since 1606 the Bishop of Durham (replacing Toby Matthew) had been the former Dean William James, and the advancement in the diocese which Henry Ewbank had hitherto enjoyed ceased

17

until the reign of the next bishop. In early 1611, indeed, Ewbank resigned one of his Durham livings. Seeing this weakening in the master's position, the Common Council in 1610/11 (controlled by the lesser burgesses) decided on a radical and formal reorganisation of St Mary's Hospital, along with the other hospitals which the town possessed (Magdalene, Bridge and – now – St Edmund's in Gateshead). Early in 1611 they petitioned the Lord Privy Seal for a refoundation by charter of the hospitals, and pointing out that St Mary's had a history of support for education 'theye desire that the foundacon thereof may be a master and usher att the nominacon of the maior and rest of the Comon Counsell . . . for the better instructinge of the youth of that towne.'[67]

But though Ewbank was not supported by his Bishop, he was now also a King's Chaplain, and had some friends at court. The charter which was eventually granted in May 1611 was a compromise: the town was given clear rights of appointment, and the Crown disclaimed all interest either in the mastership or the lands of the Hospital. But it was incorporated not as a school but as an almshouse, consisting of six poor brethren and a master, and Ewbank was named as the first Master (though not for life, something apparently which the town had feared). However, the mayor and burgesses were given the right whenever they thought fit to emend the statutes and orders of the Hospital, and this clause in effect gave the Common Council the discretion to remodel it. Similar charters were issued for the other hospitals.[68]

Accordingly, in the mayoral year of Sir George Selby (1611-12) the reorganisation of the Hospital began. The town paid for the reconstruction of the main hall of the Hospital (usually and wrongly referred to as the chapel, because of its resemblance to a church with nave, aisles and chancel) as a properly-fitted out schoolroom and election room.[69] It is because the election took place in their schoolroom that the tradition developed, which still continues, of the mayor's first duty being to address the boys of the School, and of the School having a holiday on or near the occasion (something which was the cause for celebration and holding of a mock election by the boys, at least in the eighteenth century).[70] But though Ewbank did not oppose this rebuilding, no proper educational use of the Hospital could be achieved while he was Master. In a Council meeting of July 1612 one of the lesser burgesses suggested that Ewbank should be sued before the Council of the North for non-performance of the bond he had

18

entered into in 1585, and the idea was taken up. The case came to court in September 1614, and the Council decided against Ewbank. In October 1615 he resigned.[71]

At about the same time that the case went to court, Burrowes was replaced as Master of the School. It is not clear whether he died, retired or resigned; but he was replaced in September by Robert Fowberry, attracted from the Mastership of Hull Grammar School (where he had become dissatisfied with his small prospects) by a large salary – he and his usher were paid £60 split 2:1 – and no doubt the promise of the Mastership of the Hospital if the case went well. Like most of the Masters (other than Burrowes), Fowberry was connected with the area, being one of two brothers from a decayed Northumbrian family who went up to St John's in 1583.[72] He brought with him a new usher, John Shaw, who like many other ushers received a post at St John's Church, becoming the lecturer there under the former usher Wigham, who remained as curate.[73] After Ewbank's resignation, Fowberry was duly appointed Master of the Hospital, and the intentions of the Council in 1611 had been completely realised. They now had an extremely well-paid Master, an usher who also enjoyed a salary as lecturer at St John's, a large and well-organised schoolroom and ample accommodation for the Master. The bedesmen of the Hospital continued to live in their separate almshouse, between the main Hospital buildings and the street.

In addition to this prosperous Grammar School, the freemen also arranged a writing school for their sons. This has often been confused with an elementary, pre-grammar school, but many sixteenth- and seventeenth-century grammar schools had writing masters attached to them. Their function was not to teach the basic skills of literacy, but the more refined skills of Greek, Roman and secretary hand. The modern analogy would not be with elementary literacy, but with typewriting: boys were expected to leave the grammar school capable of producing material for *publication*, for of course all public business was conducted through handwritten documents. The first known writing master at the School was Robert Johns, mentioned in 1606; he was succeeded before 1625 by Devereux Gardiner, father of the famous Ralph Gardiner. After the School's move to the Hospital, the writing master seems to have stayed in the old schoolhouse in St Nicholas's Churchyard, only moving to the Hospital when the bedesmen were transferred to a new almshouse in Pudding Chare, in 1632.[74]

The new organisation of the School, and the proven competence of Fowberry (who seems to have been the first Master of the Newcastle school to have already been the Master of an important school elsewhere), enabled it to fulfil its duties to the freemen very successfully: indeed, in 1616 the first under-usher, Robert Wante, appears in the records.[75] William Gray, writing the first history of Newcastle in 1649, remembered Fowberry as the first master of the Grammar School, 'a learned and painfull man to indoctrinate youth in Greek and Latin'[76] – a testimony to the apparently sweeping character of the reorganisation between 1611 and 1615. Fowberry was certainly well-read: his study at the time of his death contained more than 150 volumes, a relatively large private library for a provincial schoolmaster.[77]

He made his will in December 1622, and died shortly afterwards. The question of his successor therefore came before the Common Council at a time when it was still not wholly controlled by the great hostmen. One of the secretaries of state, Sir Edward Conway, wrote to the town in May urging the appointment of 'Mr Conniers' (probably the Francis Coniers who acted as his agent in various personal matters) – an illustration of the wealth and importance the new post represented. On June 10 the Common Council met to discuss the matter, and Sir George Selby the mayor reported to Conway what happened.

> According to your letter to me and The rest of our Aldermen I made them all acquainted with itt, in the behalfe of Mr Conyers for The Scholmaster of Newcastell, and Red your letter openly unto them all. And presently I Called a Common Councell Takeing every mans voice which I Sende you hereinclosed, not doubting butt your letter with divers other privye Councellors letters should not be denyed Butt yt Toke nott that effecte I looked for.

To Selby's surprise, he and his fellow wealthy merchants were outvoted by a group in which the Maddison family again featured, eighteen to seven. Sir Henry Anderson, with the caution characteristic of his family, abstained.[78]

What happened next is obscured by another legal wrangle. Fowberry had simply been appointed to the Hospital mastership by the town, and had not been presented by it to the Bishop of Durham for induction, as had previously been the custom. The new charter said nothing about whether the Hospital remained 'presentative' or had instead become 'donative', and the Bishop in 1623 (Richard Neile) now queried the right of the town to proceed

20

without consulting him first. The town sent agents to London to seek the best legal advice, but in the end the Attorney-General ruled that the law was on the bishop's side, and furthermore that he could collate without any presentation from the town once six months had elapsed since the death of the previous incumbent.[79] This was a strange ruling, as the law was quite clear that the *Crown* had the right to present on lapse, but the Bishop acted on it and instituted a new master without a presentation. The man he chose was none other than Burrowes's old usher, Edward Wigham, who had been Vicar of Ponteland since 1617 (in addition to his livings of Hartburn and St John's). Wigham had already resigned from Ponteland shortly before Fowberry's death,[80] but he continued to hang on to his other benefices. The choice of Wigham was presumably acceptable to the Maddison group on the Council, in view of his old association with Burrowes, and he may even have been their favoured candidate before the legal dispute. His resignation from Ponteland implies some confidence in receiving a better benefice shortly.

Wigham remained as Master for six years, during which period the old ascendancy of the great coal merchants began to reappear. A series of municipal disputes began in 1625, the mayoral year of William Hall, when once again the guild meeting was used to voice protests against the management of the town by the Common Council. The lesser burgesses complained that their own trading interests were being overridden by the town's magistrates, who permitted their servants and adherents to practise trades without becoming freemen, and they also accused the Common Council of letting municipal property to its members on favourable leases. The disputes continued until the end of the 1630s, with a particular explosion in 1633 when a riot by apprentices became an expression of the lesser burgesses' discontents. The Council of the North and the Privy Council again investigated the political conflicts in the town, but no action was taken.[81] The domination by the great merchants was allowed to continue; their religious attitudes were more acceptable at court than ever before, and their money (both through the coal tax and through loans) was as important as ever. This period of domination, interestingly enough, coincides with a period of great openness in the body of freemen: as the coal trade boomed as never before (and perhaps, in real values, never again) the tradesmen and artisans of Newcastle found a great deal of work, and a very high proportion of its residents were able to count on becoming independent workers.

The consequence of this change in politics for the School was of course that appointments to it were now under the secure control of the great merchants and their supporters on the Council. The problem of Wigham's successor came before them in October 1629, on his death, and they decided to split his offices between a number of different men. The curacy of St John's went to Shaw, the existing lecturer there, who may also still have been the School's usher; the Mastership of the Hospital went to a preacher at St Andrew's, well-connected to the prominent merchant families of the town, Francis Gray. He had been a friend of Fowberry's, and may have taught briefly in the school during the legal dispute of 1623.[82] All the histories of the School assume that Gray was made Master of the School as well as the Hospital in 1629, but there is no evidence that this was so, and some that it was not. Since neither the chamberlains' accounts nor the Common Council books survive from this period, we have to rely on other evidence. Walker's *Suffering of the Clergy*, the great compendium of lives of clergymen sequestered during the civil war, includes a very full and apparently highly accurate biography of one Thomas Gibson. In it, Walker said that

> This very worthy Person was born at *Keswick* in *Cumberland*, and Educated at *Queen's College* in *Oxford*; where he continued till he took the Degree in Arts; and then returning into his own Country, was preferred to the *Free School* of *Carlisle*, and from thence to that of *Newcastle*; both which he managed with great Reputation several Years; and was from the latter of them Promoted by the Bishop of *Carlisle* to the *Vicaridge* of *Horn-Castle*, (Lincs) *in the Year 1634*.[83]

Gibson was a great royalist, and after being deprived of his vicarage he was imprisoned for a time at Lincoln, and then exchanged for a Presbyterian prisoner at Newark.

> After this, in the Year 1644, Colonel K—, the Governor of *Boston* for the Parliament, gave Orders for a Party of Horse to go and fetch him Prisoner, and *Plunder his House*; but *John Lillbourn* (who had been his *Scholar*, and was then Lieutenant-Colonel to Colonel *King*) affirming upon his own Knowledge that he was a *Good and Godly Man*, got the Order, with much ado, suspended for the present: *Lillbourn* afterwards, upon some *Disagreement* with his *Colonel*, going to *London*, the Order was again Revived, and Mr. *Gibson* made a Prisoner. . .[84]

John Lilburne, the famous Leveller, whom this story puts into a particularly attractive light, had certainly been a pupil at the

Grammar School in Newcastle (his family were Durham land-owners), but he must have left the school to start on a trading career in London in or just after 1630.[85] Gibson's name does not appear in the list of masters of Carlisle Grammar School, derived from diocesan order books, but it is quite possible that he was appointed during the period between June 1627 and September 1629 for which no episcopal *acta* survive.[86] It would have been his first post, for he graduated from Queen's College Oxford, the main college for his diocese, in 1628/29; its then President, Barnabas Potter, became Bishop in March 1629 and was later to appoint Gibson to Horncastle. A new master was definitely appointed to Carlisle in September 1630, after whom there is no break in the succession of masters. It is probable, therefore, that Gibson was appointed Master of the Newcastle School in succession to Wigham at the beginning of 1630, and that the Mastership of the Hospital went to the much more senior figure of Gray. Some confirmation of this comes from Cambridge admissions registers: Henry Carr was admitted to Christ's in May 1635 having spent five years at the Newcastle school under Mr Gibson, while Henry Bulmer entered St John's in June 1633 having spent four years at Newcastle under Mr Gibson.[87] Gibson presumably owed his appointment to the influence of Bishop Potter, exercised *via* the Vicar of Newcastle. There may have been some problems at the school at the time of Wigham's death; it is suggestive that the sons of James Carr and Henry Swinburne, leading merchants, went up to St John's Cambridge in 1631 having spent one and a half years at Giggleswick School.[88]

Gibson will have been paid £40 per annum, for that was the standard sum from 1616 until 1649, a period of fairly steady prices. He brought with as usher a relative, Daniel Gibson, and appointed as under-usher Ralph Rowmaine.[89] But without the Mastership of the Hospital, the post of schoolmaster was not particularly well-paid, so Gibson's departure to Horncastle after four years is entirely understandable.

His replacement was Amor Oxley, one of the sons of the parish clerk at Morpeth.[90] Oxley's father had been a schoolmaster once, at Woodhorn, and all his boys made their careers through the educational system. The eldest, Thomas, went up to Christ's in 1598, and was usher of the Newcastle School at the beginning of the century. He was followed to the college by his brothers Charles and Amor. Amor went up in 1615; the following year Charles was given the living of Chillingham in Northumberland by the Bishop of Durham. Amor went to live with him after graduating, and acted as tutor to the family of the owners of Chillingham Castle, the Greys, until 1630.[91] He sent the boys to Christ's, as he was to do many of his grammar school pupils. Sir William Grey (from 1624 Lord Grey of Wark) was an unusual figure in early seventeenth-century Northumberland, for he was sympathetic to Puritanism and supported Parliament, albeit with some reservations, during the civil war. His position was much closer to the Earl of Northumberland's (the dominant figure in the north of the county and the other Northumbrian peer) than to that of the recusant gentry of the area. Oxley was ordained priest in 1630, and (no doubt partly through Grey's influence) became master of the Morpeth Grammar School the following year.

After only three years at Morpeth he was appointed to Newcastle, where he allowed Daniel Gibson to continue as usher until 1643. A Mr Smith briefly replaced Gibson, but the usher for the next two years after that was William Sansom. Ralph Rowmaine may also have continued as under-usher until 1637, when he was replaced by Edward Lumsden, another protégé of Oxley and the Greys, and another graduate of Christ's College.[92] Oxley is famous as the 'royalist' schoolmaster during the siege of Newcastle in the civil war; he was certainly unsympathetic to the more radical Puritans of the town in the 1630s – in a letter of 1634 to William Morton, the unofficial leader of radical Puritanism in the area, Oxley accused him of harbouring a viper in his bosom.[93] But there is no evidence that he was a particularly committed 'Arminian' or 'Laudian'; his religious attitudes can be deduced to some extent from his contacts at Cambridge and from his policy for placing boys there.

Oxley is the first Master whose contacts with the university can be traced in some detail, for from the 1630s onwards the admissions registers of many Cambridge colleges (including, fortunately, Christ's) record full details about the schooling of their entrants and which tutor in the college they were placed with. The tutor was the key figure, for he would direct the studies of the boy throughout his time at Cambridge, and would often share accommodation with him. Oxley had been himself a pupil of Joseph Mede, and remained on very good terms with him (in the mid-1620s he stayed with him in Cambridge).[94] Mede was an important figure, sympathetic both with the kind of eirenic Protestantism popularised by John Dury and Samuel Hartlib, and also with the apocalyptical speculation which they and many other

Puritans also favoured. He remained loyal to the Anglican form of church government, but disliked theological controversy – a dislike Oxley seems to have inherited.

His first pupils were placed by Oxley with his old tutor – the Grey boys in 1626, Edward Lumsden from Morpeth (later the Newcastle under-usher) in 1631, and a couple of other Morpeth boys in 1633. From 1632, however, he also began to place them with John Fenwick;[95] Fenwick was a Northumbrian (whose school we do not know) who had come up to Christ's as a sizar in 1617 and had become a fellow in 1628. During the civil war he was to keep the Essex living which he received in 1639, and he was described in 1650 as 'an able preaching minister'.[96] After Oxley moved to Newcastle he continued to use Fenwick exclusively, down to his departure in 1639; he switched then to one of his old pupils from Morpeth, Ralph Widdrington of Cheeseburn Grange. Widdrington had been admitted as a pensioner under Fenwick in 1632, and was elected a fellow to succeed him; he had a distinguished career at Cambridge, ending with his election to the Regius Chair of Greek in 1654 and the Lady Margaret Professorship of Divinity in 1673. During the war he conformed, taking the Engagement but not the Covenant; he was assisted by his elder brother Thomas, the great supporter of Parliament and the Speaker of the first Protectorate Parliament (and another Christ's graduate).[97]

Although more boys went from Newcastle to Christ's in these years than to any other college (twelve between 1634 and 1642), Oxley also continued to use the college which had always been most popular for boys from the area, St John's. We have already seen that Raimes made his career at St John's; he was one of sixteen fellows of the college between 1552 and 1630 who came from Northumberland (in most cases we do not know much more about their origins), so that there can have been few years when there was no fellow from the area resident in the college.[98] In the 1630s boys from both Morpeth and Newcastle were placed with Robert Nicholson, a Newcastle boy who went up to the college in 1618 and became a fellow in 1627 (he died in 1643).[99] These regional connections were highly important, and all colleges exhibited them: Caius, for example, catered almost exclusively to boys from East Anglia. At a time when there were no examinations for entry, tutors had to rely on personal recommendations from schoolmasters they knew; and the fact that regional dialects varied greatly and were spoken by most inhabitants of an area meant that there was a simple need to find a tutor who could understand a boy's speech.

His Cambridge connections do not suggest that Oxley was very hostile to some forms of Puritanism; his links with the Greys and his career during the war confirm this (see below). Moreover it is fairly clear that by 1642 he was not especially popular with the solidly royalist and Laudian (not to say Catholic) governing oligarchy of the town. In 1642 Francis Gray died, and the Common Council had to appoint his successor at the Hospital. Oxley was perfectly well qualified for the job, but the Council decided to keep the offices of Master and Schoolmaster separate; it appointed instead Nicholas Hall, the heir to Sir Alexander Hall, one of the wealthy Newcastle hostmen, and recently the purchaser of the old Anderson country estate at Haswell Grange, Co. Durham. Nicholas Hall had been a fellow of Emmanuel College Cambridge since 1627, and was appointed by the college to the rectory of Loughborough (Leics) in 1642; he may well have been a pupil at the Newcastle School. His appointment to the Hospital resembled Raimes's, in that the town was rewarding one of its sons who had made a career for himself at Cambridge. He was one of the three fellows of Emmanuel who supported the King in the civil war, and was ejected from both his fellowship and the rectory; but he was never removed from the Mastership of the Hospital, and spent the war living at Haswell Grange and drawing his income from the Hospital.[100]

It was in 1642, of course, that the life of both the town and the School was radically transformed. At the beginning of the war, Newcastle found itself virtually the key to the entire conflict. London and its armouries were entirely dependent on Newcastle coal, and no war effort based on the capital could be sustained for long if the North-East coalfields were under enemy control. Charles recognised this during the Bishops' War, when the Scots rapidly occupied the area and forced the English government to sue for peace; he attempted to use the same lever himself against Parliament two years later, garrisoning Newcastle two months before his standard was raised at Nottingham. His tactics almost worked: by 1643 the fuel situation in the capital was desperate. But in the autumn of 1643 Parliament (partly inspired by Lord Grey of Wark) concluded an agreement with the Scots on what were for the latter extremely favourable terms, in order to draw a Scots army across the border. On 19 January 1644 the army crossed the Tweed and the outcome of the war became inevitable.

The bulk of the royal forces in the town under the Marquis of Newcastle withdrew, leaving a small garrison behind under the command of the mayor, Sir John Marley. They held out until October, at first in the hope that the Marquis could break the forward advance of the English, though Parliament's victory at Marston Moor in July turned their resistance into merely a display of stubbornness.

During the siege the Hospital buildings (which lay close to the town walls) were hit, and both the School's Library and Oxley's own collection of books were destroyed.[101] Oxley did not commit himself to the King's cause during the siege in the enthusiastic manner of some of the other clergymen, but it was sufficient for the Parliamentary commissioners when they moved in after the fall of the town that he had stayed at his post. He was displaced from his office, along with five of the other nine clergymen in benefices within the town. But he was not wholly abandoned by his influential friends: he was first allowed to take up the rectorship of Whalton in 1647, and in 1650 Lord Grey persuaded one of his tenants to help him become vicar of Kirknewton, near Wooler.[102] His ushers were also removed, but again treated quite well – Lumsden became head of the Morpeth Grammar School in 1654.

Oxley's dismissal did not officially take place until 30 May 1645, though he had been gone from the town for more than two months before then. The newly purged Common Council seems to have decided that it now wanted as a Master of the School someone whose career had lain in the Puritan educational establishment of London, and it turned first to the Master of the Mercers' School, Nicholas Augar.[103] He was a graduate of St John's, who had been Master of the School since 1620, and had twice been considered for promotion from it to the Mastership of St Paul's School, also under the control of the Mercers. On the second occasion in 1641, a group of Puritan assessors (including the famous Edmund Calamy) found him 'an able scholar' – the Mercers were one of the only two companies before 1642 which consistently appointed Puritans to its livings.[104] During the late 1640s and 1650s, as we shall see, the Common Council of Newcastle received some extremely high-level advice about possible masters for their School from people involved in London Puritan circles; the M.P. for the town John Blakiston, later a regicide, may have been one channel for this advice, though Newcastle of course always enjoyed a special relationship with London.

Augar brought with him as usher a very recent Cambridge graduate, Matthew Gudge, who stayed for two years. In July 1647 Gudge was replaced by Edward Dobson, a former pupil of Oxley's at Newcastle who had just graduated from Emmanuel. In March 1648 the Common Council agreed that the formality of their appointing the usher should be abandoned, and the appointment left to the Master, as in practice had always been the case.[105]

The late 1640s were a period of some financial difficulty in Newcastle: the war had dislocated the coal trade, and the revenues coming into the town's treasury seem to have diminished quite considerably. Augar was forced to pay for the repairs to the School buildings out of his own pocket, the Council later reimbursing him, and Nicholas Hall apparently doing very little. The Council stopped payment of rent to him for the use of the Hospital buildings until 1658, when he was paid £17 in compensation.[106] This financial stringency may have influenced Augar's decision early in 1648 to return to London, though the reason he gave to the Council was 'his want of health this Aire not agreeing with him'.[107] Another reason may have been that while in the town he had supported the Presbyterian congregations, and a great split was now developing nationally between the two groups, loosely called Presbyterian and Independent, whose coalition had won the war. Though in Newcastle a *modus vivendi* was on the whole struck between the various congregations,[108] there is little doubt that the sympathy of its rulers in 1648 was with the Independents and with the new regime at Westminster established after Pride's Purge in November had excluded Presbyterian members: the North East in general came well out of the Purge, and Blakiston was one of the more radical figures among the Independent leadership. Symbolically, after the King's execution the Council caused to be engraved over the gateway on the Tyne Bridge a slogan from Tacitus: *Principatus ac libertas res dissociabiles* (Monarchy and liberty are incompatible).[109]

Augar's departure led the Council to concentrate their attentions not simply on the Puritan schoolmasters of London, but on one particular group of them. Since before the war a number of people in England had been fired with the idea of a programme of educational and social reform which would harness for the public good the technical and industrial developments which had been heralded by Francis Bacon, and were already being realised (apparently) in the industrial areas of Central Europe. At the centre of this activity in England was Samuel Hartlib from Elbing, who was settled in England from 1626; he acted as an intellectual entrepreneur, fostering all ideas which he thought conduced towards this end – and which he took in part (like many visionaries of a technological Utopia since) to be the realisation of a millenarian expectation. The writings of the Moravian Jan Amos Comenius were particularly important to Hartlib, but he culled his ideas from a wide variety of sources.[110]

The first contacts between Hartlib's circle and Newcastle probably came through the town physician, Samuel Rand (appropriately enough, since medicine was one of the key areas in the Hartlibian programme). Rand was the uncle of James Rand, one of Hartlib's chief patrons and himself a leading London physician; Samuel became the town physician at Newcastle in 1637, and remained there until his death in 1654, even though in the late 1640s the town's financial crisis led to his stipend being discontinued.[111] But Newcastle was an obvious place for Hartlib and his friends to be interested in, for it was at the centre of the most advanced industrial area in the country – the perfect place for the new intellectual and social order to emerge. The group later enthusiastically supported the proposals for a university at Durham.

On Augar's departure, the Council tried to appoint a series of Hartlib's protégés. First it turned to William Webbe, who in August 1646 had been appointed schoolmaster at Berwick (a garrison town against the Scots, and dominated by the Independents in the Army).[112] Webbe had come to Hartlib's attention in the late 1620s: in 1626 he had been granted a patent for teaching languages 'after a new method without Rules', and Hartlib believed that some system of this kind was necessary if technical information in Latin were to be made available rapidly to a large audience. Throughout the 1630s Hartlib fostered a Europe-wide debate about Webbe's methods, though he seems himself gradually to have been convinced of the superior merits of an alternative simplified system put forward by Hezekiah Woodward. Woodward, like Webbe at this time, was a school-master in London, though unlike Webbe he taught at a public school, St Saviour's in Southwark.[113]

Having just acquired Webbe's services, the Berwick town Council was unwilling to release him. Newcastle therefore looked for an alternative candidate, and enlisted Blakiston's help in securing Woodward himself. Some doubts were expressed by the Common Council about the desirability of his methods, but a formal invitation was sent; Woodward however refused to come, and shortly afterwards left Southwark for the church at Bray, allegedly at the personal request of Cromwell himself. He was succeeded at Southwark by Nicholas Augar, who presumably owed his appointment to these links between Hartlib's circle and Newcastle.[114]

In April 1648 a Presbyterian Scots army seized Berwick, and Newcastle was no longer obliged to defer to the wishes of its Council. When Woodward refused the invitation, the Common Council considered inviting Webbe once again. But an alternative candidate had now been suggested, once again by Hartlib or his associates: a former assistant to and fellow countryman of Comenius himself, a Sudeten German named Georg Ritschel. The Council consulted the clergy of the town, and on balance they preferred Webbe; but their advice was disregarded, and Ritschel was elected master on 29 August, at the usual £40 per annum.[115]

Ritschel was born at Deutschkahn, near the modern Decin on the border between Germany and Bohemia, in the industrial heartland of Central Europe. His father was related by marriage to a family of Newcastle merchants – the industries of Northern Bohemia being principally glass and coal, Newcastle, the centre in England for both these industries, had obvious links with the area. Like many other Bohemian Protestants, Ritschel was forced into exile in the 1620s, and eventually found his way to England. He was recruited by Comenius into the programme of providing a universal and readily accessible body of technical and philosophical knowledge, and was charged with producing a textbook on metaphysics. It appeared in 1648 at Oxford under the title *Contemplationes Metaphysicae*, but Comenius had already rejected it as too complex for his purposes. During the period of his work at Oxford Ritschel was very short of money, and Hartlib on a number of occasions tried to procure suitable jobs for him; the Newcastle appointment was his eventual success. Links between Newcastle and Hartlib were further strengthened during the 1650s, when his son Samuel was appointed the town's agent in London.[116]

The economic depression of the late 1640s in Newcastle began to lift during Ritschel's time at the School, and the Council was able to spend quite a lot of money on it. In 1649 Ritschel's salary was raised to £50 p.a., and during the early 1650s the buildings were put in better order and a number of books bought for the School Library.[117] At the same time the Council decided that the internal government of the School and its curriculum should be properly regulated, and revised orders for its management were presented to the Council on 10 August 1649. A copy of these orders was found in the City Archives and published by T. H. Rowland in 1952. He dated them to c. 1600, but the orders are partly concerned with establishing the rules governing the appointment and conduct of Visitors to the School, and this was a function which the town had to take on in the absence of episcopal visitation during the Interregnum.[118]

Rowland thought that the curriculum which they outline was rather old-fashioned, but it is in fact remarkably advanced. We must remember that the basic function of the sixteenth- and seventeenth-century grammar school was the teaching of Latin grammar, and that a Tudor proclamation had enjoined that Lily's Grammar was to be the central text in every free school. This was confirmed by the Church Canons of 1603, which were taken in law to apply to every episcopally licensed schoolmaster. The main thrust of the arguments put forward by Webbe, Woodward and the other followers of Comenius was that traditional grammar teaching was a waste of time: boys should not be instructed in formal rules of syntax, but should learn by reading and translating as soon as possible. When episcopacy was abolished, the power to enforce the Canons disappeared, and the free schools were opened up to innovations in language teaching (which is one reason why we find people like Webbe moving from their private schools into the free schools).

The Newcastle orders are remarkable precisely because they allow virtually no place to traditional grammar. While most schools' statutes of an earlier date prescribed the learning of the whole of Lily's Grammar by rote in the junior forms, those of Newcastle required them simply to learn the basic parts of speech and then to proceed directly to the business of reading and translating, with the assistance of the usher.[119] The textbooks which the orders list are the usual set that would be found in any mid-century grammar school, and do not include any of the radical works of contemporary educational theorists – works that were unobtainable in Newcastle in the necessary quantities. But the use that was to be made of these texts was exactly in line with the ideas of the Hartlib circle. As we shall see later, this may have set up a tradition in Newcastle which persisted even after the Restoration, and must have given the School a very distinctive educational character.

31

To modern eyes, the daily life of the School as laid down in these orders was an odd mixture of hard work and leisure, of anarchy and repression. Boys had to attend the School from seven in the morning until six at night, with a break of two hours between eleven and one to enable them to go home for dinner. They had to do this every day except Sunday, and even on Sundays the School had to gather for two services at St Nicholas's. They had twelve days holiday at Easter and twenty at Christmas. And yet this punishing schedule was devoted to a relatively light work-load. The boys spent most of their time, of course, learning Latin, and in the first three forms under the usher read largely modern Latin works, particularly those of Erasmus. What classical texts they read were plays, such as Terence, apart from a selection of Cicero's letters. Not until the fourth form, when the master himself took over, did they read much classical Latin, starting with Cicero and Ovid. The basic material of Latin courses today, such as Caesar or Virgil, was reserved for the fifth and sixth forms, and it was only in these two last forms that the boys began to learn Greek. It was Latin in its use as a modern language that they would have fully to comprehend; both classical Latin and Greek would be relatively advanced work.

The same disconcerting mixture is to be found in the discipline of the School. Two or three masters had to control over a hundred boys of varying ages, and they did so through physical force: beating with a wooden cane was the standard punishment for swearing and lateness in the junior forms, and for speaking English or faulty Latin in the upper forms. But seventeenth-century schools, especially in the north of England, periodically erupted into riot, particularly at the time of 'barring out', when the boys simply took over the buildings. The orders prescribed that this custom should be 'discontinued for ever', but there is no reason to suppose that Newcastle easily achieved this. The juxtaposition of harsh discipline and licensed riot was characteristic of early modern English society in general, and the School was not going to escape it.[120]

The orders end, characteristically, 'it is required and expected that every Schollar (going to university) shall forever hereafter in all his publick sermons pray for the welfare and good Estate of the Mayor and Burgesses of this Corporation' – the School was the corporation's school, and it expected gratitude from its pupils for the rest of their lives.

At the beginning of 1657 Ritschel was included as one of the

32

twelve founding fellows of Cromwell's college at Durham, the great achievement of Hartlib's circle (which did not, however, long outlast the Protector's death).[121] Ritschel's initial intention must have been to combine the post at Durham with his Mastership at Newcastle, but a new opportunity for him appeared in the middle of the year when he was invited to take over the church at Hexham. Such a post would allow him more time to spend at Durham (many of the other fellows also acted as ministers in local churches), so in July 1657 he resigned from the School. Ritschel had kept Edward Dobson on as usher until 1651, when he replaced him with William Sansom, thus restoring a link with Oxley's time. A Mr Neilson was under-usher until 1655, when he was succeeded by Alan Gilpin; Sansom and Gilpin thus had to keep the School going while the Council tried to find a replacement for Ritschel.[122] No official invitation was issued until April 1659, when the Council invited a Joseph Johnson from Oxford, about whom nothing else is known. Johnson refused, and the Council tried again, deciding by the end of the year to elect one John Newman, an equally obscure figure.[123]

Newman was initially appointed at £50 p.a., but the salary was shortly raised to £60, perhaps in recognition of the difficulty the Council had found in making an appointment without the Hospital Mastership to offer a candidate. The obscurity of both Johnson and Newman is testimony also to the political situation: the Protector had died on 3 September 1658, and the future was entirely uncertain. No one was going to commit themselves to a career as the nominee of one political group, when it might be out of power any moment. Newcastle in the last two years of the Interregnum, like much of the country, in fact came under the rule of moderate Independents for whom efficient government was more important than the 'good old cause', and they paved the way relatively easily for a Restoration. A brief attempt was made in the restored Rump Parliament, meeting in May 1659 after the resignation of Richard Cromwell as Protector, to overturn the rule of these moderates in Newcastle: a bill inspired by the 'well-affected' was considered in September 1659 for 'the better government' of the town. But the mayor, Mark Milbank, organised a counter-petition and the bill was forgotten.[124]

An indication of what men in the town thought was likely to happen is given by the fact that in 1659 the Council ordered that arrears of pay due to both Sansom and Oxley for their work in 1643–4 should be paid.[125] Even before the national transfer of livings back to orthodox ministers on St Bartholomew's Day 1662 (24 August) Newman disappeared and Oxley was reappointed to the School, on 27 April. His salary was raised to £100, a graphic illustration of the favour now shown to him by the Council. As we saw, Oxley cannot be considered a particularly extreme Anglican, and his religious attitudes fitted the new government of the town very well. He continued both Sansom and Gilpin in their offices, though Gilpin died in 1668 and was replaced briefly by George Waugh – a suggestive appointment, for Waugh was a non-conformist accused in 1669 of frequenting conventicles.[126]

Oxley remained as Master until his death in August 1669. His reputation was still high at the university – he was described by a fellow of Christ's in 1666 as 'the unwearied inspirer of the new age' *(novi indefessus seminator seculi)*, and many of his pupils continued to go there.[127] He also attracted many gentlemen's sons from the surrounding area: for example, the boys of the Delaval family of Seaton Delaval were sent to the school in the mid-1660s. Ralph Delaval, their father, was exactly the kind of person who survived the Restoration, having been in Richard Cromwell's Parliament but receiving a baronetcy after 1660. His sons while at the school boarded in the house of an only recently conforming minister, John Weld.[128]

1669 saw a number of deaths which affected the school. As I said, Oxley himself died in August, leaving in his will a number of books to the School in partial restoration of its library destroyed in the siege. William Sansom died in July, while Nicholas Hall the Master of the Hospital died in May. Both Sansom and Hall were replaced before Oxley's death, Sansom by another old boy of the school, Robert Gray, who had entered St John's as a sizar in 1665 and had just graduated B.A. Hall was replaced not by Oxley, as might have seemed appropriate, but by another survivor from the Interregnum, John Bewick. He had been a Puritan lecturer in the town just before the war, and was minister of Stanhope during it; but he conformed at the Restoration and became afternoon lecturer at St Nicholas's in 1662. The Council thus once again had only the stipend of the schoolmaster to offer Oxley's replacement.[129]

Who that replacement was to be, was a matter of some concern to the Archdeacon of Northumberland in November. Writing to Bishop Cosin, Isaac Basire said that 'I returned to Newcastle where I did earnestly entreat the present Mayor, Mr. Davison, a good man, to have a special care of three things; the maintenance of orthodox ministers, the choice of a good schoolmaster, well principled, and the suppression of conventicles.' But the town once again chose someone who had a rather equivocal record, ignoring at the same time Cosin's advice about the choice of a new vicar, for that post too was now vacant. Cosin's view of the Corporation of Newcastle was that they hoped to be 'kings and bishops' in their territory.[130] The new master was Richard Garthwaite, who had been born at Dent (Yorks.) in 1622. Educated at Sedbergh School, he had like so many of his fellow Northerners gone to St John's College Cambridge, graduating B.A. in 1644. In 1646 Parliament appointed him temporary Master of Sedbergh, the previous Master having been sequestrated, and he stayed on as usher when a new permanent Master was appointed in 1648. In 1654, however, he was dismissed on the grounds of being an 'apostate-proselyte' (i.e. having sympathy with Anglicanism). This was probably more the expression of a feud with the Master, who was himself dismissed for dereliction of duty in 1656. Garthwaite was a candidate for the post, but was not elected and accepted instead the Mastership of Kirby Lonsdale School until he was called to Newcastle.[131]

Although Garthwaite was not appointed to the Hospital, that post became vacant in less than two years, when Bewick died in June 1671. The Council seized the opportunity once again to integrate the two offices (which had not been held by one man since 1629) and appointed Garthwaite 'for and by reason that the said Hospital anciently and formerly was annexed to the said schoole and accounted as part and parcel thereof.'[132] For the next hundred years the two posts were always held by the same person.

Garthwaite continued Robert Gray as usher, until Gray's death in 1677, but he replaced George Waugh with Richard Wilson until 1674, when he was succeeded by Ralph Wilson, another of Oxley's pupils.[133] The choice of the successor to Gray in 1677 tells us something, perhaps, about Garthwaite's intellectual sympathies, for he chose the interesting figure of Richard Gower as his new usher. Gower was from Durham, but had trained as a physician at King's College Aberdeen, which he entered in 1667. He represents a remarkable survival of the attitudes of the Hartlib circle, for not only was he concerned with medicine, but he was also interested in the reform of language teaching. In 1682 he published a translation of a work on children's diseases, and two years later *A Censure uppon Lilly's Grammar* (signed R. G., 'formerly of the Free-School in New-Castle'). This is attributed in the second edition of

Wing to Garthwaite himself, but is as Laws observed clearly by Gower.[134]

The *Censure* breathes the air of the 1650s. Although the legislation underpinning Lily's Grammar had been restored in 1660, Gower urged Parliament to rescind it, and to abolish the formal teaching of grammar altogether. He drew on examples from 'our profession' of medicine, as the Hartlibians had so often done,[135] and quoted their idols Comenius and Bacon – 'the way to redeem our art is (as my Ld. *Bacon* has it) to attempt an instauration *ab imis fundamentis*, from the very foundation: and first to take off that superstitious reverence, which has bin so long paid to the antiquated Masters of the profession.'[136] If Montaigne, claimed Gower, could learn Latin without any formal grounding in grammar, the way the Romans themselves learnt it, why could not English schoolboys? 'I know not, whether any thing be better learnt, than what is learnt by play.'[137] He outlined an ideal curriculum and method which sound very similar to the orders for the Newcastle School under Ritschel, though he acknowledged that as a master in a free school he was legally obliged to teach grammar formally. If Gower's approach was typical of the School under Garthwaite (and as usher Gower was largely responsible for its grammar teaching), then Newcastle represented a remarkable phenomenon in the 1680s. This should perhaps not surprise us too much: the area saw at the same time the first example of a modern, well-disciplined and economically rational factory, of the kind urged by Hartlib and the others, in the shape of Crowley's Ironworks at Winlaton.[138] The combination of medicine, industry and a hostility to traditional grammar was likely to survive in Newcastle more than anywhere else in the kingdom.

Gower was ill from 1680 onwards, and in 1683 resigned his post. He was succeeded by John Metcal, who had graduated from St John's in 1674. Metcal stayed as usher until 1710, when he moved to the lectureship of the new chapel of St Ann's in the Sandgate.[139] Garthwaite himself fell ill in 1690, and in March the Council considered removing him from his post; but he died in September.[140] As far as we know, the School under Garthwaite had not been affected by either the Exclusion Crisis or the Revolution of 1688; throughout the reigns of both Charles and James, the town seems to have been ruled by the kind of men who took power at the end of the 1650s, and they allowed dissenters a considerable role in the town's life. James's policies did not meet with much opposition in the town (though he intruded a mayor by *mandamus* in 1687), but neither did his overthrow.

But Garthwaite's death fell in the period when the whole English social system was beginning to tighten up. The proportion of the population going to university fell dramatically in the 1680s, to stay extremely low for a hundred years. In the towns, the freemen became an increasingly small proportion of the population, and in Newcastle their School played a much smaller role in the education of the town's children. As the Tyne valley became a fully industrial area, the population of Newcastle grew at an extraordinary rate, from 11,500 in 1665 to about 20,000 in 1700, according to the best current estimates.[141] The principal concern of the Council in the late seventeenth century was simply to cope with this new and often very poor population, and it threw a lot of its efforts into developing a great charitable complex on the site of the old Manor, the former meeting-place of the Council of the North when in Newcastle. By 1700 the site housed the town's workhouse (a publicly-funded equivalent of the disciplined private industrial scheme such as Crowley's Works), the house of correction (in which there was also an elementary school), the Holy Jesus Hospital founded in 1682, and the lecture-hall and meeting-place of the surgeons of the town – a combination once again of medicine, industry and education. The privately-endowed charity school movement also began to supplement the Council's efforts at the beginning of the new century.

At the same time as access to the universities began to be restricted, the practical advantages of a knowledge of Latin also began to diminish; though Newton's *Principia* was still written in Latin, the fact that – for example – Locke's *Essay Concerning Human Understanding* was not, showed that the most complex arguments could now be conducted in English. Technical literature about mining, industrial processes and economics was all increasingly in English. An education in Latin grammar, which had had a most practical application in earlier centuries, no longer had the same point, and the history of education in Newcastle became a much wider matter than the history of its grammar school.

Although some interesting people still became masters, the story of the School for the next sixty years is not a particularly impressive one. Garthwaite was succeeded by a couple of fairly obscure figures, first John Cotteral (appointed in December 1690) and then Charles Stoddart. Cotteral was a Worcestershire man

ROYAL GRAMMAR SCHOOL

who had been at St Paul's School before going up to Oxford in 1661. In 1673 he was a candidate for the post of Surmaster (i.e. usher) at his old school, but failed to win it. In 1684 he was the Master at the Doncaster School, from which he moved to Newcastle. He died in March 1699, and the School was temporarily managed by the curate of St Andrew's, Charles Stoddart, before Thomas Rudd, who had been Master of the Durham School since 1691, was appointed to replace Cotteral.[142] The fortunes of the School under Rudd and his successors are the subject of the next chapter.

Chapter II

ACHIEVEMENT AMIDST DECAY 1700–1820

The eighteenth century has been referred to as a dark period in the history of English education. This we are told was symptomatic of an age in which private enterprise and philanthropic zeal opened up new paths while chartered institutions grew lazy and corrupt. For most of the century, it is claimed, the established church, still largely concerned with education, underwent a period of lethargy instead of activity, of worldliness instead of spirituality, of self-seeking instead of self-denial, of grossness instead of refinement. The two ancient universities were in decline, sunk in clerical and/or aristocratic obscurantism. Town government was closely controlled by a few self-indulgent families and these oligarchies, usually Tory/Anglican in complexion, failed miserably to tackle the growing problems, including education, brought about largely by a rise in population and by industrialisation.

Old foundation grammar schools were, it is maintained, no exception to this picture of decay and they reflected the apathy and slackness, even the corruption of most chartered bodies. Their government was neglected. Bound by out-of-date statutes and by tradition, they persisted in a curriculum of 'much Latin and a little Greek handled with enormous stupidity by clerical pedagogues of low status', and failed to respond to the needs of a developing commercial and industrial society. In consequence many parents sent their children to private schools and academies. This left the grammar schools either to continue with the classical curriculum, lose pupils especially from the poorer families and take boarders instead, making the schools more socially exclusive, or to sink to the level of an elementary school concentrating on the 3 Rs.

This, of course, is a very broad generalisation and presents too simplistic an analysis of the grammar schools of the eighteenth century. A recent study of the eighteenth-century grammar schools claims that they were hardly the decadent institutions they have often been described, and a local study of education during the century has maintained that 'The evidence from the north of

England suggests that the grammar schools there were more successful than in the rest of England'; that 'the popularity of these schools as worthwhile modes of training did not decline till after that century'; and that 'the grammar schools of the north were the nurseries of the northern elite in the eighteenth century'.[1]

The Grammar School at Newcastle functioned continuously throughout the eighteenth century and was one of the most successful schools in the North of England. Newcastle was as much an important educational as a religious, commercial and agricultural centre. Its Grammar School stood at the apex of a growing 'system' of education, both public and private, with the public sector receiving much support from the Corporation. Charity schools begun in the early years of the century received considerable help from the Corporation which also continued to maintain St Ann's Chapel school which it had founded in the Sandgate, the town's poorest quarter, in 1682. The Corporation strongly supported the Sunday school movement begun in the late eighteenth century and much encouragement and help were given to the new monitorial schools of the early years of the next century.[2]

The Common Council presided over a town that was already by the early eighteenth century becoming the commercial capital of the region. In 1698 that chatterbox of a tourist Celia Fiennes, noting a fine exchange and a broad quayside, concluded, 'its a town of great trade'. Newcastle remained during the century an important agricultural centre with quite thriving markets, but 'King Coal' reigned with the river almost tripling its coal exports during the period. All the industries for which Tyneside became famous had been established by the end of the century with the notable exception of engineering. Population growth in the town (from perhaps 12,000 at the beginning of the century to almost 30,000 by its close) together with increased trade and industrial development led to a demand for education, for literacy and numeracy, and also resulted in a growth of the professions, especially the law, medicine and banking. This was a very litigious age with increasing disputes in the area concerning mines, wayleaves, copyholds and enclosures, and the town could provide very lucrative pickings for lawyers and attorneys. In an age, like our own, rather over-addicted to medicine, medical facilities in Newcastle improved as the century progressed. An infirmary of ninety beds was opened in 1752 followed by a lying-in hospital in 1760 and a dispensary in 1777. The town became an important

40

money market for the region. Its first bank opened its doors in 1775, the second oldest provincial bank in England, and by 1801 the town had four.

The old town near the river might be ill laid out, overcrowded with the labouring classes and still the commercial nerve centre, but in the growing upper part of the town there were new wide thoroughfares like Pilgrim Street and Westgate Road (where the Grammar School was situated) where the 'middling sort' lived and where the country squires might winter. Even Dean Cowper, who in an earlier visit to the town in 1748 had remarked 'It has indeed the riches and trade of London in some degree, but with it the nastiness and filth of Edinburgh, the inhabitants of the poorer sort seem to vie with one another in dirt', was forced, in 1751, to admit that his former execration 'was of force changed into Compliments on the beauty and airyness of Pilgrim Street and the magnificence of the River Tyne'.[3] Newcastle had finally shed its role as a frontier town; its walls were allowed to fall into disrepair from the 1760s and the expansion into the suburbs was speeded up. The un-reformed Corporation was often accused of not spending nearly enough on the town and its development, and this charge is certainly true of its neglect of the river and its harbourage where little was done until the foundation of the Tyne Improvement Commission in 1850. However, it did spend over £100,000 between 1780 and 1832 on town improvement schemes whilst the post-1835 reformed Council, with its eye on the rates, proved distinctly more economical for many years and showed no great enthusiasm for spending money on schemes to improve the town's health and cleanliness.

As elsewhere, the town grew in importance as an island of civility in a sea of rural rusticity. Lecture series were popular throughout the century, as were subscription music concerts begun in 1736 which were occasionally held in the Grammar School. Magnificent new Assembly Rooms were built in 1776 and the old Theatre Royal opened in 1788 with Stephen Kemble, brother of Charles Kemble and of Mrs Siddons, as its manager from 1792. Coffee houses and circulating libraries were most popular. A Philosophical Society was founded in 1775 and the present more famous Literary and Philosophical Society in 1793. The latter showed a great interest and displayed much initiative in education from its earliest days. The Newcastle Courant, first issued in 1711 (a Newcastle Gazette had actually appeared the previous year but had quickly folded), was the oldest provincial newspaper in the

North, and the town at most periods in the eighteenth century could boast of having at least three weekly newspapers. Newcastle was also a sizeable centre of the printing trade, especially of books for children.

'Whoever will examine the state of the grammar schools in different parts of the kingdom will see to what a lamentable condition most of them have been reduced . . . empty walls without scholars, and everything neglected but the receipt of the salaries and emoluments. In some instances that have lately come within my own knowledge, here was not a single scholar in the schools though there were very large emoluments to them.'[4] This observation by Lord Kenyon, Lord Chief Justice, in 1795 laid the blame for this sad state of affairs at the door of governors, trustees and masters. Some years later Nicholas Carlisle in his survey of the country's grammar schools and the various reports of the Charity Commissioners between 1818 and 1837 provided many instances of neglect and consequent decay, though the latter reports mentioned very few cases of downright peculation on the part of governors or masters; rather laxity and maladministration were the main contributory causes.[5] Local examples included Hexham Grammar School where the governors were notorious for the tight secrecy they maintained about their accounts and management of the school, and at Kirkby Stephen where the governing body apparently never met between 1785 and 1797 and 'for the last fifteen years of the century no one seems to have received the major part of the school's income'. In 1783 at Morpeth Grammar School 'there were one hundred scholars in the school but from that time to 1811 it had fallen off, then there was one master the Rev. Shute and one scholar'.[6]

However, this view presents a very broad generalisation of the state of the country's grammar schools at the end of the eighteenth century, a generalisation that has been repeated in many of the textbooks covering the period. There were many exceptions, particularly among those schools where trustees and governors were open to local pressure, for example schools which came under the control of an embryonic local government organisation. This certainly seems to have been the case at Newcastle which was one of about twenty towns where the Corporation controlled the grammar school.

The Newcastle Common Council, whose members were generally referred to as magistrates, comprised the mayor, sheriff, nine aldermen chosen for life and twenty-four councillors somewhat mysteriously 'elected' by twenty-four electors from among the burgesses. In reality the government of the town was by an oligarchy – close control by a few family groups most of whom had made their fortune in trade. Clayton, Cookson, Cramlington, Bell, Brandling, Blackett, Ridley, Hood, Surtees are recurring names on the eighteenth-century Common Council. During the whole of the century the Council met regularly (usually quarterly) and, though educational matters formed only a small part of its business which was largely taken up with the management of its extensive estates, much could be done for education as already noted.

Throughout the century the Grammar School masters were paid their salaries by the Corporation in quarterly instalments, were provided with living accommodation and with coals and could be allowed removal expenses such as the £5 awarded to James Jurin in 1710 on his appointment to the headship.[7] The Common Council could also be very supportive towards masters' widows. In 1710 the widow of the late under-usher, Ralph Wilson, was allowed his quarter's salary and in the same year Henry Wilson's widow was paid £5 to help her to return to Cumberland following the death of the under-usher.[8] There is the occasional purchase of books and equipment for the school. Thomas Rudd's (Headmaster 1699–1709) request for books was met in 1700, and in 1758 it was reported, 'the Corporation, according to their usual Generosity, have ordered a pair of the best Globes to be bought for the use of the Free School in the Spital'.[9]

Crises, mainly over the staff of the School, could on occasion disrupt the otherwise uneventful administration of the School by the Common Council. The most celebrated of these concerned the headmaster Richard Dawes and this will be discussed below. Such crises were usually referred to a standing committee of the Council, consisting of eight members with aldermen being in the majority. The Common Council was well accustomed to work by committees. This particular standing committee was most probably the powerful Revenue Committee which dealt not only with routine finance but also acted as a general executive committee. In July 1737 for example, on the resignation of George Carr as under-usher, 'the low state of the said School was observed and that many freeman and inhabitants were obliged to send their children to distant schools which was a great loss and disadvantage to the town in general and the Common Council being also acquainted that the present Headmaster of the said School was

43

willing to resign his place it is ordered that the committee appointed to meet on the first Thursday of every month enquire into the yearly profit of the Mastership of the Hospital of Saint Mary the Virgin in Westgate usually given to the Headmaster of the said School and consider of and report to the next Common Council the most proper methods for retrieving the character of the said School'.[10] For its September meeting the Council had the full minutes of the committee which had considered various proposals for the Headmaster (Edmund Lodge) quitting the School but had 'not yet come to a full resolution thereupon'. After a very full debate the Council resolved to pay Lodge, should he agree to resign, £38 annually for the rest of his life, to allow him the use of an under-usher's house and to enjoy the benefits from the renewal of certain leases for the Hospital. Because of this considerable outlay, the Council ordered that the School should only have two masters during Lodge's lifetime unless increased numbers made a third necessary.[11]

In January 1765 the two assistant masters had apparently neglected their school duties, for the Common Council ordered 'that prayers shall be read in the said school by one of the masters every morning and a chapter in the bible by one of the boys in the head [top] class and that the masters call all boys constantly to attend this duty'. One of the assistant masters was to accompany the boys to St Nicholas every Sunday for morning and afternoon services. Their salaries were raised to £50 per annum but they were not to 'accept any church preferment or do any ecclesiastical duty for any pecuniary award [reward?]'.[12]

In September 1794 the Common Council was asked to adjudicate in a quarrel between Edward Moises, the Headmaster, and the usher Moses Manners. There is no record of the Council's decision in this affair, though Manners wisely resigned his office, being allowed to keep his house.[13]

Even in well-managed town schools financial crises could occur. These normally arose through misappropriation of funds, especially the leasing of school land or property at an uneconomic rent, or just through maladministration. At Manchester, for example, where the Grammar School was largely dependent on its endowments, the main source of its income came from a local monopoly of milling (including lucrative malt milling). An expensive legal action over the matter of the School's malt monopoly meant the feofees (governors) were forced to close the School in the 1730s for lack of funds. For most of the country's grammar schools inflation, especially in the latter years of the eighteenth century, was perhaps the most difficult financial problem they had to face, and many succumbed. The Newcastle School experienced no such financial problems arising from misappropriation of funds or poor handling of endowments. For one thing, there was no endowment to mishandle, for although the great tithes of the parish of Bolam in Northumberland were supposed to belong to the school, there is no evidence, at least in the eighteenth century, to support such a claim.[14] Besides, Newcastle was a very rich Corporation which took a great interest in education, as we have seen, and increasing revenues throughout the period provided unfaltering financial assistance to schools even during periods of inflation like the 1790s. The Newcastle Corporation provided that continued support and stability which Matthew Arnold in the following century in demanding a system of secondary schools called on the state to furnish.

By far the most important task of a school's governing body was the appointment, and the occasional dismissal, of staff. A headmaster could make or ruin a school. Hugh Moises, Newcastle's most successful eighteenth-century Head, by his scholarship and teaching ability could attract many pupils to the school from a very wide area. On the other hand, in 1716 the Tyneside merchant, William Cotesworth, transferred his two sons, William and Robert, from the School to Sedbergh, most probably on account of the resignation of James Jurin (headmaster 1710–15). Henry Liddell, Cotesworth's friend, maintained that Jurin had not been appreciated by the Governors and sent his own son Henry to Hackney School. 'Posterity will have occasion to curse those who have had any hand in making him (Jurin) uneasy in the Post he was possessed of. But what other can be expected from such a sett of Governors and to be succeeded by such a wretch (Edmund Lodge, headmaster 1715–38) who is not worthy of wiping his shoes is no less admirable. By this they seem resolved that the next generation shall continue in the same obscurity'. One contentious matter between Jurin and the Common Council as Governors of the School had been over the payment of pupils' fees. In 1714 the Council resolved, 'It is upon debate thought to be the intent of the said constitution that freemen living without the town ought to pay no more to the said master for teaching their children than those living within the town. It is hereby ordered that he (Jurin) demand no more for the future'.[15]

On the whole, however, Newcastle Grammar School was

fortunate in its choice of masters in the eighteenth century. Vacancies, unlike those at other northern grammar schools such as Morpeth, seem not to have been advertised in the local newspapers. It was not till 1828 that the Common Council resolved that the vacancy for the headship of the school should be advertised in the Oxford and Cambridge newspapers as well as those of Newcastle.[16] Appointments were usually by recommendation. In 1749 Walter Blackett, mayor the previous year, was requested by the Common Council to apply to a Dr Nicholls for a recommendation of a proper person to succeed Richard Dawes as Headmaster.[17] Hugh Moises who replaced him was recommended by Edmund Keane, Master of Peterhouse, rector of the rich Durham living of Stanhope, later Bishop of Chester and of Ely. The normal appointment procedure was to receive testimonies of character and scholarship often from the universities. Henry Wilson, who was actually Headmaster at Penrith Grammar School at the time, was appointed by the Council under-usher in July 1710 having produced 'sufficient testimonies of his qualifications and conformity to the doctrine and discipline of the Church of England'.[18] An unsuccessful candidate for the headship in 1737, Henry Noble, produced a letter of recommendation signed by ten fellows of Queen's College, Oxford.[19] There was some internal promotion; a number of under-ushers during the period were promoted to usher, for example, in 1781 John Brand, the historian of the town, who had held the post of under-usher at the school since 1778.[20]

Grammar school masters' salaries in the eighteenth century varied enormously, with town schools generally paying better. Very few grammar school masters in the North East received more than £50 salary per annum during the eighteenth century; the majority seem to have been paid between £20 and £30 and this was not much above the average earnings of a labourer – £11 per annum in 1700, £26 in 1790. At Darlington Grammar School at the beginning of the century the master was paid just £30 annually, the usher a mere £6. At Newcastle in the same period the Head received £50 per annum, the usher £35 and the under-usher slightly less, all paid in quarterly instalments.[21] There is some evidence to show that masters' salaries in the North of England lagged behind those in the South and this could add to the difficulty of finding suitable teaching staff. Also the North generally lacked graduate masters and had fewer in holy orders than elsewhere. Newcastle, however, was much better off in these matters than most grammar schools in the North. Of the twenty-one masters who taught in the school during the eighteenth century, just over 90% were graduates and some 60% were in holy orders.

Many grammar schools during the century could not afford to engage an assistant master. For example at Hexham Grammar School the endowment was so small that, though the statutes called for an usher, it was not till the nineteenth century that one could be afforded. The fortunes of one of the North's most successful grammar schools, rivalling Newcastle in importance, Durham School, fell so low in mid-century that for twenty-four years before 1785 there was no second master. Newcastle could afford to pay good salaries and could attract able teachers. It employed an usher throughout the century and, for most of the period, an under-usher. Usually assistant masters were young men straight from university or occasionally those about to proceed there, though none of the Newcastle masters was in this latter category. Its assistants were a little older on appointment than elsewhere with an average age of twenty-six, and often had had previous teaching experience. They were usually men of quite high quality; as John Scott (Lord Eldon) wrote of the 1760s, 'There were also excellent ushers at that school whilst I continued it'.[22]

Newcastle's masters' salaries increased during the century; the Head's was raised to £120 per year in 1750 and, as already noted, the ushers' to £50 in 1765. Edward Moises (Headmaster 1787–1829) wrote to the Common Council in 1790 asking for a salary increase. This was refused but he was compensated by being appointed to the Mastership of the Virgin Mary Hospital. In the general re-organisation of the school in 1822/3, the Head was to be paid £150 per annum, the usher or second master £120 and the under-usher £100. They were, however, to perform extra duties.[23]

Of course, these were basic salaries for the Newcastle masters and, as elsewhere, they could be supplemented in a number of ways. Quite often the headship of the School was combined with the mastership of the Hospital with its many perquisites especially for the renewal of leases and, together with the stipend from a morning or afternoon lectureship at one of the town's churches, these could add up to a very respectable salary. For example, Hugh Moises (Headmaster 1749–87) combined the headship with the mastership of the Hospital (granted in 1779) and with the office of forenoon lecturer at All Saints (1761) which carried an annual salary of £100. All these emoluments probably added up to ar annual salary in excess of £350.

The order of Common Council dated 14 January 1765 preventing assistant masters accepting any church preferment or doing any ecclesiastical duty for pecuniary reward was rescinded in December 1772 when William Hall, the usher, was appointed afternoon lecturer at St Thomas's Chapel. In 1778 the Council was assured by the Headmaster (Hugh Moises) that John Brand could faithfully discharge both the duties of under-usher at the School and those of a curate at St Andrew's Newcastle.[24]

There is little direct evidence of Newcastle masters taking boarders, a not uncommon practice to supplement salaries at this time. The School drew its pupils from a fairly wide area and, though most of those from a distance probably boarded in private houses in the town, some masters might accommodate them. In 1784 John Brand could write to a friend, 'While I was usher of Newcastle School I refused several advantageous offers of bo(a)rders'.[25] In 1818 it was reported that the headmaster, Edward Moises, 'has not taken Boarders for several years past; neither does the Second Master take any'.[26]

Many grammar school masters during the century took private pupils. This seems to have been a rare occurrence at the Newcastle School, though for a time James Jurin certainly taught mathematics to private pupils.

The provision of free housing (and coals) at Newcastle was also a welcome supplement to masters' salaries. Housing could be worth at least £10 per year, the amount proposed to be paid to John Wibbersley the under-usher, in lieu of his house which Edmund Lodge was to occupy when he resigned the headship of the School in 1737/8.[27]

The status in the local community of the Newcastle Headmaster was quite high and most treated the town Councillors as equals. If he were a university graduate the status of a school master was that of a gentleman and his place in the social scale that of a lawyer, doctor or merchant. Newcastle Headmasters' salaries were certainly commensurate with those at the top of the 'middling sort', though their high regard and that of their assistants may have come more from the fact that they were clergymen than schoolmasters. In the next century Thomas Arnold of Rugby was convinced that this was the case.

James Jurin was supposed to have saved £1000 during his brief tenure of the headship and, as we have seen, Hugh Moises by 1779 had an annual salary in excess of £350.[28] Moises had also married well: first in 1754 to Margaret Ridley, sister of Matthew Ridley, M.P. 'a very agreeable lady, with an ample fortune'; then in 1758 to Miss Bella Ellison 'a genteel and amicable lady with a considerable fortune'; finally to Mrs Ann Boag in 1764.[29] Hugh Moises was also very prominent in the town's affairs; for example, he was on the house committee of the infirmary which had been opened in 1752. His nephew Edward was very active in the management of charity schools in the town, and he chaired the general meeting in February 1793 that led to the foundation of the town's Literary and Philosophical Society, of which he became a prominent member and an enthusiast for its library. He was also known to a much wider public, for he said the prayers at the public execution on the Town Moor of Thomas Nicholson on 8 August 1795.

Grammar school statutes very rarely mentioned a retiring age for masters, and that of forty-five at Brigg Grammar School in Lincolnshire is something of an oddity. In the eighteenth century headships were usually long affairs mainly because of appointments to them being made at a relatively early age. The average age on appointment of the six heads at Newcastle in the period was twenty-eight; Edward Moises at twenty-five being the youngest. The shortest reign, just over five years, was that of James Jurin; the longest that of Edward Moises, forty-two years, though there were signs of decline in the School's fortunes during his latter years. In 1749 the long-serving (39 years) usher, James Ferne, presented a problem for the Common Council, and the committee that was set up to investigate the position of the Headmaster, Richard Dawes, was also briefed to discuss what was expedient to be done with respect to Mr. Ferne, assistant master in the said School who by reason of his great age is not now able to undergo the fatigue of a school'.[30] The difficulty resolved itself when Ferne died in the same year. The case of the Headmaster Richard Dawes was not so easily settled.

Richard Dawes (Headmaster 1738–49) had been appointed to succeed Edmund Lodge whose latter years at the School had not been particularly successful. If one is to judge the success or otherwise of an eighteenth-century grammar school by the numbers of pupils sent up to university, then the Newcastle School was very much in the doldrums in the 1730s with only five boys proceeding to the two universities during the decade. On 30

September 1736 the Common Council ordered that the 'annual sum of £5 or any other sum whatsoever shall not at any time hereafter be granted to any student or students at either of the said universities'.[31] An air of mystery surrounds this decision, but a contributory factor could have been the Council's dissatisfaction with Lodge's running of the School which, as we have seen, was reported on the following year as being in a very low state. Dawes, a fellow of Emmanuel, was already renowned for his Greek scholarship and great things were expected of him at Newcastle to revive the fortunes of the School. However, he was not particularly successful during his ten-year tenure of the headmastership. In a letter, probably written in 1744, he reflected that 'The good people in this part of the world are not very fond of Greek'.[32] The following year Dawes published his magnum opus, *Miscellanea Critica*, the production of which most probably led to the neglect of his duties as Headmaster. He was also an irascible controversialist. He had already crossed swords before his arrival at Newcastle with the greatest classical scholar of the age, Richard Bentley, Master of Trinity Cambridge, but, more to the point, nearer home with some of Newcastle's leading citizens. He lampooned the aldermen, teaching pupils to construe the Greek word for 'ass' as 'alderman' and, in 1747, he produced a pamphlet, 'The Tittle-Tattle Mongers No. 1', a scathing satirical piece on the town's leading men. Such disrespect led to cries for his resignation. Dawes proposed to resign but not till he had negotiated a sizeable settlement, what would amount to a considerable pension to purchase his retirement. After much haggling a settlement was finally agreed between the Headmaster and the Common Council on 26 June 1749. Dawes was to receive an annual pension of £80 for life (he died in 1766), and certain sums from the payments made for the renewal of leases of the Hospital of which he had been appointed master in 1738.[33] In his retirement at Heworth, Dawes, who was 'thought to be a little unsettled in his mind',[34] continued to indulge in his eccentricities and, as one commentator put it, 'as he had begun his life with the science of bell-ringing at Cambridge, he ended it with rowing on the Tyne'.[35] There was continual trouble over the Hospital leases and in 1752 the Corporation found itself involved in a Chancery case when a bill was filed against Dawes by the executors of his predecessor, Edmund Lodge.[36]

Fortunately, the School's other eighteenth-century Heads caused few problems on resigning. Jurin left to pursue a medical career, becoming Secretary of the Royal Society and later President of the Royal College of Physicians. Rudd and Lodge both took headships, at Durham and Haydon Bridge respectively, and later church livings. Hugh Moises retired to the rich benefice of Greystoke in Cumberland, though he later returned to Newcastle. No Newcastle Grammar School master apparently found it necessary to join the Association of Protestant Schoolmasters in the North of England which was founded in 1774 for 'the Support and Maintenance of the necessitous amongst their own Body, and the relief of the Wives and Children of their deceased Brethren'.[37] Both the Moises gave donations to the Association however.

After Cox's case (1700) it was decided that in the matter of episcopal licensing church courts had jurisdiction only over grammar school and not over elementary school masters. In theory therefore, eighteenth-century grammar school masters had still to subscribe as laid down by a statute of 1603 which stipulated that 'No man shall teach but such as shall be allowed by the Bishop of the diocese . . . except he first subscribe simply to the first and third articles in the thirty-sixth canon, concerning the King's supremacy and the Thirty-Nine Articles of religion, and to the first clauses of the second article concerning the Book of Common Prayer, viz., that it contains nothing contrary to the word of God, and may lawfully be used'. The statute further ordered that 'Every school-master, shall, at the Bishop's first visitation, or at the next visitation after his admission, exhibit his licence, to be by the said Bishop either allowed, or (if there be just cause) disallowed and ejected'.[38] During the period Newcastle Grammar School masters did subscribe from time to time and were sometimes cited to appear at a visitation. When they did subscribe it was quite often at the same time as they subscribed as clergy. The ecclesiastical authorities seem to have been more concerned with those grammar school masters who were not Anglican clergymen.

Along with Reverend Hugh Moises the Headmaster, Reverend Anthony Munton who had been appointed usher of the School two years before subscribed as follows:

> I Anthony Munton, Clerk M.A., to be licensed to perform the Office of Second Schoolmaster in the Free School in the Town and County of Newcastle upon Tyne and Diocese of Durham, Do willingly and ex animo subscribe to the first and third Articles contained in the 36th Canon and also

51

to the first and second Clauses of the second article thereof this eighteenth Day of July in the year of our Lord one thousand and seven hundred and fifty four.

I do declare that I will conform to the Liturgy of the Church of England, as it is now by Law established.'[39]

No copy of a licence granted to a Newcastle Grammar School master during this period has survived, nor is there any record of a licence to teach being refused any of them. This was probably not the case at Morpeth Grammar School where in 1771 after a disputed election for the headship, the Bishop of Durham on petition from the bailiffs (governors), whose candidate had not been elected, seems to have withheld his licence from the successful candidate, William Holden. At least Holden did not take up the post. Such rare cases apart, citations to appear at visitations, subscription and licensing even of grammar school masters in the Durham diocese seem to have been rather haphazard affairs in the century, more especially in its last quarter. Technically the licensing of grammar school masters continued until its abolition under the 1869 Endowed Schools Act, but long before that date it had become a mere formality, most masters never bothering to subscribe and take out a licence.

The late seventeenth century apparently saw the end of the golden age of the grammar school. Hobbes in his *Leviathan* (1651) had blamed them along with the universities for the 'late troubles' for their students' reading of certain classical authors had led to 'a habit of favouring tumults and of licentious controlling the actions of their Soveraigns'. It is significant that the most famous and influential educational work of the period, John Locke's *Some Thoughts Concerning Education* (1693), dealt with the upbringing and education of a kinsman's heir by a tutor at home. In Fielding's novel *Tom Jones* (1749), Squire Allworthy had Tom educated with Master Blilfil at home 'where he thought their morals would escape all that danger of being corrupted to which they would be invariably exposed in a public school or university'. Earlier Defoe who was a staunch advocate of a school education, was convinced that the main reason for the well-to-do educating their sons at home was social snobbery, the fear that the sons of gentlemen would be 'bred up among mechanics'. However, as the eighteenth century progressed and the home versus school debate continued, the disadvantages of education by a tutor at home were contrasted with the benefits of a school education. This debate was a very old and continuing one: as early as the first century Quintilian had defended school as against home tuition. At home a child was removed from society and was deprived of the kind of education needed to shine in society. The Georgians increasingly placed great store on sociability as well as civility in their idea of a liberal education. This was admirably summed up by Edward Gibbon who had been educated at Westminster: 'In a free intercourse with his equals the habits of truth, fortitude and prudence will insensibly be matured and his play-fellows may be the future friends of his heart or his interest'.[40] The old school tie network might be thought to be a nineteenth-century invention, but it was in evidence earlier, for as one eighteenth-century commentator observed, it was 'often the means of advancing a man's future in the world'.[41] In 1764 the High Master of Manchester Grammar School could also emphasise the competitive spirit found in public schools, whereas 'a youth spent in privacy and retirement has too often been found an obstacle to appearing afterwards to advantage in the busier scenes of life'. This sentiment, no doubt, would appeal to the growing business community in Manchester. The Newcastle Journal reported in its edition of 11 April 1776 on a debate by the town's recently-founded Philosophical Society on the question 'Is an education at a public school or by private tutors most eligible?' Newcastle society certainly favoured school education, for a majority found in its favour.

Unfortunately, very few eighteenth-century grammar school registers have survived, making it difficult to analyse the social backgrounds of their pupils. Indeed, it is difficult to find hard evidence of the numbers who attended the schools. This is certainly so in the case of the Newcastle Grammar School. In 1737 the low state of the School (presumably including numbers) was recorded in the Common Council book; by 1749 and the arrival of a new Head, Hugh Moises, the School was almost deserted of scholars; by 1761 Moises had raised the School 'from a very low to a very flourishing state'; three years later an under-usher was appointed 'on account of the great increase of scholars'.[42]

A recent study of the grammar schools in the four northern counties in the eighteenth century has argued that, unlike the south where there was more use of the 'great schools', private schools and home education, 'the grammar school seems to have been still the most frequent and most successful form of educational establishment in the north'.[43] Reasons for this are complex and far from clear, but it is certainly true that the

Newcastle Grammar School remained one of the great nurseries of the northern elite during the century.

What little evidence we have of the social background of Newcastle pupils during the eighteenth century suggests a fairly comprehensive social intake, not unlike that at Manchester Grammar School where, according to Thomas de Quincey who was a pupil there at the very end of the century, 'the parents of many boys were of artisans, or of that rank; some even had sisters that were menial servants; and those who stood higher by pretensions of birth and gentle blood were, at the most, the sons of rural gentry or of clergymen'. The bulk of Newcastle's pupils came from the 'middling sort' – merchants, lawyers and more especially clergy – but sons of watchmakers, joiners, cordwainers, tanners also attended the School. As one writer who had attended the School in the 1760s remarked, 'the Head School continued to be filled for several years with the sons of gentlemen and the sons of freemen; thus learning became generally diffused'.[44] However, as we shall see, there is some evidence to show that the School became rather more socially exclusive late in the eighteenth century.

The aristocracy and upper gentry either employed private tutors or sent their sons to the 'great schools', as they were beginning to be called – the Percies to Eton; the Middletons of Belsay to Rugby, for example. But the Newcastle School was attended by the sons of the great merchant families – the Blacketts and Ridleys, for instance, as well as those from rising entrepreneurial families such as the Cotesworths and Ellisons. Many of these were later in the century to ape their betters and send their sons to the 'great schools'. However, for most of the century these merchant families (many joining the ranks of the upper gentry) patronised the Newcastle School for the town 'afforded a situation very centrical and convenient for the four northern counties', and, in a land as yet without turnpike roads and fast mail coaches, 'country gentlemen residing far from the metropolis, were glad to find suitable places of instruction within their own reach'.[45] During the period the Newcastle School drew its pupils from a very wide area of the north.

Education in the School for the sons of freemen was virtually free at least in the classics; and many parents, especially clergy families, could not afford to send their children elsewhere. John Scott (Lord Eldon) later recalled, 'He (Cuthbert Collingwood, Admiral Lord Collingwood) and I were class fellows at Newcastle.

We were placed at that School because neither his father nor mine could afford to place us elsewhere'.[46] Many parents sought careers for their sons in trade and in the professions for which a grammar school education, even with its classical curriculum, could provide a good foundation. It should be noted that the distinction between professional and business elements in the eighteenth century was blurred; the professions served apprenticeships like tradesmen. Newcastle was quite an educational centre and could offer much in the way of variety of learning 'besides the pure classical fountain at the head school'.[47]

A grammar school could be very attractive, especially to the parent of fairly moderate means like an unbeneficed clergyman, because of the closed or semi-closed scholarships and exhibitions to the two ancient universities attached to it or its area. The sixteenth and seventeenth centuries had seen the endowment of many such awards. However, if we except the sixteenth-century Pattison scholarship, the Newcastle School did not benefit from scholarships provided by private donors until the eighteenth century. The most valuable of these were the Crewe and Hartwell exhibitions. Nathaniel Lord Crewe, Bishop of Durham from 1674 to his death in 1721, left a very considerable estate which, amongst other things, provided for twelve exhibitions at Lincoln College Oxford, worth £20 per annum for four years to natives of the diocese of Durham in the first instance. Many Newcastle boys enjoyed this privilege from 1717 (even before the bishop's death) to 1854 when the scheme was changed by the Oxford University Commission of that year. Those who benefited included John Brand (1768) and John Brewster (1772). The Hartwell exhibitions which operated from 1724 were originally worth £10 per year (later raised to £15) for four years at either university to scholars from Durham and Newcastle grammar schools. Headmaster Lodge's son Edmund was one of the first holders while at Lincoln College.

Of less importance was the Baker exhibition at St John's Cambridge, founded in 1699 and affording preference to natives of Durham and pupils of Durham School. Occasionally Newcastle scholars were awarded the exhibition, for example in 1758 William Hall who later was a master at the School. The Smith exhibition to Emmanuel College Cambridge for Durham and Newcastle Schools was claimed by John Brand to have been awarded shortly after the donor's death in 1773, but the first known award was to Humble Lamb, a former Newcastle pupil, in 1798.

Unlike today, scholarships and exhibitions were then rarely competitive. They were normally awarded to those already accepted as members of a college, what examination there was being carried out by a tutor. A notable exception was the prestigious Durham scholarship at Corpus Christi Oxford. This could be highly competitive and could be advertised in the local newspapers. The most famous holder from the Newcastle School was William Scott (Lord Stowell) in 1761.

The Common Council could on petition make awards of £5 per annum for five years to ex-Grammar School pupils studying at the university. Awards were limited to five students at any one time and were normally restricted to sons of freemen. However, in 1712 when two vacancies occurred and with no freemen's son applying, the £5 payment was awarded to two non-freemen's sons, John Sorsbie and Henry Holme, but it was ordered by the Common Council that for the future applicants should have been at the school for five or six years and should proceed straight from school to university.[48] As we have already seen, for some unknown reason (it could have been the very low state of the school in the last years of Lodge's headmastership) the award ceased in 1736. Interestingly enough, in 1778 the Common Council minutes record the award of £5 for Moses Manners, son of a mason, for Lincoln College, but this appears to have been a one-off payment.[49] John Brand could write in his history of the town (1789), 'Highly distinguished as this (the Corporation) is for every other species of munificence and charity, it appears extremely deficient in making no handsome provision, out of its ample and increasing revenues, to encourage the laudable ambition of the scholars of fortune'.[50] No doubt Brand, who had been an apprentice shoemaker after leaving the Grammar School, recalled his own difficulties in obtaining a university education. In 1768 he had been admitted to Lincoln College only with the aid of a subscription inaugurated by his headmaster, Hugh Moises, and somewhat later had been fortunate to obtain a Crewe exhibition.

University fees and expenses during the eighteenth century could vary greatly. There were, of course, those '*pauperes et indigentes scholares*' (poor and needy scholars) 'working their way through college' – the servitors at Oxford and the sizars at Cambridge, or those like John Brand who relied on a scholarship or exhibition. However, many Newcastle boys would be commoners or pensioners and a university education could be quite expensive. In 1784 Thomas Malthus's father, a man of fairly moderate means, paid £100 per annum to have his son educated at

Jesus College Cambridge, and remarked that if costs rose any higher, clergy would have to send their sons to universities like Leipzig where the annual cost was about £25. In 1803 Thomas de Quincey, an ex-Manchester Grammar School pupil, found that close economy was needed to live at Worcester College Oxford on ninety pounds a year.

Cambridge was more favoured than Oxford by Newcastle pupils, and St John's, Trinity and Christ's were the Cambridge colleges most frequented, whilst Lincoln and University Colleges were the most popular at Oxford. Unfortunately, during this period the Oxford college registers do not give the schools attended by undergraduates and those of the colleges at Cambridge are by no means complete. During the eighteenth century at least 143 Newcastle Grammar School pupils entered the two ancient universities – 50 to Oxford and 93 to Cambridge – and they came from a fairly wide social background, the majority coming from the 'middling sort'. In the North of England Newcastle's total for the century was only bettered by Appleby Grammar School (158) and was one more than the grammar school at Durham. Newcastle and Durham along with Houghton-le-Spring were the only three grammar schools in the North East to send up more than twenty students each to the two universities during the eighteenth century. For the Newcastle School there were 50 entrants for the first three decades of the century; a quite marked decline to only 13 for the next two (a national mid-century trend); a pick-up in numbers from Hugh Moises's headmastership (1749–87) onwards, peaking in the 1770s.

Entrants from the School to other universities during the century were few. At least one entered Trinity College, Dublin. Edinburgh, largely because of its medical reputation, was certainly favoured by a number of Newcastle's pupils, though the other three universities north of the border had students from the School. Of course, one of the reasons for entering a Scottish university was that Oxford and Cambridge still had religious tests and many dissenters refused to take these. One of Newcastle's famous pupils, the poet Mark Akenside who was at the school under Lodge and possibly Dawes, only managed to attend Edinburgh in 1738 to read for the Presbyterian ministry (he actually transferred to medicine) with financial help from fellow dissenters. Akenside completed his medical education at the University of Leyden.

Because of the lack of a comprehensive register for the School it is not possible to say what percentage of pupils went on to university during the eighteenth century. What very limited evidence we have of the jobs that pupils took up after leaving the School shows that about one in four went into the Church, with about one in seven into trade and one in ten into a legal career. Careers in medicine and the forces were somewhat less attractive, and teaching proved very unpopular with only one known taker, though many clergymen obviously taught to supplement their stipends.

One of the main reasons usually given for the decline of grammar schools in the eighteenth century was the existence of competition. Newcastle throughout the century possessed numbers of private schools and academies of one kind or another. These have left very few records and are known largely through newspaper advertisements. They almost defy classification and range from that described by a foreign visitor which proclaimed 'Children educated here. Shoes mended here. Funerals furnished here', to schools in Newcastle like those of Charles Hutton and Robert Harrison which operated in mid-century and rightly acquired reputations far beyond the town. Hutton's school was near the Grammar School in Westgate Street and 'a great proportion (of the Grammar School) pupils attended Mr. H to learn mathematics'.[51] Harrison's was quite unique in offering skills necessary for the legal profession.[52] Particularly after the Schoolmasters' Relief Act of 1779 (extended to Catholics in 1790/1) by which non-Anglicans became legally free to follow the profession of teacher, these institutions grew apace. At least fifty-seven private schools or academies have been identified as operating in Newcastle in the last thirty years of the century. These included classical schools, schools for clerks and schools for modern languages though, somewhat surprisingly for such a growing commercial centre like Newcastle, there were relatively few of the latter. Dancing schools and riding schools also operated. In 1801 John Baillie's History listed twenty-one private schoolmasters in the town.[53]

The likeliest rival of a grammar school was the private classical school, more often than not run by a clergyman, which offered basically the same classical curriculum as the grammar school and, because of its good staff/pupil ratio, proved attractive to many parents. There is no doubt that in many country areas the local grammar school suffered because of the existence of such a rival. Throughout the eighteenth century Newcastle Grammar School seems not to have been too much affected by competition, though Edward Moises's reform of the curriculum in 1793 was possibly occasioned by competition from private schools, and, as will be seen in the next chapter, Bruce's Academy in the early years of the next century was a different story. The register for the private classical school run by the Unitarian minister, William Turner, in his house in Percy Street lists 161 students during the period 1785–1802, just over half of these from Newcastle and Gateshead. Five of Turner's students during this period went on to the Grammar School, whereas not one left the Grammar School for Turner's.[54] Turner, a very prominent dissenting minister in the town, actually sent his own son Henry to the Grammar School in 1804.

In Newcastle the existence of public and private schools alongside each other did lead to much cross-fertilisation in educational ideas and practice. Pupils from the Grammar School could attend private schools or academies for special subjects – Hutton's for mathematics during Hugh Moises's headmastership or Samuel Dilke's for drawing in the 1780s. Anthony Munton after a spell as usher at Houghton-le-Spring Grammar School opened a private school in Newcastle in 1747 teaching the classics but also offering a course of lectures on the use of the globes and on algebra.[55] In January 1752 he was appointed usher at Newcastle. On the other hand, Moses Manners who had been an usher at the School went on to open a private academy in the town for English, Hebrew, Greek and Latin.[56]

The curriculum of the School in the eighteenth century differed very little from that of the previous century, where Latin was the 'meat course and salads and desserts were few'. Of course, religion played an important part in a pupil's education. School began with prayers and scholars repaired to church on Sundays. The church catechism, first in English and then in Latin and Greek was learnt, and the upper forms studied the Old and New Testaments. A grammar school education was basically literary (book learning) and it aimed through the study of the classics to implant in its pupils the habit of study, sound learning and good moral conduct. Younger pupils taken by the usher or under-usher would learn Latin rules from Lily's *Grammar* which was in common use throughout the century, becoming perhaps better known as the Eton Latin Grammar. With its confusing arrangement and the use of doggerel hexameters to explain many of the grammatical rules, this was a difficult text, and, no doubt, for most pupils provided a quarry of knowledge they hated to hunt. As in previous centuries much 'gerund grinding' went on at this stage. English sentences would be translated into Latin and simple authors would be attempted. Pupils then progressed to more difficult texts such as Aesop's Fables in Latin and Cicero's Letters. Great emphasis was placed on the ability to speak Latin and conversation books such as the *Colloquies* of Corderius and Erasmus could be studied. The double translation method was in common use: a Latin piece would be translated into English, then back again into Latin which, in turn, would be compared with the original. Repetition was the basic teaching method. By the fourth form under the headmaster the writing of themes commenced, together with the study of more advanced texts of Cicero and Ovid. Greek grammar was begun in the fifth form. In the sixth, Hebrew was studied alongside more difficult Latin and Greek authors. Of course, unlike today, the absence of any *de facto* university direction of the school curriculum permitted much independence on the part of a headteacher in determining programmes of study. Indeed, a variety of classical texts could be used, though teaching methods remained much the same throughout the century, despite the efforts of reformers like John Clarke of Hull Grammar School who condemned rote learning and advocated the use of English translations of texts.

Critics of the classical curriculum were numerous. Defoe, for example, early in the eighteenth century questioned, 'Is it worth any gentleman's while to go seven years to the Grammar Bridewell (school) and there beat Greek and Latin, as whores beat hemp?'[57] But it would be a mistake to think that it was an excessively restricted education, for the study of the classics could, and did, introduce pupils to a very wide range of learning – from biography through history to logic, political ideas and so on, and a code of values could be obtained. Besides, many pupils did turn to the classics for pleasure. For example, under Edward Moises late in the century pupils from the fourth class onwards always had what were termed 'private studies' which required them to read at home classical texts which were later examined.[58]

The eighteenth century saw important changes nationwide in the classical curriculum of the grammar schools. Spoken Latin declined and, as Latin became less a language for everyday use, the curriculum became even more literary. Aesop's Fables in Latin for junior forms virtually disappeared. Latin prose writers tended to take over from the poets while the study of Greek advanced, though it was still learnt through Latin, the nineteenth century seeing the establishment of English as the medium for Greek teaching.

These changes can be seen to some extent in the 'Outline of the Plan of Education' introduced by Edward Moises into the Newcastle School in 1793. Spoken Latin is nowhere specified. The Eton Grammars are still being used, though with rather more explanation on the master's part. Aesop has been dropped for younger pupils and replaced by *Delectus Sententiarum* ('easy and elegant passages from the best Latin authors'). The poets Ovid, Nepos and Virgil are the favoured authors for upper forms, though Caesar and Cicero are studied. Greek is begun now in the fifth class (there are nine classes, including the head [top] class). The seventh class begin the study of Hebrew. Scripture still forms an important part of a pupil's studies, and Eldon's recollection of his own schooldays in the 1760s still held good some thirty years later. 'I remember, that when I had the benefit of an education at one of those grammar schools, the education was carried on in what, I believe, was once a *capella* or a *sacellum*: that the boys educated there were headed by their venerable master to church constantly upon Sundays; and *that* part of the duty of a master of a grammar school was, in those days, as much attended to as teaching the scholars what else they ought there to acquire.'[59]

The eighteenth-century grammar school has usually been criticised for its rigid curriculum. It is claimed that, hide-bound by its statutes and by tradition, it was unable or unwilling to change its classical curriculum in an age that was demanding more breadth in studies, to include in particular English, mathematics, the sciences and modern languages. Refusing to change, many grammar schools found that the classics were not attractive to many potential pupils, especially those from the lower orders of society, and masters were forced to take in boarders thus making the schools even more socially exclusive. An alternative was to add 'modern subjects' to the curriculum, especially English, which could result in time in the degrading of the schools, turning them into elementary schools. For example, Nottingham Grammar School could be regarded in 1818 as 'a useful Seminary for teaching boys English Grammar, reading, writing and arithmetic but its former celebrity in classical learning is at an end', and it was reported of the local grammar school at Stamfordham, 'At present the rudiments of the *English* language only are taught'.[60]

However, there is much evidence to show that the grammar

schools, especially in the later years of the eighteenth century, were responding to the demands of a changing society for new subjects to be introduced into the curriculum. Very few new grammar schools were founded in the North East during the century, but, as elsewhere in the country, new foundations did introduce subjects other than the classics into the curriculum. One such was at Gateshead which was to teach pupils 'the Latin and Greek tongues, and also to write and cast up accounts, and also the art of navigation'.[61] Existing grammar schools could, if they wished to add new subjects to the curriculum, attempt to change foundation statutes in order to do so either through the Court of Chancery or by private act of Parliament. For example, in 1785 at Haydon Bridge Grammar School the trustees 'at the request of the Inhabitants of the Chapelry of Haydon, and at Woodshields, obtained an Act of Parliament to render the Foundation of the greatest real use and benefit of which it appeared to be capable'. Amongst other things, the act empowered the trustees to 'appoint such Master, and such and so many usher or ushers, to teach and instruct Boys and Young Men . . . not only in Grammar and Classical Learning, but also in Writing, Arithmetic, Navigation and the Mathematics, and in such other branches of Literature and Education as should from time to time, in the judgement of the Trustees be proper and necessary, to render the Foundation of the greatest real use'.[62] This act probably gave legal recognition to existing practice.

Newcastle's curriculum throughout the eighteenth century remained essentially classical, though there is evidence to show that other subjects were taught in the School. Fortunately a writing school was attached to the Grammar School where pupils were taught the 3 Rs. This was usually referred to as the Free Writing School and the arrangement was very similar to those found in Scottish borough schools, and at Berwick. Though this school did not become a preparatory school to the Grammar School till the reorganisation of 1823, it did throughout the century educate many boys who entered the Grammar School at about the age of eight. Again, numbers of boys from the Grammar School attended it for elementary mathematics and for accounts. John Scott on occasion played truant from the writing school where he learned the art of penmanship from William Banson for half a guinea a quarter.[63] Banson (or Benson) was master from 1755 (it could have been earlier) to 1776, and was a son of a previous master, Henry Banson, who had succeeded his father William in the post. In 1702 the latter published *The Merchants Penman*, a copy book for school use, the Corporation granting him in October 1700 £20 'towards printing and completing his writing book'.[64] In 1709 he published *An Arithmetical Exercise, being designed for the more speedy improvement of the Free Writing School in Newcastle upon Tyne.*

As in many other grammar schools during the period, new subjects could be added on the initiative of individual masters and, as we have seen, pupils could be sent for tuition in these to other schools. James Jurin offered a course of lectures in mechanics to the public in 1711–12 and also taught mathematics to private pupils.[65] It is not unlikely that he taught mathematics to his Grammar School pupils, though we have no direct evidence of this. John Wibbersley, at the time usher at the School, gave a course of public lectures there in geography in 1749.[66] Like Jurin, it is quite possible he included some geography in his teaching at the School. Later in 1758, as already mentioned, the corporation provided globes for the use of the school. Of course, in a highly successful school such as Newcastle Grammar School under Hugh Moises, the very fact of success could lead to even more concentration on the classics. However, even his pupils in the 1760s practised English prose composition.[67]

The 1793 'Outline of the Plan of Education' seems to have been introduced on his own initiative by Edward Moises and was most probably occasioned by falling numbers in the School. There is no evidence that the Common Council as Governors played any part in its formulation. Though the Plan owed much to Moises's own rather limited experience and, no doubt, to his uncle's example, it appears to have been based on the ideas of Vicesimus Knox who in 1781 had produced a work on the practical side of grammar school education. Knox, Headmaster of Tonbridge School (1778–1812), was a staunch defender of the position of the classics in the school curriculum, though he did recommend other subjects. However, he was at pains to point out that new subjects in the curriculum depended for their educational value upon effective methods of teaching which had not as yet emerged. 'So I would rather conduct a pupil in the beaten path (the classics), which has led tens of thousands to the summits of learning, than by untried ways; notwithstanding that they are pointed out by the truly ingenious as shorter and pleasanter.'[68] Classicists were to employ similar arguments, together with that of the lack of competent teachers, against the introduction of science teaching in the next century.

Moises's Plan provided for an essentially classical curriculum, though it paid more than just lip service to other subjects. English texts such as Goldsmith's *Abridgement of Roman History*, Pope and the *Spectator* were read in the lower classes. Upper classes read Milton, Shakespeare and, most interestingly, the top class studied an abridgement of Locke's *Essay on Human Understanding*. Cellarius's *Geography* was used in the fourth and fifth classes with 'the remarkable places pointed out in the maps'. From the fifth class onwards subjects included algebra, geometry and trigonometry, mechanics, hydrostatics and astronomy. However, these were referred to as 'lectures', were given only twice weekly and, significantly, were 'not to interfere with the usual business of the School', that is the reading of the classics.

Mention must be made of the Leeds Grammar School case because the decision made in this case in 1805 by Lord Chancellor Eldon, a Newcastle alumnus, is generally considered to have held up curriculum reform till the Grammar School Act of 1840 which, though limited in scope, permitted statute revision and therefore the introduction of new subjects. A recent writer has alleged, 'If anything were needed to hasten the process of atrophy in secondary schools, Lord Eldon's decision in the Leeds Grammar School case (1805) was admirably fashioned for the purpose'.

This particular case had a long and complex history beginning in 1779 when the School Governors decided to add mathematics and modern languages to the curriculum, a decision ignored by two successive Headmasters who contended that the foundation statutes forbade any other teaching than that of the classics. Besides, the Headmasters added, there had been no fall-off in pupil numbers and if, as the Governors argued, School funds were in surplus, then such surplus was by right payable to the staff. Though Eldon did give a decision, following Dr Johnson, that grammar schools were for teaching grammatically the learned languages, he did not rule that there was no room for any other subject in the curriculum besides the classics, or indeed that it was illegal for such other subjects to be taught. Much of his decision rested on usage, and he ruled that where new subjects were introduced to promote the direct object of the charity, then this was perfectly legal. In other words, if by the addition of, say, mathematics and modern languages parents were induced to send boys to schools to learn the classics, then such addition was acceptable as it promoted the original intention of the foundation. Though, as we have seen, the Newcastle Grammar School was bound more by tradition than by statute, this is what happened to some extent at Eldon's own school and he may have recalled this in giving his decision in the Leeds case. In the event curriculum reform did take place at Leeds and, though the length and expense of the Leeds case no doubt did deter other schools hoping to introduce new subjects to the curriculum from going to law, changes in the curriculum of the country's grammar schools did take place well before 1840.

References to the school library in the eighteenth century are few. As already noted, in March 1700 in Rudd's Headmastership the Common Council provided books, and those in the School Library were repaired or re-bound at about the same time. In 1762 the Bishop of Chester sent down from London a library for the benefit of pupils studying divinity in the school. The 1793 Plan of Education stated, 'The English books which are read in School and as private studies, are lent to the different classes out of the New Library'. The money to purchase these books was to come from the entrance fee of half a guinea. Though individual copies of library books still exist, there is no catalogue of the eighteenth-century Library but, as elsewhere, the Library would reflect the central position accorded to the classics and religion at this period.

As we have noted, the Common Council seems to have played very little part in deciding curriculum matters during the eighteenth century and to have left what changes there were in the curriculum to individual headmasters and, in effect, to market forces. However, at the turn of the century there was growing criticism of the running of the town and, in particular, of its financial dealings. An audit crisis arose in 1809 led by a prominent Wesleyan burgess, Joseph Clark, who in the previous year had published *The Newcastle Freeman's Pocket Companion*. In this publication the Grammar School did not escape Clark's strictures. He attacked in particular its classical curriculum, increasingly otiose in a utilitarian age where 'the habits of the literary world are now so changed, that almost every useful work is published in our own language, and more especially since the extention of commerce and navigation have rendered the knowledge of the modern languages and of the sciences and arts connected with ship-building, and with the manufactures on which our prosperity as a nation depends, an object of much greater importance, a correspondent alteration seems very desirable in the constitution of our public schools'. Clark went on to call for the appointment of teachers of French and German and also 'in the elements and practical application of the mathematics'. There is also a strong hint that the Grammar School under Edward Moises had become more socially exclusive, for Clark humbly presumed 'to recommend it to the Magistrates and Common Council, as a proper object of their consideration, whether it would not be highly desirable to apply a part of their ample revenues in extending the benefits of the school to those for whose use it appears from the charter to have been originally intended'.[69]

Walter Yate in an open letter to the town's magistrates in 1812 was more direct. After referring to the low state of the Grammar School he concluded 'Hence one of the greatest satisfactions a parent can feel, that of giving their offspring a good education, would, by the restoration of this school, on a scale adequate to its ample revenues, revert to the inhabitants, and be within the reach of the *poorest* of them'.[70]

In 1817 in a new edition of his companion, Joseph Clark desired the Corporation to institute an inquiry into the causes of the decline of the School which was in 'a state almost unattended to, and unknown by the public, except by the payment of the salaries of the master and usher'.[71] In that year the Common Council requested its Revenue Committee to 'make Enquiry into the grounds of certain complaints which have been made tending to show that the scholars educated at the said School are neglected by the master and report their opinion to the Common Council'.[72] Nothing really appears to have been done till late 1822, resulting in a quite radical reorganisation of the School in the following year which is discussed in the next chapter.

Even glimpses of what went on inside eighteenth-century grammar schools are rare to come by. Fortunately, a pupil of the Newcastle school in the 1760s has left an interesting account of his schooldays under Hugh Moises. The Headmaster with the senior scholars occupied what had been the chancel of the Hospital chapel which, with other buildings on the site, had been leased from the Virgin Mary Hospital; the usher, on a raised platform, occupied the east end of what had been the nave; the under-usher with the youngest pupils the west end. The upper school room also served as the election room for the Corporation and had had a fine east window of the Virgin and Child with later additions of armorial bearings of various mayors. By this time the window was apparently bricked up and whitewashed. Writing in the following century, the eminent Newcastle architect Benjamin Green was not enamoured of the 'elegant porch' (Brand's phrase) built as an entrance to the school in 1782, one of whose pillars still stands at the bottom of Westgate Road near the Stephenson memorial.[74] Masters usually appeared in full academic dress which 'offered a dignity and decorum which were not lost upon the scholars'. Prayers were read at the east end by whichever master arrived first and a chapter from the New Testament was read by one of the senior pupils. Older scholars later construed that particular chapter from the original Latin with a master giving verse by verse elucidation. As in other grammar schools of the period, pupils were arranged in classes according to age and attainment but classrooms with desks, as we know them today, were really a nineteenth-century development and pupils, either individually or in small groups, came up to a master's desk for instruction. Moises apparently kept a tight check on all pupils' (and masters') progress, for every Thursday was his day for hearing the lower classes. Under Edward Moises there were 'exercises' (home-work) for the whole School every day of the week and this was most probably the case in his uncle's time.

Entrance was usually at the age of eight and pupils could continue in the School till sixteen or seventeen. Hours were long, usually from seven in the morning till six in the evening with a two-hour break for lunch, and pupils attended six days per week. In the 1823 reorganisation of the school, hours were 9–12 in both summer and winter, 2–4 in winter and 2–5 in summer.[75] Holidays were about three weeks at Christmas and a fortnight at Easter, together with certain holy days. Under the 1793 Plan of Education, there was to be a month at both Christmas and at Midsummer. We have no direct evidence that Newcastle Grammar School boys enjoyed the time-honoured custom of 'barring out' which took place about six weeks before Christmas and which survived well into the nineteenth century in many northern schools. In 1818 Nicholas Carlisle specifically mentioned Rothbury Grammar School where the 'annual custom of "barring out" the Master and Usher long prevailed'.[76] Pupils 'growing petulant at the approach of liberty (the Christmas vacation) took possession of the school of which they barred the doors, and bade their master defiance from the windows'. Most masters sensibly gave way and granted extra play days before Christmas and the suspension of all punishments, though 'if tradition may be credited, he often struggled hard to face or surprise the garrison'.[77]

The eighteenth century witnessed a changing attitude towards children, more especially among the upper and middle orders of society. Influenced largely by the writings of John Locke, Richard Steele and others, parents were becoming more gentle and sensitive in their approach towards their children and, in particular, physical punishment became less severe. Many parents no longer regarded their offspring as sprigs of the old Adam which had to be broken. This changed attitude, especially in the matter of punishment, does not appear to have caught on in the grammar schools; however, there is some evidence to show that private schools and academies were less severe in their punishments which, in turn, made them more attractive to caring parents. Even Hugh Moises 'always tempered necessary severity with affability and kindness'. Yet Eldon, who on more than one occasion was beaten for his misdemeanours, recalled that he was 'once the seventeenth boy that Moises flogged'.[78] George Hodge, a master mariner, went so far as to petition the Common Council in 1824, complaining of Edward Moises beating his son Robert 'in so cruel a manner'.[79]

Newcastle pupils had long enjoyed the privilege of playing games in the Spital Field, specific times being set aside for such. In connection with this privilege an interesting example of eighteenth-century pupil-power occurred in 1787. In that year the boys petitioned the Common Council complaining that Hugh Moises, the Master of the Hospital, had done nothing towards remedying abuses against their use of the Spital, 'namely forming roads, breaking out doors, making drains and other encroachments'.[80] The matter ended happily with Nathaniel Clayton, the town clerk, being granted a lease of the two-acre field for twenty-one years at twenty shillings a year 'that he will permit and suffer the said scholars to have the free and unconditional enjoyment of the said croft as a place of exercise and amusement'.[81] Most schools at the time did not possess playing fields; Manchester Grammar School had none. Another favourite playground of Newcastle pupils was the nearby St John's churchyard where Eldon recalled riding on the gravestones.[82]

From Thomas Rudd to Edward Moises, the years from 1699 to 1828, the Grammar School at Newcastle experienced a period of mixed fortunes: it plumbed the depths under Richard Dawes and reached its apogee during the headmastership of Hugh Moises. The school, unlike most of its contemporaries, more than just survived. For most of the period Newcastle Grammar School remained one of the leading schools of the North of England and, though still largely the preserve of the 'middling' class, it did set many 'lads of parts' on the road to successful careers, thus aiding social mobility. The School responded, admittedly to a somewhat limited extent, to the various pressures seeking curricular change. The close connection between the School and the two universities was preserved and developed. The period witnessed a generally amicable relationship between the School and its 'government', the corporation providing throughout a secure financial base for its activities, which most eighteenth-century grammar schools would have envied. Change there would have to be, but the Newcastle Grammar School was, perhaps more than most of its kind, in a healthier position to respond to the demands of a changing society. What advantage would be taken of such a state of affairs is one of the themes of the following chapter.

Chapter III

UNCERTAIN PROGRESS 1820–1888

There is a garden and it is enclosed with high walls and planted about with shrubs; the schoolmaster tends his pots; dominating the scene, but not overpowering it, stands the Grammar School. This mellow image was established in the picture commissioned by John Brand for his *History of Newcastle* published in 1789. Whether fortuitously or by design, the scene is laden with symbols; the garden itself, sheltered, orderly and cultivated, reflects stability; the medieval church, long since the home of the School, proclaims continuity and strongly rooted tradition; the gardener, going about his task with unhurried purpose, brings his plants to useful fruitfulness. As a representation of the School's eighteenth-century heyday under Hugh Moises this picture could hardly be more apt and it makes the irony even more piquant that within a generation, at most, of publication it had lost its symbolic relevance. For much of the period under review in this chapter – from the 1820s to the 1880s – there was physical upheaval where there had been stability, uncertainty and experiment where there had been continuity, decay in both size and function in place of predictable usefulness. When, during the 1850s, circumstances, local and national, became more favourable the School began to revive, slowly and in some respects unsteadily, so that by 1888, when this chapter closes, it had been re-established as Newcastle's principal secondary school. Important problems were outstanding in 1888 but nevertheless that year has been taken as a convenient point at which to close, as it was then, after more than fifty years of debate and planning, that a measure was passed by Parliament which remodelled the School's constitution.

(i) *Decline, 1820 to 1847.*

When it entered the nineteenth century the School was in difficulties and the passage of ninety years did not see an end to them. The evidence relating to this century is dominated by problems and crises but this feature is never more apparent than it

70

was before the 1850s. The most obvious symptom of the School's weakness was its erratic and sometimes extremely poor enrolment. As the roll is a crucial indicator of how the School stood in the estimation of the town, it is unfortunate that we cannot establish with any precision how many boys were in the School at that time. No help is given by A. R. Laws's *Schola Novocastrensis* or by B. D. Stevens's *Register of the Royal Grammar School 1545–1954*. Both works present only fragmentary biographical information about a small number of the pre-1870 alumni. The registers, if they ever existed, have not survived before 1870 and consequently we must work with stray references some of which may be unreliable, as for example, statements made in Council meetings by partisan or merely ill-informed councillors. Furthermore, attendance would have fluctuated over the year. Thus, a number might reflect the size of the School in a particular week or month but it will not necessarily show what the annual average attendance was. Bearing these qualifications in mind, the evidence suggests that recruitment was very unstable in the 1820s, 30s and 40s. At the beginning of the 20s there were only nine boys in the School while at the end of the decade there seem to have been eighty; in the early 1830s the roll had fallen to fifteen but towards the end of the decade the School was described as flourishing with about 150 pupils; during the 1840s there seem to have been no more than a few dozen pupils.

The evidence concerning the size of the School is full of gaps but what there is gives good reason for believing that it was far from being the most popular school in Newcastle, or the most significant, during the first five decades of the nineteenth century. This is corroborated by various kinds of material spread over the fifty or so years here under consideration. Throughout that period the town Council fretted over the unreasonably small intakes of pupils. Signs of their concern are seen in their special enquiries of 1820, 1822 and 1846, to find out why the School was in the doldrums.[1] The opinions of well-informed, well-intentioned and reliable citizens also lend support to the conclusion suggested by the numerical evidence outlined above. Eneas Mackenzie, an active politician, writing in 1827, tried to account for 'the declension of this once flourishing institution'.[2] Twenty years later, Sir John Fife, one of Newcastle's leading personalities, and one who was very sympathetic to the School where he had been educated, took it for granted that the School had floundered. In 1865 the most eminent of the town's schoolmasters, the Reverend

Dr John Collingwood Bruce, called as an expert witness before a royal commission, was asked to 'account for the falling away of the Grammar School in Newcastle, why it should be a school of low rather than a high class'. The doctor's reply, which assumed the question to be valid, ranged over the School's fortunes during the 1820s, 30s and 40s.[3] Some contemporaries of Bruce were of a similar mind but as they are relatively anonymous witnesses it is difficult to know whether theirs were considered opinions born of solid knowledge or merely prejudice. Certainly, the Council debates during the 30s and 40s give the impression that within the Council there was increasing impatience with the School. A Councillor Preston seems to be speaking for many when in 1847 he stated that it was 'quite clear that the ancient glory of the School had departed'.[4]

There can be little doubt that the Grammar School was failing and it is the purpose of the first part of this chapter to discover the cause, or causes, of that failure. Decline, measured in terms of low recruitment, may have been at any given time the result of specific events which, viewed in a wider perspective, were as insignificant as their results were short-lived. There are examples of substantial damage being done to enrolment by untoward events, even after the mid-century when the School was on a much surer footing than it had been earlier. In 1871 the Headmaster, James Snape, resigned amid great controversy and within a year the School had lost 187 of its 280 pupils; at one stage the roll fell as low as 140. However, within five years recruitment had returned to what it had been before Snape's resignation. Another example of the acute sensitivity of public opinion is given by a fifteen per cent reduction of numbers in 1888 following a fatal playground accident which received hostile attention in the newspapers.[5] These incidents are undoubtedly illuminating but it is most unlikely that the long decline, which had probably started in the 1780s, was the result of a succession of temporary set-backs. It is much more likely that the School's loss of reputation was caused by one or more structural weaknesses.

Newcastle's Grammar School was not alone in its experience of decline at this time. Although it was somewhat unusual, being financed by an annual subsidy from the town's public treasury rather than by its own property held in trust and administered by an autonomous board of trustees, it was nevertheless one of a group of about six hundred endowed grammar schools in England. For a variety of reasons many, if not most, of those schools were labouring under severe pressures. Some had been successful in adapting themselves but most were not coping well with declining popularity. No single general explanation will adequately account for the decline of the grammar schools. Each case is individual. Some were damaged by the negligence or incompetence of their trustees; others lost revenues through misappropriation. Some were starved of funds, their income rendered inadequate by the passage of time and inflation; others suffered from the unpopularity of masters with an abrasive manner. Some were subject to successful attacks on their curricula; others collapsed because of superior competition in their localities.

Suggestive though this analogous material is, it does not provide a satisfying explanation for Newcastle's problem. The viability of a school such as this one was the product of the balance between the attractiveness of its curriculum, the ability of its headmaster, the quality of rival schools in the area, the condition of the universities, the organisation of its financing, the attitude of the governing body (the town Council until 1888), and the religious and social prejudices of the population. These eight aspects of the School's life need now to be examined in detail to determine how far each might have contributed to its decay between 1820 and 1850.

Was the School unpopular because it was only offering courses in subjects for which Newcastle families generally had no use? Edward Moises was certainly running the School as a traditional classical establishment. His primary objective was to qualify his senior scholars in Greek and Latin for matriculation at Oxford or Cambridge. Consequently everyone in the School had necessarily to learn the foundations of the classical languages so that the minority who remained beyond fourteen could proceed to advanced work in those subjects. Moises's 'Plan of Education' of 1793 shows that the youngest boys spent their time studying Latin, ancient history and English. Later they added Greek and a little geography. Mathematics is also touched on but only in thrice-weekly lectures which, in the words of the Plan, were 'not to interfere with the usual business of the School'.[6] The senior scholars continued with Latin and Greek, began Hebrew, attended mathematics lectures and dabbled in philosophy.

Missing from Edward Moises's curriculum are elementary mathematics, modern languages, commercial English (such as précis and shorthand), modern history and science. With the exception of science (which very few schools would be offering at this time) the omission of these subjects would have damaged the School's recruitment prospects because they were available in at least one secondary school in Newcastle. As Newcastle was a trading town with substantial markets in northern Europe boys destined for commercial jobs would need some knowledge of French and German. Much the same may be said of the lack of elementary arithmetic and mathematics and book-keeping. It is true that 'practical arithmetic', suitable for commercial work, was provided in the Writing School which was carried on beside the School in the grounds of the Virgin Mary Hospital. However, as we shall see, the Writing School was badly managed at this time and as it was independent of the Grammar School until 1823 the Headmaster had limited opportunities to interfere.

The narrowness of Moises's curriculum might be thought to have been the cause of the School's recruitment problem because of its lack of direct vocational relevance. However, this does not seem to have been the case. Moises's system came under scrutiny by the Council during the latter years of his headmastership. In 1822, having received a petition asking for the reason why he had only nine pupils in the School, the Council appointed a committee to look into the matter and suggest remedies.[7] As a result of the inquiry the Council, in 1823, imposed a number of changes, which will be considered below, but, significantly, they left Moises's curriculum alone saving the addition of modern history and the removal of Hebrew.[8] The changes of 1823 must have been effective, for five years later when Moises retired from the headmastership there were some eighty pupils in the School, a very respectable roll for a grammar school at this time and an important proof that there was a demand in the town for a classical school.

The Council showed their determination to maintain the traditional character of the School when they appointed George Mortimer to the headmastership in succession to Moises. Mortimer, a young man with a distinguished academic record and just down from Oxford with a First in Greats, was charged by the Council in 1828 'to restore the establishment to its former high character as a place of classical education'.[9] In the light of the notable recovery of popularity in the concluding years of the Edward Moises period, it may be presumed that they intended Mortimer should 'continue' restoring the School's classical reputation rather than rebuild it from ruins. The interval between the two headmasterships would have been the most opportune time for the Council to make changes if they had been planning to bring the curriculum in line with the demands of the market. However, between Moises's departure and Mortimer's arrival no changes were made, though there is perhaps a hint of concern when they asked the new Headmaster to give in addition to classical work, 'instruction in those branches of education more generally useful in a commercial town'.[10] But Mortimer did not remain in Newcastle for very long. When he resigned in 1834 the School was again in trouble. In 1827 there were eighty boys on the books; in the year before he left there may have been as few as fifteen.[11] The Council's 'Committee on Schools, Charities and Hospitals' (a body whose title was changed several times in the nineteenth century and which will be referred to here as the Schools Committee) were now much less emphatic than at the time of Mortimer's appointment about the desirability of keeping the municipality's public secondary school as a classical school.

When they recommended the appointment of the Reverend John Wood to the headmastership, the Schools Committee felt that 'The system of education pursued in the grammar school is still not of a sufficiently useful or practical nature, too little time being devoted to the instruction in all other branches save the learned languages'.[12] Although on that occasion they did not state how they thought the curriculum could be made more practical, they must have acted fairly quickly for reforms were very probably introduced around the time of Wood's appointment. In 1838 the committee record that they 'had the satisfaction of finding the Free [sic] Grammar School in a flourishing condition'. There were about 150 boys on the roll, of whom seventy specialised in the classical curriculum. They continue to identify the changes that had been put into effect since Wood's appointment: '. . . there has been added a complete mathematical and commercial course of instruction . . . and the boys are allowed either to go through the whole routine of the School, or to confine themselves to any particular course of instruction that may be specified, according to the views of their parents respecting their professions and prospects in life, whether for the universities, commerce, or engineering'.[13]

As well as this new flexibility of choice other noteworthy features of Headmaster Wood's establishment are the inclusion of French and practical arithmetic in the routine work of those who chose the commercial course, and the availability of German and technical drawing as optional extras. Thus, a very significant change had taken place. Between 1834 and 1838 the School ceased being the sort of grammar school run by George Mortimer and Edward Moises and their predecessors. Although there was a classical department by the late 1830s, and although it was still possible to learn Greek (the acid test of whether a school was a first-grade classical school), the classics were no longer obligatory and had therefore ceased dominating the academic careers of all the boys on the roll. The classical department coexisted with the mathematical and commercial departments, neither of which is written up in the 1838 Report as a poor relation of Greek and Latin. By 1838 the curriculum had been fixed and was to remain substantially unchanged until the end of the century.

This attempt to find out whether the School was a classical school was prompted by the question of whether the cause of its recruitment difficulties was the type of education it was offering. It appears that the School's literary bias did not necessarily deter parents from enrolling their sons. In the late 1820s, when a traditional grammatical education was offered, there were as many as eighty pupils. However, in the early 30s under the same traditional curriculum, there could be as few as fifteen on the register. Furthermore, in the late 1830s when the curriculum was more practical and more flexible than it had ever been, there were at times as few as two dozen pupils and in 1847 only eleven. Considered alone therefore the curriculum does not explain the unsteady popularity of the School. The scope of the subjects on offer was no doubt a feature of the School that prospective parents bore in mind when deciding where to have their boys educated. However, unless other things were equal, the provision of a curriculum that people found useful would not by itself be enough to fill the School. Factors other than the curriculum will need to be considered if the causes of the School's erratic recruitment are to be identified. To what extent did the day to day management of the School deter parents?

In the search for pupils the Grammar School was in competition with a number of good secondary schools which, because they were all private enterprises, were of necessity very responsive to the expectations of the market. The ability of the Headmaster was therefore of great importance if the School was to compete with its rivals. Newcastle's most successful schoolmaster-proprietor, Dr John Collingwood Bruce, said as much when asked by the Royal Commission on Endowed Schools under the chairmanship of Lord Taunton (hereafter referred to as the Taunton Commission) to suggest what could be done generally to improve grammar schools: 'Everything, almost' he replied 'depends on the masters you get, upon their learning, their reputation and their tact, and their love of their profession'.[14]

In the case of the Grammar School the Headmaster's influence was even more crucial because once he was appointed it was very unlikely that he could be dismissed. The appointment was made by the School's governing body, a committee of seven Councillors nominated by the Council. Before 1858 the Headmaster, if dismissed, could appeal to the Court of Chancery. Such an appeal would have been very costly for both parties and, as there was the possibility of reinstatement, and of formidable difficulties during a protracted vacancy while the appeal was being heard, the Council would probably wish to avoid such a step. But even if a Headmaster did not need to be removed, there was still a possibility of some difficulty because there was in the nineteenth century no normative age for a Headmaster's retirement, and, for all practical purposes, he had tenure for life. Thus it follows that a man who was not able, conscientious, reasonable, respectable and in rude health, might substantially damage the School's fortunes. Was the fluctuating popularity experienced by the School up to the 1850s the result of the inadequacy of Headmasters Moises, Mortimer, and Wood?

It was under the Reverend Edward Moises (1787 to 1828) that the School's decline became apparent. Although this decline continued under his two successors, the Reverend George Mortimer (1828 to 1833) and the Reverend John Wood (1834 to 1847), it is Moises's headmastership which is the most interesting precisely because he had picked up where the great Hugh Moises had left off: the point at which the School's reputation and fame were at their highest. Edward Moises had been educated by his uncle Hugh, then at Cambridge, and afterwards his inclinations remained sufficiently scholarly to enable him to produce in 1792 a Persian grammar and, in 1811, an Arabic translation of the Bible. The decline of the Grammar School can therefore not be attributed to any lack of learning on Moises's part. Indeed, contemporaries as far apart in social background and political sympathies as Eneas Mackenzie and Thomas Headlam, admired his scholarship.[15] That he was a conscientious man is attested by his 1793 'Plan of Education' as well as by the votes of confidence passed in 1820, 1822 and 1823, by committees appointed by the Council to discover why the School was failing to attract pupils.[16] And even when he had only nine pupils no-one blamed him for his

School's failings. Perhaps some Councillors did have reservations about Moises the schoolmaster, but if so, they were not willing to air them in public. Newcastle, before 1835, was governed by a small oligarchy and it is possible that the gentlemen who comprised the town Council were unwilling to embarrass another gentleman, the nephew moreover of the revered Hugh, by advertising his inadequacies to the generality.

The inquiry held in 1822 to find ways of improving the School's popularity has already been mentioned. The ad hoc committee's report perhaps contains a clue to a weakness of Moises as a Headmaster. The classical side of the School should continue as before. But they suggest that a third master be appointed with responsibility for 'the higher branches of mathematics, viz. algebra, geometry, trigonometry, . . . and to perfect the boys in writing and arithmetic'. A criticism is implied by another of their recommendations, that his salary be increased 'in consideration of his undertaking a general superintendence of the other department [the mathematical work] as well as the conduct of the classical department in the School'. Also, the Headmaster needs to be reminded that it is his duty occasionally to examine the pupils 'in every branch of education'.[17] The inquiry committee seem to have believed that Moises was not making satisfactory provision for the teaching of mathematics. That they were ready to recommend employing an extra master solely to teach the subject to the older boys strongly suggests they doubted the mathematical work was being adequately done.

The 1822 committee were also concerned with the mathematical work of the younger boys. Apart from giving the new mastership (which soon became known as the Mathematical Master or Third Master, a tradition continuing well into the nineteenth century) some responsibility for the arithmetic of the younger boys, they turned their attention to the Writing School. The Writing School was maintained by the corporation as an elementary school. It played a part in the life of the Grammar School when the Headmaster sent those of his younger boys who contracted to receive instruction in writing and arithmetic from the Writing Master. The Grammar School boys who would leave at thirteen or so to go into commercial employment, needed to be fluent in English grammar and proficient in arithmetic. As these subjects were important to the employment prospects of his pupils it is surprising that Moises was willing to farm the work out.

When the committee looked into the Writing School in 1822

they found that the Writing Master, Mr Askew, needed to retire on account of advanced age and infirmity. For some time past he had not been giving a sound service to the boys from the Grammar School. Yet, Moises seems to have done nothing about the problem. The Council however took action and made the Writing School the preparatory department of the Grammar School under the purview of the Headmaster. A new man, James Lowes, was appointed as Askew's replacement, to get the new system off to a good start. Six years later Lowes was dismissed by the Council who considered 'his habits gave him no claim on the Corporation'.[18] What had gone wrong is not known but it is clear that Moises had not been exercising control over Lowes. It is inconceivable that Moises was ignorant of Lowes's unsuitability. Why was Lowes allowed to continue for five years before he was removed from his post? Moises seems not to have recognised the importance to the health of his School of the subjects essential to the employment prospects of most of the boys who would attend a secondary school in Newcastle. If he did realise the importance of elementary mathematics he seems to have been unable to summon up enough enthusiasm to ensure the subject was taught as efficiently as it was in the commercial schools existing in the town at the time.

If therefore Moises was at fault it is that he was lacking in enterprise and flair. Perhaps the only thing he lacked was the harsh incentive of an empty school meaning an empty larder. The salary he received from schoolmastering contributed only a small part of his annual income. The headmastership brought him £150 a year, a free house and two-thirds of the pupils' fees. More important, however, was the £330 a year (on average) he received for being Master of the Virgin Mary Hospital (the Hospital mastership was separate from that of the School and the Master of the School was not automatically entitled to be Master of the Hospital). Another source of income for Moises was the vicarage of Hart which he held from 1811 until his death and which probably produced around £200 annually in Moises's day.[19]

George Mortimer was only twenty-three years old when he was appointed to succeed Moises in 1828. He was no doubt given the headmastership on the strength of his degree (one of the four Firsts in Greats in 1828) and rosy expectations of future promise. However, his undoubted potential did not come to fruition in Newcastle. Enrolment in the School dropped from 80 in his first year to 15 in his last. It is difficult to say what had gone wrong. There are no signs in the town's official records, or in the newspapers, or in the biographical study by A. E. Douglas-Smith, of any great quarrel with the Council nor are there any signs of scandal; indeed his subsequent very successful career as headmaster and churchman makes it improbable. His departure is probably explained by the School's poor recruitment in the early 1830s which reduced his income. Unlike Moises he was not supported by the mastership of the Virgin Mary Hospital. For the first time since 1779 the Headmaster of the Grammar School had to support himself on his annual salary of £150 salary and a share in the fees (four or six guineas per annum to freemen's and non-freemen's sons respectively). The more his pupils declined the poorer he became. Certainly his financial outlook became much brighter following his departure from Newcastle. He went first to a proprietary school in Kensington and soon afterwards to the headmastership of the City of London School where the facilities were incomparably better and the income around £1000.

Mortimer's inability to make a reasonable living from his post as Headmaster of Newcastle's Grammar School shows that the School's endowments (a municipal subsidy the nature of which will be discussed in due course) was unequal to the School's pretensions. From the early 1830s it was useless to look to the Council to increase their subsidy because during that decade they were retrenching.[20] In the absence of further help from the town and of private benefactors the School had to attract the maximum number of pupils so that their fees would augment the Headmaster's £150 salary. Why, then, could Mortimer not attract enough pupils to produce a reasonable income? A possible explanation may be the appearance in Newcastle of the first cholera epidemic which coincided with the opening of his headmastership. Brought into the country at Sunderland in 1831, by October of that year Newcastle was ravaged, not only by this new infectious disease, for which there was no known cure, but also by the panic of an urban population living in insanitary and overcrowded housing. However, as the first visitation lasted through the winter of 1831–32 and then died down, school attendance should not have suffered very long. In any case epidemics did not necessarily mean that schools would be emptied. Many, if not most, of Newcastle's families would not have been able to flee for very long and as they had nowhere else to go it was reasonable for them to send their sons to school if only to keep panic at bay. Such was the logic of Headmaster Snape's keeping the School open during the worst of the cholera in 1851.[21]

As Mortimer's failure to attract pupils cannot be attributed to his lack of discipline, learning or integrity, and as epidemics probably do not account for the continuing poor recruitment, it is necessary to look for another cause.

That reason may have been the way the teaching of mathematics was organised during Mortimer's time. When he resigned in 1834 the Council reviewed the School's management so that they could tell the new Headmaster what they wanted doing. It has been shown how in 1823 the Council had brought their old Writing School (renaming it 'the preparatory department') into the Grammar School. But this measure had not produced the desired result. Consequently when Mortimer took the School over in 1829 the Council had replaced the inadequate writing master, James Lowes, with the Mathematical Master of the Grammar School, John Weir. In one sense this was a good move for Weir was a successful teacher; in another it was a damaging decision for it took him away from the Grammar School, excepting four hours a week, and put him in charge of what was becoming a separate elementary school. Thus, the School's weakness in mathematics may have been recognised in the town with the result that Mortimer found himself with fewer and fewer pupils. It was not true that Newcastle could not support a classical school. But such schools could survive in the town only if they provided teaching in 'commercial' subjects as good as that provided in the classical languages. Accordingly the Council asked Weir to give more of his time to the Grammar School. When he refused they removed the preparatory department from the Grammar School and reinstated the Mathematical Mastership there.[22] A new appointment was made in 1834 and from that time the teaching of mathematics from the most elementary to the highest levels was done as part of the School's routine by a teacher with responsibility for that part of the curriculum and nothing else. The tinkering with the problem of mathematics, which had gone on since 1823, was over. Although the Council had recognised their mistake too late to be of any help to Mortimer surely his successor, John Wood, should have reaped the benefit.

When Mortimer resigned, the second master was promoted to the headmastership. He was John Wood, a thirty-two year old Cambridge graduate. Wood was in a favourable position even if the School was experiencing another recruitment crisis. He already knew the town, as he had been second master for six years; he was respectable, being Edward Moises's son-in-law, and a priest. Moreover the Council had just put the mathematical work on a sounder footing than it had ever been before. They had just appointed a new Mathematical Master, James Snape, a mere youth of eighteen, destined to become a patriarchal figure in the School's history. Also at some time between 1834 and 1838 the Council made changes which allowed the Headmaster to run the School as a semi-classical, or semi-commercial, establishment; no record of the decision has survived but there is no doubt that the changes were in operation by 1838 and that the School had a different character from the Moises and Mortimer periods.[23] It is therefore not surprising that Wood had notable success in the early stages of his headmastership: there had been fifteen pupils in the School when he became Headmaster in 1834; by 1836 there were 50 and 150 by 1838.

But this success was not sustained. In the closing years of his headmastership fewer and fewer boys joined the School and there is no reason to doubt the claim made in 1845 that it was almost extinct. One explanation for Wood's poor showing is perhaps furnished by one of his assistants who later recalled that Wood 'had long been failing in health and unable to devote much attention to the discharge of his duties'; a view perhaps corroborated by his premature death in his mid-forties.[24] Although he is a shadowy figure, very few records of him having survived, there are nevertheless signs of unpopularity. Dr Bruce remembered how some of Wood's pupils had come to his Academy from the Grammar School on account of the Headmaster's unpopularity.[25] And during the 1840s a number of Councillors made disparaging remarks about him. They attributed the School's decline to his negligence. In 1846, when someone asked in a Council meeting whether the Headmaster would retire if offered a pension, the question was received with laughter.[26] Whether this backbiting was based on informed judgement about Wood's pedagogic and managerial inadequacies cannot now be determined. On the other hand it is possible that he had invited the hostility of some townsmen by his reluctance to vacate the school rooms in the Virgin Mary Hospital which the Council wanted to demolish to make way for urban redevelopment.[27] As a number of Councillors were enthusiastic 'improvers' their dislike of the Headmaster may have sprung from the bile of local politicians impatient for progress.

How far the causes of the School's continuing decline under Wood were beyond his control and how far his ill-health unpopularity and, possibly, negligence, may have been responsible it is impossible to say. Certainly in times of wavering confidence in an institution it cannot have helped that the School was in the hands of a man either unable or unwilling to devote his energies to resolving its problems. In fairness, however, to Wood it should be remembered, which his critics failed to do, that Moises and Mortimer, more robust men and better scholars though they were, had a record no better than his. Nor was every one of Wood's contemporaries inclined to blame him for the School's problems: experienced and respected men like James Losh, Recorder of Newcastle, were unwilling to lay the blame at his door.[28]

This review of the qualities of Headmasters Moises, Mortimer and Wood gives no grounds for concluding that the primary cause of the Grammar School's decline up to the 1840s was their incompetence and negligence. However, although they would not seem to have been careless in general it is nevertheless a distinct possibility that each was unequal, though for different reasons, to the challenges threatening the School. Moises and Mortimer appear not to have realised that parents would generally use the Grammar School only when the non-classical or commercial subjects were taught with the same thoroughness as the classics. This never became a possibility until 1834–38 when pupils were allowed, for the first time in the School's history, to choose either the traditional classical curriculum or the commercial one (in which the classical element was slight). Why had this choice not been available before the mid-30s? The man best placed to recognise the need for reform was the Headmaster. There is no evidence that either Moises or Mortimer approached the issue with any sense of urgency. That the Grammar School was trailing behind the best secondary schools in the town is surely in part attributable to their not giving the town Council a lead. Moises may have been too set in his ways and too comfortably off, to want to become a reformer in his fifties. Mortimer, when appointed, had been instructed to conduct a classical school and as he was young and without experience he may well have lacked at that stage the self-confidence necessary for persuading the town Council to abandon their prejudice for a traditional classical school. When the Council did change its approach, John Wood espoused the transition with enthusiasm, but before he was able to consolidate his initial success his grasp on the running of the school slackened probably because of ill health.

The failure of the Headmasters of the Grammar School to keep abreast of the needs and demands of Newcastle families was especially damaging to their School's fortunes because there was no shortage of secondary schools in the town. In the first half of the century there was one establishment in particular whose curriculum was so attractive and whose results so highly regarded that it must have been profoundly threatening to the Grammar School. The opponent which posed so great a challenge was run by the Bruce family and was known as the Percy Street Academy.

The school in Percy Street was the private enterprise of John Bruce and his son John Collingwood Bruce. It was opened in 1802; when Bruce died in 1834 it was taken over by J. C. Bruce (referred to here as Dr Bruce to distinguish him from his father) who ran it until 1859 when he retired from active management; thereafter the school ran down and eventually closed in 1881. The golden age of the school lasted from the 1820s to the 1860s.[29] In his report for Lord Taunton's Schools Inquiry Commission, published in 1868, John Hammond, the assistant commissioner for Northumberland, found Bruce's Academy by far the best of Newcastle's secondary schools.[30] It is significant too that it was Dr Bruce not the Headmaster of the Grammar School who was summoned before the Taunton Commission as an expert witness.

Chief among the reasons why the Percy Street Academy was so formidable a rival must have been the personal qualities of the Bruces. John Bruce settled in Newcastle in 1793 and within a decade he had established a teaching practice in the town which included among its clients sons of some of the leading families of the area. In 1802, when two good schools in the Haymarket closed, he made an astute move by opening his own establishment; a few years later, helped by a good marriage, he took the lease of a large, well-appointed house in Percy Street. Indefatigable industry, a winning personality and a canny eye for a promising opening John Bruce certainly had; he also had enterprise: his flair and enthusiasm are reflected in the authorship of popular school text-books as well as in his tour of Edinburgh schools in 1817 where he observed Scottish teaching methods, studied curricula and encountered the system of annual examination which he introduced into his own school on returning home.[31] The examination, which parents and interested members of the public attended, was an ideal method of showing off facilities demonstrating efficiency and identifying the public's enthusiasm with his private business: Bruce's aim 'being not so much to test the efficiency of the system or the capacities of his pupils as to rouse the emulation of the boys and to gratify the pardonable vanity of their parents'.[32] The Grammar School on the other hand appears to have lacked a public examination day until 1847, the first year of Snape's headmastership.[33]

From the outset the Academy was a commercial school whose aim was to equip its pupils with the practical knowledge necessary for their entering trade and business. The nature of the school was doubtless dictated by the demands of the market which Bruce, a man of no background or capital, had to respond to or starve. By way of contrast, from the turn of the century until 1835, when a drastic change was made, the masters at the Grammar School received a fixed income paid by the Council which was quite unrelated to the number of boys receiving instruction. Another reason for the practical nature of the Academy's curriculum was the fact that John Bruce had taught himself what he knew, his subjects being mathematics and French. Thus in his first known prospectus, issued in 1802, he offered writing, mathematics, geography and French: the value of French will have been immediately apparent in an international trading port whereas in the Grammar School foreign languages were not made available until the 1830s. When Dr Bruce became proprietor in 1834 he published an 'Outline of Education' which shows the younger pupils engaged in practical arithmetic to gain facility in mental calculation, book-keeping and cartography, while the older boys studied in mathematics 'those parts that bear more immediately upon practical utility' including mensuration, land surveying, navigation, and mechanics. Classical instruction was available but it was not part of the mainstream of the Academy's work.[34] During the 1820s and 30s, therefore, when the Council were trying, rather haphazardly, to provide a course of instruction that would attract to the Grammar School respectable numbers of pupils, townsmen had in their midst a school that could meet their requirements and which moreover did what it set out to do with conspicuous efficiency: as early as 1820 the egregious William Turner publicly attested to the excellence of Bruce's teaching and when the Schools Committee visited the Academy in 1836 they found it 'a university in miniature' as they said in their glowing report to the Council.[35]

The Academy was fortunate in that the continuity of the businesslike and innovative management of John Bruce was maintained after his death in 1834 by his son Dr Bruce, a continuity more fortuitous than deliberate for Dr Bruce had intended making his career in the Presbyterian ministry but had been thwarted by a lack of openings at the crucial time: perhaps the Grammar School's problems would have been more tractable had Dr Bruce been successful in his original ambition. Dr Bruce had all his father's strengths and, in addition, had received a systematic education at Glasgow University where he had come into contact with the natural sciences. In the early 1830s he introduced science into his curriculum and by so doing placed his Academy in the very small number of English schools teaching science at that time; even in the mid-60s it was reported that the Academy was the only school in Newcastle (a leading industrial town) and Northumberland where serious instruction in the sciences could be obtained. Whatever educational or vocational value science might have had at a time when the nature and content of the subject were uncertain, it was nevertheless felt that scientific knowledge was an area of expertise essential to the prosperity of Tyneside and therefore very desirable, and for that reason alone Dr Bruce showed that he was in tune with the enthusiasms of an influential section of Newcastle society.[36]

Another of Bruce's initiatives indicates that he recognised the potential value of other developments still in their early stages. Soon after the institution in 1858 of the examinations (known as the Locals or the Middle Class Examinations) organised for schools by the University of Oxford, he escorted five of his pupils there and entered them as candidates for the examinations.[37] By way of contrast the Grammar School seems slow off the mark: when Hammond reported on the school in 1865 he made no mention of its pupils being entered for the public examinations – presumably he would have mentioned it if they were participating as it was exactly that type of indication of efficiency that he was searching for; moreover there is no record of examination candidates in the minute books of the Schools Committee until the 1870s; in fact there is no evidence of Grammar School boys taking the Locals before the 1870s.

Even if the Grammar School had been competing on equal terms, which it most certainly was not, with the Percy Street Academy, between 1820 and 1850, the Bruces would have been very formidable opposition for Moises, Mortimer and Wood. The combination of the Bruces' modern curriculum, their flair for positive publicity, their ability as teachers, their readiness to embrace new developments, explain why they outpaced the Grammar School.

The town's secondary schools flourished or not depending on how well they provided a fairly narrow service. The urban day-school catered mainly for children who would have to work for their living. Some of them would be aiming for a university education which was one way into the more solid professions especially for those without social connections or appreciable financial support. Hence, there was a close relationship between the condition of the universities and the viability of the grammar schools; demand for schooling would be determined to some extent by the attractiveness of the universities. The deterioration of Newcastle's Grammar School cannot be explained by a decline in the opportunities for higher education in Britain in the first half of the nineteenth century, because the university system was expanding and improving at the very time when the School was in difficulties. Oxford and Cambridge were undergoing reform which was to transform them out of all recognition. Moreover, in the 1820s the foundation of University College London, with its low fees and wide and modern curriculum, was an educational development of the greatest importance. In Newcastle itself the College of Medicine was set up in 1834 and was soon afterwards incorporated by the new University of Durham. Meanwhile, the Scottish universities continued to provide the cheap and good instruction which had drawn students from Tyneside for generations.

There is no doubt that Moises, Mortimer and Wood failed to keep up with the Bruces. While their failure can be explained to some extent by the limitations of their interests, experience and health, there may have been a more fundamental cause. Running through the careers of these men there is one theme, and that is money. I have already suggested that Moises's competitive edge was probably blunted by the comfortable income he drew from sources other than the headmastership. I have also argued that Mortimer lacked the incentive to remain in Newcastle because he probably had only his meagre Headmaster's salary to live on. Wood's resignation, which would have been to the School's advantage, was prevented by the Council's refusal to give him a retirement pension. How the School was financed appears therefore to merit some attention.

The School had no endowments at this time and the greater part of its income was paid annually by the Corporation from the town treasury. There were also the pupils' fees which were shared by the Headmaster (who received three-quarters) and the other masters, although in a period of unstable recruitment they were a depreciating asset. Up to the mid-30s the Borough subsidy to the School was in the range of £400 to £500. This money paid the salaries of the Headmaster and his three assistants and a pension for Edward Moises.[38]

The Grammar School therefore possessed a valuable advantage over its rivals. Much of its income was guaranteed and not related as theirs was to the vagaries of popularity. But, important though this annual subsidy was to the School's survival, it was inadequate in one crucial respect. The Headmaster's share was £150 which was not enough to attract or retain men of the highest capacity. This conclusion seems to be supported by Hugh and Edward Moises's presentation by the Corporation to the lucrative mastership of the Virgin Mary Hospital and by Mortimer's early departure from the School. Unless the Council could find additional income for the Headmaster, and they did not do so for Mortimer or Wood, there would be a slim chance of their finding someone whose talents were equal to the challenge facing the School, for such men could go where they chose as Mortimer did.

A devastating blow was dealt to this method of financing the School in 1835 when the Municipal Corporations Act was put on the statute book. This Act reformed English local government. One of the objectives of the legislators was the extension of the electoral franchise for the governing bodies of municipalities. Prior to this Act many towns, including Newcastle, had been ruled by narrow oligarchies wherein power had been held by a limited number of families from which the town Councils were coopted. As far as Newcastle was concerned it extended the social and religious base of the Council which now comprised forty-two members, chosen in triennial elections, who selected fourteen of their number to serve as aldermen for six years; the mayor, also elected by the Council, held office for one year. While the newly included elements were by no means revolutionaries they did nevertheless impart a brisker attitude to the administration of their localities. The new corporations, in Newcastle as elsewhere, became very much more accountable, especially in financial matters, and it follows that they were 'closely responsive to the opinions of the rate-paying electorate [which] proved distinctly more economical for many years and showed no enthusiasm for spending money'; 'the besetting sin of the new corporations, and of the local government as a whole, was meanness'.[39] In Newcastle the new Council conducted a clean sweep and started by selling off at derisory prices the Mansion House and its contents: 'cheap government', so powerful a cry in other areas of Victorian government, was powerfully entrenched in the views of the town's Councillors.[40]

The change to a socially broader based town government, no less than the increasingly urgent demands for civic amenities, meant that the Grammar School found itself in a less indulgent climate. A sign that it might have to work harder to justify its privileges may be seen in the Council's Schools Committee Report for 1836. Having visited Dr Bruce's Academy the Committee commented that he was showing what could be done by private enterprise 'without the resources of a chartered [endowed] school'.[41] In January 1839 the Council declined to give £10 to the School for prizes, though money had been allowed to Dr Mortimer, because such a grant might be a precedent and, more darkly, because 'this school already received great patronage, and cost the Corporation a pretty large sum, it was not thought necessary to carry that expense further'.[42]

Contained in the reforms of 1835 was a more specific threat to the School's interests. Section 92 of the statute imposed very narrow limitations on the responsibilities of the new corporations. Subscriptions to charities and all voluntary payments had to be discontinued. As far as the Grammar School was concerned Newcastle Corporation was obliged to continue paying salaries and pensions to masters appointed before 1835.[43] When vacancies occurred appointments would be made only if salaries could be paid by capitation fees, which was unlikely as an understaffed school would contract rather than expand.

The accounts of the town treasurer show that the effects of the Act were not felt for ten years. It was not until the mid-40s that the School's subsidy was reduced: in 1843 the annual pension of £100 to John Weir (Mathematical Master from 1823 to 1834) lapsed; in 1845 Moises's £100 annual pension stopped on account of his death. Strictly speaking the £200 was not being spent directly on the School. These pensions were a drain on the town's treasury rather than on the School; however, there is good reason for thinking that the unreformed oligarchy would have redirected the money spent on the pensions, once they had lapsed, to the School's account. Another example of the Council's penny pinching comes from 1847 when Wood's death left the headmastership vacant. The position was not filled until 1869 and in the meantime James Snape supervised the School on the salary of an assistant. By 1847, therefore, the Council was giving the

School £155 a year (and this level of subsidy was generally maintained until the late 60s) whereas before the Municipal Corporations Act it had provided over £500.[44]

The injurious changes in the School's financial relationship with Newcastle Corporation brought about by the Municipal Corporations Act lasted until the 1860s. The new law caused a reduction in the School's income which in any case had been quite inadequate and at the same time precluded the possibility of a future increase in the support received from the town. That the Act did not immediately harm the School is shown by the Schools Committee's glowing report of 1838. However, Wood's damaging period during the 1840s could have been avoided if the Council had been able to make his retirement possible by granting him a pension so making way for a more active man. That solution was prevented by the Act. A more positive effect of the Act was to stimulate the search for alternative finance. The School now had a moral case for a share in the surplus revenues of the Virgin Mary Hospital. That case was accepted in 1858 by the Court of Chancery. The Court accordingly endowed the School, a development which will be examined below, but the new arrangements did not come into effect until the 1860s and even then only partially.

For twenty years, as a result of the 1835 Act, the Grammar School was underfunded in comparison with its previous position. During the 40s, 50s and 60s its income came almost exclusively from fees. The Headmaster had to attract a large and stable clientele or become almost destitute. To achieve this he was forced to place much greater emphasis on commercial rather than literary education. Thus, changes in the mechanisms of municipal government were directly related to the evolution (or decline) of the School's character. Moreover, the difficulties that came in the wake of the corporation reforms cannot but have damaged morale at the very time when the problem of the curriculum was very near to resolution. No sooner had the major internal weakness of the School been sorted out than this external threat appeared.

The provision of salaries was only one of the duties that had been assumed by the Corporation in its role as the School's governing body. The range of involvement may be seen in the Council's memoranda between the 1820s and 1850s: they appointed the Head and undermasters, they determined the curriculum and fixed the fees, they maintained the schoolhouse and from time to time checked on the running of the School. As these functions concerned all the fundamental aspects of the School's work they were clearly of major importance, so it follows that if the Council had been negligent or if they had applied inappropriate policies the School's prospects might have suffered serious damage. And what were the effects of the 1835 municipal reforms? Did they weaken the links between the Corporation and the School?

It has already been shown that between 1820 and 1847 the Council frequently involved itself in the School's problems: in 1822–23 they drew up a reform programme including expensive building alterations; in 1828 the Council considered the merits of twenty-eight candidates for the headmastership; in 1829 they discussed with the new Headmaster the restoration of the School's 'former high character'; in 1834 they received a detailed report on the state of the School along with another set of reforms; in 1835 they provided a reasonable sum for maintenance; in 1845 and 1847 the Schools Committee tried to remedy the School's problems. The governors therefore were by no means inactive. It is true that they had not advanced since 1820 with an unfaltering step; several mistakes had been made such as their preference for classics in the early 30s and their removal of John Weir from full-time work in the School. These misjudgements were however recognised within a reasonable time and put right. The decline of the School was not the product of indifference or mismanagement on the part of the Council in their role as trustees. On the contrary when the School was imperilled the Council was most active.

Another issue that might be thought to have put the School at a disadvantage was the animosity between Protestant non-conformity and the Established Church. As Newcastle was a centre of religious dissent it is possible that the School's traditional connection with Anglicanism – all the nineteenth-century Headmasters were ordained members of the Church of England until the appointment of Samuel Logan in 1883 – made nonconformists disinclined to send their sons there. Of the religious background of the members of the School in this period there is next to no evidence. Between 1800 and 1850 three known nonconformists attended, of whom one was the son of the famous Unitarian minister, William Turner, while the father of another belonged to the Wesleyan ministry.[45] The most that can be said is that the School was not put at a disadvantage by being obliged by its statutes to turn away dissenters. When in 1858 a new constitution was drawn up a clause was included declaring the

School was open to all whatever their religious beliefs. This rule, like others in the 1858 Scheme of Government, formalised existing practice rather than breaking new ground. The real problem for the Grammar School seems to have been not the existence of nonconformist schools as such but rather the availability of such schools with more attractive and efficiently taught curricula. In the School of the Presbyterian minister, Dr Bruce, the majority of the pupils belonged to the Church of England which suggests that the Grammar School had more to fear from academic competition than from religious partisanship.[46]

If religious partisanship was probably not a major cause of the School's uncertain existence, what of that other great cultural value, perceptions of social status? Neither the leaders of the town's mercantile and professional families, nor the county gentry, patronised the School to any appreciable degree. In 1855 a telling observation was made in a Council debate by Sir John Fife who said he 'had always observed that the old Grammar School was attended by a number of boys whose parents had gone back a little in the world, or of parents whose families had been respectable for generations, but who had not advanced their position'.[47] Moreover, the social character of the School at this time may be inferred from the evolution of the curriculum by the 1840s from a classical to a predominantly commercial one: an indication that it was being shaped by the needs of tradespeople, artisans and clerks.[48] The well-to-do, and the socially aspiring, preferred to send their sons to boarding schools. Their reasons were nicely stated in the Taunton Commission's report which, though written in the mid-60s, represents the position thirty years earlier:

> . . . in a great measure . . . the landed gentry, clergy, professional persons, and wealthier manufacturers and merchants of Northumberland [the inclusion of Newcastle is understood] almost without exception, send their sons to be educated out of the county. There is no doubt a growing disposition on the part of the rich everywhere to patronize the large public schools, but in Northumberland the less affluent of the higher middle class who cannot afford the expense of Eton, Harrow, or Rugby, nevertheless prefer such schools as Rossall, Durham or the collegiate institution at Liverpool, to any of the Northumberland schools, which, in fact, partly in consequence of the want of boarders, cannot pretend to supply a first-class classical or mathematical education. It is true that the strong accent or "burr", which might be caught from provincial schoolfellows, is also of the nature of a deterrent . . . but the main reason for this migration of boys requiring an education for the universities or for the learned professions, is that there are no schools at hand that can completely supply it.[49]

Although this passage is explicit enough, the Report probably understated the extent to which parents were influenced in their choice of schools by social rather than academic considerations. Such attitudes the School could scarcely hope to combat: because the social elite did not put their boys into the School it could not be conducted as a first-grade grammar school and because it was not one such, the social leaders of the locality did not send their sons thither. The presence of the sons of the Duke of Northumberland, the Blacketts, the Ridleys, the Armstrongs and the Bells, would surely have acted as a magnet attracting the less influential from town and county. Pupils of distinguished families would have imparted a cachet that must have overcome the difficulties caused by the Municipal Corporations Act, the Bruces' Academy in Percy Street or the intermittent troubles of headmasters. Could any measure have been taken to combat the social prejudice against the urban grammar school? Transport was a crucial factor. Before the late 1840s it was impossible quickly to travel into Newcastle from surrounding districts, let alone from the remoter parts of the county. If the School was to attract the gentry it would have to overcome problems of distance by taking boarders. That formidable rival of the Grammar School, John Bruce, claimed to have in his Academy pupils from the upper classes; he also offered facilities for boarders.[50] In this matter, as in others, the Grammar School was less organised. By 1818 Edward Moises had stopped taking boarders. His successor, financially less comfortably off than Moises, seems to have revived the boarding tradition though the brevity of his stay in Newcastle apparently made the revival short lived. During some of John Wood's headmastership accommodation was advertised but how long and to what extent it was used cannot be established; however, the low level of recruitment during the 40s suggests that there were few, if any, boarders. Wood's successor, James Snape, took only day-boys between 1847 and 1870.[51]

To conclude this review of the School's history from the early nineteenth century to the 1850s it appears that no cause can be identified which alone explains why it was so unsteady. At a time when the State had a negligible part in education, the development of an urban school depended on how well it satisfied the social, vocational and educational needs of the people who lived near it. The recruitment crises of this period show that when the system of education it offered was unattractive to the townsfolk they could find what they were looking for in the numerous schools in the town, especially in the Percy Street Academy. However, the School's problems were more complex than the mere existence of rivals; how complex may be seen in the 1830s. By then the curriculum had been altered to produce a more attractive relationship between the commercial and the literary subjects; the teaching too had been strengthened. Now, when stronger progress might have been expected there came in 1835 the set-back dealt by the Municipal Corporations Act, the effect of which was the reduction of the Borough's subsidy to the School. The Act obliged the Corporation to continue employing people engaged before 1835, but, with the exception of the municipal officials named in the statute, when posts were vacated new appointments could not be made. So, whereas before the Act four teachers had been supported by municipal funds, from the late 40s only two masters were being paid by the Corporation, and after 1863 only one.

The problems caused by the Municipal Corporations Act were not the only difficulties the School had to face up to during the 1830s. At this time Newcastle was in the throes of rapid redevelopment and it was only a matter of time before the attentions of the speculators would fall on the district south of Westgate Road where the School was situated. That the upheaval came sooner rather than later was due to the Council's desire to encourage the railway companies to construct their lines through the old town. Plans to link Newcastle with Carlisle and with Shields were being vigorously pursued from the early 1830s and were successfully concluded in 1839. The next step would be the bridging of the Tyne to allow Newcastle to be joined with the lines to York. Furthermore, if, as it was generally hoped, Newcastle was to be the regional junction of the north-eastern network, the Council was going to have to find space for a central station. These plans were to have direct consequences for the School. The morphology of the town, as well as existing buildings (such as the castle and St Nicholas's) that could not be removed, more or less left the ground south of Westgate Road as the best, if not the only, place for the railway bridge, a central station and access roads. Thus, the School was in the way of the railway craze, shareholders' dividends and new jobs. In 1838 the Council began considering whether to have the School knocked down and the site sold. A group of proto-conservationists tried to save the ancient schoolhouse but their campaign had only a limited appeal because the building was dilapidated and, it was claimed, the space for a thorough restoration was lacking. There simply was not the will to let unattractive buildings, however old, interfere with the economic development of the town.[52] In 1841 demolition was agreed on, the objective being to widen the approaches to Westgate Road and Neville Street. In the last week of March, 1844, the School was razed to the ground.

This tearing up of the School from its historical roots must have been dispiriting. The Headmaster, John Wood, was presented with the problem of resettling his School but he was ailing and had no enthusiasm for the challenge. He was unimpressed with the alternative accommodation the Council had found in Forth House, a property standing only thirty yards away from the old School and occupying the ground at the western end of the present Neville Street; the garden attached to the priests' house connected with the Roman Catholic cathedral is partly on its site.[53]

In 1844 the School moved into the three rooms in Forth House, converted by the Council at the cost of £300. Wood was no worse off for space than he had been, indeed three rooms was a generous allocation as he had only a dozen pupils at the time. His worries were probably more concerned with the neighbourhood rather than with the building. While it was true that within living memory The Forth had been a pleasant piece of common, by the 1840s it was far from arcadian. Not fifty yards away there soon would be the building works for the new Central Station whose completion would bring much noise, heavy traffic and considerable pollution. Not a hundred yards south, on Forth Bank, there was a concentration of heavy industry, 'the smoke from which is often an annoyance'.[54] Not fifty yards to the west, there were cattle and sheep markets.

Wood did make the move but he died a few years later in 1847. The Council, doubtful of the School's chances of survival, put the second master, James Snape, in charge. They told him 'to make the best of it'.[55] Snape could not have known it, nor can anyone else, but the worst was over. A period of revival was about to open.

(ii) *Survival, 1847 to 1870.*

For obscure reasons Snape was not made Headmaster until 1869 but this was a legal nicety and can be ignored, for there is no doubt that before then he ruled the School with as much authority as any of his predecessors.[56] He had no sooner taken up the reins than he was told, in 1848, to vacate Forth House, which was about to be demolished. The School's new home was to be a domestic dwelling

a few hundred yards away in 6, Charlotte Square. Once a
fashionable Georgian enclave, the square was no longer so.
Plumbers and gasfitters had moved in, and gold beaters and retail
merchants, and commercial stables. The house Snape took
possession of in 1848 had six rooms which, though unmodified for
school use, were more than enough for him, his one assistant and
their dozen pupils.[57] However, within a few years space was at a
premium; by 1855 there were 150 pupils and during the 1860s there
were usually over 200. These numbers attest the School's
remarkable and sustained recovery from its unsteady existence
during the 20s, 30s and 40s. The measure of this achievement was
seen in 1865 when there were 800 children in secondary education
in Newcastle of whom 530 were 'in the three more important
schools', which were the Percy Street Academy, another
(unidentified) school and the Grammar School.[58] This period was,
therefore, a bridge between the insecure institution of the early
nineteenth-century and the twentieth-century School. Who, or
what, was responsible for this achievement?

Earlier in this chapter eight determinants of the School's success
were identified: the attractiveness of the curriculum, the ability of
the Headmaster, the quality of rival schools in the locality, the
condition of the universities, the source of its funding, the attitude
of the governing body (the town Council until 1888) and the
religious and social prejudices of the citizenry. In the Charlotte
Square period (1848-70) there were no major changes in these
areas, the exception being the financial and constitutional
reorganisation of 1858. However, as I will show later, the benefits
of these reforms only started coming through after 1870.[59]

The one development that might have been to the School's
advantage was the appearance in the late 1830s of the railway in
the town and its region. This new mobility certainly brought boys
into Newcastle from the outlying districts. Dr Bruce, for example,
received 'a considerable number of people' from places eight miles
away.[60] The Grammar School benefited too though there is no
way of telling how important the gain was. In 1861 Councillor
T. L. Gregson stated that 90 of the School's 215 pupils came 'from
the country'.[61] As he was a friend of Snape and an undoubted
authority on schools in the area, Gregson's statement may well
have been accurate, but as his opinion was challenged by some of
his colleagues it is perhaps better discounted. J. L. Hammond, in
1865, took the ten oldest and ten youngest boys in
the School (there were 230) and found that six travelled between

six and ten miles to school; five made a return journey of four to seven miles and the rest lived in Newcastle.[62] The appearance of the railway did not of course mean that the Grammar School would necessarily be chosen by parents who now had their first regular and convenient access to Newcastle. Their choice was presumably determined by the School's reputation. We have seen how low its standing was when Snape took it over in 1847. It is clear that by the mid-50s he was maintaining a very creditable level of recruitment. Thus, in the absence of any other significant development, the key to the School's recovery in the mid-nineteenth century appears to be James Snape.

Contemporary opinion of Snape's significance lends weight to this conclusion. For example, in a Council meeting in 1855 one Councillor after another praised him 'for restoring the School to a high degree of celebrity and usefulness'.[63] In 1864 the Sheriff of Newcastle told his audience that they 'may be assured that the name of James Snape will be remembered by posterity as teacher of that School in the same way as that of Hugh Moises, which is still so highly respected . . .'.[64] J. L. Hammond, in 1865, concluded that Snape had made 'a very useful institution . . . From all I could learn, the changes introduced by the master have met with very great approval . . .'.[65] The general opinion of his work is reflected in a comment made when he resigned in 1871: 'He devoted the prime of his life to the seemingly hopeless task of raising the Grammar School from utter uselessness to high efficiency and prosperity and he has accomplished that task to his infinite credit'.[66] Even at the time of his death in 1880 his reputation was still high.[67] Who was this man and how had he accomplished so much?

When Snape was given control of the School he was thirty years old. By the standards of the time he was not particularly young for such promotion; of his predecessors, John Wood was in his early thirties and George Mortimer was only twenty three when they were appointed. But this was about the only thing Snape had in common with the other five Headmasters of the nineteenth century. They were Oxbridge graduates whereas he had no degree and very probably had not even attended a university for he had come to Newcastle at the age of eighteen and had previously taught in Blackburn Grammar School. The claims that he had been a member of Trinity College Dublin are not supported by TCD's records. Nor was his doctorate, awarded in 1869 by Giessen University 'for his services to the Evangelical faith', a mark of any scholarly achievement or intellectual distinction.[68] It was in fact probably acquired so that he could satisfy a rule in the 1858 Scheme which required the Headmaster to have a degree. Furthermore, he was the first Headmaster of the School since 1738 not to have been in holy orders at the time of his appointment. This in itself was an indication of how low the School was sinking, for the Anglican priesthood was one of the most important attributes, both social and professional, of the respectable schoolmaster.

What Snape did have, however, in abundance was enthusiasm. He emerges from his letters, from his pupils' recollections and his obituaries, as a model of the imaginative, strict, conscientious and consistent schoolmaster. His many foibles were tolerated and savoured by his pupils who left vivid memorials of their gratitude and affection. They remembered him as an effective, if bombastic, speaker 'with a prodigious voice which he used more than necessary'. They learnt by heart his florid set-pieces. They were embarrassed by his old-fashioned courtesy – he addressed them with the Johnsonian Sir – and crossed to the other side of the street when they saw him coming. However, despite his gravitas he had a simple affection for his pupils and could be seen racing with the younger ones along the West Walls, 'laughing at the fun of being hopelessly beaten by his small competitors'.

This range of amiable eccentricities by themselves would not have been sufficient to drag the School out of the slough it was in when he was put in charge. He had other, more substantial, qualities. One of these was his frugality which no doubt enabled him to keep his School in the reach of the working class boys. He used the minimum number of books and those were the cheapest; only one of his classrooms had desks and most of the work was done orally, doubtless to save using expensive writing materials. In the period of its revival the Grammar School was cheaper than the more important private schools in Newcastle. Consistency was another of his traits which cannot have been anything other than a valuable asset to the School. When, in 1853, a cholera epidemic threw Newcastle into a panic, unlike most of the town's schoolteachers, he kept his school open, and in so doing put himself in the best company as Dr Bruce did likewise.[69] Snape claimed that he had rarely been away from the School during the 37 years of his association with it: 'Some years ago, indeed, on a memorable occasion, I visited London; but, on the second evening after our arrival, notwithstanding the novelties and splendour of the great city, and notwithstanding the very earnest entreaties of my family that I would remain with them during the limited period assigned for their stay, by express train I took my departure; and at nine o'clock on the following morning, I was once more at my post'.[70]

Of all the reasons which might explain why Snape succeeded where Edward Moises, Mortimer and Wood had failed, the most persuasive is his outstanding ability as a teacher of the School's bread and butter subjects. In the mid-century when parents put their sons into the Grammar School they did so in order to have them made proficient in literacy and numeracy so that they could find work in non-labouring jobs. Skill in the lower levels of mathematics and accuracy in English was what Snape was expected to impart. It was these very subjects that he taught brilliantly.[71] 'Few undergraduates in a college lecture room could have surpassed these lads in the repetition of propositions or in the explanation of the successive steps required for the constructions and proofs.'[72] However, it may be asked why his brilliance in teaching had not been more apparent before 1847 for, after all, he had been working in the School since 1834. The answer to this question seems to lie in the timing of John Wood's death after which the School's recruitment strongly recovered. It seems therefore reasonable to infer that Snape's talents had not been more in evidence before 1847 because he had been held back by Wood, or because he had been either too tolerant or too loyal or too inexperienced to undermine his ineffectual superior.

To conclude this consideration of Snape, what was the significance of his career? To state the matter at its least, if he had been as unassertive as Moises and Wood, the School surely would have sunk even lower. He established his reputation for efficiency at precisely the time when there was a prospect that a large sum of money would be made available for education in Newcastle. His reputation gave substance to the claims that this money should be used to re-endow the Grammar School. In the light of his success the School's supporters could argue that given better facilities he, or his like, could continue his work on a grander scale, an argument that could have carried little weight before 1847.

While Snape was making do with the supposedly temporary accommodation in Charlotte Square a movement was under way in Newcastle that brought his School the prospect of re-endowment. If this were to materialise it would prove a watershed in the School's history. In the time of Snape's predecessors the

School's funding had been seriously inadequate and the long-standing weakness had recently been made worse by the effects of the Municipal Corporations Act. It was ironic that the radicals that had undermined the School by campaigning for the reform of local government would later on play an important part in its revival. The reformers had more targets in their sights than the corrupt government. Another of their attacks was directed at charitable institutions whose wealth was being wasted, or worse. The force of the radical onslaught against complacent charitable trusts is nicely illustrated by the trials of Trollope's gentle warden of Hiram's Hospital. Among the thousands of unregenerate charities like Barchester's Hiram's Hospital was Newcastle's Virgin Mary Hospital.

Before it was reformed in 1846 the Virgin Mary Hospital was an autonomous corporation comprising a Master and six almsmen who were provided for by a considerable endowment. In the 1830s and 1840s the Hospital received from its property an average annual income of almost £400, most of which (£300) went to the Master while the almsmen received £36 between them. This sinecure was by itself enough to bruise the sensibilities of utilitarian reformers. What further increased their interest in the Hospital was the probability that the value of its property, much of it in the town, would greatly increase as the rush of industrialisation in the area pushed up the value of land. Quite apart from their contempt for such an anachronism the radicals saw in the Hospital the means of financing urgently needed public amenities thus enabling them, ratepayers that they were, to avoid the morally obnoxious alternative (as they saw it) of good works financed by public taxes.

However, the reform of a charitable trust could not be achieved quickly or easily, for like all trusts the Virgin Mary Hospital was under the jurisdiction of the Court of Chancery, a notoriously conservative and slow-moving body at this time. There had indeed been rumblings of reform during the early 1830s, but the campaign did not begin in earnest until 1836 and, significantly, it was the first reformed Council that took the matter in hand in that year. By 1839 they were ready to advise the Attorney General as to how the Hospital's revenues should be used. Broadly speaking the Council thought the Hospital's funds should provide benefits for the town at large; one-third of the annual income ought to be spent on education. By 1845 the Attorney General's office had drafted a scheme and asked the Council for their final comments. In 1846 those proposals were embodied in an Act of Parliament which remained in force for forty-two years.[73]

The Virgin Mary Hospital Act of 1846 liberated a portion of the Hospital's surplus annual income for the maintenance of schools in Newcastle. However, twelve more years were to pass before the Grammar School was named as the major beneficiary of this measure. The lack of urgency in expediting matters was not caused by the apathy of the principal parties, rather the delay is explained by the Act's provision that new almshouses and a new chapel (in reality it was an elaborate structure meant to serve as a parochial church) should be erected. Until these buildings were completed (in 1859) no surplus income was available. While the authorities were waiting for money to become forthcoming there was protracted debate about the allocation of the Hospital's educational fund. It was widely recognised that this was a landmark in the town's educational history. Informed opinion in the 50s thought that the fund would produce about £700 a year for spending on schooling. Moreover, the value of the Hospital's property was expected to increase by leaps and bounds when long leases came up for renewal at the end of the century. Interested parties were therefore inclined to take a long-term view and thus argued their case with considerable tenacity.

During the decade in which this question was thrashed out there were three main views concerning the uses to which the Hospital funds should be put. These ideas were not exclusive to Newcastle. They represented commonplace opinions prevalent throughout the country. One group believed the money should be used to support a tertiary institution for the sciences and technology; one of the variations on this theme was the demand for a university for Newcastle. Others assumed that the revenues of this charity belonged to the poorest in the area and demanded Ragged and elementary schools be built in working class neighbourhoods. A third body of opinion held that the Grammar School should receive the greater part of the Hospital endowment, though the proponents of this idea disagreed among themselves as to how far the School needed restructuring, perhaps on the model of a Scottish academy.[74]

The Council's Schools Committee had the task of distilling these conflicting views. The Committee were strongly inclined to use most of the fund to re-endow the Grammar School. However, they were unable to persuade the Council to accept their recommendation to give £600 a year to the Grammar School and to set up an elementary school with an annual endowment of £120. A compromise was accepted by the Council in 1856 to the effect that the Grammar School should receive £330 a year while the remaining £440 would go to a number of charity schools. These elaborate deliberations turned out to be otiose because the Attorney General rejected the Council's proposals and instead produced a formula which was sanctioned in 1858 by Chancery in a document known as the Scheme.[75]

This Scheme was a landmark in that it contained two arrangements which promised to put the School on a much firmer footing. Firstly, new premises were to be built for the School, to be paid for by the Hospital; additionally, the Hospital was to provide an annual fund for maintenance and furnishing. The new works were completed within a dozen years at the cost of £11,000. This was a development of the greatest importance. The fine new buildings would never have been provided otherwise. Certainly the Council would not have used borough funds. Nor could the cost have been covered by the pupils' fees, the main source of the School's income at this time. Nor was there any individual willing to assume the expensive mantle of The Great Benefactor. Moreover, the new arrangements liberated the School from rents, mortgages and maintenance, whereas private schools had to meet these costs either by keeping their fees high or by paring their costs to the bone, so blunting their competitive edge. The second financial provision in the 1858 Scheme was the provision of an annual endowment of £440. In theory this should have made up for the damage done by the Municipal Corporations Act for the endowment was to have been paid as soon as the new building was ready for use. There was, however, a serious hitch, to be considered below, which resulted in the endowment being withheld until 1881.[76]

If the Scheme had done nothing more than finance new buildings and provide the endowment it still would have been a major turning point for the School. However, it went further because its drafters had addressed themselves to three very broad questions. What academic goals should the School seek to achieve? How to maintain a better academic record? How best to use the endowment? Their responses to these questions would have far reaching consequences because they would influence, if not determine, many aspects of the School's management and social composition. Furthermore, the Scheme remained in force during a period (from 1858 to 1888) in which the School experienced considerable change and development. It cannot have been other than a formative influence in an age of transition and it therefore merits further consideration. The Scheme, although the text does not say so, sanctioned the curriculum which had been established in the mid-30s when the purely classical character of the Grammar School had been abandoned by the Council. It ordains that classical, modern and scientific subjects will be taught and is significantly silent as to whether Latin and Greek are compulsory. Moreover, the Council, as the governing body, is given wide powers over the curriculum, and may add subjects as they think fit to provide 'a sound religious, moral and useful education'. The Scheme's second main preoccupation was to ensure that the School fulfilled the social obligation inherent in its endowment by maintaining a good standard of academic work. Of course, the main incentive had already been given in the form of the promise of new buildings. Competition, the shibboleth of Victorian reformers, was also encouraged by ten new prizes of a year's free tuition and seven scholarships giving three years' free education. All these grants were to be awarded for merit shown in a public examination. The masters were also to be kept on their toes by an annual examination conducted by external examiners chosen by the Council. The examiners were expected to produce a detailed report which would be the basis of remedial action. This innovation was not put into effect until 1871 but thereafter the annual examination exerted an increasing influence on the School's values and organisation.[77]

In an attempt to protect the School a new rule was put into the Scheme which give the Council the power to dismiss the Headmaster. Though the Council had always had this right it had been severely limited by the fear of the very considerable problems which could occur if a Headmaster were to appeal against dismissal to the Court of Chancery. Affairs such as the Fremingham School case must have made governing bodies aware of the horrific possibilities. In 1844 the trustees of that school sacked their Headmaster who thereon appealed to the Lord Chancellor and was given judgement. The success of the trustees' counter-appeal was to no avail because the Headmaster refused to move and was still in his place in 1864 when the dispute was concluded. To meet the costs of the litigation the trustees had to mortgage and sell the school property and dig into their own pockets, simply for having done their duty. The final bill for the action came to £3,000 yet the school's annual income was just £80.[78] Thus, the new rule in the Scheme for Newcastle pre-empted any appeal by giving to the Charity Commission the definitive ratification of a dismissal. This important reform was not of course produced solely for Newcastle. The problem was common to endowed schools and to combat it the Court of Chancery and Charity Commission were of the opinion that governing bodies should be competent to hire and fire.

The third of the Scheme's concerns was how to use the £440 annual endowment. Opinion was divided and thereby faithfully reflected the various schools of thought nationally. One radical group argued that the money ought to be used only for financing the education of boys who could not otherwise afford to attend a secondary school, while everyone else ought to pay the full cost which would be a lot more than the four guineas being charged during the 50s and 60s. A second body of opinion campaigned to have the whole endowment used towards defraying the School's ordinary running costs. This idea was prompted by egalitarianism because by keeping the fees at the absolute minimum the School would be within the reach of boys from low-income homes. In this way the Council could cater for more working-class pupils than the proposals of the first group would have permitted. The third group favoured Justification by Competition and argued that the endowment ought to finance free scholarships which would be awarded on academic merit irrespective of the candidate's social background.

The final decision lay with the Attorney General who settled on a compromise. The Scheme reserved almost half (£190) of the School's endowment for scholarships (seven at £10 per annum for three years and three £40 bursaries, for three years, to finance a pupil in higher education). The remainder of the endowment (£250) was to go to the School's current account for general purposes. This plan was very much in line with the Council's thinking on the matter. During the 50s, as well as during the next three decades, they insisted on charging the Grammar School pupils very much less than the real cost of their schooling. Dr Bruce reckoned in the mid-1860s that it cost 16 guineas annually to educate each boy in the Grammar School.[79] However, they were being charged only four guineas a year (this charge was fixed in 1834 and was maintained until 1873 when it was increased to a maximum of £9 (including a 12 shillings charge for stationery).[80] This policy must have had some effect on the social composition, and the social function, of the School, although it is not possible to establish whether this policy made the School a working-class one. Three-quarters of the School in the mid-60s came from shop-keeping, artisan and labouring families but that was not the result of the Scheme which had not come into effect then. For the rest of the period, and indeed until 1898, when coherent evidence about pupils' social backgrounds begins, little more can be said with certainty on this important subject.

This account of the school in Snape's time is dominated by the complex process whereby the endowment was secured and a new constitution drawn up. Meanwhile, however, the routine work went on, generally unrecorded. Indeed, if it was not for J. L. Hammond's report of 1865 (brief and selective though it is) we should be in the dark about even the most basic features of the School's life and work.[81] Hammond was very unimpressed by what he found when he visited the School and dismissed out of hand its claims to be a grammar school. In his opinion Snape was providing, albeit extremely efficiently, a commercial education mainly for working-class boys up to the age of fourteen. Their so-called advanced work was not much above the elementary level consisting of rote learning and repetition. He was clearly taken aback by the absence of written work and thought it responsible for the severe limitation of the education the boys were getting. It meant that they were not being taught to think for themselves, a goal which distinguished a first-grade school from others.

Hammond's main concern was with the School's future and he had no doubt that it should not be allowed to continue in its present form. For him there was no case for using public funds to subsidise a school which was duplicating the work being done more efficiently by private establishments. In future the Grammar School must revert to its proper function of preparing its pupils, at a reasonable cost, for higher education and entry into the professions.

I will later show how the Council accepted Hammond's view of the School's future development.[82] As a result, and before too long, the School's character began to change. It is for this reason that the Snape period may be seen as a transitional one. His work was not the foundation of the modern 'RGS'. His real contribution was to restore the community's respect for the School at a critical moment in its history. There were people in the 1840s and 50s who thought the School was not worth re-endowing. That they failed to make their case was to a large extent the fruit of Snape's headmastership.

When Hammond drew attention to the very inadequate conditions in which the School was operating he was preaching to the converted. Even as he was writing his report the Council had already decided to build new premises at Rye Hill and had acquired two and a half acres lying between Westmorland Road and Cambridge Street for the purpose. This land had cost the Council nothing because it belonged to the Virgin Mary Hospital which was willing freely to dedicate it to the School's use. Another, though subsidiary, attraction of this area was its semi-rural character, a fresh environment being a major priority in current thinking on the location of schools.

In time it would become all too apparent that the choice of Rye Hill was a serious mistake which hindered the development of the School, perhaps for fifty years. Ironically, in 1861, when the Council chose the Rye Hill site, one of their number, T. L. Gregson, with uncanny accuracy told them exactly why their choice was the wrong one. Gregson drew their attention to Sir William Armstrong's Elswick Engine Works which lay just a mile away from the spot where they intended placing the new School. The Elswick factory was in its infancy but its inexorable growth would transform the West End of Newcastle from a residential area into what he called 'a manufacturing district'. There was no question of the School's being able to live off its endowment or of its ability to continue without charging fees. A working-class suburb could not produce the quantity of pupils necessary for keeping the School financially afloat. Gregson's warning was, however, ignored by the Council for whom no doubt the allurement of a free building site was overwhelming. By accepting Rye Hill, they rejected the main rival, Barras Bridge, which would have cost £3,000. How ironical it was when in 1897 the School opened the Branch in Barras Bridge to cater for the middle-class districts of Jesmond and Gosforth.

So much for the site. When the time came to choose a design again the Council cut costs and commissioned the architect of the Godolphin School in Hammersmith to adapt his design to the sloping ground at Rye Hill.[83] In 1866 the foundation stone was laid. The ceremony was an elaborate essay in civic self-consciousness and a demonstration of the new significance of the town's 'head school'. The Earl of Ravensworth performed the ceremony which was witnessed by an enormous gathering of

106

notables: the mayor and Corporation, the borough magistrates, ecclesiastics, foreign consuls, Tyne Commissioners, trade guilds, an escort of the 13th Hussars, and an artillery band. Prayers were said, speeches were made, and a 'substantial repast' eaten. Several Grammar School boys got drunk and disgraced themselves.[84] The crowning touch, the account carried by a London newspaper, must have been gratifying as it could be taken as an advertisement for the culture and confidence of a provincial community.[85]

In October 1870 the building was ready for occupation and so the School left Charlotte Square for good and settled into Rye Hill. It had been constructed throughout in stone and designed in the fashionable neo-gothic style that was all but ubiquitous in scholastic architecture at that time. The ground floor comprised classrooms and living quarters for the Headmaster's family, the latter being a valuable supplement to his salary and intended to be a bait to attract men of high academic calibre to the job. Next to the Headmaster's apartments was a dining room for the pupils. As there had never been provision for meals in the School this must be seen as an attempt to create some of the corporate spirit which J. L. Hammond had found absent in the mid-60s. In the first few decades at Rye Hill about one-third of the pupils stayed at school for their mid-day meal, the rest went home or endangered their morals by frequenting 'eating shops' in the town. The remainder of the ground floor was divided into six classrooms (see the plan on page 108), three of which (40 feet by 25 feet each) ran along the north of the building and were fitted with partitions which could be removed to make an assembly hall. The other three classrooms were situated along the east side of the building, two of them measuring 37 feet by 23 feet and the third 29 feet by 20 feet. As the School was designed to accommodate 500 pupils there was in theory one square yard for each pupil, though in practice the ratio was more generous because the roll in this period never exceeded 300.[86]

The second storey was used for sleeping quarters for the Headmaster's family and for boarders. The boarding tradition had been dead for several generations and in trying to revive it the Council were hoping to augment the Headmaster's salary, for a well-managed boarding element in a school could be very profitable. However, the reservation of all the second storey for boarders was wildly optimistic, if for no other reason, because the 1858 Scheme stated that there should be only 20 boarders at any time. If boarding ever had a future in the School, which was

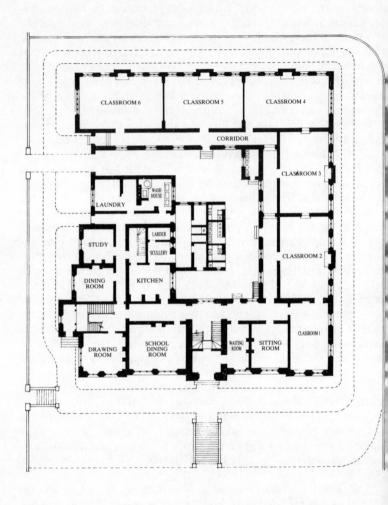

GROUND FLOOR PLAN

SCALE

THE ROYAL GRAMMAR SCHOOL AT RYE HILL

108

LOCATION PLAN

THE ROYAL GRAMMAR SCHOOL
AT RYE HILL

unlikely, then it must have received a fatal blow in 1877 when a seedy story involving some of the boarders was given wide and salacious circulation in the local newspapers.[87] The Schools Committee investigated the allegations made by the guardian of a boy who had been expelled for his part in the affair and were able to exorcise an even graver suspicion of scandal by concluding that Headmaster Brian Christopherson was culpable only in the laxity of the supervision exerted over his boarders.[88] This tiresome episode soon fizzled out without doing much damage to the School but it may have persuaded all concerned that the boarding house was more trouble than it was worth. By the 1890s boarding had been discontinued and the first floor converted into classrooms.

When it was opened few people had anything but praise for the new Rye Hill building. After the cramped and inadequate conditions at Charlotte Square the new School was impressive and indeed was known locally as 'the palace'. Some critics objected to the expense of the operation and to the unnecessary opulence (as they saw it) of the building materials, but they were a minority. For a generation or two the building seems to have worked well, the only recorded adjustments occurring in 1875 when the larger classrooms were subdivided. At the time of its inauguration the new School's lack of land for organised games, the absence of a gymnasium and of laboratories for science work, suggest that it was designed pre-eminently as a place for book-learning and nothing else. The layout of the School at Rye Hill shows how the functions of a mid-Victorian grammar school were perceived; those perceptions were about to undergo a rapid transformation during the next thirty years.

(iii) *Revival, 1871 to 1888.*

While the new premises were being built, between 1866 and 1870, the Council had been considering the School's future. Their most obvious option was, of course, simply to allow Snape to run the School as he had been doing for twenty years. The strengths of the Snapean system were apparent: he was providing a valued service for the working-class families whose sons formed three-quarters of the roll in the 1860s. But it was very unlikely that this choice would be acceptable as there were four developments that were pushing the Council towards a radical redefinition of the School's goals and character.

In the first place, the acquisition of a new building was in itself an incentive to pursue more ambitious objectives. Secondly, the

858 Scheme was about to come into effect in its entirety and this
meant that the annual endowment would be forthcoming. Thus,
for the first time since the Municipal Corporations Act had
deprived the School of much of its borough subsidy, money would
be available for reform. Thirdly, in 1869 Parliament had set up
the Endowed Schools Commission, a body with important new
supervisory powers over the grammar schools. Although the
commission's jurisdiction strictly concerned only governing bodies
and endowments, it also influenced curricula and thereby many
other features of school life. This commission (and the Charity
Commission which took over the former's responsibilities in 1874)
had innovative views on the functions of endowed schools, and it is
inconceivable that boards of governors in the localities would
remain uninfluenced by those ideas. The 1860s saw an intense
debate on secondary education and the mass of literature
produced by, for and about the Taunton Commission reflects the
fact that the grammar schools were in a critical stage of their
history. Amid such intense rethinking about the principles of
education the Newcastle Grammar School could hardly expect to
operate as if the national debate was not going on. The fourth
influence on the Council was the increasing momentum of public
examinations. Various universities in 1858 had started examinations for schools and in 1870 the government civil service
examinations began, while the military colleges were also
recruiting by competitive examination. These examinations now
provided a measure for judging a school's merits. The
considerable attention given by the Taunton Report to the social
value of examinations meant that urban schools with working- and
middle-class constituencies could not hope to be taken seriously
unless they became proficient in the examination system. For this
reason, if for none of the others outlined above, change was on the
cards for the School.

Such was the case. In March 1870, one month before the new
building was inaugurated, the Schools Committee finalised their
plans. Once they had got the measure of J. L. Hammond's
critique, and having accepted his conclusions, the committee
summoned the Headmaster and instructed him to prepare his
pupils for direct entry into the universities, the civil service, and
for participation in the universities' schools examination
(popularly known as the Locals).[89] Although this decision looks
bland enough it in fact required some fundamental reorganisation
because the School was entirely lacking relevant experience.

Accordingly, the committee divided the School into two departments 'on the same principle as Liverpool College'.[90] One of those departments (the 'modern') would cater for boys intent on careers in trade or business and its curriculum would be biased towards practical subjects (such as mathematics, surveying, book-keeping and shorthand) whose vocational value was direct. The other department (the 'classical') was to provide advanced teaching in mathematics, science and the classical languages all of which would form the bases of degree courses. The classical department was to be organised on the assumption that its pupils would remain at the School beyond the usual leaving age of 13 or 14, and that a good number of them would stay until they were 18. This department was therefore intended to become the senior school, and as such it was an attempt to restore the traditional character of the School which had been lost earlier in the century.

It will be noticed that the two-fold commercial–literary division had already been tried in the 1830s when the experiment had not met with lasting success. It is, therefore, not surprising that the Schools Committee in 1870 consolidated their measures by undertaking to replace the second master with a graduate who would be made head of the classical department. Snape himself would retain the title of Headmaster as well as his full salary but was demoted to the superintendence of the inferior modern department.[91]

The Council's desire to see improvement in the School's academic standard was only a means to a more important end. It was their intention that the School should provide as cheaply as possible for as many pupils as possible the kind of education that would gain for them admittance into the professions. Hence the all-important question of the fees which were pegged at four guineas, a sum well below a realistic rate, so that able boys of limited means could make their way to the top. One such was Thomas Bedford. He entered the School some two decades later having come from the elementary factory school of Armstrong's Engine Works at Elswick. Bedford won a scholarship to Cambridge, took a double First in science, was called to the Bar and returned to lecture in his old university. When his Headmaster wrote that 'the success of Bedford affords proof that at least from this district, the educational ladder from Elementary School to the University is complete', he was in fact summing up the objective set by the Council for the School on the eve of its translation to Rye Hill.[92] It was not going to be easy to transform the School so that it could produce as a matter of course successes like Bedford's but a start had been made. The purpose of the third and final part of this chapter is to estimate the extent to which the School was successful in achieving the academic and social goals set for it in 1870.

The establishment of a senior element was the Council's priority in 1870. Whether they were successful in achieving their goal is difficult to say because the evidence is fragmentary. Where the durations of post-1870 school careers can be established they show a tendency to be somewhat longer than they usually had been before. Between, for example, 1870 and 1876, 429 boys were enrolled and of these the careers of 242 are known: 143 of them stayed after their fourteenth birthdays but only 14 continued after they reached fifteen. Indeed, considering the 1870s and 80s overall, the material, such as it is, gives the strong impression that the School was unsuccessful in its attempt to retain pupils until their late teens.

This disappointing result was very probably related to the lack of state bursaries for those wishing to continue their education and to the absence of local funding to make good that deficiency. In theory the School at this time had four scholarships to give away. One of these had been provided in 1861 by James Dale, a Newcastle schoolteacher, who bequeathed £1,000 meant to produce £50 a year to pay the expenses of a university student from the Grammar School.[93] The first Dale award, delayed until sufficient interest had accumulated on the capital sum, was not made until 1877, and thereafter disbursements from this fund were irregular. There were also the three scholarships allocated in the 1858 Scheme from the annual endowments paid by the Virgin Mary Hospital but only one pupil benefited from this before 1880 because of the non-availability of the endowment. A number of awards were open to competition at Oxford and Cambridge and between 1870 and 1890 sixteen pupils won scholarships or exhibitions. Only one of those successful boys is known to have come from a working-class home whereas eight were the sons of beneficed clerics and another's father was the famous Newcastle cleric-schoolmaster-surgeon, Dr Rutherford. Generally, therefore, the Oxbridge awards do not seem to have been a means of social mobility for the working-class boys who comprised three-quarters of the School. In addition to Oxbridge various provincial universities and colleges offered bursaries but not more than half-a-dozen pupils seem to have won any of them in this period.

Despite the near absence of help to enable pupils to proceed
higher education some progress was made. During the 1860s,
average, only two pupils each year went up to a university where
between 1870 and 1890 129 did so and they represent eight p
cent of all those who joined the School in those two decades.
The choice of university illustrates one aspect of the Schoo
contribution to the life of Tyneside. One half of those who we
straight from the School to a university stayed in the North Ea:
39 entered the University of Durham's Medical College
Newcastle; 13 enrolled in that university's College of Science al
in Newcastle; and 14 resided in one or other of the colleges
Durham. When they had qualified about half of those 51 m
remained in the area to work. Of the remaining 63, Cambrid;
claimed 32, Oxford seven (only six of the Oxbridge graduat
returned home to practise their professions), various Scotti
universities 13, a number of English universities four, while t
universities of another seven are not known. Although th
achievement represents a step forward the School w
nevertheless nowhere near becoming an avenue to the professio
for the majority of its pupils. What was missing was a willingne
on the part of the Corporation to provide a borough subsidy (
augment the endowment from the Hospital) which would provi
the financial help on the scale necessary for turning the School in
an institution whose primary purpose was propelling its pupils
the social ladder. Quite the reverse was to happen, for as t
senior element took root in the School those who received mo
advantage from it were the children who could afford a mu
extended educational career.

An improvement in university entrance was only one of th
priorities set by the Council at the beginning of the School's R
Hill period. They were also concerned that the School shou
participate in 'the Locals'. Accordingly, new ground was broken
1872 when the School's first candidates were entered. During t
70s and 80s about 20 boys a year on average took either the juni
or senior papers. At first the School did no better than oth
establishments (Newcastle Modern School gained more pass
than the Grammar School in 1878) but expertise was quick
gained. Thus, in 1882, the Cambridge Senior Locals were taken l
605 candidates nationally but only 29 gained first class certificate
including two of the School's entrants.[95]

It was not long before the need for examination success induc
change and development in the teaching body. The older pupil

114

who were specialising more, required better qualified masters than had been usual hitherto. Shortly after the move to Rye Hill the staffing of the School was radically changed. In April 1871 Dr Snape ended his 37 year connection with the School. As he was one of the more significant Headmasters his departure merits a little attention. He had been aggrieved in 1870 by the appointment of Reginald Broughton as second master. Broughton was young and accomplished (he held a First in Greats) and Snape did not disguise his resentment of him as 'an alien; an entire stranger; an eleventh hour man', who had not shared the privations of the Charlotte Square period but who had yet been admitted to all the benefits of Rye Hill.[96] Moreover, Mr Broughton had been given control of the advanced work, which Snape had unsuccessfully requested, and exemption from the Headmaster's authority, a move as unusual as it was outrageous. In any case a chill seems to have been developing in the Schools Committee's relations with the veteran Headmaster. Were they not unsympathetic when he had complained about Broughton's inability to control his pupils? And what was their purpose in appointing a 'weekly visitation sub-committee' unless it was to spy on him?[97] Having been all but autonomous for over twenty years, Snape, who was in any case thin-skinned, was wounded by the unaccustomed atmosphere that was developing.[98] Meantime, he had been embroiled with the Council who were seeking an amendment of the method laid down in the 1858 Scheme by which the Headmaster's salary was calculated. Although the proposed change would not have damaged his interests in the foreseeable future he nevertheless took an extreme (and incorrect) line that the Council could not alter his contract unless he was in agreement. When they refused to concede on that point he resigned.[99] Miserable though this episode was in human terms it may have done some good, for the Schools Committee had established, crudely enough to be sure, that it was their wishes and not the Headmaster's, be he never so venerable, which were paramount. The Patriarch had gone. His successor, a stranger to Newcastle and to the School's traditions, would in all probability be more tractable.

When the School opened its doors at Rye Hill there were in addition to the Headmaster six teachers. They are shadowy men but enough is known about them to say that they had worked for Snape in difficult conditions at Charlotte Square, that they were effective on the level that the School was working on in the 60s, and that with one exception they did not hold degrees. If in 1870

they believed that their moving to a new building would improv
their careers, they were much mistaken, for as things turned ou
the end of Dr Snape's career in the School was also the end o
theirs. Five of his assistants left soon after him and the
replacements showed the Schools Committee seeking to improv
the teaching body; three were graduates and another had spel
some time at a university. Thereafter 'gowned masters' formed
significant proportion of the staff (34 of the 71 men appointe
between 1870 and 1889 were graduates, all but seven coming fro
Oxford or Cambridge).[100]

This was progress of sorts but the Schools Committee did no
have it all their own way. The only one of Snape's assistants wh
had not left when his dispute with the Council was at its mos
acrimonious was Dr Hans Ehrlich. He seems however to have ha
second thoughts and wrote to the press defending Snape, wa
reprimanded by the committee, whereupon (in 1874) he resigne
and opened his own establishment (Newcastle Modern School) o
Westgate Hill. This school was a considerable success and as it wa
on the Grammar School's doorstep it very probably attracted som
of the latter's potential pupils. And, what was even mor
damaging, he moved to Jesmond in 1881 and thereby provided th
middle-class families of the town's prosperous suburbs with yo
another argument against sending their sons all the way down t
Rye Hill for their schooling.[101]

The Schools Committee were having some success in attractin
better qualified teachers but were unable to retain them: of the 7
men who joined the staff between 1870 and 1889, 47 remained fo
less than two years and only eleven stayed longer than five years
This mobility was a problem that was undermining the Council
efforts to upgrade the School because the coming and going o
masters hindered the establishment of the routines necessary fo
the attainment of long-term academic goals. Explaining the men
reluctance to stay was their poor wages. In 1870 they petitione
the Council for more money but were told that although the
deserved more the School could afford to pay only a toke
increase in the form of occasional bonuses.[102] Inadequate wage
were in fact just a symptom of a fundamental weakness in th
School's constitution (its finances) that was responsible for holdin
back progress for a generation.

From 1870 until the late 80s the School could not pay its way
The annual deficits were caused by neither mismanagement no
extravagance but were the inescapable product of the financia

arrangements made in the 1858 Scheme. The Scheme ruled that (a) the Corporation should pay annually £105 to the Headmaster and provide him with a house or a further £100 in lieu; that (b) the Virgin Mary Hospital should pay £440 a year, of which £190 was for scholarships, leaving £250 for wages and maintenance; and that (c) the pupils' fees were to be divided between the masters (one half for the Headmaster, one quarter for the second master and one quarter for the rest). Thus, the assistants' salaries had to be met by a fund consisting of £250 and one quarter of the fees. However, even that arrangement, inadequate though it would have been, was not put into effect until it was too late. The delay was brought about in the first place by the provision in the Scheme that the Hospital's new chapel and the new Grammar School were to be paid for out of the Hospital's current revenues; it was not until 1870 that these works were completed and paid for. Thereafter, the Master of the Hospital, for reasons which are too complicated to be gone into here, refused to pay the School's endowment until ordered to do so by the High Court in 1881. Thus, from 1870 to 1881 the sole source of funds for the salaries was one quarter of the fees. How far this sum fell short of the bill is shown below:

The deficit in the assistant masters' wages account during the 1870s.[103]

Year	Fees to general fund £	VMH subsidy £250 from £440	Assistant masters' salaries total £
1870	294	not paid	566
1871	173	not paid	491
1872	166	not paid	480
1873	257	250	770
1874	436	not paid	911
1875	503	not paid	1126
1876	593	not paid	1254
1877	632	not paid	1515
1878	550	not paid	1532
1879	512	not paid	1695
1880	482	not paid	1580

Even when the endowment was paid regularly there was still not enough money to cover the salary bill. Crisis was kept at bay by the Borough treasury which made good the deficits, but there was no likelihood that the Corporation would allow the School to borrow indefinitely. As the debt mounted (almost £12,000 by 1888, including £3,207 loaned so that the Rye Hill building could be finished) the School came to be regarded as 'the one blackspot in the history of Corporate [i.e. Newcastle's] administration'.[104]

Something had to be done and the most obvious way forward was for the Council to persuade the Endowed Schools Commission of the urgency of reforming the financial provisions of the 1858 Scheme. Accordingly, in 1871, they submitted proposals to that effect but had to wait two years before receiving the commissioners' refusal. The commission were not unsympathetic but were unwilling to preempt the master-plan being prepared for the town's educational charities as a whole. In the meantime the Council had no choice but to seek additional money for the School from alternative sources. Their options were in fact very limited. For reasons which have already been explained it was accepted that recruitment had reached a ceiling for the foreseeable future.[105] In any case, even if the School's normal intake had been doubled the extra revenue would not have paid the salaries because the 1858 Scheme reserved three-quarters of the fees for the Headmaster and second master, and also because more teachers would have to be engaged to cope with the increased numbers of pupils; and the Endowed Schools Commission had discounted the possibility that the Scheme could be amended in the near future. The other alternative was a fee increase. This was a difficult line to take as they had resolved that the School should 'be the road to the professions and the universities' and they could hardly now put the School out of the reach of working-class families by making it too expensive for them. However, there was no escape and the fees were put up in 1873 (from £4 to £6 18s 0d for the under-14s and from £4 to £9 for the older boys) and again in 1877 (when every pupil was to pay £9, which included stationery).[106] Noticeable though these rises were, they were still very reasonable (Manchester Grammar School was charging between 12 and 16 guineas), but were, too reasonable to solve the problem of the School's debts.

During the debate on the School's shaky finances the most likely solution seems to have dawned only slowly. Was not the Virgin Mary Hospital growing richer by the year and did it not have more money than it needed? Would not the Hospital profit substantially when its leases came up for renewal at the end of the century? The

118

Hospital had been founded to help the poor; the School's goal was helping children who lacked the money to launch themselves in the world; so, why should not the one be made to help the other? In 1875 work began on the drafting of a new constitution which would jettison the anachronistic arrangements made in 1858.[107] Thirteen years would pass before that revision was complete.

The Council proposed but, of course, it was the Charity Commission which disposed. The commissioners agreed that the School should have a greater share of the Hospital's income, but before they could determine the exact amount they first had to discover how much spare money the Hospital had. The surplus was the income remaining after the payment (a) of the stipends of the master and almsmen (£772 10s 0d altogether), (b) of £150 for the upkeep of the elementary school attached to the Hospital, and (c) of the Grammar School's £440 endowment. The apparent simplicity of this division notwithstanding, it was far from easy to estimate how much was usually left over after the above disbursements had been made. The Hospital's affairs were in a state of extraordinary confusion because of the various suits which its Master, the Reverend Robert Anchor Thompson, had brought against Newcastle Corporation. It was not until 1882 that the litigation was concluded and the commissioners could proceed. By then, however, they had embarked on a complete remodelling of the Hospital's constitution. That project involved a four-cornered interchange of ideas between the Charity Commission, the town Council, Anchor Thompson (whose capacity for obstruction was phenomenal) and various interested parties in Newcastle. As the drafts of the reforms travelled between London and Tyneside they grew in size and complexity, hence the long gestation. Meanwhile the School sank deeper into debt. However, the result (the St Mary's Hospital Act, 1888) was well worth the wait because the Charity Commission had transformed the Hospital into a predominantly educational charity whose income was principally dedicated to the uses of the Grammar School. The School's endowment from the Hospital was increased from £440 to £800 (which included the endowment of the Hospital's elementary school which had just been closed); the £205 endowment from the Corporation was also to continue. Also, £3,580 was transferred from the Hospital into a new maintenance fund for the School: during the 1890s this capital produced almost £100 annually. The School was also given entitlement to a share in the Hospital's surplus, when there was any, which on occasions brought between

£800 and £1,000. Finally the Hospital money was used to discharge the School's £12,000 debt to the Corporation.[108]

During the thirteen years when they were revising the old Scheme the Charity Commissioners were concerned with securing a sound financial future for the School, though not exclusively for they had to concern themselves with other aspects of its administration. Many of those reforms concerned routine matters and were unremarkable, but there was one which initiated an altogether new stage in the School's development. Tradition was broken when the commissioners gave the School an autonomous governing body, thereby ending the Corporation's trusteeship which had been exercised since the sixteenth century. Exactly when and why this significant decision was made is not known but the Reverend Anchor Thompson seems to have been a moving spirit. When the revision process began in 1875 the commissioners gave no sign that they were intending to remove the Corporation's jurisdiction over the School. The first appearance of the idea is found in a letter addressed to the commission by Anchor Thompson wherein he dilated on the enormities of his great enemy, the Corporation, and tried to show how the School's present problems had been caused by various Council decisions in the past. In his opinion the School needed to be self-governing and certainly independent of the Corporation. During his tenure of the mastership of the Virgin Mary Hospital he believed he had learned (though whether he was right is quite another matter) that the Corporation tended to endanger the interests of individual institutions if they could gain some advantage for the ratepayers in general; 'I must', he wrote, 'beg leave to state, what an experience of seventeen years convinces me to be . . . the indispensable condition of the lasting prosperity of the Royal Grammar School in Newcastle. I am persuaded that, whether it possesses an estate or a fixed endowment, its Governors should be in a position to take an independent interest in its financial prosperity, without responsibility to the corporate body of the town. They must not be dependent for the amount of their expenditure, still less, if it possesses an estate, must they be dependent for its management and its income upon the action of officials who are the servants of another and superior body.'[109]

At first Thompson's bolt fell short of the mark and neither the Charity Commission nor the Council indicated any support for his suggestion, surprisingly, perhaps, as the School was a financial liability to the town. Indeed, the commission's official,

Mr Latham, who was co-ordinating the affair, remained unmoved even when treated to a bombardment of documentary 'proofs' by Anchor Thompson in person.[110] In 1878 Latham was proposing that the School be ruled by a 'Council of Twelve', to be appointed by the town Council who would not be obliged to seek members outside the ranks of the Corporation. By 1883, however, the commission had come round to Thompson's way of thinking although they had not decided on the principle by which the composition of the new board of governors would be determined. To begin with they were inclined to give the preponderance to the Council's nominees but during the four years in which the matter was thrashed out they changed their mind and eventually settled on a compromise.[111] Thus, in the new Scheme of 1888 it was laid down that the governing body should comprise eighteen members: nine from the city Council, three from the University of Durham, one from each of the universities of Oxford and Cambridge, and four who were to be co-opted by the representative governors.

This change was without doubt an important one and it is therefore surprising that no reason for it is found in any of the surviving materials on the subject. For an explanation, however, it may be necessary to look no further than the composition of the new board of governors whose academic and co-opted members may point to the weakness of the School's old constitution. Previously, the School had been administered only by local politicians who in general had not been through the university system and who may have lacked familiarity with all the developments going on in higher education. Earlier (in 1870) the School had been given the task of transforming itself into a bridge to link the suburbs of Newcastle with the universities and professions. The achievement of that goal was made much more certain by the inclusion of academics and men distinguished in their own right.

The reforms contained in the Scheme of 1888 were a landmark in the School's history. Problems which for generations had impeded its development were cleared away and although difficulties remained the School was more stable than it had been at any other time in the nineteenth century. From the time of Edward Moises it had mainly served one or two neighbourhoods. Now some of the conditions had been provided that would enable the School to serve a wider public. How far and how quickly the new opportunities were exploited will be considered in the following chapter.

Chapter IV

THE IMPACT OF CENTRAL GOVERNMENT 1888–1922

(i) *The Aftermath of the 1888 Act*

In two lectures on the subject of education in Newcastle given to the town's Literary and Philosophical Society in the spring of 1884 its honorary secretary, solicitor Robert Spence Watson, spoke of the mental ferment of his time. Personally involved in the promotion of education in the town, he expressed a deep concern to ensure a better future for his fellow citizens, in particular through the agency of education. During this period he was enthusiastically involved in the establishment of the Free Public Lending Library, University extension lectures, the foundation of Durham College of Science and served twenty-three years on Newcastle School Board. In secondary schooling, he shared the objectives of the educationalist Professor T. H. Huxley whom he quoted:

> Our business is to provide a ladder reaching from the gutter to the university along which every child in the three Kingdoms shall have the chance of climbing as far as he is fit to go.[1]

Four years later, as a co-opted governor, Dr Spence Watson convened the first meeting of the School's governing body, newly constituted under the Scheme of the 1888 Act, which he had actively promoted through his considerable influence in the Liberal Party, thereby significantly extending the future educational opportunities for the region's aspiring sons.

This chapter will enquire into the various influences both at national and local level which affected the fortunes of the Grammar School throughout a period of rapid social and economic change. It will also record during these years the gradual development of academic provision and the distinctive corporate life within its walls.

The St Mary's Hospital (Newcastle upon Tyne) Act 1888 received the royal assent on 24 July 1888. Although its scheme confidently expected future growth, much of the expected development remained unfulfilled for several years. Nevertheless, its finances were stabilised by the increase of income from higher fees now ranging from a minimun of £8 p.a. to a maximum of £14; by a yearly sum of £605 to be paid from the Hospital funds, and by the far-sighted requirement in clause 65 that any surplus income, after all other necessary payments had been met, should be paid to the Governors for educational purposes. A residue of the foundation's income not required for all other purposes was to be accumulated to form a fund for the establishment of a girls' secondary school in Newcastle. The closure of St Mary's elementary school, hitherto maintained out of Hospital funds and superseded by schools provided out of city rates, would finance scholarships out of an annual £150, thus ensuring access to the School for a few promising pupils from the public elementary schools, access for which the Master of the Hospital had fought so long. By 1889, the scholarship schemes provided the first fifteen free scholarships to elementary school boys, ten of whom came from the Elswick district and five from Board Schools in Heaton and Byker.

The School's new Governing Body was to be composed of eighteen 'competent persons duly qualified to discharge the duties of the office': four co-optative governors nominated by the Charity Commissioners, nine elected from the Council, and, linking the School with institutions of higher education, representatives from the Universities of Cambridge, Oxford, Durham, and Durham's Colleges of Science and Medicine in Newcastle.

As the government of the School finally passed out of the hands of the municipal Corporation, Councillor Richardson reminded them that the selection of nine council members would, he hoped, 'put energy and zeal into the work,' and would make 'the weal or woe of the future of the Grammar School'.[2] Voted first Chairman of the Governors, and shortly afterwards elected Mayor, Richardson was to give over twenty years of energetic service to the School, exerting considerable influence on its behalf through his important position in Newcastle civic life, and through membership of key council committees.

At the first meeting of the Governors, the Headmaster was asked to report fully on the position of the School, laying before the Governors his proposals for the future of the School under the new Scheme. Samuel Charles Logan, aged 38, educated at the

Perse School and St John's College Cambridge, had been appointed Headmaster in 1883, after his resignation from the Headship of Hull Grammar School when planned development had been thwarted by Hull City Council.

What were the problems and challenges which Logan faced in 1888, and how did he propose to deal with them? Despite the steady rise in the birthrate in the North East of England, numbers in the School had remained disappointingly static since his appointment; there were wide variations, from nine to sixteen, in the age of entry to the School, an irregular length of school life, and a marked tendency towards early leaving: of the fifty-nine boys who entered in 1888, only sixteen stayed for five or more years in the School. Furthermore, frequent changes in staffing inhibited improvements in the quality of academic education and more especially the development of the practical sciences, which had been strongly recommended in the new Scheme. The development of science teaching was also hindered by the poor supply of chemistry apparatus and limited laboratory accommodation: 'We may well hope to take a higher rank among Science teaching establishments,' Mr Logan reported, 'when properly appointed laboratories are attached to the School.'[3]

Physical activities were also seriously curtailed and the Headmaster was anxiously looking forward to the time 'when our playground shall be fit for use and when the opportunity for healthy recreation which this indispensable portion of a well equipped school affords shall no longer be denied to us.'[4]

Although a part time drill master had been appointed in 1886, the condition of the playground, already reported as unsatisfactory in 1885, had made the provision of a gymnasium an urgent need. An earlier proposal of the Council's School and Charities Committee for an ambitious recreation ground at Fenham, 'three and a half acres for the purpose of a cricket field and football ground and a portion of the lake for a swimming pond' was rejected both on grounds of cost and also by a representative of Fenham Hall Estate who declared the plan exceedingly detrimental to the Hall.[5]

The new Governors put forward a more modest suggestion for the construction of three level terraces for sport, incorporating the playground of St Mary's elementary school on the Rye Hill site but it was delayed because, as the Town Clerk put it, 'neither the Trustees nor the Governors had at present any money available for the purpose.'

There were to be recurrent difficulties in playing team games because of the lack of pitches. In 1892, the Headmaster's stern dictum that 'No Association Football is to be played in this School in any form whatever' may have resulted in improved rugger, but the loss of the rented pitch at Burdon Terrace, required for the building of the Fleming Memorial Hospital, was to be a blow. It was the opinion of one young contributor to the 1894–5 *Novocastrian* that the provision of a playing field was 'the one thing needed to bring the School to the place it should occupy among the schools of the neighbourhood.'[6]

However, the *Novocastrian*, which had been launched in 1885 to create and maintain an esprit de corps among past and present members of the School' revealed the Headmaster's dogged promotion of physical activities despite the curtailment of cricket and football. Paper chases were run from Rye Hill when not prevented by 'the state of the roads'. A cycling club, formed in 1889, visited Morpeth, Tynemouth and Shotley Bridge and participated in a two-mile Bicycle Handicap as part of the annual Athletic Sports held on the Newcastle Constabulary's ground. The magazine earnestly reported other innovations. The creation of twelve prefects would 'bring a wholesome moral influence to bear upon the boys'. The newly appointed prefects had resolved to wear 'college caps when on duty'. The writer hoped when the new scheme was fully in operation to see a new Prefects' room 'wherein a library may expand and it will make a prefectship a thing to be sought after . . .'

By 1890, Mr Logan had introduced school caps with red cords upon which the Royal and Newcastle Arms were embroidered at a cost of two shillings and two pence per schoolboy head. But old boys showed a lack of respect for the article, and in 1897 a *Novo* correspondent sorrowfully recorded 'a growing antipathy to the wearing of the school cap' by members of the School, though 'the wearing of mortarboards by the VIth form has a considerable number of backers'.

A. S. Bibby, who attended Rye Hill from 1897–1900 after winning a school scholarship of £30 to cover the cost of fees, books and equipment wrote a brief but evocative account of the School in the late 1890s.[7] He recalled the Rye Hill building as 'rather imposing' with a main South facing entrance 'which we boys were forbidden to use'. He described the setting for Morning Assembly on his first day in the IVth Form room:

The room was very wide. The door was at the middle of one long wall, and a very gently sloping gangway of broad steps led down to the master's desk. From each side of the gangway, long desks stretched to the end walls with a long form at each desk for the boys to sit on. Everything about these two galleries was of the most solid and immovable construction. I was intrigued to see the amount of carving that had been perpetrated on these desks. There were even wide peepholes cut through to the bookshelf below.

Allocated at first to the IVth Modern and launched on commercial subjects such as book-keeping and shorthand, he later transferred to IV Classics to take Latin, a compulsory subject for passing matriculation in order to go to college, and was given extra coaching at home by the Latin Master, Mr Luzmore. He recalls the lessons of 'Daddy' Laws – a skilful teacher of both physics and chemistry – in a physics lab equipped only with a large central table and balances in glass cases along the walls.

French was taught by Mr Stallworthy, nicknamed Bulldog:

He never spared himself. . . . He had a funny habit of smacking the side of his nose with his right forefinger. We knew that something serious was coming. He must have been one of the first to teach French by the Direct Method. . . .

He described one particular encounter during the season of 'pluffers' with intense schoolboy relish.

These (pluffers) were pieces of glass tubing through which we blew grains of rice at each other, and while Bulldog, that day, was toiling up the stairs he could hear the row we were making. When he entered the room we were sitting as good as little boys can be, but his boots crunched the grains of rice so he knew what had been going on. For punishment he dictated three lines, each to be written twenty five times.
(1) I must bring to school carefully prepared work, not rice.
(2) I must fill my mind with knowledge and not litter the floor with rice.
(3) I must throw my faults and evil tendencies away, NOT RICE.

By the beginning of the next decade two of the problems which Mr Logan had identified in 1888 were approaching a solution, partly as a result of central government policy. The Charity Commissioners' insistence in the 1888 scheme on the closure of St Mary's elementary school had provided potential space for conversion into much needed laboratories or a gymnasium. An independent report perhaps influenced by the higher standards in Board School buildings was, however, critical of either possibility:

A gym should be essentially a place for healthy exercise. Considerable enlargement of the gable windows would be necessary for the admission of healthful sunlight of which there could hardly be too much.

As for using the building as a laboratory, it was very ill designed for a school room and light and air are not less essential for a laboratory and it appears deficient in both.[8]

Clearly the cost of conversion or of new building could not be met out of school income. The Governors sent a deputation to the Charity Commissioners to win support in persuading the Trustees to allow the use of capital funds out of Hospital endowments. The Charity Commissioners, in receipt, under clause 58 of the Scheme, of the examiners' annual reports on the School, would have read the 1889 comment by H. R. Norris that 'the science teaching which I cannot praise too highly, is sadly handicapped by want of proper accommodation both for lecture purposes and for laboratory work', and his comment the following year, 'I am sorry it has not been found possible to start some practical work in experimental physics'.[9]

The Governors received the support they were looking for from the Charity Commissioners, and built a new gym on a site to the south west of the old elementary school with a loan of £1800 from capital funds made by the reluctant Trustees. The formal opening of the gym took place on 3 July 1891, and was welcomed by a contributor to the *Novocastrian* who pronounced: 'Too much time has been bestowed upon intellectual excellence to the neglect or partial neglect of the physical condition'.[10] The Chairman of the Governors thought the School should now 'quickly rise to the position of supremacy in the North which it ought to hold'.

At the same time the Governors drew up a plan to convert the old elementary school for use as a lecture room and two laboratories, and Professor Garnett, the representative Governor from the Durham College of Science, visited the Science and Art Department to obtain approval for the plan so that the School might qualify for a grant paid annually by that Department on the basis of approved instruction given in suitably equipped rooms.

The conversion proved timely. The activities of a National Association for the promotion of Technical and Secondary Education founded in 1887 had resulted in the passing of a Technical Instruction Act in 1889, an apparently insignificant piece of legislation giving permissive powers to the newly created county and borough councils to levy a rate not exceeding 1d in the pound, for the giving of technical instruction. Financial backing for the

Act was secured the following year in the Local Taxation Act which diverted approximately £750,000 raised by a tax on spirits (sometimes referred to as 'Publicans' or 'Whisky' Money) to the County Councils for the purposes of secondary education. Thus a state subvention for a limited part of secondary education was secured almost accidentally 'by a side wind'.

In December 1890 Newcastle City Council held a lively debate on the application of this unexpected windfall. An earlier opinion of Lord Armstrong that 'almost any amount might be advantageously utilised in diffusing technical instruction' was quoted approvingly. It was thought that funds, obtained somewhat by a fluke, should not be used simply to reduce the burden of local taxation, but 'if applied to technical instruction might come again'. All agreed that the grant would be amply sufficient for distribution among the various schools and therefore a local rate need not be levied.[11]

However, marked differences of opinion were expressed concerning the allocation of the funds. Alderman Richardson forcefully refuted the principle that no school with endowment should receive a share and in particular he defended the School's claim against one critic who declared that it 'must have a great deal of money for he found the Governors had levelled a piece of ground, destroyed a beautiful greensward, and made a sort of mud-hole, and they had also put up a building called a gymnasium in front of one of the finest elevations in the city'. The Alderman's answer was that his Governors' actions had been forced upon them by an Act of Parliament and that, being 'so hard up they did not know where to turn for money', they had found it impossible to carry out the provisions of the Act with the amount allowed them under that Act. He added that the School was already involved in scientific instruction, with 168 boys in the Science and Art classes, earning the School £32 that year. A grant to the Grammar School would go towards a demonstrator's stipend and laboratory equipment. His intervention secured the Council's vote and an annual grant of approximately £150, which persisted well into the twentieth century and stimulated local interest and involvement in the School in a new way.

The School's finances, however, remained insecure and inhibited a solution to another problem Mr Logan faced, the frequent changes in staffing. Mr Logan had requested an increase in the salaries of the assistant masters, but the application for the increase and for the formation of a pension fund under Section 61 of the Scheme had been quietly shelved. In July 1891, following the suggestion in the examiners' report of that year that languages, especially German, required urgent attention, Mr Logan asked his Governors to approve minor reorganisation of several salaries in order to appoint a specialist modern languages teacher at a salary increased from £140 to £200. He told them:

> I shall then be able to secure a really efficient teacher and great improvement in this most important part of school work will be the result.[12]

He had found it necessary to remind them yet again of their undertaking given to the Council to appoint an extra science teacher and to purchase apparatus following their grant of £150 towards the promotion of technical education in the School.

Mr Logan's request was remitted, but he submitted it again unaltered the following week with the stubborn observation: 'I am not able to make any change in my proposals'. The Governors finally accepted the proposal the following year but with great reluctance, because the disappointing numbers and income 'scarcely appeared to warrant it'.

Other repercussions for the School through the implementation of the Technical Instruction Act were the fresh influx of able boys from the Board Schools in addition to the fifteen under the 1888 Scheme, bringing a modest increase in overall numbers by the mid-nineties, and a widening of the geographical area from which pupils were drawn. Six boys, awarded secondary school scholarships by Northumberland County Council, requested to hold them at the Grammar School. By 1894 the County was also contributing a sum of £28 per annum out of the Whisky Money for several other boys, not scholars, attending the School from its district, in addition to a scholarship of £30 to enable one boy to go on to University. An additional nine scholars were expected in the autumn of 1894. The Headmaster, urging his Governors to accede to the request for a Northumberland County representative governor, wrote:

> The County Council is practically in its infancy and I should hope that we may get still greater help from them as time goes on.[13]

From 1893 Durham County Council was also contributing a sum from its Whisky Money for several of its boys. One effect of the

Counties' introduction of examinations to provide a fairer distribution of free scholarships was to induce even the unsuccessful candidates to consider coming to the School as fee-payers.

The slight improvement in the School's fortunes is reflected in the Headmaster's yearly report to his Governors in February 1895, with a record 274 pupils by the end of the year and ten boys electing to remain after seventeen. Two open scholarships had been won to Cambridge University; one by R. J. Paterson the son of an assistant master at the School. The second, T. G. Bedford, was felt to be particularly deserving of special mention because he had won a school scholarship from Elswick Works school, thus affording clear proof that at least for their district 'the education ladder from the elementary school to the university is complete'.[14] Both boys would go on to take first class honours in their Tripos examinations.

The School's published accounts reveal that, for the first time since the new Scheme, and for three years in succession, its annual expenditure had been less than its income, and the Trustees had informed the Governors of surplus income from Hospital funds which could be handed over to the Governors for educational purposes under the 1888 Scheme.

The School's location at Rye Hill had caused problems well before 1888, and in 1895 the Governors once again turned their attention to it. At their meeting in February of that year the Governors agreed, on a motion from Dr Spence Watson, to form a 'New Schools Committee' which would inquire into the necessity and advisability of erecting new school buildings with sufficient ground for all physical purposes; the best site in the city to be secured for any such new buildings and their probable cost; and the value of the existing school property and the prospect of disposing of it advantageously.

The committee's report was cautious. Though they saw the desirability of removal to a site adjacent to playing fields, and had considered the Headmaster's report on the geographical distribution of pupils, they could not recommend a move at that time. But if such a move became practicable, one site in particular should be seriously considered: the land at the north end of the city, belonging to the Corporation as Trustees of the Magdalen Hospital, which was currently being laid out as building sites. Consideration of the third issue was deferred.[15]

The decision to defer action was taken on financial grounds, but at least two men continued to explore practical ways of effecting a move. The Charity Commissioners had ordered the Hospital Trustees to invest the surplus income now beginning to grow significantly as the rateable value of land and property in Newcastle increased through economic development. The investment of the current year's £800 would form a fund for the establishment of a girls' school under the terms of clause 68 of the Scheme, but the Vice-Chairman, Dr Spence Watson, argued that the money should be used for 'the general improvement of the Grammar School'. Shortly afterwards a deputation of Governors persuaded the Charity Commissioners to sanction the application of the surplus £800 for the School's purposes and thereby established a most useful precedent as the Trust's properties increased in value in the following years. Dr Spence Watson, who with his wife had keenly promoted the opening of a girls' school in Gateshead under the auspices of the Girls' Day Schools Company in 1876, must have been aware of that school's plans to transfer to Newcastle and their negotiations in 1896 to buy land in Eskdale Terrace from Newcastle Corporation. The Church Schools Company had already established a high school in 1885, which now occupied a new building in Tankerville Terrace. Girls' education, it would seem, had been adequately provided from parental pockets, and would not immediately require the charitable support of clause 68 of the St Mary's Hospital Act.

The Headmaster, ever watchful of variation in the number of pupils, now took an important initiative. In 1896 he presented to the Governors, in their clerk's words, 'an exhaustive report which he had prepared with a view to an enquiry as to the advisability of either removing the School to, or opening a branch at, a position equally accessible to all parts of the city of Newcastle'.[16] Presenting a tabular statement, he analysed the possible causes of the fluctuation of numbers in the School since his appointment. During 1896 the numbers had once again decreased alarmingly to 227. His explanation was that the School depended for its boys almost exclusively on two sources, the train and the west end of the city. The number of boys coming by train from Northumberland and Durham would tend to diminish as efficient local schools were established, and as the Armstrong Works had developed the west end had become more artisan and less residential: there was a distinct gravitation towards Jesmond. He believed that the School was now taking almost every boy whose parents desired for their children an education superior to that obtained at the Board Schools. At the same time, he had observed an absence of boys from the Jesmond district. During the previous weeks, he had been discussing the question with a number of parents resident in Jesmond who, assuring him that distance was the deterrent, pledged themselves to send their boys to his school if it were transferred to a more convenient site. In conclusion, Mr Logan strongly recommended either the School's early removal to a more accessible site, or failing this, the temporary opening of a branch to the main school in the Jesmond district the following term. He supported the latter recommendation by reference to the increase of numbers at other endowed schools such as Latymer Upper School Hammersmith, Liverpool College and Southampton Grammar School, all of which had moved successfully from decaying neighbourhoods in recent years. Included in his report was an abstract of replies received from several Headmasters in response to an earlier circular from Logan.

In a unanimous resolution, Jesmond residents, meeting at the Grand Assembly Rooms on 18 January 1897, petitioned the Governors to open a Branch School in Jesmond without delay 'with a view to supplying the educational needs of the large population residing at the north end of the city'. The meeting, instructed by Mr Logan, had discussed the example of other town grammar schools which had followed the migrations of the population which supplied them with funds and scholars.[17]

Faced with a deficit as numbers declined, and a list of anxious Jesmond residents' signatures, the Governors wasted no more time. A house was rented in St Thomas's Place and the Branch School opened in May 1897. It immediately ran into trouble, provoking an outburst from nearby residents that it 'would create a great nuisance and annoyance to occupiers and would destroy the quietness of their houses and lower the value'. In the Council chamber, Alderman Richardson's sardonic response, that it was a strange thing that some of the signatories to the petition received by the School Governors were now signing against having the School near to them, drew laughter among the councillors. The move, he assured them, was only a temporary one. 'If the thing was a success, they would have to remove and that very shortly. If it was a failure, they would shut it altogether.'[18] He gave his personal guarantee as Chairman of the Governors that if the Branch School should prove a nuisance he would ensure its immediate dissolution. Would the Council say, he demanded, that a Branch School of intelligent and respectable boys – members of

132

the Council were fathers of some of them – was going to be 'noisome and offensive'? (A voice: Yes.) He did not believe it for a single moment. He entirely rejected the accusation that the Governors had acted precipitately without authorisation from the Council by 'smuggling it through'. The final motion in favour of the opening was described as 'Vote for Progress' and was carried by 28 votes to 18 with 4 abstentions.

Sixteen boys enrolled in the first term, but by the end of the first year there were 52, and when Mr Logan gave his annual report to the Governors in February 1898 the numbers stood at 69 with every prospect of further increase. Though numbers at the Rye Hill School continued to fall, the overall total had risen from 224 to 247. He urged his Governors:

> The time is fast approaching, if not already arrived, when they should consider policy as to the future site of the school.[19]

Additional support for this view came from an independent educational expert. Following a fierce Council debate over the allocation of Technical Instruction funds in 1896, the Council had invited Sir Joshua Fitch, Assistant Commissioner in Yorkshire under the Schools Inquiry Commission earlier in the century, to report on the distribution of the Technical Instruction grants to various institutions in the city. In his section on the Grammar School, he observed that it was unfortunate that the School was situated 'in a part of the city in which there is less need for advanced instruction than in the North East or Jesmond quarter in which the bulk of the richer inhabitants reside'.[20] He thought that the School should flourish if means could be found to 'plant this institution in the Jesmond district, thereby increasing its opportunities of usefulness to the city'.

Another meeting of Jesmond residents, while expressing approval and appreciation of the valuable extension at the Branch School, urged the provision of more permanent buildings. On that occasion, Mr Logan had told them that he 'looked forward with a strong personal desire for the centralisation of his work in Jesmond'. The report in the Newcastle Daily Chronicle the following day saw it as a 'bold coup' of the Governors to capture the other large funds of the Virgin Mary Hospital 'to secure a palatial collegiate establishment'. Their Rye Hill School, built at great cost in 1870, it was suggested, had an airy situation, embracing every feature conducive to health. Young Jesmond could 'easily get to the station by a penny tramcar' and five minutes walk brought him to Rye Hill. If not, the enterprising and influential residents should put their hands deep enough in their own pockets to establish another grammar school.[21]

In bold contrast to such criticism, the zeal and commitment of the RGS Governors emerged clearly as consultations concerning, in the Governors' phrase, 'the urgent necessity for the removal of the grammar school from the present buildings at the West end to Jesmond' began with Charity Commissioners, Virgin Mary Trustees and the City Councillors. Alderman Richardson appeared personally before the Trustees to plead the case for removal and to gain support in applying to the Charity Commission. He had already opened negotiations for the land behind Windsor Terrace with colleagues on the Estate and Property Committee, 'where there would be ample space for a Boys' School and also for a Girls' School as contemplated by the St Mary's Hospital Act 1888'. Was his reference to the girls' school calculated to reassure the Trustees of the Governors' firm adherence to the spirit of the 1888 Scheme? Certainly, the Alderman did not anticipate any financial difficulty in carrying out the proposals. After a visit by Mr L. A. Selby-Bigge, Assistant Charity Commissioner, the Trustees accepted the Commission's suggestion that the purchase of land should be treated as an investment of funds derived from the sale of other lands belonging to the Trust.[22]

The approval of the City Councillors for the project required even more powerful oratory. In Alderman Richardson's persuasive speech on the School's behalf, in March 1900, he declared that the school in Rye Hill had never been a success, that even in the palmiest days of Dr Snape it had never exceeded 261 and that well before the present Headmaster came it was a failing institution, running gradually into debt. The new governing body had felt concern that the school was not answering the object of its foundation. It was not progressing at a rate which was consistent with its ancient history, its prestige and its endowments, and it was not meeting 'the wants of this great community'. They were legislating, he told the Council, 'not for today only, or for tomorrow, but for the future'. The population, increasing rapidly, might have doubled within fifty years. Annual reports of independent inspectors had stated that the school was giving education of a high standard, sending out brilliant boys, including two years previously the son of a mechanic in Armstrong Works, to the best universities. The reason for the School's comparative failure was: first, that it was not in the right place, and secondly, that they needed ample playgrounds. Physical education was essential in any modern school curriculum, in some measure because of its moral effect. 'Just let the Council look at what the army had done recently in South Africa.' The Branch School was now 'chock-full' with 107 boys and the Headmaster was forced to reject many more applications. The step proposed by the Governors would equip, not only the present, but future generations of citizens for the struggle for life.

The Council gave him a round of applause and voted 34–15 approving his proposal for the time being, though some Councillors, particularly those representing the West end of the city would return to the attack during the year that followed, and there would be protracted wrangles over the price of the Magdalen Hospital Land, the loss of public right of way from Brandling Park to Eskdale Terrace, and the sale of the Rye Hill site.[23]

To the educational and administrative difficulties of running the School on the two separate sites during the years of planning and building were added the recurring financial problems. The decisions to appoint extra staff for the Branch School and to raise a few salaries of individual masters were only taken in July 1900, and again in 1903, after careful enquiries to several other endowed schools had confirmed that their annual expenses, like those of the Grammar School, were exceeding the revenue from the school fees and that their survival now seemed to depend upon extra income from endowments.

For these reasons in addition to the building project the question of the availability of surplus income from the Hospital funds in an amended scheme for the Newcastle school would again become of paramount importance to its Governors. Two grave omissions in the work of the Charity Commissioners had become apparent: in legally fixing the scale of fees in the schemes of the endowed schools, they had failed to allow for possible shrinkage of endowment or even for the inevitable rise in the cost of efficiency under the new conditions prescribed by their schemes; secondly, in their failure to monitor the operation of the schemes an opportunity for evolving national standards of efficiency had been missed.

As the School entered the twentieth century, an assessment of its academic life was offered by His Majesty's Inspectors. The *Novo* editorial in 1903 informs us that 'for three whole days the boys were kept in a state of anxiety, by the sight of the gentlemen flitting about the various classrooms and doubtless great interest will be shown in their report'. The 'gentlemen' were the Inspectors from the Board of Education conducting their first general inspection of the School, and their report provides for the first time a valuable objective assessment of the School's academic standing on a national scale. They reported that the 1888 Scheme was substantially in operation except in one minor respect, the non-observance of the requirements under clause 58 of the Scheme for the yearly examination of all scholars by an external examiner. As for the School buildings, the classrooms were pronounced 'inconvenient being too large and too high and the windows are in all cases so arranged that the light falls on the boys' right side or else the boys directly face it . . . the walls are very dirty; it is understood that they have not been cleaned for several years'.[24] The labs in the converted St Mary's building were deficient in apparatus, one observed lesson having been given 'with the crudest makeshifts'.

Despite these limitations, the staff had achieved considerable success. The Headmaster had shown a pleasing readiness to accept suggestions and to introduce improvements: 'it is clear that he is constantly making strenuous efforts to improve the School by giving more time to the work of supervision.' In a full-time staff of eight masters there was at least one teacher of high qualifications and ability in each main subject, though additional specialist appointments for classics and modern languages were urgently needed to replace too large a proportion of masters qualified only for general teaching in the lower part of the School.

The inspectors noted an imbalance in time spent on maths and science in the curriculum to the detriment of work in classics in the upper forms, nor was the science course 'in keeping with that usually found in schools of this type', since physics was merely ancillary to chemistry. It was commented that since Newcastle was becoming a very important centre of industrial enterprise, particularly through expansion in coal-mining, engineering and ship-building, the School should respond to the needs of scholars and neighbourhood by devoting more time to physics in its various branches. Time given to shorthand was considered excessive, and its compulsion inadvisable, even on the modern side, while English subjects were being badly neglected.

The difficulty in arranging a satisfactory course of education appeared to arise from 'a want of clearness as to the class of boys to be educated, and the position to which the School aimed'. The inspectors were challenging:

> Is it to be a school for professional men, whose sons would naturally remain till at least 17? Is it to depend chiefly on those who wish to become clerks, and will require a commercial education, leaving at 15 or 16? Is it to provide for sons of skilled artisans from Elementary Schools, who require chiefly a thorough grounding in Science and Maths with English?

The School appeared to be performing all three functions at once and to be unable to do any of them thoroughly. The classification and promotion of boys were thus made more than usually difficult, particularly because boys entered at different ages and from widely different educational backgrounds. These difficulties appeared so serious that there was an obvious need for a thorough investigation of the whole scheme of education in the city. The inspectors observed that the division of the School on two separate sites had created problems. The experiment of the Branch School had probably proved wise, but was putting too great a strain upon the' Headmaster and his time, half of which was already spent in teaching. On a minor organisational point, the inspectors had observed that some sixteen boys who travelled in daily from a distance used the gym as a dining room at midday, but that the remainder appeared to disperse 'to eating shops or father's office'. Greater control should be exercised since 'in a town like Newcastle, boys may easily get into undesirable quarters and company'.

The report concluded that in general the School did much good work, but could obtain a much higher rank than it held. In such an eminent town of large population, the Grammar School should in future 'take its place with quite the most important of the great day schools in the country, not only in numbers, but also in its standard of work'.

The Inspectors' 1903 report had an immediate significance for the future of the School in that it provided additional and influential evidence to support the Governors' efforts to move the School into more modern buildings and to secure adequate income with which to maintain them. Equally importantly, it advised higher standards of teaching through better qualified and paid staff, and suitable equipment, and a considerable shift in emphasis in the curriculum, with properly thought-out time tables, with an eye kept upon the particular needs of their district. The report itself heralded the expansion of state responsibilities into the general provision of national education following recent government legislation.

(ii) *The School and the Government*

The local interest in technical and secondary education which, as we have seen, was stimulated amongst councils and their committees and among elementary teachers and boys' parents, coincided with a new and powerful groundswell of public opinion, particularly in parliamentary circles. Voicing their anxieties for an efficient national provision of education, especially secondary, men of widely different social and political beliefs frequently based their arguments on utilitarian grounds. R. B. Haldane warned of the 'peril of German rivalry' if England continued to neglect education. There was fresh evidence coming through diplomatic channels and from figures collated by the Board of Trade, of the country's failure to compete in new industrial and scientific processes. The schools, universities and laboratories were represented as the battlefields of international commerce. In addition a growing empire presented opportunities for development of trade and investment. Trade would follow the flag if education preceded it.

The case for parliamentary intervention was also argued on philosophical grounds: state aid for educational provision rightly directed could 'extend the bounds of liberty' and avert a 'dangerous cleavage of classes', wrote two young Liberal politicians, H. Samuel and C. P. Trevelyan. Finally there were persuasive financial, as well as educational, reasons for radical restructuring of secondary education. In response to the local parental demand through the previous decade, there had been fragmented, uncoordinated and frequently wasteful provision of secondary schooling: in many areas ingenious use of local rates and central Science and Art grants had supported the growth of low-fee Science and Higher-Grade schools. Inevitably the vote on Education had risen steeply, making Education the biggest-spending home department. During the same period, many of the old endowed grammar schools like the Newcastle School, were being forced by competition to adopt an increasingly commercial and scientific bias in their curriculum in order to survive.[25]

Public recognition of the need for state intervention in secondary education was now beginning to emerge. A royal commission in 1894 under the chairmanship of James Bryce considered 'the best methods of establishing a well-organised system of secondary education in England'. The recommendations of its report in 1895, providing a valuable point of reference, would be widely scrutinised by both politicians, industrialists and educationalists in the coming years. They raised expectations for a fundamental re-appraisal of current secondary provision and organisation leading to a more rationalised development throughout the country.

Specific problems facing endowed schools were raised by a number of witnesses such as Charity Commissioners Sir George Young and Sir Henry Longley, and in submitted memoranda. The Charity Commissioners had supported the endowed schools in forming new schemes wherever possible, but many of the schemes had subsequently proved inflexible and cumbersome as the schools endeavoured to meet rapidly changing circumstances in their localities. Their fees had often been fixed by their schemes at less than cost price. Such a level still remained a deterrent to deserving children of poor parents, nor did it allow the payment of adequate salaries to the teachers. Local rate-supported schools' fees were still lower, at an average of 9d a week. The Commissioners' formal powers had not included the 'good supervision' advocated earlier in the century by the Schools Inquiry Commission, nor any check on the efficiency of schemes when formed, nor any form of registration of schools or their teachers.

Several witnesses provided evidence of the dangerous distortion of the secondary school curriculum encouraged earlier in the century by the Science and Art grants from Kensington, and now compounded by the material inducements of Technical Instruction grants from the councils. These grants, the former dependent on a variable pass rate in annual examinations, and the latter upon an unpredictable income from the national tax on the consumption of spirits, administered by councils in a variety of ways, still failed to provide the security of guaranteed income. Because of a drop in tax returns on spirits in 1893–4, the Newcastle Council cut its grant to the Grammar School by 10% in 1894–5. In his evidence, Mr Bidgood, Headmaster of the Higher Grade School in Gateshead and President of the Association of Higher Grade and Science Schools, admitted that steady access to rates had enabled the new Higher Grade schools to compete successfully with the older grammar schools. Registered as public elementary schools, they qualified for a more liberal rate of grant from the Science and Art Department and benefited from the stimulus of official government inspection. In the counties of Northumberland and Durham the number of children attending Higher Grade Schools had already exceeded those in all other secondary schools in the two counties. Asked whether the Grammar School in Newcastle had proved a success, Mr Bidgood thought it was 'beginning to be successful now'. He was sure this was because the School's curriculum had gradually been adapted to that offered by his own school.[26]

The Science and Art Department's days were numbered, however. An unobtrusive but far-reaching Act of 1899 created a central authority, amalgamating the old Education Department with its responsibilities in elementary education, the Science and Art Department (which the Bryce Commission Report had scornfully described as 'a highly centralised grant-distributing machine') and the Charity Commission, with its specialised duties connected with endowed schools. The new Board of Education contained within it, in Inspector Fitch's favourite phrase, 'possibilities of usefulness', still not fully grasped, in bringing a unity of purpose to the whole educational machinery, and most significantly conceded that secondary education was a state matter, an interest which it had hitherto recognised only indirectly and haphazardly.[27] Its influence upon secondary schools was already beginning to emerge both through the terms of its grants-in-aid and through its powers of inspecting schools.

This reorganisation of the central government's education administration was soon followed by the Education Act of 1902 which was to have a decisive influence on educational administration throughout the country. It created new local authorities, county councils and county boroughs, to deal with education as with other public services in their localities. Under Part II of the Act, state recognition was given to the need for relating all types of education and for a sound general education before, and as a basis of, technical and professional education, by requiring the new authorities to consider the educational needs of their area and 'to take such steps as seem to them desirable, to supply or aid the supply of education other than elementary'.[28] How would these two Acts affect the course of a northern provincial grammar school?

Under the terms of the 1899 Act, the Grammar School's clerk had applied to the new Board for recognition as a secondary day school for certain forms under Clause 73 and 74 in its Directory, and for recognition of yet another part of the School as a School of

Science qualifying for higher grants under Paragraph 65. Somewhat defensively, he had added that the Governors were actively engaged in arranging for the removal of the School to new buildings 'to be constructed in the most approved manner, with every facility for giving manual instruction'.[29] The Principal Assistant Secretary, newly promoted from the Charity Commission, the Hon. W. N. Bruce, noted privately:

> 'This school has Science and Art classes in its main and also in branch buildings. Instruction and equipment in the main building has been well reported on but in the branch the lab is unsatisfactory. I think we should send forms for making application for recognition for both types of schools starting at the same time. . . .'

The School's grant as a secondary day school was temporarily confirmed, subject to an inspector's visit from the Board. The clerk's letter reflects the confusion in many secondary schools over proper schemes of instruction and within a system of grants administered originally by the Science and Art department which had been strongly biased towards scientific subjects. The position would be clarified in the new Board's Regulations for Secondary Schools in 1904. The Board's new powers were also exercised in their recognition of 'efficient' schools. Members of the teaching profession could apply to be registered, qualifications for which included three years' experience of teaching in an efficient school. Had the inspector's earlier visit constituted merely approval for the continuation of grants or had the Royal Grammar School been recognised as 'efficient'? The question concerned E. W. Bookey, an assistant master at the RGS who wrote anxiously to the Board:

> It is of the utmost importance to the staff of the school to learn at as early a date as possible whether they are qualified for registration or not.[30]

The Board's response in March 1903 had been, as already noted, a full inspection, to be repeated every three years, to ascertain 'efficiency'. On the last day, there was an exchange of views between the team of inspectors and the Governors. Approval of the new site was expressed; the Governors should consult the Board's new regulations for the erection of new schools, however. But there was some regret concerning the poor performance of many boys on the Modern side and their early leaving. In general it was felt that the School could attain a higher standard. Particular criticism was levelled at the 'exceedingly small' annual 'Whisky Money' grant from the Corporation (£148) which was compared unfavourably to those of other large towns, for instance, the £1200–£1400 grant of Bradford to its grammar school. Since the corporations would have new powers under the 1902 Act, the Governors should make strong representation for a considerable increase.[31]

The report of the conference in the *Newcastle Daily Journal* on 2 April 1903, tactfully omitted all reference to criticism and concluded:

> The chief school of Newcastle has had a great past: it promises to have a great future.

The Act of 1902 had expressly directed the new Local Authorities in considering the secondary provision in their areas 'to have regard to any existing supply of efficient schools'. What would be the response of the City Council to the tasks devolved upon it by the 1902 Act and how would this affect the fortunes of the Grammar School?

During the course of her inquiry into English local government, Beatrice Webb spent five weeks in the summer of 1900 in Newcastle to study its municipal government. Her notes were unflattering:

> In contrast with the Birmingham Town Council and in the last decade of the century also with the London County Council the capitalists who dominated the Newcastle City Council were honestly devoted to the doctrine of laissez-faire which yielded conclusive arguments against undertaking improvements in the housing, education and sanitation of the poorer inhabitants of their city as matters of public concern and common well-being.[32]

There was no reason to expect vigorous and prompt municipal reaction and the Council showed marked reluctance to incur further rate expenditure, ignoring the option to rate up to 2d in the pound under part II of the 1902 Act. The Governors' pressure for direct representation on the newly established education committee was also resisted; two elected representatives from all the secondary schools of the city were accepted. However, when the Advisory Higher Education Sub-committee met, its appointed chairman was Dr Robert Spence Watson, Vice Chairman of the Governing Body, and at least one other Governor, Principal Gurney of the College of Science, was also a member.[33]

One of the first documents tactfully forwarded by the Board for consideration at the Higher Education Sub-committee's meeting on 30 November 1903, was a copy of the report of the Board's inspection of the Grammar School. The allocation of the grant under the Local Taxation Act remained firmly at £148 despite a letter from the Governors urging reconsideration of its distribution. By contrast the Council voted £1,150 of its 'Whisky Money' to Rutherford College, which lacking endowments had been organised as a flourishing science school and had benefited from rate support also. By far the most pressing problem before the committee would be the training of elementary teachers in view of the Board's new regulations, regarding their education and training. The Board's circular 494 showed a marked preference for the intending pupil-teachers to be educated between 12 and 16 in secondary schools. The congested state of the city's secondary schools necessitated the immediate organising of a Pupil-Teacher centre, but the Board's policy would bring in new pupils to secondary schooling from the elementary schools, in the years ahead.

Two further matters were raised, with implications for the secondary schools already in existence: the advisability of 'acquiring a secondary school to be conducted by the education committee' and of granting free scholarships to be held at secondary schools. The latter had always been of special concern to Dr Spence Watson. Both questions were postponed, and the Committee resolved to invite Professor Michael Sadler, of the Victoria University of Manchester, to undertake an inquiry into the present condition and future requirements of secondary and higher education in Newcastle on their behalf.[34]

The choice was a happy one. Characteristically plain-spoken and independent in judgement, Michael Sadler (until his resignation in 1903) had been the Director of the Board's Office of Special Inquiries and Reports. In his earlier membership of the Bryce Commission, in his advisory role in government legislation of 1899 and 1902, and in his personal contribution to the section's published volumes of research on educational matters, he had worked unstintingly for the establishment of harmonious relations between the State and existing secondary schools. His reports on education have since been described as 'an object lesson in the art of arousing the popularly elected representative by an appeal to his area and by providing him with just the right arguments with which to still the murmurings or rebut the arguments of his constituents'.

He presented his *Report on Secondary and Higher Education in Newcastle upon Tyne* to the City Council in 1905. After a tactful mention of 'signs of educational advance' in this 'metropolis of North-Eastern England' he pointed out some of the regional prejudices hampering secondary schooling: 'a half contempt for subjects which at first sight look unpractical or detached from the work-a-day duties of life'; a 'certain indifference to school training' and the attachment of too little importance to the Humanities, and too much to what was 'material and apparently capable of yielding direct profit'. Employers in the locality were only too eager to take on apprentices well below the age of sixteen.[35]

Professor Sadler's graphs demonstrated the irregular pattern of school attendance at both the Rye Hill School and the Branch School. Only 31% of the pupils had been in the School for three years or more; and only 6% had reached the age of sixteen or over. Further statistics gave information about the School's composition at the time: over 50% of the pupils came from public elementary or Higher Grade schools. Those pupils from outside the city boundary were mainly living in Gateshead, Tynemouth, Gosforth or Wallsend. Only 10% of the boys went on to universities or other places of higher education. The absence of linkage between the region's educational establishments generally, and the widely differing categories of pupils entering the School undoubtedly undermined the effectiveness of its intellectual work, causing the 'lack of precision in its educational aim' already diagnosed in the 1903 Inspectors' Report.

Nevertheless, once the School had been transferred, escaping from its present surroundings which gave 'a certain air of forlornness to its work', it should visibly make a new start and would thus gain a 'more commanding position in the thoughts of the citizens of Newcastle' and its wider neighbourhood. In Professor Sadler's estimation there was every reason to hope for a bright future for the School; it certainly deserved an immediate increase in its annual grant from the Newcastle City Council.[36] The Council, reluctantly shouldering the rate burden of its new responsibilities for all primary schools, ignored this latter recommendation, But the Report itself, and Professor Sadler's

144

ersonal interest in the Grammar School's development, gave
imely encouragement as the Governors grappled with problems
osed by their ambitious plans to move to Jesmond.

Much depended, of course, on the School's financial position.
he Governors looked for an increased fund at their disposal
to give the school a better chance pending the erection and
ompletion of the new schools, when no doubt an adequate
ncome will be provided'. The terms and wording of the revised
cheme put forward by the Governors and Trustees, particularly
hose clauses touching upon finance, had occasioned considerable
iscùssions among senior officials at the Board. The legal adviser
or the Charity Commission had found difficulty in apportioning
he capital endowment between educational and non-educational
lements of the Trust. Upon whom did the work connected with
he new building actually devolve? Why, queried W. N. Bruce, in
flurry of office memoranda, was the yearly income appropriated
or both boys' and girls' education to be limited to £2500 as in the
roposed amendment? Why could not the whole endowment be
ducational, subject to the specific requirements for non-
ducational purposes mentioned in clause 7 of the original 1888
cheme.[37] The limitation was retained but the question is of
nterest. The figure of £2500 was well above the surplus income for
hat year (£342) or in the foreseeable future. The clerk's letter
o the Board of 11 September 1903 refers to the careful
onsideration of this point by Alderman Richardson in his dual
ole as Chairman of the Grammar School's Governors and as a
Trustee of the Virgin Mary Hospital. Was there a tactical
alancing of the future needs of the Hospital brethren with the
nore pressing and immediate demands of the Grammar School
oys? The clerk also mentioned that the chairman was strongly of
he opinion that the Charity Commissioners should consent to the
se of the Girls' School fund in the unlikely event of there being no
urplus income available. 'It seems to him that it would be fatal in
ny way to jeopardise the interests and welfare of the grammar
chool for the sake of the prospective girls' school for which (I may
afely say) the governors consider there is no demand nor
ecessity.' Nevertheless, a specific sum of £4195 (significantly
ltered from the 1888 Scheme's 'the Residue') was allocated for
he education of girls in the revised Scheme.

The amended Scheme was signed by Governors and Trustees
n 18 September and the purchase of the land completed by
October 1903 through the Trustees' sale of land at Fenham

and Bolam. Soon after, the Governors were anxiously requesting approval of additional sums from surplus income for maintenance to which the Board and the Trustees consented.[38] On Prize Day the previous July, in a strange mixture of apology and confidence the Chairman had claimed some progress won with a 'dilatoriness entirely foreign to his tastes, feelings and business habits', and had concluded his speech with a quotation from a fellow alderman that 'the future grammar school would be the Eton of the North of England'. The phrase might be linked with the *Newcastle Journal* article the same day describing the School's building scheme in which there was 'a portion of the new place to be set apart for resident students who will considerably widen the geographical area from which scholars, now nearly all day boys, are drawn'.[39] However, there would be no further mention of Eton or boarding provision as the Governors concentrated upon the practicalities of building within a ceiling of £20,000. The projected number of boys was scaled down from the original 600 to 450 and the Headmaster pressed for economies, admitted that they could forego a dining room and workshops. The lowest tender of over £21,000 was accepted and the discovery of sewers beneath the site required an entirely new alignment of the buildings in the architects' plan.

On 28 September 1905 the foundation stone from Idle Moor was laid in the presence of Governors, Trustees, the Mayor and Sheriff and members of the corporation, the Bishop, L. Selby-Bigge from the Board of Education, Professor Sadler, members of the Newcastle Education Committee, Headmaster, masters and scholars of the School. A leaden box was later placed behind the stone containing newspaper reports of the proceedings, copies of the schemes of government, and a list of Governors, masters and other officials of the School.

At the official luncheon Professor Michael Sadler congratulated everybody on an undertaking 'which might, in the long history of the school, prove to be second only in importance to the original foundation of it'. But he also took the opportunity to mention some educational weaknesses: 'Did they not need greater precision of aim in higher secondary schools?' He hoped the Board of Education might see its way to select all over England a limited number, of which their Royal Grammar School would be one, of higher secondary schools to which it would devote special encouragement and special grants. Early attention should also be paid to the professional position of the masters serving the School

Everything in the long run depended on that.' The history of the School over the next quarter century was to show the wisdom and far-sightedness of his remarks. Almost two years were to elapse before the School was finally transferred to the new buildings. The new premises would embody many of the most recent schemes of government, changing policies in curriculum and teaching methods and new aspirations in education, generated and disseminated in the main from the reorganised Board of Education, through the advice and high standards of its inspectorate and departmental officials. 'The organisation and development of the education given in secondary schools is the most important educational question of the present day,' wrote Robert Morant, Permanent Secretary, in the Board of Education Report for 1905–6. 'It is the pivot of the whole situation as it affects the efficiency, intelligence and well-being of the nation.'[40]

The Board was now setting the pace. In its regulations for 1904, it published for the first time in the history of education a definition of a secondary school: one which offered to each of its scholars up to and beyond 16 a general education, physical, mental and moral, given through a complete graded course of instruction, of wider scope and more advanced than that given in elementary schools. Through its scale of *per capita* grants, increasing progressively from £2 to £5 in the four years, it stressed the importance attached to the secondary schools' retention of pupils for at least the full four years.[41]

Higher national standards in buildings, equipment and staffing, however, together with high local expectations, were placing increased pressure upon the School's finances once again. There were protracted negotiations with the city Council over the sale of the Rye Hill buildings to be used by them as separate accommodation for girls in the Council's newly acquired Rutherford School, on the advice of Michael Sadler. Powerfully backed by the Charity Commissioners, the Governors forced up the Council's original offer from £12,000 to over £14,000; they would need every penny.[42] Arguing that 'it would be suicidal to open out a building which only looks half finished', the Governors boldly decided to complete all stages of their building plans. Costs rose steeply from an estimated £25,000 early in 1905 to approximately £44,000 by 1906, and over £78,000 for site, buildings and fields by 1907.

Annual cash deficits continued with increasing severity as the yearly intake dropped significantly from 80 in 1901 to 49 in 1906. It is likely that some anxious parents whose sons received basic

commercial training in the elementary schools chose the security
of early openings for them as engineering apprentices or as clerks
in insurance, shipping or trading companies in a period of decline
in traditional Tyneside industries such as glass, pottery and
alkali.[43] Nationally the first decade of the twentieth century was
marked by a decline in real wages and an increase in
unemployment following the end of the Boer War. At the same
time professional associations concerned with secondary
education, backed by the Board's Inspectors' reports, were
endeavouring to promote improved salary structures for secondary
school masters. Shortly before the next Board inspection in 1907,
the Governors extended the maximum salary to £250 (granted to
the Senior Language Master, A. Stallworthy, after fifteen years of
service) only to be advised in the 1907 report that they should be
offering a higher commencing salary with prospects of regular
increments to a respectable maximum of not less than £300.

The Governors met the earliest cash deficits by raising a loan
from the Girls' School fund set aside under clause 68. The clerk
had assured the Board that there was little prospect of the fund's
use to establish a girls' school since 'the education for girls in this
city is of a high standard and already well catered for . . .'.[44] In
November 1906, he wrote again informing the Board of the threat
of proceedings against the Governors who owed the contractor
£4650. A loan of £5000 was sanctioned on security of the new site
and buildings and a further £6500 loan, in February 1907. Tem
porary relief from the 'awkward position' of the School's finances
was also found by raising the fees to a scaled nine to twelve guineas
per annum, a step recommended by the Headmaster after
consultation with similar schools. Since the 1888 Scheme Greek
had been charged as an optional extra and as a result had almost
ceased to exist. Now it was to be incorporated in the syllabus in an
attempt to keep some boys longer, and to encourage university
entrance. The Board disapproved of the Governors' increased
scale of graduated fees, arguing that this would rather deter
scholars from staying through the full four year course. The
question of fee paying was soon to become a major issue between
the Governors and the central education department.

The School's move to the Brandling fields had taken place in
September 1906 against a national background of considerable
political ferment. A general election, during which national
education had been a fiercely debated electoral issue, had resulted
in a landslide victory for the Liberals after ten years of

Conservative and Unionist government. Locally, Newcastle 'went Liberal' by a 7000 majority of votes. The Governors' list of personages to be invited to open the new buildings was tactically headed by Augustine Birrell, the new Liberal President of the Board of Education, followed by his Conservative predecessor, the Marquess of Londonderry, Lord Rosebery, the Duke of Devonshire and Professor Sadler, all of whom declined, the President of the Board because he was involved in the new government's first abortive attempt to legislate on education. The Duke of Northumberland, described by one member of the Northumberland county council's Higher Education Committee as 'the rate-payers' friend' because of his resistance to the introduction in the county's rates of a non-mandatory levy for higher education, ceremonially opened the new buildings on 17 January 1907.[45]

(iii) *The School at Eskdale Terrace*

The palatial buildings, as Alderman Richardson remarked, presented a striking contrast to those recently vacated at Rye Hill which now 'would not receive the permission of an exacting education authority for a single minute'. (The *North Mail*, Liberal in politics, noted dryly that the same authority had not hesitated to acquire the old buildings for local girls' secondary education.) But there was undoubted civic pride in the earlier published description. The visitors would be struck by 'the artistic carving and sculpture work: appropriately enough, cherub faces peep out from many pillar capitals at the main entrance . . .'. A magnificent clock, costing 150 guineas subscribed by old boys, an association of which had first been formed in 1900, was to be placed later upon the building. The main hall, 'a noble room', was capable of seating 700–800 on 'heavy oak seats, handsomely carved'.

The chairman took care to stress the close identification of the region with the life of a school which could fit its sons, the citizens of the future, for 'any service in the scientific professions and the industries for which the Tyne and neighbourhood were conspicuous. They would not be given esoteric education'. The School deserved the warm and cordial support of all sections of the community.[46]

And what were the boys' first impressions of their new premises? E. Anderson (O.N. 1904–11) recalls that, after his first two years in the dim darkness of the Rye Hill building, which 'went down . . . a long way down with several flights of steps away

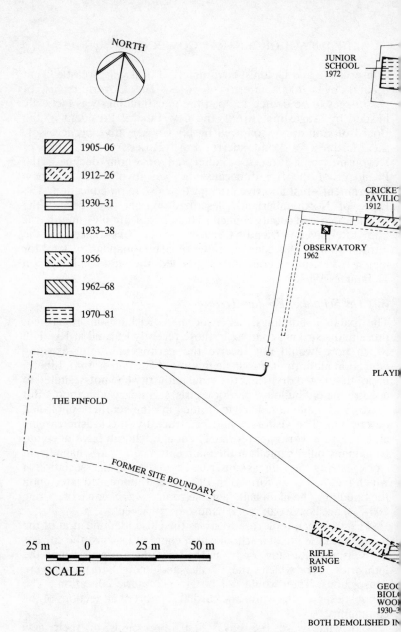

NORTH

▨	1905–06
▨	1912–26
▤	1930–31
▥	1933–38
▨	1956
▨	1962–68
▤	1970–81

JUNIOR
SCHOOL
1972

CRICKET
PAVILION
1912

OBSERVATORY
1962

PLAYING

THE PINFOLD

FORMER SITE BOUNDARY

25 m   0   25 m   50 m

SCALE

RIFLE
RANGE
1915

GEOG
BIOLO
WOO
1930–3

BOTH DEMOLISHED IN

THE ROYAL GRAMMAR SCHOO
AT ESKDALE TERRACE, JESMO

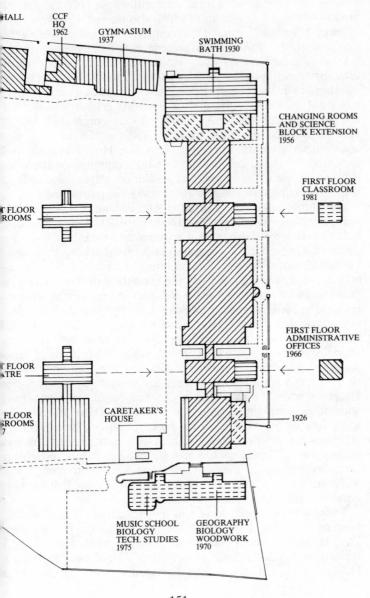

HALL

CCF
HQ
1962

GYMNASIUM
1937

SWIMMING
BATH 1930

CHANGING ROOMS
AND SCIENCE
BLOCK EXTENSION
1956

FIRST FLOOR
CLASSROOM
1981

FLOOR
ROOMS

FIRST FLOOR
ADMINISTRATIVE
OFFICES
1966

FLOOR
TRE

FLOOR
ROOMS

CARETAKER'S
HOUSE

1926

MUSIC SCHOOL
BIOLOGY
TECH. STUDIES
1975

GEOGRAPHY
BIOLOGY
WOODWORK
1970

to the depths in the direction of the river Tyne', the new scho
had seemed a change from 'midnight to sunny midday', lil
moving into a 'blaze of sunlight'. After the rigours of 'the flat' (tl
ground outside Rye Hill upon which was played a primitive for
of rugger called 'Lennary') a contributor to the *Novo*'s fir
publication from Eskdale Terrace admitted feelings of pleasure
a football field 'just outside'. House teams had been prompt
established and were confidently expected to improve the gener
standard of play. The assertion was in marked contrast to tl
mournful question at the end of the 1903 cricket season: 'WI
do we always lose?' A house trophy presented by tl
Northumberland Rugby Union in 1907 would bring a kee
competitive edge to the sport, and the House system itsel
indicated by varied colours in the cord trimmings on the scho
cap, according to boys' areas of residence, might have reflecte
some social divisions but also generated local patriotism.

An altered school day started at 9.00 instead of 9.30 am with
ten-minute mid-morning break. Dinner break lasted an hour and
half, but despite the new dining room and tuckshop (the latt
declared to be a 'decided success') large numbers, by 1912, wou
be 'cutting out of lessons' to walk home and back. School finishe
at 4.30, though there remained the institution of 'Four Thirty' fe
misdemeanours or – worse – 'Saturday morning' for a serio
crime. The facilities in the new School, so different from Rye Hil
long dark draughty corridors and battered, initialled and in
stained desks, provided each form with its own classroom, an
encouraged by Mr Logan, enabled a new flourishing of scho
societies and ethos. There was a dark room for the Photograph
club, a room for Chess devotees, a stage for the newly-forme
Dramatic Society who rehearsed 'Twelfth Night' and sympathise
with ladies complaining about 'the servant question' after they lo
some four or five 'Marias' from the cast in quick succession! Th
Debating Society periodically denied women the vote, considere
the House of Lords should not be abolished nor the chann
tunnelled but agreed that education could eradicate crime, Hon
Rule should be granted to Ireland, and that Great Britain was
grave danger of invasion by foreign power.

There was renewed interest in military affairs, which had fir
been stimulated by the participation of Old Boys in the Boer Wa
Despite the debaters' defeat of motions 'that every man l
trained as a soldier' and 'conscription should be adopted', N
Haldane's visit to the North East for recruits to the Offic

152

raining Corps was noted with keen interest. An increasing number of boys, observed *Novo*'s editor in November 1909, were wearing the fleur-de-lys badge of the scout; he would have preferred an organised cadet corps rather than the 'game' of scouting. It was recorded that a Junior Training Corps had already been instituted at a rival school, 'a near neighbour'. Two meetings were held in support of the formation of an OTC, the second summoned by the Headmaster himself who finally yielded and requested authority of the Governors early in 1911 to institute a Junior Training Corps open to boys over thirteen.

During these early years in the new building, the prefectorial system was extended, the prefects being distinguished by sporting the gowns of the Oxford commoner – 'the black gown of a nameless life'!

The first annual swimming gala was held in 1911 and would become 'as essential a part of the lighter side of school life as the field sports'. The editorial committee of the *Novo*, surprised by a modest profit, had presented a shield to be awarded to the best all-round athlete each year.[47]

The stimulus given to the corporate life of the School in its new buildings and grounds was also observed in more official quarters. In April 1907, seven months after the School's removal to Eskdale Terrace, a team of eight Inspectors from the Board of Education recorded their judgements following the second inspection of the school. After praising the splendidly healthy building liberally equipped for about 500 boys, they nevertheless found the School still disappointingly limited in nature and scope. Of the 300 boys, only fourteen per cent were above 16; the average leaving age was under 15; only two boys that year had gone on to university or university college and none to Oxford or Cambridge. Though individual departments were commended, notably Modern Languages, their success had been impaired by the absence of clear classification of pupils, some of whom were entered for two years only anywhere between the ages of twelve and fifteen. A higher ideal of the duties and position of the school should be encouraged if boys were to remain longer and closer links were to be developed with universities. The Governors' attention was directed towards two main recommendations. The first, that the qualifications of the staff should gradually be improved as finance allowed, by offering a higher scale of salaries, had been recognised 'an urgent matter' which was 'at the root of all improvements and developments' in secondary schools in the Board's Report.

153

The inspectors regretted that few of the assistant masters ha previously had experience in the country's best secondary schoo The second recommendation was that intellectual 'undesirable should be excluded by enforcing entrance examinations proper graduated according to age, as had been previously required und Clause 56 of the 1888 Scheme. Though the latter policy mig seem drastic, for a School with 200 spare places, it was thoug that the gain in prestige would bring with it the necessary increa in numbers in the long run.[48]

The report also contained a simple analysis of the classes fro which the three hundred pupils were drawn. The largest numbe were 104 sons of commercial managers, followed by 62 fro professional men or those of independent means, 57 fro merchants and manufacturers, and 56 from retail trading. Only were drawn from artisan or proletarian classes.

Correspondence in February 1907 between the Permane Secretary of the Board, Robert Morant, and a Treasury offici reveals that, in anticipation of the proposed government allocatio of £250,000 for the extension of secondary education, the Board inspectors had been steadily pressing for improvements in staffi and buildings in their inspection reports about the country.[49] Th inspectors could not fail to have been aware of changes in soci and political attitudes towards educational institutions among ci servants and politicians at Westminster. The report of departmental committee appointed in February 1905 ha contained the seeds of the 'direct grant' system whereby 'tl interests of the poor could be safeguarded, not by closi state-aided schools to the children of the rich, as by requiring certain proportion of places to be reserved for children fro elementary schools without, or with reduced fees'.[50]

During the parliamentary debate on Supply in March 190 radical supporters within the Liberal ministry, already roused the educational controversies which had surrounded the 1902 A more recently humiliated by the failure of the Liberal 19 Education Bill, demanded administrative action to clear aw obstacles impeding the progression of working-class elementa school children to secondary schooling. 'The rungs of tl educational ladder should not be too far apart.' Such views, t President of the Board of Education assured the House, would carefully considered in the allocation of the new Exchequer gran later that session.[51]

The new Regulations for Secondary Schools raised t

government grant to £5 on each pupil between twelve and eighteen in those secondary schools which satisfied certain conditions in respect of freedom from denominational restrictions, representative local control and accessibility to all classes of pupils. It was this last condition which posed a particular problem to the Governors of the Royal Grammar School.

The government offer of an increased grant was to be used to secure a proportion of free places, equal to twenty-five % of the total admissions the previous year, to be awarded to public elementary school pupils passing an approved entrance test of attainment. During further departmental discussions on the qualifying conditions, the Board's Assistant Secretary of the Secondary Branch pointed out the financial hardships such conditions would inflict upon many schools and argued that the new money should be deployed to secure a higher level of efficiency rather than new scholarships. The argument was overruled by the President, in closer daily touch with complaints in Parliament and from educational pressure groups that many state-aided secondary schools were closed to children of the poor, particularly where fees had been recently raised. But he thought in some cases the percentage of free places could be lower.[52]

The RGS Governors had met in self-congratulatory mood in July and October, following the inspection, and unanimously agreed to appoint an additional language master and a visiting music master in response to the recommendations; the raising of fees to meet overdrafts was also discussed. But at a special Governors' meeting in December, the implications of the Board's new grant regulations were discussed anxiously. Without binding themselves in the future, the Governors at once applied for the increased grant to the School, to be paid retrospectively on the grounds of ten or eleven per cent of free-place pupils the previous year. They received a generous waiver from the Board with additional advice on the introduction of a uniform scale of fees and of a suitable examination for free-place candidates.[53]

The Governors' dilemma over future policy remained acute. Would not the enforced annual inclusion of elementary school children deter the very parents of middle-class children the school had aimed to attract by moving to Jesmond? Would not their finances be more directly strengthened by a judicious increase of fees and of fee-paying pupils, rather than by submission to the Board's Article 20 and its twenty-five per cent in order to secure the modest status and rewards within the public grant system? The

Inspectors had described the School's future financial position as 'hopeful' despite its immediate yearly overdrafts. A number of original sixty-year leases of Hospital properties were due to terminate in 1908 and could be renewed at considerably higher rentals. There seemed a reasonable prospect that within a few years the School might be receiving the full endowment of £2500 from the Trustees, subject to reduction for the Girls' School fund.

During the intervening years before the Board's inspection of 1912, its officials tenaciously deployed its range of administrative powers to retain the School's commitment to the minimum of ten % free places, in particular through the Board's dispensation of increased capitation grants and through further revision of the school's scheme of government as a consequence. Governors' minutes and the Board of Education Office memoranda chart frequent exchange of opinion and information, requests and advice concerning School policy.

On the one hand, the Board's officials clearly considered most undesirable the possibility that a more financially secure school could withdraw from its free place commitment. Such an 'in-and-out arrangement', in Robert Morant's judgement, would effectively prevent the Newcastle education authority from assessing its secondary school provision accurately and would place it 'at a great disadvantage in making its own schemes and erecting its own schools'. The Board's president, Walter Runciman, minuted his final decision: 'We cannot allow an in-and-out arrangement'. Instead, the Board should pursue a flexible interpretation of the actual percentage of free places allowed, though the president did not 'wish the Newcastle people informed of this'. The Board's telegram to the School read: 'Regulations do not contemplate that a school should have the right to revert to lower scale of grant. Letter follows'.[54]

Reports of the debates within the Governing Body and of the subsequent deputation to Whitehall also reveal a significant difference of opinion between some of the Governors and the Headmaster; the former wished for more time to judge the effect of the free-place grant system in operation, but the latter was openly critical because of 'frequent intimation from parents that they object to the compulsory admission of free scholars' and because the 'private adventure' schools were, in his opinion, using the argument to prejudice the Grammar School.

One of the Board's Inspectors, who had been a member of the school's inspection team, contributed his own personal assessment

156

of local attitudes prior to the interview with the deputation. There was evident disappointment among the Governors that, though numbers were rising slightly in the lower school, the School generally was still not appealing to the better middle-class population.[55] The Headmaster and Governors apparently blamed the new secondary regulations for a local impression that 'the school is flooded with boys from the elementary schools and is not a fit place for the son of a self-respecting shop-keeper'. They would like to have been in a position to say: 'We have refused the bait offered by the Board of Education. You may now send your sons without fear of contamination'. Describing the town as 'the most snobbish of its size in the whole of England', Mr Piggott provided statistical evidence of the successful absorption of a much higher proportion of ex-public elementary school boys into the flourishing grammar schools of Manchester, Birmingham and Bradford.

During the interview, it was made quite clear that there could be no promise of substantial waiver in the Board's free-place requirements. To the Board the Governors' persistent request was not merely a matter of compromise on figures, but a fundamental contradiction in policy; 'no school which confined admission to the middle and upper classes was a public school or eligible for state aid'. As for the School's numbers, if the Governors increased its efficiency the numbers should follow automatically. Questioned about 'defects', the Board's representative, Mr Mackail, hinted more tactfully than had been expressed in his colleague's preparatory private note, that the School now needed a more vigorous, scholarly and adaptable Headmaster, a suggestion with which both chairman and clerk apparently agreed cordially.

In the correspondence which followed the interview, the Governors' mounting anxiety about the effect of the free-place requirements upon the School's financial prospects can be detected. It was met by a corresponding determination on the part of the Board's officials to extract guarantees for the continuance of the scholarship scheme, to be written into the revision of the School's Scheme of Government currently under discussion. At the same time the Board missed no opportunity to disseminate more enlightened social attitudes. It was their intention 'that holders of free places shall be placed as far as possible on the same footing as ordinary fee-paying pupils and there appears to them to be no valid reason why any pupils should be allowed to remain in a secondary school longer than they are reasonably well behaved and diligent and make good progress . . .'.[56]

Though they acknowledged the 'apprehension' of the Headmaster concerning alteration of the new scale of fees by postponement of its operation to 1910, they appear to have forced the pace of policy-formation over the revised draft Scheme to the chagrin of the Governors. A copy of the revised Scheme was sent by the Board to Newcastle education committee who responded by requesting a deputation to the Governors' meeting in September 1909. The committee would not insist on the full twenty-five per cent free places at the Grammar School but they asked that the Governors 'should leave the door open for the admission to the Grammar School of bright and promising pupils from the public elementary schools'.[57] Receiving the Chairman's assurance that they had finally agreed to the Board's modified terms of ten per cent free places, the Newcastle Education Committee would offer no further criticism of the proposed Scheme. The Board promptly affixed the seal and published the Scheme on 10 October without waiting for further comment from the Governors and in so doing incurred a wrathful letter expressing the indignation of well known public men whose suggestions should not have been flouted in the way they had been. The Governors were all prominent citizens accustomed to dealing with public questions and fully acquainted with the educational requirements of the district. 'They feel their existence as a governing body has been ignored and thus prejudiced.' A further complaint of 'contemptuous treatment' personally addressed by the chairman, Thomas Richardson, to the President of the Board, Walter Runciman, maintained that 'such treatment by the Education Department is not calculated to encourage them in their duties nor to promote harmonious working between the Department and local bodies who have to bear onerous responsibilities in the administration of their trusts'.

The clauses to which the Governors took particular exception and which they had proposed to discuss further in a specially convened meeting on 13 December, were 25, 40 and management rule 8. Clause 25 had been inserted by the Board and represented its policy of promoting the professional status of secondary school teachers by ensuring them greater security of tenure: under the new Scheme assistant masters would be employed under written contract with the Governors and could not be appointed or dismissed solely by the Headmaster. The requirement had already

een defined in the Endowed School (Masters) Act passed in 1908
hile the revised scheme was still under consideration. Mr Logan
ad complained that this procedure would be most inconvenient
n actual practice'.

The Governors accepted the maximum fee of sixteen guineas,
ut objected to the paragraph stating that the rules of payment
ould be 'subject to the approval of the Board'. Clause 40 and the
lanagement Clause 8 concerning surplus cash which, unless
therwise ordered by the Board of Education, was to be treated as
apital and invested, were interpreted as evidence of the Board's
esire 'to fetter the exercise of discretion of the governing body in
s administration of the school'. The Board was implicitly
pplying coercion in Clause 40 by cutting off their source of
lternative finance in the event of a Governors' decision not to
emain on the grant list.

Walter Runciman's subsequent replies both to the Governors
nd to their Chairman were more tactful and conciliatory in tone.
1 the first place, the Board's speed of action over the Scheme had
een specifically in order for the School to earn the government
rant on a higher scale. The Board had incorporated in their
cheme 'the latest practice formed upon knowledge of affairs
roughout the country', but were not the least desirous of 'forcing
ny cast-iron code on schools'. He had himself taken 'a personal
terest in the affairs of the School' but could not of course
terfere in a matter with which he, as President, was involved in a
emi-judicial capacity.[58]

The Governors finally accepted the Scheme of 1909 as printed
arly in 1910. It is worth noting in passing that it increased the total
umber of Governors to 21 by raising the number appointed by
e City from 9 to 10 and providing for one representative each
om Northumberland and Durham County Councils. The
omposition of the Governors was not to be changed again until
)75. Almost certainly there were other pressures upon the
overnors which also influenced the decision to accept the
cheme and which ensured that the School, at this point in its
istory, remained within the national system of grant-aided
econdary schools, still accessible through its free places, as the
everend Anchor Thompson had hoped, to aspiring sons of
oorer citizens. There is evidence in the minutes of the Virgin
lary Trustees that the increased surplus income which should
ave accrued to the Grammar School by 1908, giving its
overnors considerably greater freedom in their policy-making,

had not been forthcoming 'owing to large expenditure (
almshouses repairs and improvements then pending'. Reference
also made to a visit to Virgin Mary Hospital property in April 19(
by Mr Piggott, HMI, who had 'quite agreed that the repair of tl
property was the first charge on the funds of the Hospital'.[59]

A further letter from the Board to the Trustees, requiring tl
replacement in the Girls' School fund of the £4000 appropriated
the building of the new Grammar School in 1903, was received
May 1909 also coinciding with the Governors' deliberations up(
free places and the revision of the Scheme. The Trustees asked f(
the matter to be held in abeyance, after urgent representatic
from the Chairman of the Governors. During the following ye
the Governors also received a request from the assistant maste
for an improvement in salary scale, and an Inspectors' report
connection with the School's recognition as a Pupil Teach(
centre, which criticised overcrowding in the lower forms resultii
in serious understaffing. The recommendation for the immedia
appointment of two masters at an improved level of salary
strengthen the School's scholarship was held over.[60]

At the same time the Newcastle Education Committee reduc(
its customary annual grant to the school of £148 to £129 following
drop in Exchequer grants from whisky reserve, first earmark(
twenty years before for the promotion of technical and seconda
education, incorporated in the 1902 provision and now tota]
inadequate. The Committee ceased all contributions in 1913.
Parliament, Lloyd George, author of the 1909 Finance Act heavi
taxing spirits, had commented dourly on a ludicrous situation
which the less whisky people drank, the worse for the
education.[61] In Newcastle, the Grammar School Governo
refused a parental request for exemption from payment of fees '
consequence of the alleged effect which the Finance Act had up(
him'! A cabinet committee was set up to devise a better gra
system in April 1910, but its deliberations would be disrupted t
the political crisis which forced two elections upon the natio
followed in 1911 by a legislative session dominated by the passa
of the Parliament Bill to cut the power of the House of Lord
Financial checks upon the Education Department imposed by
delayed budget and a rapidly rising naval vote were creatii
resentment among ratepayers who were shouldering
increasingly heavy burden of educational and soci
responsibilities. The government's failure to act over the gra
system seriously threatened local enthusiasm for progress

econdary schooling and at the same time fanned resentment of central bureaucracy, interpreted as 'unwarrantable interference' and as scant sympathy of the Board with local administrators. The Governors' next consultations with the Board over the School's development were to be conducted without the President or his Permanent Secretary both of whom were by then deeply involved in a politically and educationally damaging row over a departmental circular.[62]

By the end of 1910, the School's immediate financial plight had eased considerably. Fee income had increased with 388 boys on the roll. The Trustees had at last conceded £500 more per annum to be allocated from surplus funds of the Hospital; they were even prepared to increase this to a sum not exceeding £800 per annum in the future, though they considered a definite arrangement should first be made concerning the loan from the Girls' School fund.[63] A joint deputation of Trustees and Governors to discuss the endowment directly in Whitehall occasioned a preparatory exchange of confidential memoranda among the Board's officials.

The financial position of the Virgin Mary Trust was still obscure, Mr Piggott had noted earlier in 1909. For instance, he had learned of the Trustees' 'discovery' of a sum of £6000 belonging to the charity which had been paid into court fifteen years previously and which, for some reason, had remained in Chancery ever since. In November 1910, he wrote that, since 1903, the Governing Body had received from the Trustees only the minimum surplus income to which they were entitled under the Scheme. Once again in April 1911, Mr Piggott minuted the case for the School's further endowment to strengthen the staff, increase their salaries and, above all, 'so that the governors should have enough money at their disposal to pension off its headmaster' without which he could see 'no chance of the grammar school taking its place in the educational life of the city . . .'. Personally, he was 'extremely anxious that the grammar school should not be crippled'.

Mr Bruce of the Secondary School Branch advised that the Girls' fund should not be entirely released since there were so few endowments for girls in the city and plenty of demand for their assistance in higher education. At the Whitehall meeting with the Newcastle deputation, headed by the School's new chairman, Sir Alfred Palmer, Charles Trevelyan, Parliamentary Secretary at the Board, followed his officials' advice in withdrawing the request that the Governors repay the loan. His solution, that the Girls' fund be converted into a permanent loan, to be repaid by the

Trustees at three per cent, thus raising a sum of between £130 an
£180 per annum, to be devoted to scholarships for girls attendin
secondary schools within the city, proved acceptable to all partie
The Governors were particularly heartened by Trevelyan's furthe
ruling that the surplus income of the Virgin Mary Trust shoul
now be fully available for the purposes of the School. The vexe
question of separation of the non-educational and education;
parts of the endowment would continue to stand *sine die.*
Ironically, the necessary revision of the Scheme for the Virgi
Mary scholarships would ensure its reintroduction within tw
years in a political climate less favourable to the educationa
interests within the charity.

It was regrettable that neither Alderman Thomas Richardso
nor his successor as Chairman for two months only, Dr Spenc
Watson, was alive to rejoice in the confirmation of a more stabl
financial position for the school made explicit during the Whiteha
consultations in the spring of 1911. The whole School attended th
funeral of Alderman Richardson on 23 January and little mor
than six weeks later the sixth form were present at the funeral o
Dr Spence Watson. Both men had served the school wit
unflagging loyalty as Chairman and Vice-Chairman respectively o
its governing body since its inauguration in 1888. Both ha
exercised considerable influence on its behalf through thei
involvement in the civic and educational life of the region. D
Watson had been honoured nationally by being made a Priv
Councillor in 1908; his charm, eloquence and wit were recalle
with affection.

Sir Isambard Owen had described Richardson as 'almost (th
School's) second founder' and the Governors commissioned an oi
painting (by John Charlton R.A.) of their late Chairman in hi
aldermanic robes seated beside an elaborately carved oak table i
possession of the School for many years. Still hanging in the hall o
the School today, it was unveiled in December 1911 by Earl Grey
at which ceremony the cadets of the newly formed OTC provide
a guard of honour. On the School's governing body, the new
Chairman Sir Alfred Palmer, shipbuilder, Councillor Georg
Lunn, Chairman of the city's Education Committee and soon t
be Lord Mayor from 1915 to 17 and Dr Hadow, Principal o
Armstrong College, later to chair the consultative committe
which produced the Hadow Report of 1927, ensured the continuit
of the School's close links with commerce, local government an
higher education in the region.

162

Further change, however, was in the air. The third government inspection which took place between 12 and 15 March 1912 had once again revealed a disappointing absence of change in the academic achievement of the School. The five Inspectors had found little evidence of 'essential development' in the senior end of the School: in fact the position compared unfavourably with that of the previous five years. Only 6.5% of the boys were over sixteen; the average leaving age was fifteen years nine months, and the length of schooling only three and a half years. 13% of the boys in the School were receiving free education; 28% had come from elementary schools. All scholarships held in the School had been awarded by the Governors and there were no boys holding any scholarships awarded by the local authority. The connexion between the School and the universities had remained slender.

The Inspectors paid tribute to Mr Logan, whose long term of office had seen considerable development, and they noted that the previous four years had been particularly taxing on his ability and physical strength because of the new buildings and the rapid increase in numbers. More openly critical in a private office memorandum following the inspection, they doubted his ability to run a school of such scope and size. In addition, there were still within his staff of eighteen some 'relics of the former days and some of these men have little claim to posts in a school that has to accomplish what is before this school'. Staff timetables were overloaded and there was no system of staff meetings. The curriculum, too, drew their criticism:

> The School can no longer remain content with work of the second grade, with an occasional flight into the regions of first grade work in the case of the odd one or two scholarship boys.

As for the social composition of the School, the classes from which the two largest groups of boys were drawn were the professional and retail traders and contractors. Only seven boys came from the artisan class.

Some aspects of the School's corporate life were specifically commended – the 'important formation of an OTC' the prefect system and games successes. But, in the anxiety for numbers, Mr Logan had accepted an irregularity and low standard of admission and the intellectual calibre of the School had suffered in consequence. Yet again, the Inspectors recommended a more stringent entrance examination to secure a longer duration of school life and to encourage further development of advanced work in the upper forms. Only then would the School 'take and retain the high place to which it has a right to aspire in the educational system of the country'.[65]

It would appear that the provisional resignation of the Headmaster which he sent in to the private conference between seven Governors and the five Inspectors on the last day of the inspection caused no great surprise, since the Chief Inspector at once responded with advice concerning the salary of Mr Logan's successor: it should be at the fixed rate of £1000 rather than dependent upon numbers in the School. All agreed, however, that he had 'done good work up to a point' in face of severe competition from local schools and in particular from a neighbouring prep-school, and deserved 'generous treatment'.

The tone of Mr Logan's formal letter of resignation suggests his own uncertainty about the Governors' treatment. He was prepared to resign only if the Governors would offer him a reasonably generous pension, for instance £500 per annum. Some of the Governors might be unaware that the presence of the School on its new site was

> to some extent due to me. I suggested the site and more, when the governors decided to try the experiment of a Branch school at Jesmond before committing themselves to the longer policy, I bought the house in which the School was first carried on, 3, St Thomas Place, in order that the experiment might be made. I do not like speaking about myself, but perhaps I may be pardoned for saying as much as I have.[66]

It was his misfortune to outstay influential Governors with whom he had worked most closely during the exciting and uncertain times of the Jesmond experiment. Only one of the seven Governors at the private conference on 15 March had been a member of the Governing Body at the turn of the century. We may well echo the question of another Governor at the next meeting on 30 April 1912 as to 'whether the resignation of the Headmaster was voluntary'. But we too must be satisfied with the Chairman's response that it was 'so far as he was aware, voluntary but, whether or not, it had been accepted on the terms of the letter; it was therefore imprudent to reopen the matter.' In any case, the Governors had already received covering approval of the £500 pension from the Board.[67]

The evidence suggests that Mr Logan, sharing his clerk's

onviction that the School had been 'originally intended for the enefit of the middle and higher middle class population of the own', had incurred official disapproval and signally failed to ppreciate the new educational philosophy behind the Liberal overnment's 1907 Regulations for Secondary Schools. Quite part from the immediate political exigencies, the intention had een 'to bring the advantages of higher education, so far as the mited funds at the disposal of the Board would permit, within each of the children of the poorer classes and to place them on the ame footing as pupils whose parents were in a position to pay chool fees'.[68] In the yearly reports of the Board and those of the nspectorate about the country, it is also clear that quality even nore than quantity was the foremost objective in their work mong secondary schools during this period.

During the farewell ceremonies, much was made of Mr Logan's wenty-nine years of devoted service to the School, and par-icularly of his encouragement of 'high moral tone and healthy ublic spirit'. One example of such encouragement had been the chool's participation in civic celebrations of Collingwood's entenary in March 1910. The same year the School received a opy by Harry Fogan (O.N.) of the original Mansion House ortrait of Lord Collingwood; a prize given by A. B. Collingwood ne following year was to be awarded to a boy about to leave chool who 'in the opinion of the boys and masters had exhibited he most honourable and upright character'. Expressing his thanks o the Governors for their provision of a generous pension, amuel Logan wrote sadly: 'How deeply the departure from chool affects me, I cannot find words to express.'[69]

v) *Progress and Frustration, 1912–21*

he 'new Grammar School chief' as the *Newcastle Journal* eadlined him on 20 June 1912 would be in significant contrast to he classical scholar from a struggling grammar school in Hull rhom the Municipal Council had appointed to the nineteenth-entury Rye Hill school. Selected from some hundred applicants, ohn Talbot held a Natural Sciences degree (1st class) from Trinity :ollege Cambridge, and had conducted research at the Cavendish ,aboratory in 1899 before his appointment to Harrow School as cience Master. During his period there he had become a captain 1 the OTC and in charge of the Harrow School Corps from 1908, nd was keenly interested in all sports including Rugby, Rifle-nooting and Hockey and also in Photography. The

appointment of a man of outstanding academic, military an
public school experience undoubtedly brought prestige to th
School, which was confirmed by Mr Talbot's election to th
Headmasters' Conference in 1914.

Mr Talbot saw exceptional opportunities, he told his first Speec
Day audience, in the School, situated as it was 'in almost solitar
state' in the midst of one of the greatest industrial districts of th
world. His arrival had coincided with reviving trade nationally
marked in the North East by thriving activity in ship-building an
supply industries. Applications for entry to the School steadil
increased. In the spring of 1913 the new Headmaster, respondin
to his Governors' assurance of backing for 'any changes he migh
desire to effect in the School', after staff consultations, produced
three-page policy statement.

The School building was in imminent danger of overcrowding
He asked searching questions about its management:

> If the School is to be regarded as a factory for turning out university scholar
> (which means the average boy is to be neglected) then the larger it is th
> better. If on the other hand, the average boy is to be regarded as the stapl
> product of the School, and the scholar is a valuable by-product, then th
> number of boys must be limited.[70]

The Governors approved his preference by fixing an upper limi
of 475 boys. By 1914 the School building was officially 'full' for th
first time since its opening. A special sub-committee of th
Governors considered the Headmaster's strong recommendatio
that the lower school should be reorganised into a preparator
school for boys of seven to eleven years (already an option i
clause 45 of the 1909 Scheme) with the declared objective o
ensuring 'that boys have received a thorough grounding in th
elements of English and arithmetic before passing into the mai
portion of the School'. In a later report to the Governors, he agai
referred to the pressure of numbers. Alterations and extensions t
the changing rooms and another building for the Junior Schoo
were 'essential and urgent unless work of the school is to b
crippled seriously'.[71]

John Talbot's ambitious plans for the School's developmen
were to be frustrated, first, by the local breakdown of agreemen
and cooperation between the school's Governing Body and th
Trustees of the Virgin Mary Hospital. Nationally, they were als
to be affected by the hopes raised by the President's parliamentar

166

statement in July 1913, of a 'dynamic stimulus' to the nation's education through a new improved system of Exchequer grants. These, in turn, were dashed by the Liberal cabinet's abrupt abandonment of projected legislation on education, in the parliamentary session of 1914, in face of conflicting pressures from political factions, shortage of parliamentary time and mounting inter-departmental competition for resources.

On his own initiative, the Headmaster had already requested an interview with the Board early in 1913. His Governors were probably unaware of his visit since there is no report or reference to it in the minutes of their meetings. According to the Board's officer, Mr Simmonds, the topic of conversation was the financial position of the School. Mr Talbot's purpose seems to have been to persuade the Board to authorise the maximum possible grant from the Hospital surplus income. He had also mentioned the crippling effect of his predecessor's pension, his anxiety to pay better salaries to his assistant masters, and the necessity of obtaining full knowledge of the Trustees' accounts in order to ascertain what precisely that surplus income would be.[72] Later the same month two of the Hospital Trustees also talked with Mr Simmonds about the new Scheme under consideration. They made clear to the Board that local feeling was against any possible move by the Board to take the administration of the charity out of the Hospital Trustees' hands and to give it to the Governors.

The quickening of interest in the Trust's administration and in its surplus income, clearly evident in the records of the Governors, the Trustees and the Board of Education, was not simply a result of renewed discussions over the revised Scheme incorporating the girls' scholarships, but also because, in 1913, for the first time, the surplus income of the Trust exceeded £2500, the maximum sum for education purposes in the Scheme. Surplus income would continue to increase with the development of about thirty-seven acres of land in Fenham. Anticipating substantial increases, the Governors voted to improve staff salaries and authorised the appointment of an additional master as head of the preparatory department. Meanwhile the finance committee had reported in favour of proposed building extensions. But if reviving trade had brought some prosperity to North-Eastern commerce, Lloyd George's Insurance Act had focused national and local attention on other areas of social action for the poor, sick and elderly.

At their meeting of June 1913, one of the Trustees, the Bishop of Newcastle, won strong support when he moved that the proportion of the Trust's income devoted to educational purposes should in future be limited, a larger proportion than hitherto to be made available for non-educational uses. It was agreed that the surplus income should be divided in equal portions. More immediately, the Trustees would also require £1600 for the building of new almshouses and an additional £480 for non-resident brethren. Representatives of both bodies met, without agreement; the Trustees' proposals were later declined by the Governors.

The new proposals threw the whole draft Scheme, as the Board's officials minuted glumly, 'in the melting pot'. It so happened that the President was engaged that month in a bitter cabinet struggle to retain the Exchequer grants pledged earlier for education, the reality of which seemed to be steadily diminishing. His officials advised him of the difficulties for the Minister of Education 'to go to Parliament at a time when everyone was calling out for money for education and to ask for power to divert a £1000 to non-educational purposes'.

'Resist application', instructed the President.[73] When yet another deputation, this time representing Governors, Trustees and the City Council visited the Board, they presented a compromise, unanimously agreed upon, that two thirds of the surplus income should be given to the Governors and one third to the charity. Since the Grammar School, catering for the middle class, could expect increased grants from the State very soon, and had already expended £70,000 of charity money on its new premises, it was time a new Scheme enlarged and extended the pressing work of the original charity – its support of the poor of Newcastle. The planned legislation on education might have relieved the localities to some extent of the cost of education and would certainly have strengthened such a claim. 'I agree with the secretary. We'd better temporise', Charles Trevelyan advised his President before the deputation's arrival. But by July, the prospects of legislation having waned, the Board printed the amended Scheme without fundamental re-allocation, increasing the maximum surplus income for the school to £3000 and incorporating the new scholarships for girls. The shelving of their proposals brought a considerable worsening of relations between Governors, Trustees and local councillors, several of whom served in all three roles. 'An ancient charity: How it has been diverted from the Poor,' proclaimed the headline in the *Northern Echo* in March 1914. Governor of the School and also Chairman of

Newcastle Education Committee, George Lunn, considered the School should give a much more liberal share of free places out of its surplus income, 'to satisfy the demands of democracy'.

The opening of refurbished almshouses three years later would occasion a public outburst from one Trustee who felt dismayed 'about the money of the charity having been captured for education, especially in connection with the Grammar School, as the parents of students there could, as a rule, well afford to pay for educational facilities'.[74] There were to be frequent recriminations over the precise amounts of surplus income, due to or received by, the Governors and the disagreement was not settled until November 1921 when more cordial relations were re-established. Local misunderstandings were to be overshadowed by international events, however.

Indefinite postponement of the Governors' plans for all new building developments was inevitable following Grey's fateful announcement on 3 August that the country was at war. There are no indications in the School records or those of the Trustees or of the Board's officials that war had been envisaged as an immediate contingency in the months before that dramatic declaration. Indeed Mr Talbot's reports to his Governors and those of boys in *Novo* indicate a cheerful flourishing of academic and corporate life in the School – the establishment of a tutor system 'of great value in the future', and new methods of marking and reporting, the gift of a cricket pavilion by the Chairman of Governors, Sir Alfred Palmer, the printing of the new school song, written by J. B. Brodie, Senior English Master, and its first public singing in April 1914 . . . 'Fortiter defendit . . .'. There had however been one memorable disruption of School defences and routine for nearly a week, much enjoyed by the boys, when a freak rain storm on Tuesday 16 September, 1913 had caused a huge mass of water to pour off the Moor, nearly drowning a man picking mushrooms. Then it had flowed across the North Road where it swept away the School's western perimeter fencing, formed a lake of the field and, filling the School basement, flooded the main hall, gym and science blocks to a depth of over eighteen inches. The surplus water and evil smelling mud was later removed with the help of the city's fire brigade; a small fish was found in one of the lecture rooms![75]

A year later, much of the familiar life of the School was undergoing radical change. Two assistant masters had already left on military service and many others would follow. During the four war years, there would be serious understaffing partially met by a succession of temporary appointments including part-time clergymen from reserved occupation, and women teachers to the preparatory department. Mr Talbot's energy, enthusiasm and undoubted organisational abilities were to some extent channelled into military activities through recruitment and training of the first volunteers in the city. He was gazetted Major of the 1st Commercials (Quayside) Battalion of the Northumberland Fusiliers and went with them to Alnwick for several weeks' training. The *Novo* reported a 'military presence on the School field'. The School had also become the headquarters of the Newcastle Citizens' Training League and the playing field must, at times, have seemed more like a barrack square. A wooden hut was built on the Pinfold as an army office, later to be used by the School's OTC and woodwork classes. It was small wonder that the School OTC numbers rose to 140 strong. A former pupil, Arthur Munro Sutherland, later to be an even more munificent benefactor as Chairman of the Governors, gave a rifle range to the School at the opening of which, on the south boundary of the field, in April 1915, Major Talbot, to his schoolboys' pride, was the only member of the official party to register a bull's eye! At Prize Day that year (the occasion and the prizes were abandoned for the sake of economy during the remaining war years) Principal Hadow wittily quoted from the poet Thomson's 'Seasons: "On Spring".'

> Delightful task, to bear the tender thought
> And teach the young idea how to shoot. . . .

On the same occasion, the announcement of 107 Old Boys holding commissions and 113 serving in the ranks drew long applause.[76] Already, the first of many tragic deaths had been announced in November 1914 – Trooper Harry Thwaites (O.N. 1897–1900), killed in action at Ypres with the Imperial Yeomanry, Northumberland Hussars. The mounting losses of old boys were sadly recorded by the Headmaster in his annual reports, as well as the proud mention of those wounded in action, or winning honours or special mention in despatches. During the Prize Day of 1921, the Headmaster would announce 1114 past scholars and masters on the school roll of honour, of whom 138 had died, 150 had been wounded and approaching 100 had won decorations or mention in despatches.

In addition to the playing fields, the School premises were also

1ade available wherever possible: St John's Ambulance groups
)ok over the lecture room on Wednesdays and Fridays. A
esearch team from Armstrong College used a Chemistry
1boratory three afternoons a week and on Saturday mornings,
arning the School a commendation from the Ministry of
1unitions in July 1917:

> The research work now going on will have results of permanent value after
> the war . . .[77]

A more serious threat to the continuity of school life had first
)me in November 1914 with the request from military authorities,
ot in the event pressed, for the School buildings to become a
illet for six hundred soldiers in consequence of a feared enemy
1id on the North-East coast. Again in 1916, the War Office
eriously contemplated taking over the premises as a military
ospital. In response to urgent letters from the School's clerk and
Ieadmaster (the latter also personally visiting the Whitehall
ffices) the Board of Education officials weighed the adverse
ffects, in particular, upon the kindling of 'the fine public school
)irit which the present Headmaster since 1912 had worked so
ard and done so much to inspire' and the impairment of serious
cience work by the loss of laboratories were the school to be
elocated in Sandyford Road Council School. Such a step would
1flict 'a very great blow on the school and retard its progress
esides causing great hardships to scholars . . .'.[78] The arguments
f the Inspectors and of Permanent Secretary Selby-Bigge against
1e War Office request, backed by strong representation by the
overning Body and in particular by the Chairman of Newcastle
'ducation Committee, Councillor George Lunn, persuaded the
resident to refuse the use of the premises 'unless the War Office
ut the case higher'; the main hall of Armstrong College was to be
tilised instead.

In addition to the military training of cadets in the OTC, in
)ecember 1916 the cadets assisted the Engineer Company of the
'olunteer Training Corps in the digging of trenches for the
efence of Newcastle.The Grammar School boys also contributed
ractically to the war effort in the formation of an agricultural
)ciety whose twenty to thirty members cultivated over a quarter
f an acre of land adjacent to the school on which they grew
otatoes and artichokes. In August 1917 fifty boys and three
1asters assisted in potato picking near Ely, and the following

summer the Headmaster organised an agricultural expedition ▸
Thropton in Northumberland. Lord and Lady Armstrong visite
the camp, during which sixty boys helped in hay-makin¡
turnip-weeding, sheep-dipping and thistle-cutting in the Coqu▸
valley. Boys could also turn their hands to clerical work whe
required; in February 1918, upper forms had written out rath◂
more than 13,000 meal cards for the local Food Contr◂
Committee!

It is not easy to assess the direct consequences of the First Worl
War upon the School's development. Some of its side effects a▸
identifiable, some more positively beneficial, others less so. If th
long-term building programme was badly disrupted, eve
necessary repairs and renovations accumulating, the subseque▸
overcrowding from a steep rise in numbers (516 in 1916 and risin
steadily in the 1920s) at least indicated improved local support f◂
the School. Though pressure on places in the lower school wou▸
at last necessitate more rigorous and competitive entrance test
numbers in the upper forms continued to fluctuate with boy
leaving earlier during the war for national service. 'War wage
earned in much wider sectors of the local population had mad◂
consideration of fee-paying more attractive to a new generation ◂
parents. There was clear evidence nationally of growth ▸
appreciation of secondary schooling.[79] At the same time, the ris
in the cost of living during the war would bring in its wake acut
financial strains for the School as inflation continued into th
post-war period.

If, nationally, the war stimulated interest in, and wide
recognition of, the value of education, it also revealed grav
deficiencies in scientific training and in the teaching of moder
languages. The tragic loss of young lives provided both incentiv
and resolution to repair the intellectual wastage of the war year◂
At least two years before the November armistice, department◂
and government committees had been considering post-wa
national policies. Reconstruction became a political rallying cr▸
that reconstruction, in Lloyd George's memorable phrase, of a 'f
country for heroes to live in' included that of the country's syste▸
of education in order to strengthen national efficiency and t
weaken class divisions by extending access to secondary school
and universities for working-class children from elementar
schools.

On behalf of the Headmaster's Association, Mr Talbot gav
evidence before a Privy Council Committee on Science ▸
Education early in 1917 and later produced a memorandum fo

s Governors on the 'tentative and experimental proposals' of
e Board's Circular 1023. These proposals, based on
commendations of the Consultative Committee on Scholarships
r Higher Education, and later included in the Regulations for
econdary Schools, were specifically designed to encourage larger
umbers to stay on in schools and to form stronger links with the
niversities through State Scholarships. They took the form of
ock grants for schools already grant-aided, to develop Advanced
ourses in three subject areas – maths and sciences, modern
ubjects and classics. A fundamental condition of course
ecognition was the provision and adequate remuneration – a
inimum of £300 was stipulated for men – of staff especially
ualified to teach these courses. Once again, through the 'potent
iducement of ever-increasing grants' the Board was forcing the
ace of improvements in the schools' educational standards.[80]
rder was brought into the tangle of unstandardised examining
odies by the introduction the same year of a first school certificate
t 16+ and a second examination at the end of the two-year
dvanced course.

The Governors' decision to apply for extra grants for two
dvanced courses meant staff salaries, rather than building
evelopments, would become a major priority in future allocation
f their resources. Over the next few years, the Governors' modest
alary scales and belated contributory pension scheme for masters
ere overtaken by government legislation. Fisher's Act of 1918 for
ue first time imposed on the local authorities the duty of
rganising secondary education and declared the principle that no
hild capable of profiting by higher education should be prevented
y inability to pay fees. The School Teachers' Superannuation Act
ollowed at once. 'We want a real improvement and development
1 the status, salaries and the conditions of work of teachers,'
eclared Francis Acland in Parliament on 13 March 1918. *The
imes* backed the legislative plans of the President of the Board of
iducation, H. A. L. Fisher, who would 'play no inconsiderable
art in the rebuilding of all that has been shattered in England
uring the past four years of violence and upheaval'.[81] So
esperate did the immediate post-war shortage of graduate
aasters become, and so fierce the competition among schools over
andidates for appointments, that the Association of Local
iducation Authorities asked for the Board's assistance in
ontrolling salaries. Fisher's appointment of the Burnham
'ommittee would propose a system of national pay scales which

the Governors of the Royal Grammar School could not enterta
until the end of 1921. The Headmaster regularly pressed home th
urgency of the situation: 'I am anxious that the Grammar Scho
should be well staffed,' he told his Governors in 1919, and th
following year, 'I am having difficulty in finding masters.' His mo
senior science master, Dr Todd, had recently been appointe
professor of experimental physics at Armstrong College an
recognition for the school's modern subjects Advanced course wa
still being withheld by the Board.

Faced with annual deficits of over £1000, rising inexorably wit
the new incremental salary structure, the Governors took the
problem once again to the Board. They could increase the
income in three ways: firstly, by increasing the fees significantl
secondly, by increasing the percentage of free-place scholarshi
in the hope of a subsidy from the city Education Committee; b
the Labour Party on the council would not agree to aid the Scho
from rates unless the School gave 25% free places, which course c
action the Governors still considered not to be in the best interes
of the School. The third possibility was access to increase
amounts of surplus funds from the Trust, also tactically difficu
while the disagreement with the Trustees remained unresolved.[8]

Even as the School's finances were being discussed at the Board
the country's economic climate in the late summer of 1920 wa
changing dramatically. Reconstruction would rapidly turn t
retrenchment and the Board, vulnerable to the Geddes axe itsel
would soon be under further pressure from the Treasury to reduc
its estimates. There could be no increase in grants-in-aid. Th
Board's objection to the Governors' proposal to double the fee
(to £30) would deter parents with slender resources from sendin
their sons to the school. The Governors argued that parents coul
afford the increased fees, and that full Burnham scale could not b
sustained otherwise, but they agreed, on the Board's insistence, t
provide £1000 for total or partial exemptions of fees out of th
increase in fee income. The city's Higher Education Committe
also compromised, resolving that the Board be informed that

the R.G.S. will probably always form an important part of the educatio
system of Newcastle-upon-Tyne, the committee had no objection to a
increase in the fees charged at the school, and the committee wa
considering the granting of financial assistance to the school.[83]

The pre-war 'whisky grant' of £200 was to be revived and the local authority once again made a modest contribution through the provision of assisted places at the school.

As might be expected there were protests in the local newspapers signed 'Heavily Hit', 'Uphill' and 'Fair Play', in response to Mr Talbot's printed letter informing parents of the increased fees and the 'system of assisted scholarships to meet the case of proved necessity'. Nevertheless the School gained much-needed financial stability. Despite the changed economic conditions of the years that followed, the doubling of fees did not check the growth in numbers which continued to climb steadily from 480 in 1921 to 554 in 1924.[84]

John Talbot left the school in July 1922 to become Headmaster of Haileybury. It is conceivable that he returned with some relief to a school more independent of the control of the gentlemen of Whitehall.[85] Though his plans for extension of buildings and Junior School were never realised during his period as Headmaster, his own status and that of the School had been enhanced nationally by his membership of Headmasters' Conference and Presidency of the Incorporated Association of Headmasters in 1918, and locally by his appointment as Deputy-Lieutenant of Northumberland in 1919. His interest in curriculum matters, in particular his promotion of an Advanced science course in the sixth, strengthened the School's links with universities. One of his last requests had been for honours boards to record the names of past scholars to universities, and he had been delighted to announce the establishment of a new leavers' University Scholarship by an Old Novo (1874–6) Sir William Plender, who spoke at the Prize Day of 1919 and would become an important benefactor. The discipline and tone of corporate life in the School, though necessarily military in the war years, had also been significantly improved. It is true that the School had not yet enjoyed a 'period of unexampled prosperity' confidently forecast by Samuel Logan in 1905. But by 1922, its aims and objectives more precisely defined, its academic organisation and the professionalism of its staff strengthened, the School was at last earning greater support and esteem from the community it served.

Huxley's nineteenth-century metaphor of the secondary school as a narrow 'ladder reaching from the gutter to the university' no longer satisfied the twentieth century's widening concept of education. 'A ladder after all is a shaky thing,' declared one speaker in the parliamentary debates on the education bill of 1918.

In the first decade of this century, it had become 'an unbroken bridge or causeway' (W. S. Churchill's phrase in *The People's Rights*, 1909) later to be extended to 'a broad highway' as the post-war demand for secondary education for all was felt.[88] The principle of access to the School for able, aspiring boys from any social class, asserted so forcefully by the Revd Anchor Thompson and affirmed by the Governors' scholarships in the 1888 Scheme, but always under threat from the inexorably rising fees, was upheld by the Newcastle Education Committee's bursaries, exhibitions and scholarships (described in their 1915 booklet as 'rungs of the education ladder'). The principle had been urged by Professor Sadler – 'a good deal ought always to be done in the way of offering scholarships or reduction of fees.' Its retention was zealously guarded by liberal and far-sighted officers and Inspectors of the Board of Education in the face of much opposition from powerful local manufacturing bourgeoisie, many in municipal positions, and aspiring middle-class parents who felt the social prestige of the School would be damaged by extended admission of elementary school pupils. The Board's 1921 compromise of assisted scholarships foreshadowed the School's greater accessibility in the direct-grant years ahead.

Quite apart from the all-important, yet for the historian most elusive, influence and interaction of infinitely varied personalities of masters and pupils, the School's striking progress during the years 1888–1922 could be measured by its visible transformation from an insignificant endowed municipal school of 'but small scope and ambition' in Rye Hill to the nationally 'recognised ' and grant-aided city Grammar School housed in substantial and spacious buildings in Eskdale Terrace with, as Professor Sadler foresaw, 'a brilliant future'.

The formation of policies for the School's development undoubtedly benefited from the wider experience and enthusiasm of the new Governors under the 1888 Scheme – academics, bankers and lawyers as well as local business men and Councillors. But a crucial factor in its progress was also the influence and motive power of the Board of Education, the central authority created at the turn of the century. Through involvement in the revisions of the School's Scheme of government, through discussion and dissemination of sound educational practice in conferences and reports, and by means of the financial leverage of Exchequer grants-in-aid administered by Regulations, the Board's officials and Inspectorate, more closely in touch with changing economic and social needs and political exigencies, with an element of 'bluff and cajolery' (in the words of Selby-Bigge) as well as keen personal interest, ensured that the School kept pace with educational advances in the best of the nation's secondary schools, in response to those changing needs and philosophies.

Durable institutions, it has been observed, have usually endured precisely because they have proved capable of adapting to changes in their environment. In education, wrote Robert Morant in 1906, 'as in civilisation, there is no finality.'[87]

Chapter V

TOWARDS THE FRONT RANK 1922–1945

The appointment of Ebenezer Rhys Thomas as Headmaster in January 1922 inaugurated a period of steady growth in the School's academic reputation, in its self-confidence, and in the variety and strength of its extra-curricular activities. By the mid-1930s the RGS had become one of the foremost schools in England in terms of the academic achievements of its pupils, and the educational philosophy of the Headmaster had given the School a distinctive character which has endured, in fundamentals, to the present day. The School's progress was, of course, interrupted by the four years of wartime evacuation to Penrith, but the success with which the School surmounted the problems that evacuation brought owed much to the high morale and sense of cohesion which it had acquired in the years since 1922. The academic progress of the School was maintained under Mr Thomas's successor, O. W. Mitchell, who held office from 1948 to 1960. Mitchell was a very different personality from Thomas, but he had great respect for his predecessor's philosophy and his achievements at RGS, and the essential characteristics of the School which had developed in the 1920s and 1930s were maintained and enhanced. By the time Mr Mitchell retired in 1960, the School regularly figured amongst the top ten in the country in terms of entrance scholarships at Oxford and Cambridge, and most boys concluded their school careers with two years in the sixth form and two or three passes in the Advanced Level examination of the General Certificate of Education. It was a far cry indeed from the complaints of the Inspectors in 1910 about the short duration of school life and the poor development of advanced work.

This achievement was made possible not simply by the personality and commitment of Mr Thomas, important though these were. The teaching staff in the 1920s and 1930s were more numerous, better qualified, and willing to stay in post much longer than their predecessors at the turn of the century; this in turn reflected not just Mr Thomas's judgement of men but also the

tional improvement in teachers' salaries and status after 1918. In
th national and local educational politics the 1918 Education
ct inaugurated a long period of bi-partisanship which began to
ow signs of breaking up only in the mid-1950s; and the
portance of a good standard of secondary education became
dely recognised not just amongst those concerned with
ucational administration but more generally throughout society,
Tyneside as much as elsewhere in the country. The School also
quired, at last, a stable financial basis. As Dr Wilkinson has
own, Mr Talbot's plans for the development of the School were
strated partly because of the breakdown of negotiations
tween the Governors of the School and the Trustees of the
rgin Mary Hospital over the apportionment of the Trust's
rplus income; but in 1927 an agreement was reached between
e two sides which endured for fifty years and provided a solution
this aspect of the School's financial problem. The system of
ants from the Board of Education was not to be seriously
estioned until the late 1950s, though it was modified by the
rect grant regulations of 1945; and the relative price stability of
e 1920s and 1930s enabled fees to remain unchanged in the
e-war years after the controversial decision of the Governors to
uble them in 1920.

The academic progress of the School was accompanied by a
eady increase in the number of pupils, from 500 at the time of Mr
omas's appointment to 650 in 1930 and 760 in 1933. In the
20s, Thomas often stated publicly that the expansion in numbers
s almost more than the School could sustain;[1] but the growth in
mbers was financially advantageous to the School, and reflected
e importance which parents attached not just to secondary
ucation in general, but also to the distinctive style of education,
d the good academic results, which developed at RGS under Mr
omas. The expansion in numbers imposed strains on the
hool's accommodation, which the Governors were in part able
relieve by liquidating investments purchased out of capital
rived from the Virgin Mary Hospital Trust. But of much greater
portance in providing the School with the facilities appropriate
its status and the range of its activities was the munificence of Sir
rthur Munro Sutherland, the only benefactor of real significance
the School's entire history. Sir Arthur had been a pupil at the
hool in the 1890s, and had built up a highly successful shipping
mpany. He was an example of the self-made business man
rhaps more commonly found in the industrial areas of

179

Lancashire, Yorkshire and the Midlands than on Tyneside, and
retained a lasting affection for his school.[2] He became a Govern
of the School in 1919, and Chairman of the Governors
succession to Sir Arthur Palmer in 1929, an office he held until I
death in 1953. In the late nineteenth century the School had fe
pupils who became successful in the world of industry a
commerce, and it was fortunate to find in Sir Arthur Sutherland
benefactor who was willing to finance a significant part of t
building development without which neither its academic nor
extra-curricular progress could have been so successful
maintained.

(i) *The Constitution and Finance of the School*

The conflict of interest over the apportionment of the surpl
income of the Virgin Mary Hospital Trust, which had led to t
breakdown of negotiations between the Governors and t
Trustees in 1913, was not satisfactorily resolved by the amende
Scheme approved by the Board of Education in 1914 under whi
the School was to receive £3000 a year as an endowment, with £1
to fund scholarships for girls, while surplus income in excess
£3180 was to be capitalised and the interest used 'in augmentatic
of the Hospital Education Endowment pending a further Schen
or Act.'[3] The Board of Education had taken the view that t
proposals of the Trustees in 1913 amounted to the diversion
money to a non-educational purpose, and the effect of the 19
Scheme was to benefit the School rather than the Hospital. I
1925 the accumulated surplus income amounted to more th
£13,000, and between 1922 and 1925 alone the School had receiv
over £3500 in capital for investment. It is not surprising, therefor
that in 1924 the Trustees reopened the issues of 1913.[4] Th
argued that the income of the Trust was insufficient for t
payment of pension to the brethren and the maintenance of t
Hospital. This time they received a more sympathetic heari
from the Governors of the School. The Governors and t
Trustees agreed to a proposal that henceforth the surplus incor
of the Trust should not be capitalised but should be divided in t
proportion of one third to the Trustees and two thirds to t
Governors. In June 1925 the Clerk to the Governors wrote to t
Board of Education seeking approval for the proposed Schem
The Board deliberated over the proposal for six months, and
December 1925 turned it down. The Board raised the san
objection that it had made in 1914: it was not prepared to agree

To the Reverend HUGH MOISES A.M. / Master of S.Mary's HOSPITAL and of the / Free VIEW of part of the Antient Church of that / Hospital converted into a GRAMMAR SCHOOL / happy is the Exercise in / By his ever oblig'd and most devoted / most respectfully Inscribed / faithful humble Servant John Brand / Morning Lecturer of the CHURCH of ALLSAINTS, / ROYAL GRAMMAR SCHOOL at Newcastle upon Tyne

The School in the Virgin Mary Hospital as seen in an illustration published in 1789 by John Brand in his History and Antiquities of Newcastle (See p. 70).

PLATE I

The School at Charlotte Square, 1867, showing Headmaster James Snape with some of the cast of that year's play.

The School at Charlotte Square, 1867.

PLATE II

The School at Rye Hill showing the gymnasium (centre foreground) and the science laboratory (centre right) converted from the discontinued St Mary's Boys' Elementary School.

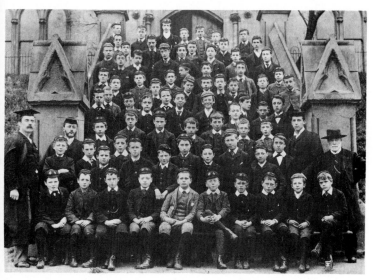

The School at Rye Hill, around 1890, showing Headmaster Samuel Logan (bottom left).

PLATE III

The exterior of the School at Eskdale Terrace, around 1910, soon after its opening.

The interior of the School at Eskdale Terrace, around 1910, soon after its opening.

PLATE IV

The School at Eskdale Terrace: aerial view of 1928 from the west showing the buildings before the additions of the 1930s.

PLATE V

Outside the Wordsworth Street Methodist Church, Penrith, after Prayers.
Throughout the wartime evacuation the church was used by the RGS for Morning
Prayers and Assembly.

PLATE VI

The School at Eskdale Terrace from the air, 1985, with motorway, University and Civic Centre in the foreground (see p. 311).

PLATE VII

Mʳ Iohn Lilburn, a pious young Gent:
leman, of about 22 or 23 yeares of age
for Suspition of printing & divulging
certain of Dʳ Bastwickes & other bookes, a:
gainst Popish innovations, was censured
in the Starr-Chamber to be whipt at a
Carts-tayle from the ffleet to Westminster,
had therby about 200 lashes with a whip,
was then, presently upon it set one a pil:
lorie, with a gagg in his mouth, was fined
500ˡ and kept close-prisoner in the ffleet
where day & night hee lay in iron shacles,
and long time indured most barbarous
and cruell usage.

*John Lilburn (c. 1614–57) republican writer during the Civil War and
Commonwealth. (Oxford, Bodleian Library, Rawl. Prints A.8. fol. 37b).*

PLATE VIII

James Jurin F.R.S. (1684–1750), Headmaster 1710–15, secretary to the Royal
Society 1721–27. (With the permission of the Royal Society, London).

PLATE IX

*Edward Moises (1763–1845),
Headmaster 1787–1828. (With the
permission of the Literary and
Philosophical Society of Newcastle
upon Tyne).*

*G. F. W. Mortimer (1805–71),
Headmaster 1828–33. (With the
permission of the City of London
School).*

PLATE X

James Snape (1815–80), Headmaster 1847–71.

John Talbot (1876–1937), Headmaster 1912–22.

PLATE XI

E. R. Thomas (1885–1979), Headmaster 1922–48.

O. W. Mitchell (1898–1963), Headmaster 1948–60, with Dr C. I. C. Bosanquet (Chairman of Governors), Mr S. Middlebrook (Second Master) and Mrs Mitchell, on the occasion of the first Founder's Service (1954) at Jesmond Parish Church.

PLATE XII

Headmaster S. C. Logan with his assistants at Rye Hill (date unknown).

The Lord Mayor's visit of 1936, showing Sir Arthur Sutherland (Chairman of Governors), the Lord Mayor of Newcastle, Alderman Graham, and the Sheriff of Newcastle, Alderman Taylor.

PLATE XIII

Field-Marshal Viscount Montgomery of Alamein inspecting the CCF in 1953, with Major Bertram in attendance. (With the permission of the Editor of the Newcastle Journal*).*

The Collingwood Ceremony, 1971, whereby three representatives of the School, with the Headmaster and civic leaders, honour one of the School's greatest men.

PLATE XIV

Pupils at work in the Plender Library, 1951.

A biology lesson with a gerbil, 1975.

PLATE XV

Gymnastics, 1940.

Newts Night, 1961.

PLATE XVI

Noye's Fludde: *a school performance in St Nicholas' Cathedral, Newcastle, in 1980. The large cast of animals was drawn from the Junior School.*

PLATE XVII

An orchestral rehearsal under the Director of Music, Mr Jack Wolstenholme, 1974.

PLATE XVIII

The set of the Agamemnon, *performed in 1932.*

PLATE XIX

The 1956 performance of Dr Faustus.

Rugby: First XV versus Sedbergh (1984).

PLATE XX

First VIII (1981).

PLATE XXI

Senior Basketball Match (1982).

PLATE XXII

RGS workers at a war agricultural executive camp in 1945.

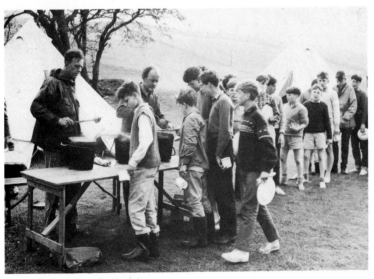

Camp Week 1963: at Littondale.

PLATE XXIII

The Crop-spraying Hovercraft, winner of the B.B.C. Young Scientist of the Year Award in 1978, on display in London's Science Museum.

PLATE XXIV

any Scheme which involved the diversion of 'educational money to non-educational purposes.' But the Board now went further than it had gone in 1914, and suggested that the surplus income of the Trust could more appropriately be used to support the fuller development of other educational activities in Newcastle, such as the award of scholarships and maintenance allowances to pupils at secondary schools and students at university. The local Inspectors had earlier argued that the provision of adequate premises for Dame Allan's School was 'the most urgent Secondary need in Newcastle,' but the Board did not persist with the suggestion that the surplus income from the Trust might be used for the benefit of the Dame Allan's foundation, perhaps because it was already aware that the negotiations between the Dame Allan's Governors and the Virgin Mary Hospital Trustees for the purchase of land in Fenham where the Dame Allan's Schools now stand were proceeding without apparent difficulty.

After receiving the Board's letter rejecting the new Scheme, the Trustees, the Governors of the School, and the Schools and Charities Committee of Newcastle Corporation sent a delegation to the Board of Education to press their case even more strongly. The delegation argued, with some justification, that the charity had not originally been established for educational purposes, and that the Trust could no longer maintain its almshouses and brethren out of its existing yearly income. But the Board took the view that the delegation had not made out a case for an increase in the Trust's non-educational funds, and offered only a minor concession that satisfied neither the Trustees nor the Governors. Despite a further written representation from the Clerk to the Governors, the Board remained adamant, and on 5 May 1926 wrote to the parties involved finally declining to approve the new Scheme. At the meeting with the Board of Education, the Town Clerk of Newcastle had hinted at an Act to secure what was wanted, and in face of the Board's rejection of the Scheme the Trustees, the Governors, and the Schools and Charities Committee now decided to resort to legislation. In March 1927 they promoted the St Mary's Hospital (Newcastle upon Tyne) Bill, under which the surplus income of the Trust up to £1800 would be divided in the proportion set out in their original proposal, and if the surplus income exceeded £1800 the excess was to be apportioned between the Governors and the Trustees in such proportion as they might agree, with the approval of the Board of Education and the Charity Commissioners. The bill also provided

181

that the surplus income which had accrued as capital since 1914 should become the sole property of the Governors, and the official trustee of charitable funds would be required to sell the securities in which the capital had been invested and pay the proceeds to the Governors. The Board of Education objected to the bill, on the grounds that it sought 'to deprive the educational foundation of moneys that should have been properly made available for educational purposes.' Under pressure, the Board offered to consider a scheme which would increase the stipend of the brethren of the Hospital from £30 to £52, but by this stage neither the Governors nor the Trustees were interested in a scheme which appeared to give the Board most of what it wanted. They proceeded with the bill, and the Board did not formally press its opposition in Parliament. The bill received the royal assent on 29 July 1927. The costs were shared between the Governors and the Trustees in the proportion of two to one.

In the autumn of 1927 the surplus income investments were sold, and realised a total of £10,851 17s 9d, which was immediately reinvested in 5% war loan.[6] Over the next few years this investment produced a small but useful income of about £600 a year, but, more importantly, the investment could if necessary be partially liquidated to meet expenditure on additions and alterations to the School buildings. The Act of 1927 satisfied both parties; but the surplus income of the Trust continued to grow in the early 1930s, partly because of the Trust's policy of selling land from its Fenham estate as building sites, and between 1928 and 1937 the surplus income exceeded £1800 on five occasions.[7] In September 1937, therefore, the Clerk to the Trustees raised the question of the division of surplus income in excess of that figure, which the Act had left to be determined by agreement between the Governors and the Trustees. The discussions between the two sides proceeded speedily and without acrimony: on 8 February 1938 a sub-committee consisting of two representatives of the Governors and two representatives of the Trustees agreed that the surplus income in excess of £1800 should be divided equally between the Governors and the Trustees and that this arrangement should endure for five years in the first instance.[8] Under the Act, the two parties to the agreement had to obtain the consent of the Board of Education and the Charity Commissioners, and in the light of their experience in 1927 the Governors advised caution, suggesting that they and the Trustees should not approach either body 'until there is income in hand available for distribution. We are . . . agreed that if the matter is dealt with in this way we are more likely to get a favourable decision than if we apply for consent before any surplus income is available for division.' The Clerk to the Trustees disagreed, however, and suggested seeking immediate approval from the Board and the Commissioners. The Clerk to the Governors gave way, and the two sides made a joint approach to the Board and the Commissioners. Approval was given on 30 March 1939:[9] it had taken over two years from the first discussion about the division of the surplus income, but the delay arose more from the long illness and death of the Clerk to the Trustees than from any great disagreement between the two sides or opposition from the Board of Education.

The agreement was renewed without serious argument in 1945, when both parties had more pressing concerns on their minds, and it endured until 1978.[10] Thus from 1939 onwards, the RGS received from the Virgin Mary Hospital Trust £3000 endowment, £180 for girls' scholarships, two thirds of the surplus income up to £1800, and half the surplus income in excess of that sum. Between 1940 and 1945 the surplus income amounted to an average of £2735 a year, of which the Governors received an average of £1668 a year, together with the interest on what remained of the capital realised by the sale of investments in 1927.[11]

The Act of 1927 and the agreement of 1937–39 provided a stable basis for the School's endowment over the next forty years; but the significance of the surplus income from the Trust for the School's recurrent income should not be exaggerated. The endowment income of £3000 a year laid down in clause 5(b) of the 1914 Scheme had not been in question either in 1927 or in the 1937 discussions, and the surplus income which accrued to the School under the 1927 Act and the 1937 agreement seldom amounted to more than one twenty-fifth of the School's annual income. The capital sum of over £10,000 which the School acquired under the Act was perhaps of greater significance, at least in the short and medium term, for it provided a source of funds which could be liquidated to finance building developments.

Board of Education grants and income from fees were of much greater significance than income from the Virgin Mary Hospital Trust in determining the financial position of the School. From 1899 onwards the Board of Education paid grants on a capitation basis to recognised secondary day schools, and by 1907, when the rate of grant was £5 per pupil, the School was receiving over £1000 in grants. Income from grants increased significantly in the 1920s and 1930s as the number of boys in the School steadily grew and the rate of grant was increased from time to time. Special additional grants for advanced courses were introduced in 1921, and these became of greater importance to the finances of the School as its advanced work developed. In 1922, when the standard rate of grant was £7 per annum for each pupil over 11, the School received £3420 in grants. The rate of grant was gradually increased over the next eight years, and stood at nine pounds in 1930. The rate of grant was reduced in 1931 as part of the national economy measures, but it was gradually restored over the next four years, and in 1935 the grant for advanced courses was replaced by an extra capitation grant for sixth form pupils, a change which benefited those schools such as RGS which had large and flourishing sixth forms. By the time the School was evacuated to Penrith in 1939, total grant income stood at more than £6000 a year.[12] In 1926, under the Board of Education's Circular 1381, schools which were not provided by the local education authority were given the choice of receiving their grant aid either indirectly through local authorities or directly from the Board, as in the past. The RGS chose the latter course, and if the direct grant system as a method of financing certain schools aside from and parallel to the system of paying grants through local education authorities can be said to have originated at any particular time it is with the publication of this circular in 1926.[13]

The conditions under which the grant was paid, however, as well as the rate at which it was paid affected the School's financial position. The most important of these conditions was the requirement that a proportion of free places should be offered to boys from elementary schools maintained by the local education authority. Until 1945 the grant regulations laid down that a school should normally offer 25% of its places free to pupils who had spent at least two years at a public elementary school; but the regulations allowed a school to offer a lower percentage of free places with the approval of the Board. As Dr Wilkinson has shown, the Governors of the RGS successfully argued in 1907 that they should be permitted to offer only 10% of their places free of fees, on the grounds that their endowment was small and that other schools were offering sufficient free places to meet the local demand for secondary education.[14] Throughout the years from 1907 to 1945 the School continued to offer only 10% of its places free, but the Board of Education remained unhappy about the

School's attitude to the free-place issue. When the Board finally approved the large increase in fees in 1921, it was 'disposed to consider that as a further condition (of approval) the percentage of free places should be increased.' The Governors argued that this was simply not possible, mainly because the Newcastle Education Authority would not bear the cost of additional free places. The Board reluctantly accepted this argument, saying 'We are almost bound to take greater risks with a school like this than we would be disposed to take with one which can look for substantial support from the local education authority,' and dropped the suggestion that the School should increase its percentage of free places, agreeing instead to the Governors' proposals for a scheme of assisted scholarships which would cost the School about £1000 per annum when fully implemented.[15] The Governors' view on the free-place question did not change substantially until change was forced upon them in 1945. The Board of Education raised the issue during its controversy with the Governors over the reduction in teachers' salaries in 1931,[16] but it never pressed the matter to the point of confrontation with the Governors.

The Board of Education grants were important to the School both in financial terms and in the opportunity they offered the School to broaden the social range of its intake. By far the greatest part of the School's income, however, was derived from fees. The doubling of the fees in 1920, though highly controversial at the time, did more than anything else to give the School a measure of financial stability, and as the number of boys in the School rose steadily over the next eighteen years, so fee income increased. In 1923 the fee income of the School was £14,302, but it had risen to £17,112 by 1929 and £19,824 in 1934, without any increase in the rate of fee, £30 per annum, which had been set in 1920.[17] The School had no other significant sources of income. The annual grant of £205 from the corporation of Newcastle under the Scheme of 1888 continued, but the 'Whisky Money' grant from the Newcastle Education Committee was reduced from £200 in 1922 to £166 13s 4d in 1923 and to a nominal £1 in 1926 and thereafter. In 1922, the Board of Education announced that it would phase out the arrangement under which expenditure by local education authorities on non-maintained secondary schools qualified for reimbursement by the Board, and although the grant to the School from the Education Committee in 1924 was the same as it had been in 1923 it cost the ratepayers of the city more.[18] It is not surprising that the Education Committee virtually extinguished the grant in 1926.

Thus by 1926 the financial links between the School and the city had become little more than nominal, and of course the Newcastle Education Authority had never had any administrative or legal authority over the School, though the Schools and Charities Committee of the Council formed a link between the School and the city since it nominated Council representatives to the governing body of the School. The links between the School and the city were seen at their clearest in the composition of the Governors. Under the Scheme of 1909 the city Corporation appointed ten of the twenty one Governors, and most of those who served also held important and influential positions in the government of the city. Sir George Lunn, for example, who was a former pupil of the School and a prominent shipowner on Tyneside, became a member of Newcastle City Council in 1901 and served as chairman of the Education Committee from 1905 until his death in 1939. He became a Governor of the School in 1928. Another distinguished former pupil who served as a Governor from 1929 until his death in 1948 was Sir Arthur Lambert, a Newcastle businessman who became a member of the City Council in 1910 and served as Lord Mayor and Sheriff. His most valuable contribution to the School came with his appointment as North Regional Commissioner for Civil Defence on the outbreak of war in 1939; he established his headquarters in the School buildings after the evacuation to Penrith, and did much to ensure that the buildings were handed back to the School in good order when it returned from Penrith in 1944. Dr J. W. Leech, who became a Governor in 1932, was not only a consulting surgeon at the RVI, but also Lord Mayor of the city, and Conservative MP for Newcastle West from 1931 to 1940: such a wide range of interests and experience was unique amongst the Governors of the School in the 1920s and 1930s.

The universities of Oxford and Cambridge each appointed one member of the Governors, and the University of Durham had three representatives, one from the Durham Colleges, one from Armstrong College, and one from the College of Medicine in Newcastle. The reorganisation of Armstrong College and the Medical College into one institution, King's College, in 1937 made no difference to the representation of the Newcastle division of Durham University on the Governors. Some of those who served as representatives of the universities were men of great distinction. Sir Theodore Morison, who was Principal of Armstrong College from 1919 to 1929, and his successor, Sir William Marris, who held office from 1929 to 1937, had both had successful careers in the Indian Civil Service before coming to Armstrong College. Professor H. V. A. Briscoe, who was Professor of Inorganic and Physical Chemistry at Armstrong College from 1921 to 1932 also served as Secretary of the Durham University Schools Examination Board from 1923 to 1932, the period when the School was rapidly developing advanced work and preparing a growing number of candidates for the Higher School Certificate examination of the University of Durham. Professor Godfrey Thomson, who was a member of the Governors from 1921 to 1925, was Professor of Education at Armstrong College, but perhaps better known for his publications on educational psychology and his work on the Moray House Tests of intelligence, which were published after he became Professor of Education at Edinburgh University and Director of Moray House in 1925. Professor Sir David Drummond, Professor of Medicine at the College of Medicine from 1911 to 1924, and a second Professor of Medicine from 1911 to 1927, Sir Thomas Oliver, represented the College of Medicine on the Governors throughout the 1920s and 1930s, and no doubt encouraged the development of the pre-registration examination in medicine at the School. All these men were in a position to offer the Headmaster informed advice on the development of the School's academic work, and in this respect there can be little doubt that the Governors were a most effective and valuable group.

(ii) *The Work of the School*

Amongst the problems identified by the Board of Education's Inspectors in 1910, perhaps the most serious was the lack of development of advanced work at the School, and the Inspectors' criticism of the poor intellectual standard of the School and the irregular length of school life contributed materially to Mr Logan's decision to resign in 1912.[19] Mr Logan's successor, John Talbot, showed himself well aware of the School's problems when he observed at Speech Day in 1920 that 'if the School was to fulfil its true purpose, it was very necessary that boys should remain for a greater length of time than they had hitherto done, in order to build up a strong upper school.'[20] Mr Talbot made some progress towards this goal, but the School's financial difficulties and the war-time emergency frustrated his plans. In December 1921 he was appointed Headmaster of Haileybury, and the task of raising the academic standards of the School fell to E. R. Thomas.

E. R. Thomas was born in 1885 and educated at Aberystwyth Grammar School, University College Aberystwyth, and Emmanuel College Cambridge. In 1912 he was appointed science master at Rugby School. During the war he worked for a time at Cambridge under Professor W. J. Pope, FRS. In 1916 he became chemist-in-charge at HM Ordnance Factory at Queensferry, and between 1917 and 1919 he was engaged in special training in ammunitions and served on several missions to French technical ammunition officers. He was promoted to the rank of major, and at the end of the war he was sent to inspect and report on chemical factories in Germany. In 1919 he returned to Rugby as Head of the science department, and moved to the RGS in January 1922. After he came to Newcastle he maintained his academic interest in science: he edited four volumes in the series entitled *Classics of Scientific Method*, which appeared between 1922 and 1928 and which were intended to make knowledge of elementary scientific principles available to laymen. In 1934 he and Michael Roberts jointly published a work entitled *Newton and the Origin of Colours*. Mr Thomas gave Michael Roberts credit for the greater part of the book, but much of the material was in all probability drawn from Mr Thomas's own knowledge of the subject. After he retired in 1948, Mr Thomas accepted an honorary part-time lectureship in the Department of Engineering at King's College, teaching students to write clear scientific reports. He also took up his research interests once again, publishing three papers on the phenomenon of singing sands in collaboration with lecturers in the Department of Physics.[21] His own energy and commitment to academic work were beyond doubt, and he expected the boys at RGS to follow his example. In his first address to the School he urged the boys to 'work till it hurts,'[22] and he was unsparing in his efforts to ensure that boys worked to the limit of their ability. Those who idled their time away were liable to find themselves subject to a monthly special report, and if this did not encourage them to improve the Headmaster might require them to withdraw from the School.

Between 1922 and the general inspection in 1926, the number of boys who left at 15+ fell from twenty five to sixteen, and the number of boys leaving at 17+ and 18+ rose from twenty two to thirty eight. By 1926 the average school was four years, and the inspectors observed that 'the advance since 1912 may be gauged from the statement made in the last report that the average school life over twelve was then two years and ten months.'[23] Ten years later, at the time of the inspection in 1936, the average school life had risen to five years and ten months, and the average leaving age was seventeen years and four months. 'These extraordinarily good figures,' the inspectors reported, 'are well above average for the country and reflect great credit on the Head Master for his success in persuading parents that a sixth form education for their sons is worth while.'[24] The establishment of a large and flourishing sixth form was not the least of Mr. Thomas's achievements in the late 1920s and early 1930s.

The strengthening of the sixth form was accompanied by increasing emphasis on advanced work, and a steady improvement in the School's record in advanced examinations. In the Michaelmas term of 1923 the Headmaster reported that there were 'twice as many boys over sixteen in the School as there were last year, and advanced work is being carried out in all subjects.'[25] But the number of candidates who achieved passes in the Higher School Certificate examination remained small: two in 1922–23, four in 1923–24, two in 1924–25, and seven in 1925–26. In the following year, however, twelve candidates passed and the Headmaster declared that 'the results in the HSC examination are far in advance of anything which the School had produced in the past.'[26] The HSC was not, of course, the only advanced qualification open to sixth formers at the School. In 1924 the Durham College of Medicine recognised the School as a suitable place for the instruction of intending medical students in botany and zoology, and in that year two candidates passed this pre-registration examination. In the following year candidates for the first year B.Sc. examination in engineering at Armstrong College were permitted to take the examination at School, and each year thenceforward a handful of candidates passed the examination. At Speech Day in December 1928, in the presence of Mr Justice Roche, the guest of honour, who had been one of Mr Thomas's referees when he applied for the headship of RGS,[27] he spoke with justifiable pride of the progress the School had made in advanced work: 'Some five or six years ago only three or four members of the School obtained distinctions in examinations above the School Certificate stage, and this year we are able to report that twenty three members of the School have achieved such distinctions. Thirteen have passed the Higher School Certificate of the University of Durham, many brilliantly. Four have passed the Durham University B.Sc. Engineering Examination, four have passed the Pre-Registration Examination of the University of Durham College of Medicine, and four have won entrance scholarships to Universities.'[28]

The Inspectorate agreed with the Headmaster. In their 1926 report they commended the School on the great advance it had made in its educational standard, and observed that the increasing numbers in the sixth form had led to the firm establishment of advanced work. There was to be no going back on this achievement: the number of boys passing HSC and the other examinations never fell below twenty after 1929, and the number of scholarships and places gained at Oxford and Cambridge steadily increased from one or two a year in the early 1920s to five in the early 1930s and ten in 1937 and 1938.[29] In their 1936 inspection the HMIs congratulated the School on 'the large number of open awards at the universities it succeeds in winning, on the average from four to five a year for the last ten years.' The whole tone of the Inspectors' report in 1936 was markedly different from those of their predecessors in 1912 and 1926. They observed that the staff was *now* 'exceptionally strong in teaching ability;' and concluded that 'the teaching reaches an exceptionally high level and the standard of work in all the main subjects leaves little to be desired.'[30]

In explaining this achievement the Inspectorate gave great credit to the Headmaster, whose foresight, energy and tact, they said, had in large measure been responsible for the School's rise to the front rank. To these qualities they might have added good judgement in appointing staff, for the improvement in the academic qualifications of the staff and their length of service at the School underpinned its academic progress. But the attraction and retention of good staff was not just a matter of sound judgement on the part of the Headmaster: it also depended upon the existence of adequate funds to pay them. Towards the end of the nineteenth century, as Dr Mains has shown,[31] the School began to attract better qualified staff, and by the turn of the century most of those who were appointed had degrees. But the School still experienced difficulty in retaining those who were appointed, and almost certainly the main reason for this was the low salary level, which in turn reflected the financial problems of the School in the late nineteenth and early twentieth century. In 1918, however, the Burnham Committee laid down nationally agreed salary scales for teachers, and the Governors of the RGS insisted that they could not afford to pay the new salary scales unless the fees were doubled. Despite much opposition, as Dr Wilkinson has demonstrated,[32] the Governors won their point, and fees were raised to £30 per year, though as one condition of approval for the increased fees the Board of Education insisted that the School should not pay salaries higher than the Burnham scale.[33] The financial stability which the School achieved by doubling the fees and by attracting larger Board of Education grants as numbers in the School increased and more pupils undertook advanced work, allowed the School to continue to offer attractive salaries to its staff, and the development of advanced work offered opportunities which were likely to prove stimulating to gifted teachers. The School also adopted the provisions of the Teachers' Superannuation Act of 1918, which for the first time provided a national pension scheme for the profession, and a more open system of promotion developed, with all graduate members of staff eligible for appointment to senior posts.

During the 1920s and 1930s the social status of the teaching profession rose, and it acquired some of the characteristics of a middle-class profession. The Superannuation Act of 1918 and the Burnham agreement provided teachers with greater financial security than they had enjoyed in the early years of the century, both while in service and in retirement, and as more graduates and certificated teachers entered the profession so the esteem in which it was held increased, while the greater value placed on secondary education by parents after the war enhanced the standing of teachers in secondary schools. Thus circumstances nationally favoured an improvement in the quality and length of service of the staff at RGS, and there is no evidence that Mr Thomas faced difficulties either in recruiting or in retaining his staff.

Mr Thomas inherited twenty eight staff from John Talbot, four of whom continued to serve under O. W. Mitchell.[34] Three of the twenty eight, who taught PE, music and art, had appropriate specialist qualifications; but of the remaining twenty only nine had an honours degree obtained by full-time study at university, and a further ten had either a pass degree or an external London degree obtained while in service. Six had no advanced qualification at all. On the other hand all but two of the staff appointed by Mr Thomas to the Senior School had honours degrees (except the specialist teachers of PE, music and art), and a handful had higher degrees. Mr Thomas showed a marked preference for Cambridge men, following, no doubt unconsciously, the bias of recruitment to the staff in the late nineteenth century: twenty five of the fifty six staff whom he appointed had Cambridge degrees, whereas only ten were Oxford graduates. The School was now able to retain such well qualified men: thirty eight of the staff who were appointed between 1922 and 1939, when the demands of war service necessitated a series of short-term appointments, served for more than ten years at the School, and twenty one of these men were still in service when Mr Thomas retired.

Some of the staff whom Mr Thomas appointed were men of a distinction and a richness of experience unusual in the earlier history of the School. The Theakstone brothers Anatole and Louis, for instance, who were appointed in 1925 and 1931 respectively, had been brought up in St Petersburg and had begun courses at Moscow University before the Revolution, whereupon they came to Scotland and took degrees at the University of Edinburgh. Anatole Theakstone remained at RGS for the rest of his career, becoming head of the modern languages department and introducing the teaching of Russian in the sixth form in 1954. His brother, who taught mathematics, acted as an interpreter for the western powers at the Yalta conference in 1945. His departure to be head of mathematics at Gateshead Grammar School in 1954 was a surprise, and a blow to the School. Max Black, who joined the mathematics department in 1931, had taken his degree at Queens' College Cambridge in 1930 and had then undertaken research in mathematics at Göttingen University. In 1933 he published a book entitled *The Nature of Mathematics*[35] in which he examined and criticised the more important mathematical theories of his contemporaries, notably Russell and Whitehead. In 1936 he was appointed a lecturer at London University Institute of Education, and after 1940 spent the rest of his career in the United States, becoming Professor of Philosophy first at the University of Illinois and then at Cornell University. A. R. Laws is best remembered as the author of *Schola Novocastrensis*, discussed below, but he shared with Sydney Bowie, who taught science at the School from 1918 until his sudden death in 1924, an interest in the measurement and testing of intelligence. Laws and Bowie received advice and encouragement from Godfrey Thomson, whose own work on intelligence testing was appearing in print in the early 1920s, and in 1921 they administered American Army intelligence tests to a group of seventy boys in the lower fifth and fourth forms. The results, which were published in the *British Journal of Psychology*,[36] suggested that there was a substantial number of boys, particularly the older ones, of only limited ability: a conclusion which perhaps should occasion little surprise in view of the HMIs' critical observations on the School some years earlier.

A. A. le M. Simpson, a graduate of New College Oxford who joined the staff in 1929 as head of the English department, published two volumes of his own poetry and edited a number of text books, including the widely used anthology of verse for schoolchildren, *Young Pegasus*. At RGS, he was perhaps most celebrated for his translation of Aeschylus' *Agamemnon*, which was performed in December 1932 and which was the first really distinguished production at the School. Simpson's successor as head of the English department, M. G. Robinson, who was appointed in 1934, was the first member of staff on the arts side to have a research degree, and he brought to the teaching of English a particularly fine sensibility.

Perhaps the most outstanding of those whom Thomas appointed between 1922 and 1939 was W. E. Roberts, better known as Michael Roberts.[37] Roberts graduated in chemistry from King's College London in 1922, and then went to Trinity College Cambridge to read for a second first degree in mathematics. At Cambridge his interests became as much literary and political as scientific: he read much modern literature, became involved in a play-reading society, and was elected vice-president of the university socialist society. He also did some work for the Cambridge branch of the Communist Party. The story of his appointment as physics master at RGS, on the strength of a two hour interview which was concerned mainly with Elizabethan poetry, has been told in print before. Mr Thomas had been warned that he was 'distinctly left wing,' and his unconventional appearance and conversation were regarded as shocking or stimulating at RGS, depending on one's point of view. He continued his political activity when he came to Newcastle and was appointed to the district committee of the Communist Party, with responsibility for the Agit.-Prop. Department. He also spent much time writing, but neither a lengthy novel nor *Critique of Poetry*, a critical study which owed much to I. A. Richards and Robert Graves, yet found a publisher, though in 1930 he published a small volume of poems, *These Our Matins*. His most important poetry, however, did not appear until the later 1930s.

At school he was both a stimulating and an exasperating teacher: a remarkably frank appreciation of him, published in the *Novo* when he left RGS, temporarily as it turned out, in 1931 said of him that 'no one can be so annoying, no one delights in being so

annoying – yet no one has had a more electric effect on the school.'
The anonymous author concluded: 'I pity his new colleagues. But
justice must be done. However much we may have resented it he
has forced us all to see clearly, think clearly, speak clearly: hauled
us by the scruff of our necks from the seventies into 1931.' His new
colleagues at Mercers' School in London proved much less
sympathetic to him than either the *Novo*'s correspondent or his
colleagues at RGS. His outspoken and irreverent style, and his left
wing politics, soon got him into trouble, and he was dismissed
from his post in February 1934, in the middle of term. Mr Thomas
had in all probability kept in touch with him while he was in
London, for they were working together on *Newton and the Origin
of Colours*, and he had no doubts at all about his worth as a man
and a schoolmaster. After he was dismissed, Mr Thomas offered
him a job immediately, teaching Latin and geography; but in the
event he took a short-term post more suited to his experience, and
returned to RGS in September 1934 to teach mathematics, physics
and English.

The impact Michael Roberts made on his pupils at RGS is
described elsewhere by William Lough;[38] but he also made a vital
contribution outside the classroom. He had always been an
enthusiast for camping and mountaineering, and together with
R. F. I. Bunn and T. T. Anderson he played a leading part in the
development of school camps, discussed more fully below.[39] In
1941 he moved to London to undertake war work with the
European service of the BBC, and in December 1944, as the war
was drawing to its close, he was appointed Principal of the
College of St Mark and St John, a teachers' training college then at
Chelsea. In December 1948 he died of monocytic leukaemia. He
was perhaps the most distinguished person to teach at RGS in this
century: he was a man with a remarkably broad range of interests
and the ability to stimulate and inspire enthusiasm in his better
pupils, stretching and challenging them and irritating them as well.
During his service at RGS he pursued an increasingly successful
literary career, and, as with many of his generation, his enthusiasm
for communism faded and he became more sympathetic and
receptive to religious ideas. To those he taught, his distinctive
contribution, apart from his enthusiasm for outdoor activities, was
his familiarity with both the world of literature and the world of
science and his understanding of the tension between the language
of science and the language of poetry. As he said in his

introduction to *Elizabethan Prose*, 'The poet is constantly at war with the scientist; his sensibility perceives similarities where the instruments of the scientist (always visual and tactile) detected differences . . . and language in the course of the struggle becomes more and more complex.'[40] He had no time for the extreme claims either of the scientist or the literary critic; neither alone could provide a full understanding of experience, but together they could advance a student's appreciation of the world.

Mr Thomas's judgement, and his appreciation of qualities in a man which went beyond his political associations, were seen at their best in his decision to re-employ Michael Roberts in 1934; but Mr Thomas was also at pains to maintain the loyalty and morale of all his staff in the difficult circumstances created by the recommendation of the Committee on National Expenditure in July 1931 that teachers' salaries should be reduced by 20%. The Labour cabinet under Ramsay MacDonald agreed to a cut of only 16%, and after the formation of the National Government in August 1931 the cabinet agreed that the cut should be only 15%. Circular 1413, issued on 11 September 1931, set out the government's intention. At this stage, Mr Thomas hoped to protect the staff of the RGS from the full impact of the cut, and he proposed that their salaries should be reduced by only 10%. After protests by the teachers nationally, and within a week of the Invergordon mutiny, the cabinet backed down on its proposal to reduce the salaries of both teachers and servicemen; and on 21 September 1931 the government announced that teachers' salaries would be cut by only 10%. Mr Thomas still hoped to impose a smaller reduction at RGS, but he came into conflict with Sir George Lunn, a Governor and Chairman of Newcastle Education Committee, who was said to be 'out for the full 10% reduction of salary for all masters,' on the ground that the staff of the RGS should not be treated differently from teachers employed by the authority of which he was Chairman.[41]

In the early stages of the argument Mr Thomas carried the Governors with him, and at their meeting in October 1931 they agreed by eleven votes to four that salaries should be reduced by only 5%. Lunn was furious: he 'left the meeting breathing fire and slaughter and vowing that he would take steps to bring the Governors into line.'[42] The majority of the Governors believed that a reduction of 5% was sufficient to compensate for the reduction in the Board's capitation grant from £9 to £7 12s 6d that formed part of the national economy measures, but Lunn argued that if the full 10% cut were applied the additional sum saved might be used to provide more free places, scholarships and maintenance grants. Lunn resigned from the Governors, and made representations to the Board of Education about the issue; the Board, displaying its usual sensitivity to the opinions of powerful figures in local educational politics, took his side. The Board even went so far as to suggest, in an internal minute, that 'it is necessary to consider whether the Board should not take action in regard to the suitability of the School to earn grant . . . The connection of Lunn with the Burnham Committee [he was a member] does rather pick the School out and raise the question of special rules.' The high fees charged by the School still rankled with the Board: 'We do not care very much about having such high fee schools as this on the grant list,' and the Board recalled that it had agreed to a lower free-place requirement partly on the grounds of the School's difficult financial circumstances. The School could not, in the Board's view, at one and the same time claim special treatment over free places on grounds of poverty and, in effect, pay its staff above Burnham rates; and in any case, the School had undertaken not to exceed Burnham rates when the Board approved the increase in fees in 1921.

The Board had already decided that any grant-aided school which did not reduce teachers' salaries to the full extent would have its grant reduced *pro rata*, but in January 1932 the Clerk to the Governors met the Board to urge the view of the majority of the Governors that the full cut should not be enforced at RGS. The Clerk explained that the Headmaster felt that in recruiting staff he was 'in competition with other schools of a quasi-public school character, some of which paid above Burnham salaries, and that he could not hope to compete successfully with such schools if a 10% reduction of salaries were made.' The Clerk also voiced his suspicion that the Board's decision to reduce grant if the School failed to implement the full reduction was the result of Lunn's machinations, but he received an assurance – which was surely correct – that this was not so. However, faced with the threat of losing grant, the Governors capitulated, and the full reduction was implemented retrospectively from 1 December 1931. The Board's insistence on some measure of retrospection undoubtedly caused hardship for the staff, but Mr Thomas received some recognition when they presented him with a formal written address thanking him for his efforts on their behalf.[43] The episode has, however, significance beyond the immediate issue of the reduction of salaries. It revealed the tension between the School's aspiration to a status where it could compete with public schools in recruiting staff and charge high fees while still attracting large numbers of able boys, and its dependence on Board of Education grants and the Board's reluctant acquiescence in the School's continued exemption from the 25% free-place rule. The policy of raising the status of the School, which had been implemented so successfully since 1922, entailed taking some risks in its relationship with the Board of Education.

(iii) *Outside the Classroom*

Mr Thomas's concern to develop the academic work of the School was accompanied by an equally significant emphasis on the 'social training,'[44] as he termed it, of each of his pupils. This was best accomplished, in his view, by extensive participation in extra-curricular activities and by taking lunch at school. The large family of the Victorian era, he argued, had been capable of providing shared activities and some measure of social training within itself, but the trend in the 1920s and 1930s towards much smaller families meant that these functions had to be performed by the School if they were to be performed at all.[45] Mr Thomas's educational philosophy, as it developed in the late 1920s and early 1930s, thus laid great stress on the virtues of leisure hour activities and the practice of taking lunch in common at school. In 1936 the HMIs observed that these aspects of school life had been developed to a wholly exceptional degree, and Mr Thomas himself suggested in 1930 that 'The boy who can find no help from school in any of his hobbies must be both amazingly fortunate in his home surroundings and of a singularly unsociable disposition. The opportunity which these school activities offer will never recur in the boy's life; it will never be so easy for him to pass through the initial stages of acquiring skill in any of those accomplishments.'[46] This emphasis on the value of leisure time activities at school was very widely accepted, by boys, parents and staff; and it has done much to shape the character of the School ever since, surviving even the social and generational conflicts of the 1960s.

To those familiar with the tradition of residential universities, the belief that dining in common is an essential part of community life, and provides some social training for young adults, is commonplace enough; but it had never been widely accepted at day schools, and at RGS in the late 1920s Mr Thomas's zeal to encourage boys to lunch at school was novel and was treated initially with some suspicion and scepticism, particularly by the Governors, who saw school lunch as a financial liability. During the years when the School was at Rye Hill only one third of the boys lunched at school, and even after the move to Jesmond lunch was provided only for those boys who came to school by train or tram from more distant parts of Newcastle or Tyneside. For Mr Thomas, however, lunch was not just a matter of convenience: its importance as a means of social training meant that all boys should be encouraged to stay at school for lunch, even if they lived only a few minutes' walk away in Jesmond, and by staying for lunch they would also have the opportunity to take part in some useful leisure hour activity. The Governors had doubts about the wisdom of providing lunch on such a large scale, not least on financial grounds. Mr Beckingham, the Vice-Chairman of the Governors, believed that when it began it was 'a certain source of loss,' and the Governors reluctantly approved the scheme on condition that the Headmaster covered the loss. In fact, school lunches made a healthy surplus throughout the 1930s, and Mr Thomas gained considerable satisfaction from the steady increase in the number of boys taking lunch. In 1936 the HMIs observed that some 400 boys took 'the excellent school lunch in very attractive surroundings' in three sittings.[47]

By staying at school for lunch, boys were able to join in the various extra-curricular activities that developed so extensively from the later 1920s onwards. In 1922 the School had little to offer boys except the debating society, the photographic society, and sport, mainly rugby and cricket. Music was scarcely developed at all, and the inspectors in 1926 severely criticised the low level of musical activity.[48] 'Music does not occupy a worthy position in the curriculum or practice of the School,' they complained, and they recommended that the subject 'should be much developed and brought into much greater prominence in the life of the School.' In the following year the Inspector of Music noted some improvement:[49] a newly appointed visiting master had, 'with the backing of the Headmaster . . . already accomplished a great deal towards putting the subject on a proper foundation.' An orchestra had been established, and the JTC apparently marched to the Northumbrian pipes played by boys! But the Inspector regretted the lack of class teaching in music above form III, and recommended that class work should be carried right up the School.

The Inspector's advice about the development of music soon bore fruit. In September 1927 Mr Thomas appointed as Director of Music Arthur Milner, a former pupil of Dame Allan's School who became an ARCO in 1913 and an ARCM in 1915; he came to RGS after experience as a Lecturer in Music at Armstrong College and at Lemington Adult School. He was a man of great drive and energy who, with the Headmaster's enthusiastic support, soon transformed school music: little more than a year after his appointment the *Novo* declared that 'he is entirely changing the character of our music.'[50] The orchestra which had been formed, in a somewhat tentative manner, in the year before Milner's appointment, grew in size and technical accomplishment, and in 1930 a second orchestra was established, to be followed in 1936 by the third orchestra. The number of boys playing an orchestral instrument rose from 10 in 1929 to 74 in 1936, and visiting teachers were recruited to provide instrumental tuition. The Governors gave their support by authorising the purchase of instruments which were then loaned to boys, and they also provided funds for the purchase of a grand piano. The Headmaster himself played in the school orchestra, and his example encouraged a number of other members of staff to follow his example, so that by 1936 the first orchestra had acquired the character of a joint staff-pupil orchestra which it has retained ever since. At the general inspection in 1936 the HMIs reported on school music with great enthusiasm: 'There must be few schools in the country (even the largest) which can boast of having three orchestras, but such is the stimulus and inspiration of the Headmaster's leadership in music that his ambition to have every boy in the school learning an orchestral instrument is on the way to becoming realised';[51] this was an exaggeration, but it was understandable in the light of the enormous progress made since the HMIs' report ten years earlier. Mr Thomas was himself an accomplished 'cellist, and he believed that learning to play an orchestral instrument was one of the best hobbies available to all except those who had no ear at all for music and no sense of rhythm. He believed that playing an instrument not only taught a boy to master technical skills, but also provided him, when he played in an orchestra, with valuable social training. In a broadcast talk entitled 'Outside the Classroom', delivered in November 1934 and subsequently published in *The Listener*,[52] he argued that 'playing in an orchestra can give just as good training in what is known as the "team Spirit" as any game that I know.' The philistine assumption common to many public schools that team games possessed unique character-building virtues had no place in Mr Thomas's educational philosophy, and although the two most important team games at RGS, Rugby football and cricket, were well supported and successful, they do not seem to have received quite the same degree of encouragement from the Headmaster as music, drama and other outdoor activities, above all school camps.

School drama was perhaps slower to develop than school music, partly because of the inadequate facilites for performance until the building of the School theatre in 1930. When A. A. le M. Simpson joined the staff in 1929 he founded the XXI Club, which began as a society limited to twenty one members and concerned with play reading rather than production. Such productions as there were took place in the School dining hall, which was obviously an inappropriate venue for most plays, but with the opening of the School theatre there was a burgeoning of dramatic activity in all parts of the School, notably amongst the modern linguists, who established a tradition of producing plays in French and German which has continued until the present day. Perhaps the most notable production in these years, however, was Aeschylus' *Agamemnon*, produced in the school hall - a suitable venue for classical if not for modern drama – in December 1932. This production illustrated the development of the musical and artistic, as well as the dramatic life of the School over the previous seven years. The translation was the work of A. A. le M. Simpson, the music the work of Arthur Milner, and the scenery was designed and painted by boys and members of staff. As Mr. Thomas himself remarked, 'everyone connected with the play worked in such a way as to produce a remarkable effect of unified effort.'[53]

Of all the school's extra-curricular activities the establishment of school camps has generally been seen as the most significant, and as contributing decisively to the distinctive pattern of life at the RGS over the past half century. The initiative in establishing school camps came in 1926 from two newly appointed members of staff, Michael Roberts and R. F. I. Bunn. While an undergraduate Michael Roberts had undertaken an extensive walking tour in France and Switzerland, and was to develop into an accomplished mountaineer. In the summer term of 1926 the two men, with the enthusiastic support of the Headmaster, took a party of boys to camp at Dipton Mill near Hexham over a very wet Whit weekend. The experiment was highly successful: weekend camps were soon held regularly at Dipton Mill, and at Race Week in the same summer (the last full week in June, and a holiday in Newcastle schools until the late 1950s) Michael Roberts took a party of boys to the Lake District. A full week's camping provided a much better opportunity for the boys to explore the countyside in which they were staying, and over the next four years other Race Week camps were established elsewhere in the Lake District, in the Yorkshire dales, and at Stratford upon Avon. The Race Week camps had become an institution.[54]

Michael Roberts also had ambitions to take the boys abroad, and in 1930 he led a party to the Jura, on a much more adventurous programme than anything that boys had attempted at Race Week camps in England. After his return to Newcastle he took parties on even more demanding mountaineering expeditions to the Alps, and set a pace which astonished, and exhausted, many of those who went with him. Michael Roberts' own enthusiasm and leadership made such expeditions possible, and they were not resumed after the war; but other members of staff, especially Bunn and T. T. Anderson, did quite as much as Roberts to ensure the establishment of the camps as an integral part of school life. The Headmaster's own enthusiasm was not in doubt: in his broadcast talk in 1934 he argued that the school camps offered another opportunity for social training, and observed that 'Camp life seems to be able to offer certain boys unique opportunities for development. Time and time again I have found that boys who were of very little importance in the School, often dull and backward, even in the lowest form for their age, who did not shine at games, turned out to be leaders in camp, and thereby gained a sense of achievement and an increased self respect which has been of the very greatest value in their development, and did undoubtedly, within such powers as they had, improve their work in the School.'[55] The range of school camps, and their popularity with the boys, may have been exceptional, but here, as in many other respects, the Headmaster and his staff were working with the grain of public opinion, which had the examples of the Duke of York's summer camps and the permanent camps established by other schools to reinforce the virtues and the acceptability of the RGS camps.

(iv) *Building Development*

As the School grew rapidly in size in the years after 1922, and leisure hour activities assumed an increasingly important place in the life of the School, so it became obvious that the 1906 buildings were inadequate to cope with the expansion in numbers and activities. The need for some extension to the buildings had become apparent by 1925, and the Inspectors in 1926 recommended alterations and additions that would provide more changing room accommodation, better library facilities, and a new art room. The new changing rooms were provided immediately: they cost a total of £2449 11s 0d, and were paid for out of income.[56] There was little prospect, however, of the School being able to finance more extensive alterations and additions solely out of income or capital, since the School's investments, before the Act of 1927, amounted to little more than £12,000. The substantial development that the School needed was made possible in large part through the generosity of Sir Arthur Munro Sutherland. Sir Arthur had given a rifle range to the School in 1915, and in 1922 he presented the School with the War Memorial Organ, which transformed the appearance of the school hall and formed a fitting memorial to all those former pupils of the School who had given their lives in the war. The Memorial was dedicated in a moving ceremony on 1 June 1923 and the occasion was marked by the publication of a book in which the names of all the fallen were inscribed.[57]

In 1929 Sir Arthur became Chairman of the Governors, and within a few months of his appointment he announced his intention of presenting a swimming bath to the School. At the same time the Governors undertook the provision of a new art room, a new music room, a theatre, and alterations to the science block. The art room and the theatre were built on top of the single storey pavilions at the north and south ends respectively of the 1906 building; the alterations to the science block were internal, to provide laboratories suitable for the more advanced work in science which the School was undertaking. The total cost of these alterations and extensions was over £12,000, one third of which was met by liquidating investments purchased with surplus income from the Virgin Mary Trust.[58] In 1931, after this work was completed, the old art room at the north east corner of the main school building was converted into a new library and reading room, and once again the School found amongst its former pupils a generous benefactor, Sir William (soon to be Lord) Plender, who provided the oak panelling, bookcases, tables and chairs to furnish the library which thenceforward bore his name.[59] William Plender had attended the school for only a year, between 1875 and 1876; he qualified as a chartered accountant, and had a long career as an adviser to government on matters ranging from railways to national insurance and company law. He was knighted in 1911, created a baronet in 1923, and raised to the peerage in 1931. Unlike Sir Arthur Sutherland, however, he did not retain close links with Tyneside: indeed his career would probably have precluded it. He lived in Kent and was President of Kent County Cricket Club. His benefaction to the School was, of course, less substantial than those of Sir Arthur Sutherland, but in one respect it was perhaps more significant: Plender made his career away from Tyneside, in a manner more characteristic of former pupils in the twentieth century who have migrated to London to practise their profession; but such was the standing of his old school by 1931 that he was willing to endow it not just with the furnishings of its new library but also with a history prize and a leaving exhibition.

The Sutherland swimming bath was handed over to the school in May 1930[60], and swimming became not only an important school sport, but also a skill which every boy now had the opportunity to acquire. No sooner had this been completed than work began on the construction of a new building for woodwork, metalwork, geography and biology. This building, situated on the southern perimeter of the playing field, was to be the main casualty of the motorway construction in the 1970s. Although awkwardly sited in relation to the rest of the School, it provided badly needed accommodation for two subjects that had been unduly cramped in their previous quarters in the science block; while the metalwork rooms incorporated facilities for technical drawing which benefited those sixth formers taking the first year engineering examination of Durham University at school.

The great increase in the number of boys taking lunch at school created pressure on the existing dining hall accommodation, and in 1933 the dining hall was enlarged and the kitchens were entirely re-equipped. At the same time the Governors took the opportunity to begin the process of separating the Junior School from the main body of the School by building three classrooms and a hall above the newly enlarged dining hall on its western side. The alterations were paid for by liquidating investments.[61]

The additions and alterations undertaken between 1929 and 1933 eased the pressure on accommodation and provided much more satisfactory facilities for the library, for art, and for the burgeoning musical life of the school. In 1936 the HMIs congratulated the

Governors on what they had achieved so far, but recommended yet more improvements. They reported that the buildings 'cannot yet be considered adequate to the needs of such a large and important school as RGS,' and they suggested a whole series of developments, including the provision of two new gymnasia, the housing of the Junior School entirely in one block, more music practice rooms, and more classroom accommodation, which they considered barely adequate. They also advised the School to enlarge its playing field accommodation by exercising the option to purchase the eight acre field at Benton which they leased from Sir Arthur Sutherland's firm, B. J. Sutherland & Sons.[62] By good fortune, the general inspection in May 1936 was followed two months later by the conferment of the freedom of the City of Newcastle on Sir Arthur, and the Inspectors' comments were fresh in his mind. In his address on that occasion, which was published and presented to the boys of the RGS by 'one of Sir Arthur's old friends,' he declared that he would 'like to do something' for this old school. In characteristically blunt style, he went on, 'We have recently had Board of Education Inspectors going through the School, and I am glad they have given a very good report . . . They say they have one of the best swimming baths they have ever seen, and that is a great satisfaction to me. They are also pleased with the buildings, but they want a better gymnasium and say the masters want a better room. They also thought that new rooms should be built for the Junior School. It is all very well saying these things are needed. If I went to the Governors for £10,000 to pay for these, I am afraid Mr. Beckingham and Sir George Lunn and Sir Arthur Lambert would hold up their hands in righteous horror and say "We haven't got the money." Well, if they haven't got the money, I have.'[63] In just under a year, all the new buildings which the Inspectors had suggested and which Sir Arthur had promised to finance were completed: the double gymnasium, a reorganisation of office and classroom space to provide a large staff common room behind the organ, together with new classrooms and a new entrance for the Junior School which enabled it to become a self-contained entity within the School until its move to quite separate buildings in 1972. The new work cost £12,000 rather than the £10,000 which Sir Arthur had envisaged, but he paid for it in full.

The School by now had adequate buildings and facilities, but it would be wrong to suppose that even after the extensive additions undertaken in 1930–31 and 1936–37 the School was lavishly provided for. Classroom and playing field accommodation in particular remained a problem: no further alterations or additions were undertaken at the school before the war, and in the 1950s the problem of overcrowding again became a matter of concern to the Governors.[64] In 1938, the Governors began negotiations to exercise their option to purchase the Benton playing field from B. J. Sutherland & Sons. The purchase price was £10,000, and the Governors proposed to raise a mortgage to finance it. The Chairman of the Finance Committee of the Governors, Mr Beckingham, expressed some doubt about whether the Governors could raise a mortgage for so large a sum, and advised them that they might have to 'draw on their holding of War Stock for the balance.' The Governors began negotiations with an insurance company to raise a mortgage of £10,000, but the negotiations foundered on the question of the personal liability of the Governors for the repayment of the loan. Mr Beckingham argued that the Governors acted as quasi-trustees, and could not accept personal liability. He drafted a rider to the proposed deed of mortgage, excluding any personal liability on the part of the Governors, but the rider was evidently unacceptable to the insurance company and the negotiations were abandoned. Sir Arthur Sutherland now offered to lend the Governors £8,000 at 4% towards the purchase of the playing field. The Governors gratefully accepted this solution to their dilemma, and agreed to find the balance of the purchase price by selling investments.[65] The transaction was completed, and for the next forty-five years Sutherland Park proved a useful addition to the School's outdoor facilities. At Sir Arthur's death in 1953 his Executors demanded the repayment of the mortgage so that they could pay Estate Duty.

(v) *The Wartime Evacuation*[66]

The purchase of Sutherland Park proved to be the last important development undertaken by the Governors before the outbreak of war in 1939. As Donald Shipley shows later,[67] the Governors had been contemplating since February 1939 the possibility of evacuating the School in accordance with the Government's voluntary scheme to move schools out of danger areas, and when war was declared on 3 September the school moved to its pre-arranged quarters in Penrith. In the forty years that have passed since the end of the war, the success of the evacuation has come to assume an important place in the tradition and the corporate consciousness of the School, but such success could by no means be taken for granted in 1939. The danger which such disruption presented to the maintenance of the School's integrity, its solvency, and its relations with parents should not be underestimated, and some schools suffered irreparable damage as a result of evacuation. The Headmaster saw from the outset that it was vitally important for the School to make a success of evacuation. He described the decision of Dame Allan's School, evacuated to Wigton in Cumberland, to return to Newcastle in February 1940 as 'a great pity', and he sought to reassure parents of RGS boys that the School had 'over six hundred boys happily billeted at Penrith with practically full-time education.'[68] Mr Thomas was determined that the School should not be defeated by the challenge it now faced, and he used all his very considerable personal authority – and for a time some of his own money – to ensure that the School held together in evacuation.

It was by no means obvious in the spring and summer of 1939 that the Governors or the parents shared the Headmaster's belief that the School should co-operate with the Government's voluntary evacuation scheme, and even when evacuation was an accomplished fact friction arose between the Headmaster and the Governors over the extent of the Governors' financial responsibility for the School in evacuation, while the resolution of this difficulty brought with it another, in the form of local education authority involvement in the control and finance of the hostels for the boys at Penrith.

At an early stage in the discussions about the possibility of evacuation the Governors expressed their misgivings. In February 1939 the House Committee reminded the Governors that the School had no funds to defray the costs of evacuation, and warned that parents might not be willing to co-operate with an evacuation or pay the increased fees that might result.[69] The Governors accepted the evacuation when it took place but distanced themselves from it for a time, partly to avoid financial responsibility, but partly because of a feeling that control over their school was being taken out of their hands. As Sir Arthur Sutherland put it in March 1940, 'the Governors have nothing whatever to do with taking the boys to Penrith,' and he reiterated the point in a letter to the Headmaster in July 1940, adding that the boys 'were taken away from their homes by an Authority who have power to do so.'[70]

In the summer of 1940 a difficulty arose between the Headmaster and the Governors over the question of the payment by the Governors of maintenance allowances to boys whose parents could not afford to supplement the billeting allowances paid by the Ministry of Health. The disagreement was apparently over the degree of financial responsibility the Governors should take for the School in evacuation, but it may have had as its underlying cause a difference of opinion between the Headmaster and some of the Governors about the advisability of evacuation.[71] By February 1940 the Headmaster had started to pay small supplementary billeting allowances to some boys out of his own pocket, and from this grew his idea for a billeting fund or 'Sponsor Fund' out of which the Governors would assist boys whose parents had limited financial resources. Initially the Headmaster was reimbursed by the Governors on an *ad hoc* basis for his out-of-pocket payments to needy boys, but when he wrote to the Clerk to the Governors in early March 1940 asking for a cheque for £30 towards the Sponsor Fund, the Clerk raised objections. He replied to the Headmaster saying that 'both Sir Arthur and Mr Beckingham are "dead against" our contributing anything towards the billeting expenses of the boys beyond the £20 already sent you (in February), which was paid mainly in order that you might reimburse yourself for the money you personally paid. It was never intended to create anything in the nature of a permanent Fund, and there are obvious objections to doing so.' Mr Thomas argued, however, that the Governors had the power to pay maintenance allowances under the Regulations for Secondary Schools, and that the Government hoped that such allowances would be paid. By now he was considerably out of pocket, but the Clerk to the Governors was unsympathetic to his difficulties: writing to Mr Beckingham, the Chairman of the Finance Committee, he observed 'He (i.e. Thomas) states that he is considerably out of pocket himself. This goes to the root of the matter, because Mr Thomas chooses to take upon himself to make these payments, relying on getting recoupment afterwards, which is a very easy way out for him.' Faced with the reluctance of the Governors to establish a sponsor fund, Mr Thomas turned to the Board of Education in the hope that they would welcome the idea and that their approval would persuade the Governors to change their minds. The Board's initial response gave Thomas grounds for optimism, and he communicated this to the Clerk, who in turn informed Sir Arthur Sutherland. In a revealing comment, Sir Arthur expostulated: 'Why should we give money to a Sponsor Fund? What does it do for us? I think we give enough away in *Free Places* and should therefore curtail, as much as possible, our funds for our own school and its facilities.' His sense of detachment from the School in Penrith could hardly have been more vividly conveyed.

Mr Thomas's optimism proved to have been misplaced. The Board of Education declined to give official approval to the proposal to award maintenance allowances, on the ground that the allowances laid down by the Ministry of Health had to be regarded, by another government department at least, as adequate to meet the cost of billeting. But the local HMI pointed out that under the School's scheme of government, which she had asked to see, the Governors were in any case empowered to award maintenance allowances up to £10 per annum for each boy in need, and this point was conveyed to the Governors. Although Sir Arthur Sutherland and Mr Beckingham were still unhappy about the proposal to pay allowances, the Headmaster had some support amongst the other Governors, and in July 1940 the Finance Committee recommended that the Governors should make such payments, and that the Headmaster should be reimbursed for all his out of pocket expenses.[72] Payments continued to be made until the School returned to Newcastle.

The problem of maintenance allowances was soon, however, to be overtaken by events. By the autumn of 1940 many boys were accommodated in hostels rather than in private billets, and in the previous May responsibility for such hostels had been transferred from the Ministry of Health to the Board of Education.[73] The Board introduced a scheme under which schools could apply to the Board for grants to cover the costs of running hostels for evacuated children, though the grants were to be administered by local education authorities, who would assume control of the hostels. The scheme seemed at first glance to be an admirable solution to the financial problems faced by the School, but the Headmaster's initial reaction was cautious. After his difficulties with some of the Governors over maintenance allowances, he feared that the Governors would still wish to keep their distance from the evacuation and would not be willing to apply for such grants; he even suggested to the Clerk to the Governors that 'the best thing to do is to go ahead with the idea without worrying Sir Arthur about it at all officially.' But the Clerk hastened to reassure the Headmaster that the Governors were quite happy to accept responsibility for the evacuation and apply for a grant since it would be financed by the government: their earlier concern had

208

been about the extent of their own financial responsibility for the school at Penrith.

The Headmaster was also concerned about the implications for the School of receiving a grant via the local education authority. Both he and the Governors were reluctant to yield any control to the local education authority, 'as once they get a grip, so to speak, it is difficult to shake them off.' He hoped the Board of Education would understand the School's wish to retain its independence, and he proposed that the School should receive direct grant from the Board to finance the hostels. Mr Thomas's fears about local authority control were understandable, though it is doubtful whether the local authority would ever have attempted to maintain control over the School once the emergency was over and the school had moved back to Newcastle. The Board, however, proved unsympathetic to the direct grant proposal, and insisted that the grant should be channelled through the local authority. The Headmaster and Governors felt that they had no alternative but to agree to this, and Newcastle Education Committee therefore took over full financial and administrative responsibility for the hostels from 1 January 1941. The arrangement worked well for the remaining years of the evacuation, and the fears of the Headmaster and the Governors about local authority control proved groundless. When the School returned to Jesmond in September 1944 local authority involvement in its finances ceased.

Despite the financial difficulties of the first fifteen months of evacuation, the Headmaster achieved his object of holding the school together, and he fully deserves the credit he was given both at the time and subsequently for maintaining the integrity of the school in circumstances which proved too much for some of his contemporaries in other schools. The success of the evacuation crowned an outstanding career and the sense of community, status and pride which he had encouraged in the School before the war undoubtedly helped to sustain it during the years of evacuation. Although, as we have seen, Mr Thomas was developing the school at a time when both public opinion and national policy were sympathetic to the extension of secondary education and were particularly aware of the value of sixth form work and success in public examinations, the distinctive character that the School acquired after 1922 was in large part his own creation, helped by an able and sometimes distinguished group of colleagues on the teaching staff. He gave the School more than academic standing and a reputation for encouraging a very wide range of extra-curricular activities. He also enhanced its national standing, and encouraged a sense of pride in its past. In 1925, to mark the fourth centenary of Thomas Horsley's will, a ceremony was held in the School hall at which portraits of Lord Eldon and Lord Stowell were presented to the school, and the President of the Board of Education, Lord Eustace Percy, whose father had opened the School buildings in 1907, addressed the School on the part played in the history of education by the old grammar schools of England and the role of the state in trying to foster and maintain the ideal of the old grammar schools in the twentieth century: an apposite theme for a school celebrating its fourth centenary yet dependent for part of its income on state support.[74] Another, more enduring achievement in 1925 was the publication of the first volume of the most detailed history of the School to appear so far, *Schola Novocastrensis* by A. R. Laws, a work which unfortunately remained unfinished but which brought together not only much material about the history of the School itself, but also biographical information about pupils who had attended the School from earliest times.[75] Laws had preceded his substantial history of the School with a much shorter account, written jointly with his colleague J. B. Brodie, author of the School song, and published in 1924.[76] This brief history was given to each boy on entry to the School, and thus brought some understanding of the history of the School within the reach of every pupil. By coincidence, the publication of the short history took place at the same time as the presentation to the School of two pillars which were the last surviving remnants of the medieval hospital building which had housed the school in the seventeenth and eighteenth centuries, and, as the Headmaster remarked, their presence outside the Jesmond building would 'serve to remind many generations of boys that they are members of a School with a distinguished history and great traditions.'[77]

Some other developments were of a more symbolic character but were nevertheless intended to reinforce the School's sense of status and pride. In 1930 the coat of arms which the School had used since the nineteenth century, and which symbolised both the royal and civic associations of the School, the arms of Queen Elizabeth I juxtaposed to the arms of the city, was replaced by the arms familiar today. The cost of obtaining the grant of arms was met by Sir Arthur Sutherland.[78] At the same time the names of the four houses were changed from Reds, Greens, Browns and Blues to Stowell, Collingwood, Eldon and Horsley, thereby establishing in the minds of the boys another link with the School's past. In the following year the motto 'Progrediendum Est' was dropped in favour of 'Discendo Duces.'[79] The emphasis on leadership may have been imitated from public schools, but the implication that education qualified one for leadership was likely to have been a rather more acceptable sentiment both to the Headmaster and to the School.

These developments and changes served to foster a corporate pride in the School and a sense that it had enjoyed a long and distinguished history: the rise in status which they demonstrated was a necessary and proper accompaniment to the School's growing academic success. But Mr Thomas was wise enough not to overestimate the importance of outward symbols. He appreciated that a day school in an industrial city could not flourish without the confidence of the parents who sent their sons there, and that this confidence would depend not just on the academic success of their sons, but also on co-operation and understanding between school and parents. There is little evidence that social conditions on Tyneside between the wars discouraged parents from sending their sons to the School or led them to withdraw their sons before the sixth form stage. In 1926 the HMIs had suggested that 'the prevailing trade depression' had restricted entry into the advanced course in mathematics and science; but the steady growth between 1926 and 1936 both in the size of the School and in the numbers taking advanced courses would seem to imply either that parents placed an increasing value on advanced education at a time of high unemployment or, more likely, that the School drew its pupils mainly from those parts of Tyneside where mass unemployment was not an immediate family experience. The School had never drawn many pupils from those districts most severely affected by the depression and even within Newcastle its pupils came mainly, though certainly not exclusively, from middle-class residential areas such as Jesmond, Fenham and Heaton. There was a slight increase between 1926 and 1936 in recruitment from Gosforth and the Coast, so that in 1936 only 47% of pupils came from Newcastle itself, whereas in 1926 the figure had been 52%; but this minor change is attributable to the development of middle-class housing outside the city boundary. The Headmaster was therefore working with parents who understood the value of sixth form work and expected good results, while at the same time they had the resources to fund their sons' school career to Higher School Certificate level and beyond.[80]

Parents' conferences were first held on an experimental basis in 1925, and their success encouraged the Headmaster to make them a regular part of the life of the School.[81] In 1929 he observed that holding parents' conferences each year over the past five years had 'shown an improvement in the measure of co-operation between parents and masters,' and by 1935 he had become much more positive about their value: 'In no other way,' he said, 'can parents gain so much knowledge of the organisation and of the working of the School; and the knowledge they gain is at least equalled by the assistance which they give to the masters in discussing in detail with them the problems and difficulties which their sons have in connection with their work at school.'[82] Mr Thomas went on to argue that the great advantage which a day school had over a boarding school, where of course he had spent the early part of his career, was that it allowed a boy to remain a member of his family and take advantage of all the opportunities offered by both family life and school life. The good relationship which Mr Thomas established with parents, and the positive manner in which he encouraged them to become involved with the school life of their sons, almost certainly played an important part in convincing parents that their sons would be in good hands during the evacuation.

The status and the achievements of the School in the years before the war are scarcely open to doubt; but in the last analysis Mr Thomas's concern was for the individual boy: indeed, the friction with the Governors in 1940 arose from his concern that a small number of poor boys should not be placed at a disadvantage or be compelled to withdraw from the School because of their parents' financial circumstances. He expected each boy to take full advantage of the opportunities both for academic work and for leisure time activities that the School offered, but the ultimate goal was not so much the prestige of the school – though this came in abundance – but the full development of the individual. In a letter he wrote to a friend and parent in January 1940 he succinctly summed up his own philosophy: 'I have a dictum which I am believing in more and more as the years go on. I believe that what is the best thing for any individual boy of the School . . . is, in the long run, the best thing for the School.'[83]

Chapter VI

POST-WAR ACHIEVEMENTS 1945–1960

(i) *The Government of the School*

The School returned from Penrith in time for the start of the autumn term in 1944; but well before this the Governors had turned their attention from the problems of evacuation and the arrangements for the re-occupation of the Eskdale Terrace buildings to the much broader question of the future of direct grant schools. With post-war reconstruction in mind, and with opinion running strongly in favour of the provision of free secondary education for all, the wartime coalition government had established the Fleming Committee in July 1942 to consider how 'the association between the Public Schools and the general educational system of the country could be developed and extended'.[1] While the Committee deliberated there was much speculation that it might recommend the ending of the direct grant system, and this speculation was reinforced when the Association of Directors of Education recommended that direct grant should be abolished and that 'all grant-aided schools should henceforth receive their grant from the local education authorities.'[2] The Governors of the Royal Grammar School were well aware of this current of feeling, and in 1943 the Finance Committee recommended that the Governors should apply for membership of the Governing Bodies Association: it was argued that this would be advantageous to the Governors 'in connection with the present proposals for State control of schools'. The Governors accepted the advice of the Finance Committee, and Mr Beckingham was appointed as the Governors' representative.[3]

In the event, the preliminary report of the Fleming Committee, published early in 1943, recommended the retention of the direct grant system, on the grounds that it was desirable to 'retain in our educational system a combination of initiative by the central and local authorities and traditional independence in the schools'.[4] The majority of the Committee, however, also recommended that tuition fees in direct grant schools should be abolished, and this proposal must have caused the Governors of the RGS some alarm. The final report of the Fleming Committee, published in 1944, recommended retention of the direct grant system, and also accepted the minority recommendation in the preliminary report that direct grant schools should continue to charge fees.[5] Before the final report was published, however, the President of the Board of Education, Mr R. A. Butler, had announced in the House of Commons on 19 January 1944: 'We intend to preserve tradition and variety and for that purpose to keep in existence a direct grant list.'[6] He made it clear that the list would be revised and that schools on the existing list would have to reapply for inclusion on the new list, but he also indicated that direct grant schools would retain the right to charge fees. This announcement came as some relief to the Governors of the RGS. At a special meeting held on 19 June 1945 they agreed to apply to continue to be recognised as a direct grant school, and at the same time they applied to increase fees from £30 p.a. to £42 p.a. Both applications were successful.[7]

The inclusion of the School on the new direct grant list did not, however, mean that it could continue in its pre-war state. Both the Education Act of 1944 and the Direct Grant School Regulations issued by the Ministry of Education in 1945 brought about a number of important changes in the character and in the financial position of the School, not all of which were immediately apparent. The 1944 Act abolished fees in maintained secondary schools altogether, and the direct grant schools were thus left as the only secondary schools in receipt of grant which were empowered to charge fees and which were free from control by the local education authorities. In the longer run, this position of isolation within the secondary school system was to be a source of weakness to the schools. The Direct Grant Regulations of 1945[8] laid down that schools in receipt of grant were obliged to offer 25% of their places free of charge, and the provision for exemption from this rule which had been contained in the pre-war regulations for secondary schools was dropped. The RGS thus had to raise the proportion of free places it offered from 10% to 25%, and this was achieved with only a brief transition period.[9] The regulations also allowed local eduction authorities to 'take up' (i.e. to pay for) these free places, and in order to reduce the burden of fees for parents of limited means a system of fee remission according to an income scale approved by the Ministry was introduced, paid for by government grant. If local education authorities could be persuaded to 'take up' all 25% of the free places, the School could thus receive full fee income for all its pupils, as indeed some direct grant schools, generously assisted by LEAs, had been able to do under the pre-war regulations. In the case of the RGS, however, it was ten years before the local education authorities could be persuaded to 'take up' free places at the School.

The result of the progressive increase in grants and of the eventual local education authority provision for free places is shown in the annual accounts of the School between 1948 and 1960.[10] In 1948 capitation grants amounted to £10,918 and grants in respect of fee remissions to £8340; while the fee income was only £17,553 and the cost of internal scholarships (i.e. free places under the direct grant regulations) met by the Governors stood at £6341. In 1960 the corresponding figures were: fee remissions £9132; capitation grant £44,063; fee income £56,737; and internal scholarships £13,768. It is important to note that the 1960 figure for fee income includes substantial but unspecified amounts paid that year by Northumberland and Newcastle Education Authorities in respect of free places; without that help the cost to the Governors of internal scholarships would have been very much higher, and they might have had difficulty finding the money. Thus in the post-war period income from grants and later from local education authorities exceeded that from fees paid by parents, a reversal of the pre-war position.

The Direct Grant Regulations of 1945 were remarkable for the scale on which they were intended to operate, for local education authorities were empowered to take up not only an initial 25% of free places, but also a further 25% of 'reserved' places. It is not known in how many schools this 50% free places scheme came into existence (it may have done so in some of the Roman Catholic direct grant schools), but it is significant as an attempt to associate the direct grant schools very closely with the maintained school system.

The Ministry of Education were well aware that the provision of free places was not easy for schools with small endowments; but they also pointed out that co-operation with local education authorities would help to solve the problem, and they consistently refused to permit an increase in fees in order to fund free places, since it was obviously wrong for the parents of some pupils to pay for the free places of others. Two other points are significant. One is that legislation in 1953 made it impossible for local education authorities to take advantage of the fee remission scheme in paying for free places;[11] the other is that when the Newcastle Education Committee were negotiating about free places with the Governors they proposed to cease to pay the £205 which had been the Corporation's contribution to the School from very early times, but the Governors pointed out that it was in the School's Scheme of Government which had the force of law.

The 1944 Act continued the provision of previous legislation that all grant-earning schools were to be inspected by His Majesty's Inspectors, who provided a further link between independent and maintained schools. The 1945 Regulations required direct grant schools to obtain approval from the Ministry for any extensions to school buildings, which had to comply with the building regulations, but they made no provision for capital expenditure, as they did for Voluntary Aided Schools. The schools had to provide milk and meals at prices approved by the Ministry, were required not to charge parents the fees for public examinations, to obtain the approval of the Ministry for increases in fees, to observe a consistent standard for all boys of similar ages in their entrance examinations and to arrange for one third of the Governors to be appointed by local authorities, though in the case of the RGS this condition had been more than observed in the Scheme of 1909.

The salaries of the teaching staff continued to be based on the national Burnham scales, increases in which were periodically negotiated. In order to meet these and other increases in their commitments, the Governors had from time to time to apply to the Ministry for permission to increase the fees.[12] The fees for the Senior School rose to £51 in 1951, £57 in 1954, £66 early in 1956 and £75 later the same year, while in 1960 they reached £81.[13] The difference between the Senior School fee and that charged for the Junior School gradually widened with the Junior School fee reaching £90 in late 1956 and £96 in 1960. These fees covered little more than 55% of the economic cost of a place at the School, the remainder being covered by the endowment and the grants from the Ministry of Education (which also covered the cost of internal scholarships). The Ministry had to examine the school accounts in detail and compare them with the accounts of other schools, and to consult local education authorities before agreeing to a proposed fee increase, and they often approved a lower increase than the Governors had applied for, because of course taxpayers' money was involved. The balance between the level of grant and the fees was therefore determined by the Ministry, who must share with the Governors the credit for keeping the School solvent.

In the 1950s, as a result of negotiations undertaken by the Headmaster and some of the Governors, some progress was made in persuading local education authorities to take up free places. In 1954 the Newcastle Education Committee appeared willing to co-operate if the Governors could arrange for additional city representatives on the Governing Body to be appointed by the Education Committee rather than the Schools and Charities Committee. The Governors pointed out that this would be inconsistent with the Scheme of 1909 and the negotiations broke down, some of the Governors, notably Sir Angus Watson, being anxious that control of the School should not fall into the hands of the city Education Committee.[14] It seems that the Education Committee still preserved School Board traditions and thought of themselves as a separate organisation for some purposes from the Corporation, although all their major policy proposals and their financial affairs had to be approved by the city Council. In 1955, however, a successful arrangement was made with the Northumberland Education Committee, who took up 6 places in that year, 16 in 1958 and as many as 26 by 1960.[15] Meanwhile after consultation between the Governors and the Ministry a further approach was made to the city, who agreed to be responsible for up to ten places, provided that the candidates had passed both the 11+ examination and the School's entrance examination, details of the procedure for which should be furnished to the Director of Education. The Governors had no objection to these conditions but only four boys appear to have been successful in the first year.[16] However, since about 30 free places had been taken up by 1959, and this constituted nearly 25% of the entry, the Headmaster and Governors had relieved the School of a substantial financial burden, though with the attendant risk of a change in policy which political developments might induce the authorities to make.

By comparison with the income derived from Ministry of Education grants, local authority free places, and fees paid by parents, the School's endowment income in the post-war period was of lesser significance. The agreement between the Trustees of the Virgin Mary Hospital and the Governors of the School about the distribution of the Trust's surplus income, which had been reached in 1939 and renewed in 1945, remained in force until 1978. By 1948 surplus income handed over to the Governors by the

217

Trustees had risen to £4758 and by 1960 to £8000,[17] pitifully small figures compared with income from other sources.

In adjusting to the educational changes of the post-war period, the School was guided by a body of Governors only slightly less distinguished than those of the pre-war years. Sir Arthur Sutherland continued as Chairman until his death in 1953, when his many benefactions to the School were recalled in a fulsome tribute in the *Novo*. He was succeeded by Dr Charles Bosanquet, D.C.L., M.A., Rector of King's College and Vice-Chancellor of the University of Durham, who was experienced in financial administration and who is still a landowner and farmer in Northumberland. Dr Bosanquet relinquished the Chairmanship in 1960, though he remained a Governor for several years, and Sir Henry Wilson Smith, O.N., a senior civil servant and industrialist, who travelled long distances to attend meetings, was then appointed Chairman. The representatives of the University of Oxford were two Deans of Durham, first the Very Revd Dr C. A. Alington, who retired in 1951, and then the Very Revd J. H. S. Wild, who had previously been master of University College Oxford. When Dr Wilfred Hall, who had been the representative of Cambridge University since before the war, died in 1952 he was succeeded by Mr Peter Hunter Blair, a distinguished historian of Anglo-Saxon England, and when he resigned in 1954 he was succeeded by the present writer. The University of Durham had three representatives, one appointed by the Senate of the federal university, and two by King's College, one of whom was a medical professor. Professor G. B. A. Fletcher, Professor of Latin and for years Chairman of the Scholarships Committee of the Governors, Professor W. E. Curtis, F.R.S., Professor of Physics, and Professor R. V. Bradlaw, Dean of the Dental School, were the Durham University nominees from 1948 onwards.

There were four co-optative Governors, one normally an O.N. The Chairmen were all co-optative members; another was Mr E. L. Beckingham, who had served as Vice-Chairman and Chairman of Finance Committee since 1928. When Mr Beckingham died in 1949 Dr E. R. Thomas was appointed to the co-optative vacancy that then arose, a rare honour for a former Headmaster. Sir Arthur Lambert, O.N., who as North Regional Commissioner for Civil Defence had had his headquarters in the School during the war, served until his death in 1948, when he was succeeded by another former pupil of the school, Mr Lionel Markham. Mr Henry Armstrong, son in law of Sir Arthur Sutherland, served as

218

another co-optative Governor until his resignation in 1951, and he was succeeded by Sir James Spence, Professor of Child Health, a paediatrician with an international reputation who died in 1954.

Northumberland County Council regularly appointed the Chairman of their Education Committee, in 1948 Viscount Ridley, who was also Chairman of the County Council, and later Alderman W. H. Kirsopp-Reed and Alderman the Revd R. E. Robson. Durham County Council appointed one member, and the remaining local authority members, ten in number, were all appointed by the city Corporation. They consisted of Aldermen, many of whom had served the city and School for years, and Councillors, some of them members of the Labour Party but nevertheless always loyal to the School. Aldermen appointed by the city included J. G. Nixon, who was first appointed in 1932 and in later years served as an active and devoted Vice-Chairman, Sir Angus Watson, famous chairman of a fish-canning firm, Arthur Howell, for many years Chairman of the Finance Committee, and Mrs Violet Grantham, the first lady Lord Mayor of Newcastle. Councillors included J. F. Trevor Fenwick, a director of Fenwicks Department Store, who for some time represented the School on the Committee of the Governing Bodies' Association, Mrs Gladys Robson, for several years Chairman of Newcastle Education Committee, Mrs Teresa Russell, who was prominent in social work in the city, Mrs C. C. Scott, and Mrs M. Shaw. These ladies were regular attenders and took a great interest in the affairs of the School.

The School's Scheme of Government gave the Governors power to appoint a clerk 'or any necessary officers' for the conduct of their business, and from the early years of the century it became the practice to appoint a Newcastle solicitor who used his own staff to type and have printed the agenda, minutes and accounts, and to conduct the Governors' official correspondence. E. G. Harvey, who served as Clerk between the wars and was a member of the delegations that met the Board of Education in 1926 and 1931, retired in 1943 and was succeeded by another Newcastle solicitor Henry Gandy, who held office for only five years. His successor was H. J. M. L. Criddle, whose grasp of legal and financial matters was excellent and who co-operated well with the Headmaster until in later years he suffered from ill health and other misfortunes. A full time Bursar was appointed in 1960, but Criddle continued as Clerk for some years.

The major function of the Governors was of course the

appointment of the Headmaster, and in 1948 when Dr Thomas announced his intention to retire at the age of 63, after 26 years of outstanding service to the School, the Governors advertised the post, appointed a sub-committee to sift the applications, and after interviewing three applicants, appointed Mr Oliver Worden Mitchell, Headmaster of Owen's School Islington, at a salary of £1500 a year.[18] (Twelve years later the Headmaster's salary had reached only £3000.) Mr Mitchell, like his predecessor, had served in the forces in the First World War, and had experienced a school evacuation in the Second World War. Born in 1898 in London, he attended Owen's School and joined the Royal Naval Air Service in 1916. While on leave he was awarded an exhibition at Magdalen College Oxford, and on his return to Oxford in 1919 took a shortened degree under the regulations for ex-servicemen, satisfying the examiners in Modern History in 1920, and being placed in the second class in the final honours examination in English Literature in 1921. He taught History and English at King William's College on the Isle of Man, where he was also a housemaster, and in 1932 became Headmaster of King's School Peterborough, following this up by the Headship of his own old school in 1939.[19]

A vivid description of Mr Mitchell's career at Owen's School is given in Mr R. A. Dare's *History of Owen's School*.[20] Mr Dare also refers to another former pupil of Owen's School, Professor W. E. Curtis, who was Mr Mitchell's brother in law and, as mentioned above, a Governor of the Royal Grammar School. Mr Dare writes of Mr Mitchell's appointment as Headmaster on the eve of the evacuation of the school: 'He possessed all the qualities such a situation demanded . . . His appointment proved the most fortunate thing that could have happened to Owen's at that crisis in its history. He carried through the difficult experiment of evacuation with brilliant success. His unconquerable spirit, his sympathetic approach to hostesses, parents and boys, the fertility of his improvisations, his tact and firmness in dealing with officialdom, and especially his friendship with Mr Liddle [O.N. and Headmaster of Bedford Modern School to which Owen's was evacuated] carried the school through its ordeal triumphantly.' Mr Dare regards Mr Mitchell's successful holding together of his School during evacuation as alone entitling him to be regarded as a great headmaster, but he paid high tribute to him as a man. 'Those who knew him will not easily forget his scintillating mind, his taut nervous energy, his sudden and disconcerting resolutions, his essentially boyish outlook. Few men can have relied so little on the extraneous trappings of authority for their influence, yet few men can have won so wholehearted a respect and affection.'

No one could have been better qualified academically and by experience for the post of Headmaster of the Royal Grammar School, but, as Mr Dare suggests, his temperament was certainly unusual for such an office. He was quick, excitable and adventurous, and sometimes shocked his colleagues and friends; but under him the School was alive with ideas and novelties of all kinds. He had great enthusiasm, sympathy for others, and loyalty to a wide range of causes. He was available to everyone, boys, staff, parents, Governors and friends of the School. He placed his study in a small room adjoining the entrance to the School so that he could be the first to welcome visitors. His war experience (he once described an incident where his aircraft descended into a tree) made him a keen supporter of the CCF. An arts man, he respected and even venerated his scientist predecessor, and like Dr Thomas he had no difficulty in holding a balance between the arts and sciences. He did much to develop a connection between the school and the University of Oxford, while not neglecting the traditional contacts with Cambridge which Dr Thomas had fostered. He had a genius for personal relationships, above all an understanding of boys, their development and their problems. He was quick to generate and share amusement, but deeply serious about his ultimate ends and convictions. He gave personal attention to even minute details and his correspondence was voluminous, written in his personal style, always courteous, friendly and enthusiastic. Most of the boys' reports had individual comments in his own handwriting, and he wrote long testimonials on behalf of university applicants. His literary skill is demonstrated not only in his Speech Day reports, but also in his occasional contributions to the *Novo*. His appreciation of Mrs E. R. Thomas, who was the grand-daughter of Dr Robert Spence Watson and who died suddenly in 1956, is most moving, and his generosity to colleagues is shown in his tributes to S. Middlebrook and Mrs Owen, School Secretary and wife of the head of the classics department, on their retirement, in his reference to T. T. Anderson, whom he described as 'a saint', and also in his enthusiastic welcome of his successor in 1960.

Mr Mitchell was frequently involved in controversy and some of his decisions were criticised whether they were mistaken or not, but no one ever doubted his sincerity or failed to respond to his personal charm, his independence of outlook, his originality and his loyalty. Mrs Mitchell, who was in some ways a contrasting character, capable, practical, level-headed, friendly and reliable, was a constant source of support and strength to her husband, and made many contributions to the life of the School. At the time of writing she is still active in retirement in Oxford.

(ii) *The Conduct of the School*

The educational situation in the years following the 1944 Act was one of optimism; there was a general feeling that after the war years educational developments which were overdue were about to take place, and they included the introduction for the first time of universal secondary education. The popular realisation of the importance of secondary education led to a huge demand for grammar school places in both maintained and independent schools, and it soon became obvious that this would increase as the children of the post-war birth-rate bulge reached secondary school age. But the future of the grammar schools, including grant-aided independent schools, was by no means certain. Anyone coming from London, as Mr Mitchell did, was bound to be fully aware of the plans put forward by Sir Graham Savage, Education Officer of the London County Council, for a drastic re-organisation of secondary education in the London area, with the establishment of comprehensive schools (formerly known as 'multi-lateral'),[21] and it was clear, even before this issue became a major matter of political controversy, that this movement would spread to the provinces, and in some places had already done so.

The parents of children approaching secondary school age soon began to believe that the secondary modern school was little better than the senior elementary school under another name. The priority given to the development of the secondary modern school created the impression that the grammar schools were outmoded, neglected and out of touch with the times. Teachers in the grammar schools were apprehensive about the consequences of the introduction of common salary scales for all secondary schools, and the extent to which what was called 'parity of esteem' would be implemented at the expense of the grammar schools.

The decision of the Ministry of Education to change the examination system in the grammar schools, and the issue of the pamphlet 'the Road to the Sixth Form'[22] (which Mr Mitchell recommended parents to read) did a great deal to restore a feeling of confidence in the grammar schools, and to make them conscious that they also were participating in the general advance. For twenty years after the war, until the establishment of the CSE in 1965, grammar schools remained the only secondary schools in which all pupils could obtain examination qualifications and proceed directly into higher education. Parental preferences were clear: the prestige of the grammar schools was restored, yet at the same time the 11+ examination became unpopular in the eyes of the parents of those children who did not, or who it was thought would not, qualify for a grammar school place. And so by their very success the grammar schools were threatened with extinction, and it was by no means clear whether the direct grant schools would be able to survive unscathed.

All these considerations were fully understood by Mr Mitchell, whose aim was to foster and protect the interests of the School, the future of which lay largely in his hands. The powers and duties of the Headmaster required him to take the initiative in relation to every aspect of school life and policy, responding to both internal and external pressures. His educational philosophy emerges clearly from his printed Speech Day reports and his reports to the Governors. He wished to preserve the traditions of the School, and was keenly interested in its history, having a photocopy of the recital of Horsley's will placed in his study, and instituting a formal commemoration of Horsley on Founder's Day.[23] He continued Dr Thomas's custom of presenting boys with a copy of the short *Story of the Royal Grammar School* by J. B. Brodie and A. R. Laws, and at one time a pamphlet on Admiral Lord Collingwood was also distributed. In addition he arranged for the first time for the compilation of a *Register* of the School which was laboriously and generously carried out by Mr B. D. Stevens, LL.B., O.N., and published in 1955 with a supplement in the following year.[24]

Mr Mitchell aimed not only at maintaining the already high academic standards of the School, but also at securing a balance between academic and other activities. In his own words he wished to foster vigour, variety and vitality, and to combine boldness with caution[25] (not necessarily, some would say, in equal proportions). He held that the purpose of education was to get the best out of each individual boy, partly because this was natural to someone who was intensely interested in people, their characters, reactions and interests, but partly also because it was consistent with his deeply-held philosophy of education. Institutions mattered, but their ultimate justification was the quality of the human beings whom they existed to serve, and the test of success lay not in the order and clarity of a system but in the characters and achievements of those for whose benefit the system existed. His philosophy is clearly expressed in the following sentence from his Speech Day report in 1950: 'The history of a school is written in the hearts and minds of its sons more emphatically than it can ever be expressed by the pen or tongue of its most ardent and loyal biographer.'[26]

Mr Mitchell thought of himself, with true humility, as a member of a team, and lost no opportunity for praising the achievements of his staff, prefects, sixth-formers, boys at all levels in the School, and of Old Boys, often by naming them. He did not care for rigid rules, wishing to combine flexibility with freedom: he thought of the School as a provider of opportunities which should be seized with courage; he taught the principle that one should be enterprising, and his own activities set an example of both courage and enterprise. He was fully aware of the place of the School in the wider community, nationally as well as locally, and he did not overlook the importance of other institutions with different aims and purposes, like the secondary modern school, which he defended in one of his Speech Day reports.[27]

His advocacy of balance in the curriculum led him to stress the importance of the study of Latin for its own sake, and of supplementing it with Greek in order to restore classical studies to their former position, while at the same time taking pride in the high proportion of boys studying scientific subjects in the sixth form. He was as proud of the fact that Russian was taught as he was of the sixth-form courses in geology and engineering drawing. And he promoted with enthusiasm the introduction of general studies in the sixth form to counteract the risk of over-specialisation. It is true that this was fashionable at the time and that boys had a free choice of subjects, but it exemplified his belief that both breadth and balance were necessary.

One of the first problems the new Headmaster had to deal with was the question of the size of the School. Before the War numbers had reached a peak of about 800, with two forms entering the Junior and three forms the Senior School. Numbers had declined during the years 1939 to 1944 when the School was evacuated to Penrith, entries during these years being little more than half what they had been. But Dr Thomas had rapidly re-established the situation when the School returned to Newcastle in 1944, for in September of that year there was a record admission of 177 boys, and in the three following years admissions remained

t over a hundred, the number of boys in the School standing at
719 in 1948. Mr Mitchell rapidly concluded that the pressure of
applicants justified increasing the size of the School substantially,
and he approached the Governors in February 1949 asking them to
authorise four forms of entry at the age of 11, pointing out that
here were 650 applicants for only 90 places, 30 of which would go
o Junior School boys. The Governors agreed, and the numbers
admitted each September rose to 131 in 1949, and 165 in 1950. It
must have appeared that these figures were excessive, because in
he four following years admissions varied from 101 to 111, and the
otal number of boys in the School rose to 803 in 1949, 874 in 1950,
976 in 1956, 1,040 in 1959, and 1021 in 1960.[28]

This increase in numbers required additional forms, staff and
accommodation, though the last of these requirements was not
met as promptly as would have been desired. The size of classes
was increased, rising in the Junior School to 35 or 37 in 1956, and
other forms frequently exceeded 30. However, the staff-pupil ratio
did not deteriorate, except momentarily in 1950, for it appears to
have improved from about 19.5 in that year to about 17.3 in 1959,
figures which compare favourably with maintained schools at that
time. The number of forms in the Junior School was increased by
splitting J3 into J3A and J3B in 1949, and gradually, in the Upper
School II4, III4, R4 and IV4 were added, though in some years,
for unknown reasons, the Removes and fourth forms appear to
have remained three in number. As the size of the fifth and sixth
forms increased the fifth forms were divided into V arts A and B,
V science A and B and V general, more than the four fifth forms
which existed in 1948, and the sixth form was divided into LVI
arts, LVI science, UVI arts, UVI science, 3rd year arts and 3rd
year science instead of the simple lower and upper sixth forms of
1948. In all, over a very few years about ten extra forms were thus
created, though the 3rd year sixth form groups were small, and the
staff was increased by about twelve. A more complicated and
diverse community arose, soon outgrowing the pleasant buildings
which had been designed for a School of about 500 boys.

The progress of plans to enlarge the building was indeed slow. A
small development occurred in 1950, when Mr Lawrence
Richardson presented a telescope to the School, and the
Governors arranged for the small Observatory which housed it to
be re-erected in the School grounds.[29] In 1953 two additional classrooms were provided by the conversion of two locker rooms, while
a much more ambitious plan to improve the science

225

accommodation, first formulated in 1954 in consultation with the architects Spence and Price, resulted in the provision of three additional laboratories for physics and chemistry, with accompanying preparation rooms, stores, dark room and a large lecture theatre. The cost was at first estimated at £30,000, but the final bills totalled about £66,000. Two grants of £2000 each were made towards the costs of equipment by the Industrial Fund.[30]

There are several points to note about this scheme. First, the Governors decided not to make a public appeal for the money required (though in later years for further extensions such an appeal was highly successful) but to borrow on mortgage £35,300 from the Corporation at a low rate of interest of 4¼%, redeemable over 30 years.[31] Secondly, no provision was made for biology which remained housed in a somewhat unsatisfactory building on the playing field, along with woodwork and geography. Thirdly, the lecture theatre was not the most appropriate of additions to the accommodation at the time: few regular school activities needed a room with 140 seats, and though it was invaluable for society meetings and addresses by visiting speakers, it failed to prove useful for sixth-form private study though it may have been intended to be used for this purpose. The building was opened in September 1956 by Alderman Mrs Violet Grantham who was Lady Mayoress at the time, in the presence of a large gathering. In one of the walls was incorporated a stained glass window from the old Grammar School building in Rye Hill, which after serving as the home of Rutherford High School for Girls for many years, had recently been demolished, along with the beautiful gothic revival church of St Mary the Virgin which adjoined it, to make room for the Charles Trevelyan Technical College.

Thus seven years after the post-war expansion of the School had started, only five additional classroom spaces had been added, and the only further accommodation provided by 1960 was improved teaching and storage space for the music department. New accommodation for the CCF, however, was under discussion with the service authorities, plans were made to build a new boathouse on the river, and a second larger phase of building development was envisaged. There had been as early as 1951 warnings that the new urban motorway would probably invade the School grounds, and the Governors had taken steps to protest at an early version of the plan,[32] but it was the eventual construction of this motorway, and the success of an appeal, which made it possible to achieve in a short space of time a spacious dining hall, a magnificent new library in the old dining hall, and a substantial new class-room block.

It must not be supposed, however, that the School lacked important amenities in the 1950s; in fact the Headmaster pointed out that it was possible to manage with the existing classrooms, which must have been very fully used. The swimming bath and gymnasium were excellent, and few schools enjoyed the benefit of their own, admittedly small, theatre with good lighting equipment, even if the backstage accommodation was inadequate. The hall was a dignified place, with its war memorial organ, the ancient table and the row of portraits and honours boards, and even the Plender Library, small as it was, where the Governors used to meet, retained the furniture and glazed bookcases given by Lord Plender in 1931. The library also housed some important early printed books which were repaired, rebound and catalogued in the 1960s.[33] The major weakness in the 1950s was certainly the lack of suitable rooms for private study by the sixth form, who had to try to find empty class-rooms or to work in corners of the hall or later in the lecture theatre, or in the Plender Library if it was free.

In the 1970s, as Professor Dennison shows,[34] the problem of sixth-form study accommodation was solved by converting the Junior School building of the 1920s and 1930s into a sixth-form centre, while the Junior School was found new premises in Lambton Road. But during the 1950s the whole question of the future of the Junior School called for a policy decision by the Governors. The immediate cause was the general inspection of the School which took place in 1956. The Inspectors' report[35] described in great detail the organisation of the School and the teaching of each subject, giving also a considerable amount of attention to extra-curricular activities. Most departments and activities received high praise, especially the high proportion of boys going to universities and the impressive scholarship record. There were however a few adverse comments about accommodation, and the work of the Junior School and the teaching of religious knowledge were the chief objects of criticism. The detail about the Junior School was in fact quite appreciative, but at the end of the report its very existence was called into question. This did not seem to follow from the assessment of the work of the School, which was criticised mainly because French was taught and there was insufficient co-ordination of the teaching of subjects. It seems therefore that the Inspectors thought that it was a mistake to have junior departments in such schools as the

Royal Grammar School, no matter how good their work might be. On the other hand it is possible that their comments imply that the work was more 'formal' than was at the time usual in maintained primary schools.

The Governors were disconcerted at these observations by the Inspectors and eventually appointed a sub-committee to consider the matter, which reported in 1958.[36] In their view the strength of the Junior School lay in its value as a feeder to the Senior School, especially for fee-paying pupils. They did not think that the fact it did not attract grant was a great disadvantage, but they did feel that the building could be improved and that as far as the teaching was concerned an effort should be made to align it with the best practice in the maintained primary schools. This report was accepted by the Governors and eventually the Junior School was re-housed.[37]

There was another issue connected with the Junior School which was not regarded as important at the time. The Inspectors had stated that although Junior School boys took the entrance examination to the Senior School, they did not compete with boys from outside, although every year a few boys were found unlikely to succeed in the Senior School and their parents were persuaded to withdraw them. In later years this matter caused some difficulty, and it is still a problem in independent schools which have junior departments. Mr Mitchell's attitude was generous and accommodating. His interpretation of the direct grant regulations was that as long as a boy had reached the standard required for admission to the Junior School in the first place, it was not necessary for him to compete with boys from outside at a later stage. Therefore unless it was obvious that his lack of progress was such that for his own sake he would be happier in a less exacting atmosphere, he should continue in the School. It is less easy to discriminate between applicants at 7 or 8 than it is at 11, and the competition for entry to the Junior School would have been less keen because younger boys would not normally be encouraged to make the long daily journeys that many of the older boys made, and so the number of applicants was smaller. In addition, of course, free places were not available to Junior School boys. Mr Mitchell also believed that it was not healthy for a school to be over-selective, for he held that the community was the better for the presence of some boys who were less able or even handicapped.

The staff of the School was quickly built up by Dr Thomas in

228

he years following the war, and when Mr Mitchell took over in 1949 it included a strong group of able and devoted men whose names and characters will be familiar to many Old Novos, though none of them, perhaps, was as outstanding as Michael Roberts, whose untimely death was mourned by the School in 1948. The Second Master, H. N. Smith, head of the classics department, died in 1950 and was succeeded by S. Middlebrook, head of the history department, who in the same year published *Newcastle upon Tyne: its growth and achievement*,[38] a book which was highly regarded at the time. It was commissioned by and printed for the Kemsley Press, and copies of it were presented to the senior boys. Middlebrook sent a large number of historians, some of whom achieved eminence, to the universities, and he retired with much acclaim including the honorary degree of M.A. of Durham University in 1958. He was followed as Second Master by G. S. Dean, who taught science, and whose wisdom and quiet judgement were appreciated by both Mr Mitchell and his successor, and by all his colleagues. T. T. Anderson, now Head of the Junior School, continued to play an important part in the organisation of school camps, and combined his school work with a great deal of charitable work especially for the Save the Children Fund, in recognition of which the University of Durham conferred on him also the honorary degree of M.A. when he retired in 1960. Arthur Milner, the head of the music department, who had built up the music of the school in the years before the war, retired in 1948 and was followed by J. Wolstenholme who led the music department to even greater achievements which are recorded in the survey *50 Years of Music at the Royal Grammar School*.[39]

As the School grew in size, and as those members of staff appointed by John Talbot and E. R. Thomas gradually retired, so Mr Mitchell's own judgement began to determine the character of the staff. Mr Mitchell early adopted a policy of appointing young men, mostly straight from the universities, some of whom moved elsewhere after a short period at the School, with the object of bringing the work of the sixth form up to date, with university entrance in mind. Some of these men were only a few years older than the sixth-formers themselves, and they promoted lively discussion and new ideas which the sixth form clearly appreciated. W. A. Thornton, who had been a pupil of Mr Mitchell's at King William's College and who taught English at the RGS, published a novel and contributed to *Punch*; D. Layton, who taught physics, pioneered the General Studies course and later became Professor of Education at Leeds University. J. C. Nichols, a geographer, eventually succeeded G. S. Dean as Second Master; J. A. Bruce succeeded S. Middlebrook as head of the history department and moved on to two headships; D. R. Shipley did much to revive the teaching of classics, establishing the Classics Society at whose inaugural meeting Professor Sir Ian Richmond gave an address,[40] while John Elders, who later became England Rugby coach, was appointed especially for the contribution which he could make to school games coaching.

One consequence of the appointment of Sir James Spence to the Governors was that they asked him to draw up a schedule of duties for a School Medical Officer which was approved in 1954, and Dr Errington Ellis of the Child Health Department of the Medical School was appointed. His early reports included strong advice to improve the sanitary arrangements at the School, which was acted upon. In an analysis of the results of an early examination of the boys and their family backgrounds he commented that the standard of physical health was excellent, that a large proportion of the boys came from families of high social status, and that these families were smaller than the national average, facts which were hardly surprising.[41]

The curriculum of the School was in many ways conventional. The Junior School curiously in the early days divided English into divinity, composition, literature, history, dictation, reading and writing, though later history appeared as a separate subject. Science was originally divided into nature study and geography, and art into drawing and painting, though in later years geography appeared separately. French was taught in J3 (a practice which, as mentioned above, the Inspectors had questioned although shortly afterwards a movement began to establish French in primary schools), and the rest of the curriculum consisted of arithmetic, music and physical education.

In lower forms of the Senior School a common curriculum obtained, consisting of English, history, Latin, French, general science in Form II, followed by physics and chemistry in Form III, geography, mathematics, art, woodwork, physical education and music. All boys were expected to swim and many to learn a musical instrument. In the Removes Greek could be started at the expense of science, and woodwork could be dropped, while in the fourth form German could be started instead of geography, and anyone who did both Greek and German did no science at all, and no geography. In V Arts the choice was between Greek, German and geography, while general science or music replaced physics and chemistry; in V science no second language was possible and there was a choice between history, geography and music. In the sixth form, of course, specialisation was necessary, and the Inspectors noted that no fewer than 21 different combinations of advanced subjects could be taken. Biology was available (other than as a constituent of general science it was not taught below the sixth) either as a single or as a double subject. Engineering drawing could be taken, and also Russian to Advanced Level although started only in the lower sixth.[42] The normal practice was for sixth-formers to take three Advanced Level subjects (though the arrangements for the Higher School Certificate, as we shall see, had been different), but subsidiary non-examined courses were also available in music, economics, Russian, the history and philosophy of science, art, English, mathematics, Latin and French. Thus a real effort was made to broaden the curriculum of the sixth form even before the full programme of general studies was introduced, though even then it was possible for boys to choose subjects which hardly counteracted their major specialisation, since there was complete freedom in the choices made.

In 1958 in the general studies programme the following courses were offered: history and philosophy of science, social biology, physical science, art, music, social studies, English literature, 'methods and relations of science' (whatever that meant), recent history, economics and philosophy. The major weaknesses of these arrangements were that boys on the arts side could dispense with the study of science at too early an age, while apart from the few who took German, the linguistic work of the science specialists was limited. In addition the introduction of biology only at the sixth-form stage was regrettable. In the pre-war years and just after the War it had been the custom for a number of sixth-formers who intended to enter the medical profession to take at least one subject in the 1st M.B. examination of Cambridge University or in the Pre-Medical Examination of Durham University, while others intending to take engineering degrees took subjects in the 1st B.Sc. Engineering examination of Durham University.[43] These arrangements were gradually phased out, the last being recorded in 1957. By this time the two universities had reorganised the first-year courses in their Medical Schools while Durham University Faculty of Applied Science had earlier ceased to examine school candidates. Normal GCE qualifications were henceforward sufficient.

In 1948 the government decided to reorganise the system of school examinations, replacing the School and Higher School Certificate examinations by the General Certificate of Education, Ordinary and Advanced levels.[44] All examining boards were required to adopt the new system, and if they had not done so presumably 'recognition' would have been withdrawn, though it is interesting that the Cambridge Syndicate retained the old system for overseas candidates for many years. As far as the Advanced Level was concerned, there was no change in the standard from that of the principal subjects of the Higher School Certificate, but the examination of subsidiary subjects at a lower standard was discontinued. Instead of the requirement that a candidate should pass in a group of three or four usually related principal subjects, or in a selection of principal and subsidiary subjects, the examination could be taken in any number of subjects whether related or not. Scholarship papers, which it was hoped would help in selection for university places, were introduced, but were not taken into account in Advanced Level results. These arrangements left the schools free to determine the amount of specialisation to allow, but the effect of removing the subsidiary examination was inevitably to reduce the number of subjects examined, and so to increase specialisation. On the whole however there was no need for major changes in the standard of sixth-form work.

The conversion of the School Certificate examination into the Ordinary level of the GCE was much more complicated. Here again it was laid down that the examination could be taken in any number of subjects, and this was a major change, because the School Certificate requirements had been that candidates had to pass in 6 subjects, one of which had to be English language, one a foreign language, another mathematics and a fourth a science. These requirements had been modified by 1948, by which time the compulsory foreign language had been removed, and either mathematics or a science was permitted, but the old pattern tended to persist in many schools, dictating much of the fifth-form curriculum, and ensuring for those who obtained credits automatic exemption from the matriculation requirements of universities, provided Latin was included for those universities which required it. Many schools entered pupils for eight or nine subjects in the old School Certificate examination. The new arrangements also decreed that the 'O' level pass standard should be the credit and not the pass standard of the former examination, and that candidates could not take the examination if they would be below the age of 16 on 2 September in the year of the examination. This situation presented the schools with a number of problems. It had been the aim of the School Certificate examination that whole forms should be entered, in substantially the same large group of subjects, but from now onwards it would be necessary to enter pupils only in subjects which they stood some chance of passing at the higher standard, and therefore probably in fewer subjects. In addition either younger candidates (and therefore brighter ones) would have to be held back, or the 'O' level examination would have to be taken by some candidates in the first year of the sixth form. University entrance requirements and the requirements of professional bodies would have to be watched carefully in order to make sure that pupils took all the essential subjects at the appropriate level. To make matters more complicated the Ministry of Education urged that pupils should be encouraged not to take the 'O' level examination in subjects which they proposed to take at 'A' level.[45] This practice was called 'by-passing' and, like the age limit as long as it lasted,[46] led to a great deal of controversy. The new arrangements came into force in 1951.

In the case of the Royal Grammar School the practice had been to enter boys for as many as eight or nine subjects in the School Certificate at the end of the fifth-form year and the examination regulations determined some of the subjects to be taken. In the Higher School Certificate a large number of boys took subjects at subsidiary standard at the end of the first year in the sixth, which were often repeated at principal standard in the following year, while other boys took a mixture of subjects at principal and subsidiary standard at the end of the second year, some taking two and others three principal subjects, with one or two subsidiaries. Four subjects were thus commonly examined in the sixth form, or in some cases five. The transition to the GCE system therefore presented a number of serious problems and it is not difficult to imagine the long debates at the staff and department meetings which took place to decide on the new policy. Since the revised regulations left the question entirely open, decisions had to be made about the number of subjects to be taken at each level, and the age limit dictated that some boys would have to take the 'O' level examination in the first year of the sixth. Those members of staff who felt that the boys needed to be motivated by examinations were in favour of continuing to enter boys for a substantial number of subjects at 'O' level, in spite of the higher standard required, while those who felt that examinations should not be the main motivation, and should be 'taken in the stride', were in favour of reducing the number of 'O' level subjects to the minimum and of practising 'by-passing'. The former group thought that it was safe and sound to stick to the old system as closely as possible, since it ensured a reasonably general education in the fifth form, and enabled boys to 'make sure' of subjects needed for university entrance. The latter group thought that to cut the number of subjects examined would allow a greater degree of freedom in the fifth form, with a gradual approach to sixth-form work, and that it would be difficult to teach classes of boys only some of whom would be taking the examination. This would not have been a wise policy in a school where many pupils left after the fifth form, but at the Royal Grammar School a majority could be expected to go on into the sixth.

The Headmaster argued that the School must be adventurous and must set an example to other schools by a wholehearted acceptance of the new system, including by-passing.[47] He held the progressive view that examinations had been overdone in the past, that able boys needed to get ahead with advanced work and that with proper care the risk of over-specialisation, or of eventual failure in essential subjects which had been by-passed, could be avoided, but he felt, as everyone did, that the age limit was a nuisance, and he was relieved when after two years it was in practice removed by a decision that 'under-age' boys could take 'O' level if the Headmaster certified that they were fit to do so.

The outcome of all these debates and discussions was what amounted to an individual examination time-table for each boy, agreed on in consultation with parents at the end of the fourth-form year, taking into account the boy's age (until this became unnecessary), his 'A' level intentions, his likely university entrance requirements and his specialised abilities and interests. The result was a drastic reduction to at most four or five in the number of subjects taken at 'O' level, regular by-passing at least by all the able boys, and at first the postponement of the 'O' level examination for 'under-age' boys until even as late as the end of the first year of the sixth. Many boys took 'O' levels in stages, one or two subjects in the fifth and others in the sixth, and full advantage was taken of the December examination, which had previously been used almost entirely for re-sits. By 1955, however, with the relaxation of the age limit, the 'O' level settled down once more as mainly a fifth-form examination, with some boys re-taking usually single subjects in the December examination while in the irst year of the sixth. The idea of some work in subsidiary subjects was continued by the unexamined courses which as we have seen were part of the sixth-form curriculum, though much less ambitious than the subsidiary HSC courses.

That the new arrangements led to increased specialisation is shown by the suggestions made in later years that some kind of intermediate examination should be introduced between 'A' and 'O' levels; many examining boards introduced alternative (and more exacting) 'O' level syllabuses and in due course Royal Grammar School boys were entered for some of these examinations as well as the examinations in general studies and oral English. The general rule at 'A' level was that every boy took three subjects, but university entrance requirements were eventually stabilized at two 'A' level passes, with a complementary spread of 'O' level passes in a modern or classical language, English and science subjects which in fact perpetuated the general pattern of the old School Certificate. Under the new arrangements it was less usual for science boys to take languages in the sixth and for arts boys to take two languages as well as history and English, which had been quite frequently done under the HSC arrangements. The risks associated with the new system were whether boys would continue to work as hard without the pressure of so many examinations, and whether, under the by-passing arrangements, a few boys who needed to have a pass in a particular subject which they could have obtained at 'O' level, would fail to obtain it later at 'A' level. One or two cases of the second kind did happen, but there is no evidence that the boys did not work as hard or that the higher standard at 'O' level proved a real difficulty. Some commentators have taken the view, which it is impossible to substantiate, that in a few years the pass standard at 'O' level reverted to what it had been under the School Certificate.

With regard to Scholarship papers in the early days of the GCE, about one third of the 'A' level candidates took these papers, and in later years perhaps nearly two thirds. Of course the results, which, as has been mentioned, did not affect 'A' level grades, were, like the 'A' level results themselves, not available at the time of application to universities except in the cases of boys who spent a third year (or part of it) in the sixth, but they may have influenced the final selection in the autumn of some of the applicants. In any case the value of these papers was to provide a stimulus for wider reading and study beyond the limits of the 'A' level syllabuses. The universities continued to use 'O' level results, school reports and interviews, as they still do, when deciding on 'conditional' offers, which were confirmed when 'A' level result were published.

The School was and is justly famous for the strength of it extra-curricular activities, which have a long history, and of which successive Headmasters have been proud. The list seems endless and almost every year a new activity appears. Mr Mitchell wondered at one time whether saturation point had been reached Each member of staff regarded it as part of his professional duty not only to know and to teach his boys, but also to devise some way of interesting a group of boys in activities, whether academic or not, in which he himself found delight. The fact that the Headmaster of the day has been traditionally the President of every club and society is testimony to the interest shown and support given by Headmasters to these institutions, though only very detailed inquiry would ascertain how many of them arose through the initiative of Headmasters, of members of staff, or or the boys themselves.

In the years preceding 1950, the *Novo*, in addition to the reports of the major games, Rugby Football, Cricket, Boxing and Swimming, contains notices of the following clubs and societies: the Debating Society (with its annual Toast List to which distinguished guests were invited, and which claimed in 1953 to be 116 years old), the XXI Club (devoted to play reading and an annual major dramatic production), the Science Society, the Linguists (a club which often produced plays in French or German), the Chess Club, and societies for Woodwork, Philately, Photography, History and Bird-watching. A Scripture Union existed, a Leisure hour Art Group, Chamber Music, and Musical Appreciation groups and a Senior Choir in addition to the three Orchestras already mentioned. Race week and summer camps were regular, and periodically particular forms, lower sixth Science, the Removes, III1, II2 for example, produced their own plays. In subsequent years an Astronomical Society was formed with the arrival of the Richardson telescope, and an Entomological Society, a Transport Circle, a Golf Club, a Sixth Form Club run jointly with the girls of the Church and Central High Schools, a Scottish Dancing Club, a Model Railway Club, a sixth-form magazine club, a Shooting Club, a Gardening Club, a Classics Society, a Record Club, an Electronics Society, Middle School Debating, History and Science Societies, and a Gilbert and Sullivan Society.

In 1949 the Junior Training Corps was reorganised as a Combined Cadet Force with Army, Navy and Air Force sections, the latter jointly run until 1959 with Dame Allan's Boys' School. One of its functions was to provide a guard of honour on special occasions, such as when Lord Montgomery visited the School, and annually on Lord Mayor's Day when the Lord Mayor after election traditionally made it his first obligation to visit the School, a custom derived from the fact that in early days the Mayor was elected in the Hospital building used as the School. In December 1950 the *Novo* printed a special section on the history of the School camps, and in 1957 it was noted that the record number of 10 camps had been held in one year. The Headmaster, in addition to attending many of the School's games activities, made it a special duty to visit as many of the camps as he could. In addition to most of the clubs and societies whose officers were boys, the editing of the *Novo* was in the hands of senior boys (with gentle supervision by masters). The magazine contained valuable short items about individuals, and a judicious selection of prose and verse exercises as well as reports of games and the full range of school activities, together with letters from Old Novos at the universities and occasional contributions on the early history of the School. The Plender Library also was run by boys who from time to time tried to improve the cataloguing and issuing system, and who sometimes published lists of acquisitions, even with reviews, especially of gifts from benefactors, in the *Novo*. For purposes of games competitions the School was divided into four houses, Collingwood, Eldon, Horsley and Stowell, but there is little evidence of house meetings, and indeed one boy wrote to the *Novo* saying that the system needed drastic reorganisation.[48] House reports refer only to games, though occasionally trying to stir up a 'house spirit'. If the houses had not existed internal games competitions could not have been satisfactorily organised. Two interesting points about the House system are that boys were allocated to houses according to the district where they lived, and the tutor groups were sub-sections of Houses. One isolated activity which is worth mentioning, since no film club appears to have existed, is that in 1953 Form IV4 produced a film of their own about the School, called *School of the North*.[49]

There was a constant stream of visitors to the School. Every year 'assistants' from France and Germany contributed to the teaching of languages: Professor John Butt provided prizes for reading from 1950 and came to the School to judge the

competition; in 1957 the fiftieth anniversary of the opening of th
Jesmond building was celebrated, and was attended by th
Duke of Northumberland and Mr Laidman Browne, O.N.,
professional actor; Dr Chalmers Burns came to judge a hous
music competition in 1950; Speech Day principal guests include
Lord Eustace Percy, who at the time was Rector of King's College
Dr A. L. Goodhart, Master of University College Oxford, D
R. W. Moore, Headmaster of Harrow, Dr Eric James, Hig
Master of Manchester Grammar School, who caused som
amusement by referring to the sweepstake on the length of hi
speech which he knew the boys would be holding, Sir Georg
Thomson, Master of Corpus Christi College Cambridge, M
P. H. B. Lyon, who was Chairman of the Public School
Appointments Bureau, Sir James Duff, Warden of the Durhar
Colleges, Lord Runciman, Dr E. F. Collingwood and Sir Thoma
Armstrong, Principal of the Royal College of Music. In 1956
Russian teacher of English, Mme Tsvetkova, visited the School
One of the Headmaster's innovations[50] was an annual Founder'
Day Service in November in Jesmond Parish Church, speakers a
which included Mr M. H. Bates, the Vicar of Jesmond, who late
became Archdeacon of Lindisfarne, Canon P. M. Martin
Diocesan Education Officer and author of *Mastery & Mercy*, a
study of Gerard Manley Hopkins, and the Bishop of Newcastle
Hugh Ashdown. Talks on careers were given by Miss Brenda
Calderwood, Youth Employment Officer in Newcastle and now
Chairman of the local Governors of the Central Newcastle High
School, and by various members of the Public School
Appointments Bureau.

School plays and concerts were public occasions attended by
many Governors, Old Boys, parents and friends of the School, and
the Headmaster took special delight in these occasions
accompanied by Mrs Mitchell and a group of his guests. The
School premises were frequently used for meetings of outside
bodies, such as subject associations, educational conferences, or
even meetings of Freemasons of which order Mr Mitchell appears
to have been a member. The theatre was regularly used by King's
College Staff Dramatic Society, but perhaps the largest outside
body to use the School was the Education Section of the British
Association which met there in 1949, other sections using
University buildings. Evidence of the loyalty to and regard for the
School over many years shown by Old Boys and friends is the long
list of endowed prizes and sports trophies presented annually, the

prizes alone numbering nineteen, with two more donated by the Headmaster.

The regular series of parents' conferences for different groups of forms which Dr Thomas had established continued under Mr Mitchell. At these conferences, the Headmaster spoke first, and then released parents to be taken by their sons to meet their tutors or form-masters or subject teachers, to discuss their sons' progress. At these conferences the parents were consulted, and School policy, for instance over the new examination system, was fully explained, and their co-operation sought. Systematic attention was also paid to advice on careers, a careers department was set up, with a mass of reference material, and the careers talks already mentioned were supplemented by regularly organised 'careers interviews' of individual boys.

Thus life at the Royal Grammar School in those days was busy, exciting, various and exacting. The amount of thought and care which went into the organisation which the staff shared amongst themselves was enormous, and boys were encouraged to take responsibility and use their initiative as soon as they were able. No one worked harder than the Headmaster, whose enthusiasm seemed inexhaustible, and who was the first to praise the efforts of the staff and boys in keeping this large and complicated organisation in a constant state of purposeful activity.

(iii) *The Achievements of the School*

There is no general agreement about the criteria by which an educational institution should be assessed. Certainly its achievements cannot be objectively measured. It is sometimes assumed that this can be done by looking at examination results, comparing school with school, and compiling tables, like those for university scholarships or first-class degrees, which are diligently worked out by some contributors to the press. The central government and local education authorities put a good deal of trust in inspections, and we have seen that Her Majesty's Inspectors liked most of what they saw at the Royal Grammar School. But the most powerful means by which educational institutions are judged would seem to be reputation, which is an insubstantial thing, the product of many contributory factors of which one is the recollections of former *alumni*; the gossip of those (parents and others) connected with the institution who either know it or hear about it from those who do know it; and the impression created in academic circles by the staff and head of the institution by what they publish (if we are thinking of a university) or what they say and do and achieve (if we are thinking of a school). The professional work of a teacher is in many ways, like that of a writer or an artist, a constant exercise in self-criticism, but it also includes (as did the work of the artist in days when they took apprentices in their studios) the constant criticism and appraisal of the work of their pupils. Where this pre-occupation with excellence is strong and the second-rate is constantly shown up, the quality of an institution rises, and its reputation is enhanced. What is certain is that it takes many years of endeavour to develop an institution of the first rank, which the Royal Grammar School could now claim to be.

Mr Mitchell knew that he had taken over the Headship of one of the great schools of England, and he recognised that the School owed its high reputation very much to the work of his predecessor. Dr Thomas's work was recognised on his retirement by the award of an honorary D.C.L. of the University of Durham, and he remained in close touch with the School as is obvious from his appointment as a Governor. Mr Mitchell was bent on maintaining and enhancing the reputation of the School. Perhaps because he was a Londoner and used to being at the centre of things, he seemed to know everyone in the educational world and beyond. He believed that if he kept up a large number of contacts, with officials in national and local government, aldermen and councillors (many of whom were, of course, Governors), heads of other schools, prominent people in the services and in industry, this could not but be for the benefit of the School. He put an enormous amount of work and energy into fostering the relationships with the Masters and Senior Tutors of Oxford and Cambridge colleges, which bore fruit in the large numbers of boys who entered their colleges, with or without open awards. If he himself kept in the public eye, by accepting appointments to a variety of committees, making ambitious journeys and lecture tours in addition to the functions connected with the School and the Old Novos, the School also would be kept in the news and its activities would be widely known.

The list of his commitments beyond the School is formidable. He was of course a member of the Headmasters' Conference, and held office in the Northern Division; he served on the Central Advisory Council for Education under the Chairmanship of Sir Geoffrey Crowther, and on the English Panel of the Secondary Schools Examinations Council; he was a member of the

Educational Advisory Council of the R.A.F., and founder Governor of the Army College established at Welbeck Abbey; he served on selection boards at both Sandhurst and Cranwell, and on the councils of the Public Schools Appointments Board, the R.A.F. Benevolent Fund, and the Girls' Public Day School Trust, where he participated in the appointment of the Headmistress of the Central Newcastle High School. He was a member of the Professional Classes Aid Council, and locally of an Oxford Society that was formed in Newcastle and of the Academic Committee of the Durham University Institute of Education. He even accepted appointment as President of the North-Eastern branch of the Science Masters' Association, and was a Fellow of the Royal Society of Arts. At the invitation of the Foreign Office he went to Germany, once to Hamburg and on another occasion to Bavaria to lecture on English education, and he went also to Cincinnati, Ohio, to one of the earliest of the Childrens' International Summer Villages, one of which was later held at Alnwick Castle. He spoke to the students of King's College Education Department on grammar school education, and asked them to visit the School to observe classes in progress.

This constant round of activities took its toll: in 1954 he was ill with pneumonia and in 1957 was injured in an accident: in the same year, feeling exhausted, he informed the Governors that he proposed to retire in 1958 at the age of 60.[51] They persuaded him to serve for two further years, but his health remained uncertain, although outwardly he remained lively and exuberant, and his activities continued to be strenuous. He finally retired in 1960, with generous tributes from all connected with the School, but he did not enjoy a long retirement and the School learnt with great sorrow that he had died on 25 October 1963. S. Middlebrook in a moving obituary said that it was impossible not to warm to his zest and energy, and his buoyancy of spirit, and that he would always be remembered with affection.[52]

The School had for years an excellent record in sending boys with open awards to Oxford, Cambridge and other universities. During the years 1938 to 1948, in spite of the disruption caused by the War, the extraordinary numbers of 38 awards were obtained at Cambridge, six at Oxford, 11 at King's College Newcastle and one at Manchester, an average of 4.5 per year if we omit King's College, which shortly ceased to offer open awards. The corresponding figures for the period 1949–61, with a larger School and free from the abnormalities of war time, were 45 awards at

Cambridge, 28 at Oxford, and five at other universities (omitting a final one at King's College). The average had risen to six per year, with three vintage years: eight in 1957, eleven in 1958 and nine in 1959.[53] These figures put the Royal Grammar School high on the list, often headed by Manchester Grammar School, of those schools which were most successful in obtaining open awards, and allowing for the changed circumstances it could be claimed that the earlier record had been maintained if not surpassed. Mr Mitchell was largely responsible for the increase in the number of awards obtained at Oxford, for he set out to achieve this end; the Governors negotiated a 'closed' award at Balliol, which was partly financed by endowments known as the Dale and the Plender funds,[54] but it was agreed that successful candidates must have reached the standard for an open award, and the Dale–Plender Scholarship was awarded four times in the years 1956–61.

In addition to scholarships and exhibitions the number of boys who obtained university places rapidly increased to 60 and later to 80 in each year. In the years 1955–7, five boys won service cadet-ships, and from 1953 to 1961 in varying numbers each year some 22 boys were awarded university scholarships by the National Coal Board, Consett Iron Co., the Central Electricity Generating Board, and the GPO, all no doubt due to the keen interest of the Headmaster and staff in career opportunities. In addition some boys were awarded scholarships on the Hartwell Foundation, an endowment from the rent of an estate at Fishburn left by Dr Hartwell, to be divided between Durham and Newcastle Schools and administered by the Dean and Chapter of Durham.[55]

Both Dr Thomas and Mr Mitchell frequently pointed out that examination results were not the most important measure of quality of the work of a School, but nevertheless some attention must be paid to them. In the days before the GCE it was relatively easy to tabulate the number of School and Higher Certificate awards, and to analyse the latter into arts and science, but without a careful analysis of grades they indicate little more than the approximate size of the fifth form and the second year of the sixth. The figures of certificates awarded from 1946, the year in which Dr Thomas claimed that the best results in the history of the School were obtained, to 1950 are given below in Table 1.[56]

Some of the fluctuations in these figures are due to the exceptional years of the war with erratic admissions, but the increase in the proportion of arts candidates for the Higher School Certificate in 1948 and 1949 is less easy to explain.

POST-WAR ACHIEVEMENTS 1945–1960

Table 1
Number of boys obtaining

	(i) School Certificates	(ii) Higher School Certificates		
		Arts	Science	Total
1946	73	11	27	38
1947	68	10	23	33
1948	74	16	17	33
1949	92	14	16	30
1950	77	7	25	32

From 1951 onwards, however, since the GCE was a single subject examination, and most boys spread their 'O' level examinations over more than one year, comparable figures cannot be given. The following table shows the number of candidates passing in 'O' level subjects in the July examination only (but including the few who passed in only one or two subjects) and the number who passed in at least two subjects in the Advanced level examination, again analysed into arts and science. It should be remembered also that the 'O' level figures will include a few boys who took 'O' level subjects in two successive July examinations and who are counted in both years. In order to achieve some rough comparison between the HSC results and the 'A' level results, passes in two or more 'A' level subjects are included since this became the minimum university entrance requirement, but the comparison with the HSC is not at all accurate.

Table 2

	No. of Candidates taking 'O' level in July	No. of Candidates passing in 2 or more 'A' level subjects		
		Arts	Science	Total
1951	65	20	24	44
1952	88	16	33	49
1953	153	25	34	59
1954	159	15	31	46
1955	159	21	28	49
1956	130	27	39	66
1957	118	40	57	97
1958	173	22	44	66
1959	164	22	41	63
1960	197	27	53	80

Again it would take a close analysis of grades to indicate any changes in the quality of the work done and there is no doubt that the staff did this with care at the time. But the rise in the numbe of 'O' level candidates is a measure of the growing size of th upper part of the School, and the fluctuations are no doubt partl due to changes in admissions policy. As far as 'A' level i concerned the total figures show the same steady rise with som fluctuations for the same reasons, but although the science figure show a regular preponderance over the arts figures, it is noticeabl that the arts proportion increases substantially after 1955 and i particularly high in 1956 and 1957. These movements are no mor easy to explain than they were in the 1940s. The 'O' level figure for 1951 and 1952, when the age limit was in force, it should b noted, are not a measure of the size of the fifth form because som of the boys were already in the sixth form, while on the other han the omission of the figures for the December examination mean that the figures quoted are not an accurate measure of the numbe of 'O' level candidates either. But these tables do indicate th increase in the size of the examining exercise, and the amount o detailed organisation which lay behind it was vast.

Some general reflections on the standards obtained can b made, however. In the School Certificate no distinctions wer awarded, but Very Good was the highest grade; in the HSC distinctions were awarded, and the following table shows th number of boys who reached these top grades in at least one (an very frequently more than one) subject.

Table 3

| | Number of boys awarded | |
	(i) *SC Very Good*	(ii) *HSC Distinction*
1946	40	17
1947	36	9
1948	39	8
1949	58	7
1950	39	8

With the introduction of the GCE the School lists printed fo Speech Day gave no grades for the first two years,[57] and no grade at all for the 'O' level. After 1952 the number of boys who gained distinctions in at least one subject at 'A' level is recorded, however, and is as follows:

244

POST-WAR ACHIEVEMENTS 1945–1960

Table 4

Number of boys awarded Distinction at 'A' level			
1953	5	1958	9
1954	12	1959	16
1955	6	1960	14
1956	15	1961	19
1957	25		

These figures show the usual fluctuations from year to year in the number of boys capable of top level performance, but the average is creditably high. On the other hand a cursory examination of the lists suggests that there were too many boys who obtained only an 'O' level pass on their 'A' level work. Another set of data which throws light on the standard of the boys' performance is the numbers who were awarded State Scholarships and Local Education Authority Major Awards, which are given in the following table.

Table 5

Number of boys awarded State Scholarships & Major Awards by LEA					
	State Schols.	Major Awards		State Schols.	Major Awards
1949	5	6	1956	12	23
1950	3	19	1957	14	47
1951	6	25	1958	4	33
1952	6	18	1959	7	38
1953	7	22	1960	7	22
1954	13	20	1961	8	40
1955	11	19			

These figures do not reflect the same variations as the number of 'A' level candidates and the number awarded distinctions, but there is some correspondence. They do illustrate the number of boys who were successful in obtaining university places, though some of course went to universities without obtaining awards, for the days of the automatic award of a grant lay in the future. State Scholarship numbers depended on the Ministry's decision about how many should be offered nationally, and were highly competitive. LEA Major Awards were made after careful scrutinising of examination results and in some cases after interviews, and the number depended to some extent on the budget of the local education authorities. A considerable number of boys in later years qualified for LEA minor awards, but they are not included in the above figures.

The School more than held its own under the conditions of the new examination system, and the advice given to the boys eems to have been wise. There was a period of uncertainty in the first two years of the new examination, but this was soon overcome. The new system happened to fit the atmosphere of independence and confidence which was characteristic of the School, and there is evidence of this in the frequency with which one or two boys took unusual subjects at 'A' level, like art, music, Russian, geology, subjects in which the teaching groups must have been small. It is a pity that economics did not appear as one of these subjects: its time was to come later.

Although the School was recognised to be the major secondary institution in the North East, it rarely became the subject of adverse criticism by other schools or by the community in the area. This was partly a consequence of the careful policy of public relations, which began with parents, through the painstaking arrangements which were made to keep in touch with them, through the regular conferences which have already been described, the fullest publication of information about School arrangements by circular, with letters to individuals where necessary, and the time-tabling of extra-curricular activities throughout the week, so that parents knew in advance what their boys were undertaking. Relations with King's College were very close not only through the Governors but through the examination arrangements and the subject departments, including the Education Department, which regularly sent students on School practice to the School, some of whom were later appointed to the staff. Some of the boys attended some of the College functions and visited the gallery and museums, and attended concerts, while some also used the City Libraries and the Library of the Literary and Philosophical Society. Co-operation with the Church High School and the Central High School included the use of the swimming bath by the girls' schools, and joint musical, dramatic, debating and dancing activities as well as many informal arrangements.

Mr Mitchell fully shared his predecessor's belief in the importance of extra-curricular activities, and the school's achievements in music, drama, on the sports field, and in the great variety of less organised leisure-hour activities was perhaps even more substantial than it had been before the war.[58] One of the longest-established school institutions, the Combined Cadet Force, came under discussion when the National Service which followed the war was discontinued, but it was concluded that it should be retained, because for career purposes it preserved important links with the services, while the extension of the boys' experience and the opportunity to practise self-discipline, to undertake exacting tasks and to learn responsibility and leadership were considered to be an important part of the boys' education. But membership was never compulsory.

When conditions returned to normal after the war, school camps were re-established with T. T. Anderson once again playing an important part in their organisation. In the 1950s camps for different age-groups were held in Dentdale, Swaledale, Wensleydale, Eskdale, Ribblesdale, Connemara, Langdale, Buttermere, Grasmere, Mallestang, Ryedale, Skye and Eigg. Three expeditions to Norway were organised and two cruises on the Norfolk Broads. Harvest camps continued annually on farms at Burnham Beeches and Barton on Humber in Lincolnshire. History camps were held twice at Norwich (where the first one had been held), at Ludlow, Stratford upon Avon, Shrewsbury, Berwick upon Tweed, Bury St Edmund's, Tewkesbury, Winchester, Aylesbury and Canterbury, in each case with visits to places of historic interest in the neighbourhood. The historians also made day excursions to castles, abbeys and interesting sites nearer to Newcastle. One boy went on the British Schools Exploring Society Central Iceland Expedition in 1952.

An important feature of School policy was that every boy was expected to learn to swim, and beginners' classes were followed up by displays at what was known as 'Newts' Night', and by inter-house and inter-school competitions at which last the School was remarkably successful. The swimming teams competed not only with local schools, but also with schools further afield such as Bootham School York, Leeds Grammar School, George Heriot's School Edinburgh, The Leys School Cambridge, Bishop's Stortford College and the City of London School, while they also swam against older competitors in the clubs of King's College, the Medical School, the Old Novos and R.A.F. Cranwell. Life-saving awards were made to those who qualified and water polo was introduced.

In Rugby Football the first XV played neighbouring schools, but they also travelled to Carlisle Grammar School and St Bees School in Cumberland, to George Heriot's School in Edinburgh and Kelvinside Academy in Glasgow, to Ampleforth College and Leeds Grammar School and to the City of London School, and once (at home) they played against Springs High School, South Africa. But they also competed with more mature players (a practice no longer permitted), for they are recorded as having played the University Air Squadron, the 81st HAA Regt. R.A., Bede College Durham, Cambridge University, Old Novos, R.A.F. Acklington, and The Royal Military Academy Sandhurst, though in this case Sandhurst's second XV.

In cricket the pattern was similar, the first XI playing not only local schools, but also King's College, the Medical School, the Durham Colleges, the County Club, ICI staff, the King's Hussars, 65 Training Regt. RAC, HMS Battleaxe, and South Northumberland, while schools further afield were Manchester Grammar School and University College School. In July the custom was developed of spending a cricket week in Cambridge, where the 1st XI played 'Long Vacation Clubs' at Emmanuel and St John's Colleges, and sometimes against Cambridge High School and a team known as 'The Cambridge M.A.s.'

In boxing regular matches were arranged with Ampleforth College and St Paul's School, Haberdashers' Aske's School Elstree, Tiffin School Kingston-on-Thames, and on occasions with the Royal Military Academy Sandhurst and Welbeck College. The Tennis Club played Manchester Grammar School, Leeds Grammar School, Fettes College, George Watson's College Edinburgh and Stoneyhurst College among schools, but also King's College, Bede College Durham, the Old Novos and Jesmond LTC The School also took part in the Public Schools tennis week at Wimbledon. In cross-country running also the School Club ran against King's College, the Durham Colleges, and University College Durham, as well as against local schools. The pattern of fixtures of the Chess Club was even more varied, for matches were arranged not only with local schools and some not so local, but also with the Chess Club of King's College, Magdalene College Cambridge, LNER Gateshead, Parsons, Customs & Excise, Newcastle YMCA, North Shields, Whickham, Newcastle's City Club, and the Ministry of National Insurance. The Boat Club, which was started in 1950 with the use of boats and the boathouse lent by the Tyne Amateur Rowing Club, soon began to compete in regattas on the Tyne and Wear, and in the Tyne Head of the River Race. They raised money to buy their own boats, and eventually to purchase the boathouse and rebuild it. Quite a few boys went on to row for their Colleges at Oxford and Cambridge.

The above details of games fixtures show how the wide range of fixtures, both geographically and in age and expertise, added to the boys' contacts beyond the School and beyond the local area. In some cases it meant that they were meeting tough opposition, and the results often show that the games were as frequently drawn, or lost, as won. But the experience gained was the important thing.

That music and drama were major features of life in the School has already been mentioned, and is well known. The First Orchestra continued to give concerts with programmes that were very ambitious for a school orchestra (even with members of staff taking part, as they did). Symphonies and overtures by Beethoven, Schubert, Mozart and Haydn, ambitious choral works with the help sometimes of the girls' schools, works by modern composers, violin and piano and even horn concertos are included in the programmes, chamber music recitals and concerts by the Second and Third Orchestras were regularly held, and at least one boy went on to play in the National Youth Orchestra.

The XXI Club produced Henry IV Part I (twice), She Stoops to Conquer, Arms and the Man, The Importance of Being Earnest (twice), The Lady's not for Burning, The Rivals, Hamlet, The School for Scandal, and Murder in the Cathedral. At least one boy went on to make a professional career in the theatre.

The major event in the School hall was the annual Speech Day, with the usual short speech by the Chairman, brief remarks by the Headmaster, whose considered report was printed in the programme, and the presentation of prizes and trophies was organised so that it took place with no delay and almost at the double. After the speech by the chief guest, the School song, written by J. B. Brodie, was sung. After the Speech Day parents visited a series of exhibitions of work by the boys which was arranged by most departments of the School.

It is not easy to draw conclusions about the achievements of the School during this period. Of activities that might and did not form part of the School's programme, school journeys abroad to France, Switzerland, Germany and the low countries, as also excursions to Greece for classical studies, which were made by some schools at the time, are noticeable for their absence, Norway being the only European country regularly visited. Another omission is the fact that the School did not attempt to participate in social work, by for instance helping with Boys' Clubs in the poorer districts of the City, which was commonly done by schools of similar standing in pre-war days, and it is not true that the social security introduced from 1948 onwards meant that there was no longer any need for this kind of work, since the 1950s saw some real poverty and plenty of unemployment among those who had just left school. Although the situation in Newcastle was nothing like as bad as it had been in the 1930s, there was still scope for social work of this kind, and also among the elderly, in which sixth-formers could have participated, and to which T. T. Anderson (in his private capacity) made such an outstanding contribution. As far as the Governors are concerned one might ask why they did not arrange for the Scheme of 1909 to be brought up to date, but in practice it was not obsolete in essentials, and did not conflict with the direct grant regulations, although later, when the direct grant ceased, it obviously called for revision. One might also criticise the Governors for dilatoriness in developing the School buildings so slowly, and not arranging for free places to be taken up earlier than they were by local education authorities. Indeed there seemed to be something very old-fashioned about the slow-moving way in which they conducted their business. But the important tasks, those connected with the financial business of the School, were taken very seriously, handled methodically and bore fruit in the very considerable resources which were put at the disposal of the School and in the fact that at no time was it in danger of insolvency.

As far as the staff are concerned the above pages are testimony to their hard work, their belief in what they were doing, their loyalty to the leadership of the Headmaster, though tempered no doubt with occasional criticisms, and the satisfaction they felt in the high reputation of the School. Both the older and the younger members of the staff seem to have devoted not only their working hours to the School but also most of their spare time, for which their pupils were grateful even if at times their wives and families saw little of them. They belonged to the old tradition of grammar school masters, whose conception of their profession and of the pastoral duties which were part of it would have made any thought of the so-called 'industrial action' which afflicts some members of the teaching profession today quite unthinkable.

It is too soon to assess the numbers of Old Novos from this period who have achieved eminence in their professions. After the First World War the cult of distinguished Old Boys became strong in the School, as the portraits displayed in the hall, the School song, and the biographical nature of the massive two-volume history, *Schola Novocastrensis*, by A. R. Laws, demonstrate. Some of the boys from the 1950s are known, like a good many of their predecessors from Dr Thomas's time, to have achieved standing as academics and to have had successful careers in the universities, and it is not unlikely that the number who achieved important positions in other walks of life and whose success has yet to be recorded, will be considerable. But if, as one may assume, the aim of a school is to offer stimulus and opportunity to boys to develop their individual capacities and enthusiasms, to work hard and seriously at their studies, and to reach high standards of performance in other enterprising activities, then the Royal Grammar School was outstandingly successful in these years.

The quality of a school is, as we have said, to be measured partly by its reputation and this (more even than the other factors which contribute to quality) is in the hands of its Headmaster. We have seen what kind of a man Mr Mitchell was, what he believed, what he did and what his personal achievement was, in enlarging and keeping alive and active this school which could claim to be great in more senses than one. To those who were members of the School in whatever capacity in his day, there will be no hesitation in attributing much of its success to him personally and it is fitting to close this chapter with the sensitive and moving words about him used by Mr G. S. Dean in his contribution to the *Novo* on the occasion of Mr Mitchell's retirement in 1960.

'He has shown us the way to keep up with the quickening rhythm of life and yet maintain our stability. He has remained enviably young in spirit and outlook . . . We shall remember him for his broad humanity: his concern for the happiness and welfare of the individual; his compassion for those in difficulty or afflicted by misfortune; for the help and comfort so readily extended. Everyone of us will recall some act of kindness of which only the beneficiary could be aware. He leaves us now, after being our Headmaster, our guide, our friend for close on twelve years, a period in which he has achieved much, and done it all with the quiet undramatic inevitability which is so typical of him. As for judging his achievement impartially, no-one can judge Mr Mitchell impartially – the affection in which he has been held is too real and insistent for that.'[59]

Chapter VII

POLITICAL THREATS AND OPPORTUNITIES, 1960–84

(i) *The School Buildings 1960–84*

An Old Boy of any time between 1910 and 1930 visiting the School in the early 1950s would have found little that was unfamiliar in the physical environment. He would probably have noticed the swimming bath (1930) and the gymnasium (1937) on the Lambton Road boundary, the woodwork and geography block on the southern boundary, and would perhaps have visited the art room (1931) and theatre (1930), which had been added to the main buildings of 1906. By the early 1960s he would find the addition of 1956, with laboratories for physics and chemistry and the new changing rooms and lecture theatre,* but little else. By this time the School had outgrown its accommodation, and a radical re-assessment was needed. Several elements combined to bring this about.

The first was the growth in the number of boys. The buildings of 1906 had been designed for 600 pupils, then an ambitious target. By 1960 there were over 1020 but, as Mr Hennessey shows, the policy of the Headmaster in the early 1960s was to reduce numbers sharply. In the late 1960s and early 1970s, however, numbers rose again. A particularly notable feature was the increasing numbers in the sixth form, rightly regarded as the particular glory of the School, as of others of comparable status, and for which physical provision was seriously and increasingly inadequate. Along with higher numbers went broadening of the curriculum, with development of existing and introduction of new disciplines, and a greater range of choice for the individual boy. This did not reach its full flowering until the late 1970s, partly because of the earlier restraints imposed by lack of accommodation. The same was true for the increasing range of so-called 'extra-curricular' activities which are so important in the all-round education of the individual boy.

*See above, pp. 202–3 and 225–26.

The second major factor was the impending re-organisation of the maintained schools in accordance with the egalitarian theories of the Labour Party, coupled with attacks on the 'privilege' of grammar and direct grant schools. Although the full force of this did not become apparent until late in the decade, the implications were clear at the outset.

Thirdly, what might appear to be a minor incident proved to be the catalyst. This was that the building of the motorway along the west and south boundaries of the School, planned by the city in the 1950s* and expected to start in 1968–69, would require surrender of part of the playing fields and demolition of two buildings on the south perimeter, one housing the rifle range and the other the geography, biology and woodwork departments. It had been accepted that the School would receive compensation for the land and a reinstatement building. It was this which led the Governors to commission an outline Development Plan, in which these various elements were combined.

The most urgent needs were a new dining hall, to be built on the northern boundary of the playing field next to Lambton Road, and the conversion of the existing hall into a new library, which would in turn release space for conversion to sixth-form accommodation. There was also need for new accommodation for the Junior School. As Professor Tuck has described earlier, a somewhat critical report from H.M. Inspectors in 1956 had led the Governors to consider the whole question of the Junior School.† While they did not share the view of the Inspectors that schools such as the Royal Grammar School were better without Junior Schools or Departments, they recognised that the accommodation, then on the first floor at the south end of the main building, was unsatisfactory, and that some changes in teaching arrangements were desirable. In 1965, it was proposed that the Junior School should move into a house or houses, suitably converted. The space released in the main building would be converted mainly for sixth-form use.

The total cost of these developments was put at £150,000; the dining hall needed about £100,000, and the cost of moving the Junior School was put at the absurdly low figure of £20,000, which seems to have been no more than somebody's guess. Direct grant schools received no financial help from government or local authorities for building except that they were allowed to borrow

*See above, p. 226.
†See above, pp. 227–28.

up to 80% of the cost of new buildings and meet the loan charges out of fees, which were partly subsidised from public funds. It was estimated in 1970 that about 15–20% of buildings by the schools had been so financed, and it has been seen that the 1954–56 developments at the Royal Grammar School were financed by mortgage from the city's superannuation fund. In 1965 the Governors decided to launch an appeal, with a target of £150,000 and employing a firm of professional fund-raisers. In just over a year, £120,000 (the interim target) was reached, including about £60,000 from parents, £40,000 from Old Boys and £18,000 from local industry and commerce. The final total was just over £140,000.

In launching the appeal, the Governors took the opportunity to make a statement on the future of the School, in view of the possible effects of the major changes to be expected in the state system. They declared their intention to 'do their utmost to preserve the present character and identity of the School and to enable it to continue to fulfil its function'. While they would also do their utmost to preserve direct grant status, 'if necessary, the School will continue as a separate educational institution'. An explanation was added, that the School could not become a comprehensive school 'without completely losing its identity and character'. Newcastle Local Education Authority had decided to establish eight comprehensive schools for pupils aged 11 to 18, with 'all children from a district being admitted without selection'. But, the Governors went on to point out, 'the RGS has always served the North-East region and will continue to do so while parents will pay fees and while it can compete as a fee-charging establishment providing good teaching and up-bringing and reasonable amenity'. This statement was to provide the foundation for much that followed in the next years.

There were many discussions about the form of the new dining hall, including the possibility of a prefabricated structure, of the type then being used by York University, but in the end it was decided to have a 'traditional' building within a total building cost of £85,000 and at the end of September 1967 the architect was instructed to seek estimates from two contractors, for completion by 1 September 1968, ready for the new school year. This was achieved. Adaptation of the old dining hall to a new library, with certain other improvements including a new sixth-form common room, were carried out in 1968-69.

The move of the Junior School was left in abeyance while the building of the dining hall and the consequent conversions were in progress. It became the main project late in 1969. By then the School had bought a pair of large, but somewhat decrepit, semi-detached houses at 5/7 Lambton Road, at a cost of about £25,000 which was £5000 above the estimate of the total cost of the move included in the appeal. It soon became apparent that there was no possibility of converting the houses for use by the Junior School, on several counts; the needs of the School could not be met, while the cost of fire precautions would be prohibitive, even if approval could have been obtained, which was doubtful. There was no alternative to demolishing the houses and erecting a new building, for which the site was adequate, with careful planning. Again there was much discussion about possible kinds of building, including various forms of prefabrication, and again it was finally decided to have a 'traditional' building, even though at a somewhat higher cost. The design proposed by the architect, which met with general approval, was estimated to cost about £60,000, bringing the total, with cost of the two houses and of their demolition, to £85,000. As there was only about £38,000 available from the appeal, there was a problem of financing.

The only course was again to borrow, and after exploring various possibilities, including one or two Building Societies (which at the time were extending their operations to include financing of, e.g. university residences), the Governors obtained a further mortgage of £36,000 over 20 years, with repayment of £3927 a year, from the city's superannuation fund. Approval of the building plans, the costs, and the arrangements for borrowing had to be obtained from the Department of Education and Science, even though the Junior School received no grants and there were no free places or remissions. Building operations started in July 1971 and were completed in May 1972. The new School proved to be highly satisfactory, and the relief to the Senior School by the removal of the small boys from the rooms above the 'new' library and classrooms at the south end of the main building (the old dining hall) was palpable. These rooms were now converted for use mainly by the sixth form.

The developments consequent on the building of the motorway had coincided with the planning of the new Junior School. The loss of part of the playing field was met by securing the use of intakes on the Town Moor. The reinstatement building, on a new site on the southern boundary, next to Jesmond Parish Church, was ready in 1970, and provided accommodation for the rifle range, in the basement, and for biology, geography and technical studies. The new accommodation was better, and more spacious, than the old. Moreover, the building was designed with a view to future extension, which was not to be long in coming. A problem of some concern was the proximity of the motorway, mainly because of noise, but also because there was some danger from loose balls from the playing field. This latter problem was met by providing high wire fences along the perimeter, and so far (1985) there have been no accidents. As far as noise was concerned, the School was assisted by a report from the Building Science Section of the University's School of Architecture, which considered that the problem was manageable provided that various measures of sound insulation were adopted for the new building. It was thus designed with virtually blank walls on the side adjacent to the motorway, and with various sealed, in some cases double, windows. These have proved satisfactory, while the other buildings suffered no detriment.

Almost as soon as the Junior School was occupied, the Governors turned their attention (or had it turned by the new Headmaster) to other needs. The most important was music, long an outstanding feature of the School, but housed in cramped and unsuitable quarters in the main building. Others were additional accommodation for mathematics, and for biology and technical studies, both of which were already outgrowing their new premises. The solution was a new building to be added to the reinstatement building, principally for music, with an auditorium, practice rooms etc., but also for mathematics, and extensions to the biology laboratory and technical studies workshops. It was decided to have another appeal, this time without professional fund-raisers, and within a little over a year £180,000 was raised, sufficient to pay for the new building, and also for hard tennis courts on the space between it and the motorway. In accordance with the usual practice, the space released by removal of music from the main building was converted to classrooms, offices, and a careers room.

By this time it had become clear that the end of direct grant would not be long delayed, and that the School would become free from any controls by the Department of Education and Science, including those over new buildings and major conversions. Although no major new buildings were intended, there would be continued need for renovation, adaptation and conversion.

Previously no regular or specific financial provision had been made for this. Major building had been financed by appeals or borrowing, with interest charges met from the general income of the School. Maintenance, adaptation and conversions had been financed as they arose, and the costs included in the annual estimates of expenditure, which also had to be met from income, mainly consisting of fees. It was accordingly decided to include an earmarked element in the fees, in 1975–76 of £30 for the Junior School, with total fees of £495 a year, and in 1976–77 of £45 out of £750 for the Senior School. In both cases any increase in fees was little more than that needed to meet generally rising costs, and of course the change was partly one of book-keeping, though of some importance for the planning of physical improvement.

It has been through this that it has been possible to undertake a steady programme of refurbishment and two larger projects. The former included improvements to the art rooms and theatre, completion of the sixth-form common room, and emergency repairs to the swimming bath, to keep it going in safety for a few more years. The latter were the conversion of the north locker room, including the addition of an extra storey, to provide more room mainly for computing, and the reconstruction of the chemistry laboratories at a cost in current prices well above that of building the Junior School.

By 1984, a programme of new building and renovation over twenty years had made good the deficiencies of the 1950s, and the School was well-equipped to cater for the multifarious needs of a population of over 1200 boys, with up to 300 sixth-formers. Even so, there were still some shortcomings, while new needs continued to appear. At the time of writing, the Governors are considering plans for the improvement of sports facilities, including a new sports hall, needed to cater for the increasing demands for indoor activities which cannot be met by the existing gymnasium, and for the rebuilding of the swimming bath.

(ii) *The End of Direct Grant*

In 1965, the Secretary of State for Education and Science had outlined proposals in Circular 10/65 for the reorganisation of schools into a 'comprehensive' system, involving the abolition of selection and the 11+ examination. The exact forms of re-organisation were left largely to local education authorities, who had to submit proposals to the Secretary of State. As little guidance other than the negative abolition of selection was given, the schemes showed enormous variety, which still persists. The voluntary aided grammar schools and those controlled by local education authorities could be included in such schemes, and in fact they were mostly abolished by conversion or absorption into comprehensives. Direct grant schools, which included many of the leading and old-established grammar schools, were not under local education authority control. They were governed by independent bodies, with their own Schemes or Articles of Government – in some cases Royal Charters – and local authorities were involved only to the extent of taking up some places and nominating some governors; by the 1960s many were not even doing this. The Department of Education and Science was only marginally involved, in enforcing the requirement that 25% of the places should be free and allocated to pupils from maintained schools, determining the amount of capitation grants and levels of remission of fees to parents, approving fees charged to all classes of pupil, approval of new building projects and their financing, and holding periodic inspections to enable a school to continue to be recognised as efficient and therefore eligible for direct grant status. For a government determined to end any form of selection, these schools presented a problem, and in October 1967 the Secretary of State re-convened the Public Schools Commission, which had originally advised on 'the best way of integrating the public schools with the state system of education', though with little result. It was now provided with a new Chairman (Professor David Donnison) who had been a member of the original body, and its terms of reference were confined to direct grant schools, as follows:

> 'To advise on the most effective method or methods by which direct grant grammar schools . . . can participate in the movement towards comprehensive reorganisation, and to review the principle of central government grant to these schools.'

This was a good example of the establishment of a body to advise on how pre-determined policy could be carried out, without questioning that policy, as distinct from the great tradition of the nineteenth and earlier twentieth centuries, when royal commissions attempted to diagnose the causes of problems and propose solutions to them. In this, as in other cases, the government was to get most of what it wanted.

The Commission accepted that reorganisation of schools into

comprehensives was desirable and inevitable. It should be remembered that this was an early stage, when the aim of reorganisation was said to be provision of 'a grammar school education for all', with the prospect of widening educational opportunities and raising standards. Even so, two members of the Commission had doubts, considering that 'too much attention has been focussed on the theory of the comprehensive organisation of secondary education and too little on the direct grant grammar schools themselves', and they even subscribed to the heresy that 'an element of academic selection must and should continue in the secondary system for a number of years'. They were, however, voices crying in the wilderness, and the Commission concluded that 'schools which want to play their part within the national framework that serves children throughout the country . . . must enter a comprehensive system of education in which no fees would be charged to parents'. The 'national framework' had become a state monopoly and 'participation in' the movement towards comprehensive education had become 'entering'.

Although several specific issues were considered, and various possible forms of collaboration between the schools and the state system suggested, with emphasis on local consultations in order to secure adaptations of arrangements to suit local needs (and one or two actual examples of co-operation were given), these were largely window-dressing, and there was no doubt that the essential matter was abolition of direct grant and any form of selection. The only question (as in the terms of reference) was how best to do it. Here the Commission was divided. Seven members, including the two who had reservations, suggested Scheme A, which would establish a national body to administer grants to schools which were prepared to accept a new function as 'comprehensives' alongside the maintained schools. Eight members wished to see Scheme B, under which the schools would become more or less voluntary aided, financed by the local authorities, but retaining some limited control over their operations subject to there being no selection. Four members, including the Chairman and Vice-Chairman (Lord Annan), were happy with either Scheme, as achieving the essential objectives, of abandonment of selection, said to be 'creaming' or 'poaching' abler children from the maintained schools, and securing a 'proper' representation of 'social class' and range of ability in the schools.

The Report was published in January 1970, and the Governors again considered the position of the School. In view of the emphasis in the Report on the desirability of local consultation, local authorities in the region were approached. They were presumably too busy re-organising their own schools to be able to evince any interest. The Governors therefore decided that the original decision to remain independent if direct grant were withdrawn should be re-affirmed. At this stage, there were various uncertainties, including the financial implications as well as the possible changes in areas of recruitment. These, of course, were considered by the Governors, insofar as this was possible in the absence of firm information, but they were overwhelmingly outweighed by the fundamental consideration of 1965, that there was no other way in which the integrity of the School could be preserved. The commission had drawn attention to the damage which could be caused by uncertainty, making this a reason for an early government decision, and at the RGS there was much speculation among staff, parents, boys and others. Thus opportunities were taken, for example at Prize-givings, to make clear the intentions of the Governors. The announcements were received generally with relief and approval, particularly by the staff. There were only a few critics, including a boy writing in the school magazine, who deplored what they considered to be a move which would favour better-off parents and hence (a wonderful *non sequitur*) lead to a fall in academic standards.

With the fall of the Labour government in June 1970, the threat receded. The incoming Conservative government was committed to maintain the system, and even encouraged it. In 1971–72, for example, the capitation grant was increased, allowing a reduction in fees, while the income scale for fee remission was made more generous. The School now had four years in which to consolidate, which in various ways it proceeded to do.

With a change in government in February 1974, and Mr Harold Wilson's wafer-thin majority increased in a second election in October, the comprehensive reorganisation proceeded apace, even though the Prime Minister had said that grammar schools would be abolished over his dead body (he was the product of one). Within a few months it was announced that the direct grant system would be phased out. So far as some local authorities were concerned, this had already happened; the two which had originally taken up places at the RGS had ceased to do so, though the school necessarily continued to award free places to boys from their primary schools.

Phasing out would start in 1976, with no capitation or other grants paid for pupils admitted in September, no new free places awarded, and no local authority places taken up. Capitation grants and fee remission would continue to be paid for pupils already in the schools until they left. The alternatives suggested by the Public Schools Commission seem to have been forgotten, and the schools were given only one option, that of entering the state system by becoming the equivalent of voluntary aided schools under the local authority, on condition that they did not indulge in any selection for 'ability or aptitude'.

There was never any doubt that this could not be accepted by the RGS Governors. As had been emphasised in 1965, the School was highly selective, and catered for the whole region; a non-selective comprehensive school serving part of the residential district of Jesmond was a manifest nonsense. It would be even worse if the local authority had decided that it was to draw pupils from a wider catchment area, in order to secure a 'proper social mix', by bringing in some 'working-class' children from, say, the area of the late nineteenth century building at Rye Hill. Another factor was that the Junior School would have been either closed or taken over by the local authority as a non-selective primary school. The Public Schools Commission had considered the 'problem' of the junior and lower schools maintained by many of the direct grant schools and concluded that they could have no place in the new system. The Governors still considered the Junior School to be an integral part of the School, providing on the one hand a very good primary education for selected boys, with many activities supported by the Senior School, and on the other a significant part of the intake to the Senior School, though not as even an implicit right, but, at least from the early 1960s, in open competition with boys from state and other primary schools.

Above all, the Governors felt strongly that they should provide, so far as possible, a first-class education for abler boys throughout the region, which had been the School's function for many decades before Circular 10/65. The Department was therefore informed that the School did not wish to exercise the option of entering the maintained system, and would become completely independent. From a total of 178 direct grant schools in England, 139 decided likewise, including three others* in the Newcastle area. The majority of those opting for incorporation into the state system were Roman Catholic schools, which could manage to retain much of their original identity.

*The two Dame Allan's Schools and the Central High School.

Complete independence had two main implications: firstly for the financial position of the School, secondly for the character of its intake. The two were to some extent linked. It was thought by many that loss of direct grant would involve so substantial an increase in fees, and be so crippling, that schools would be unable to fill their places, and that entering the state system was the only alternative to closing. The Public Schools Commission itself thought that not many schools would opt for independence. Like most critics of non-state education, they misread the character of the schools (as two of their members pointed out) and under-estimated the determination of parents to secure good education for their children. Like most of the leading schools, the RGS was in a strong position. At the time of publication of the Commission's Report, there were eight applicants for every place in the Senior School. It is true that these included some who hoped for a free place, and some who would qualify for fee remission even without one. These numbers could not be estimated, as free places did not depend on parental income, while the amount of fee remission could be quite small. The Senior School fees at this time were £220 a year, and it was estimated that the abolition of direct grant would involve an increase to about £280, which it was thought would not have a substantial effect on demand for places. This proved to be correct. Although there were to be drastic changes which make direct comparison difficult, it is worth noting that after the abolition of direct grant the number of applicants per place in the Senior School fell from eight to four. The number for the Junior School, for which there were no free places or remissions, remained constant at about three.

For various reasons, the relative importance of state support had been dwindling in the 1960s. Some figures for the financial year ending 31 March 1960 have been given in Chapter VI. Of a total income of £133,000, which left a small surplus over expenditure, support from the Department in the form of capitation grants and remissions of fees came to £53,195, or about 40% of income, and fees paid mainly by parents came to £56,737. By 1976, the last year in which direct grant was fully operative, total income and expenditure had risen to £670,000. The amount coming from the Department was £192,000, or 29%, and after remission of fees, free places, bursaries, etc., parents were paying £460,000. By the time abolition of direct grant was complete, in 1983, total income and expenditure was £1.35 million. Capitation grant, at £6,500, was the tail-end for boys who had stayed on for a term to take scholarship examinations, but there now appeared £85,000 for remission of fees under the Assisted Places Scheme, to be discussed below. Fees paid by parents, after remissions and bursaries, came to £1.2 million, or 87% of the total.

The general picture, therefore, was that the School managed to surmount the financial problems of the ending of direct grant. This was made possible by two elements, the phasing out of grant over six years and a coincidental onset of major inflation. One is tempted to say that the government could not have planned it better if it had tried. The increases in fees which would have been needed to compensate for the ending of grant were dwarfed by those needed to meet steadily rising costs, especially of staff salaries. In the event, it is a remarkable result that the increase in fees over the period was slightly less than the rise in prices generally, as measured by the retail prices index. This was in part due to careful management. The School had always been economically organised, and the Governors now paid particular attention to the need to control expenditure so as to ensure that waste was minimised. The achievement in keeping the increase in fees below the level of inflation can be contrasted with the experience of the state system, including the local authorities in the regions served by the School, which had a steady increase in real costs per pupil, financed by the taxpayer.

Of greater significance, at least in the opinion of the Governors, was the possible exclusion of able boys from poorer homes, who previously had free places or remission of fees. There was also the possibility that higher fees would bear hardly on parents in the middle range of incomes, especially those with several children, and again exclude some talented children. It was therefore decided to introduce the School's own scheme for remission of fees, in partial replacement of free places and remission offered under the direct grant regulations. The amount of remission was to be dependent on parental income, with a scale much the same as that of the Department. The limitation was in the number of boys who could be helped; the resources did not permit of automatic remission, and help had to be based on a combination of merit and need. Finance was partly available from the Virgin Mary Hospital Trust whose income was rising, the main source being ownership of property, much of it commercial, in the city, with rising rentals. The School shared in this, by receiving part of the 'surplus' income of the Trust, as defined in the Scheme of 1927. But, further, in

1978 the Charity Commissioners approved a new Scheme for the Trust which, in addition to revising various provisions for managing the Hospital Funds, increased the participation of the School, which now was to nominate two Trustees and also receive a larger share of the 'surplus' income, as newly defined. Whereas in 1960 the School received about £8000, by the mid-1970s this had risen to about £20,000 and by 1984 to almost £50,000. In the revised Scheme, the provision for the award of scholarships for girls to go to university was retained, and at the suggestion of the School, which continued to administer the awards, the total annual sum was increased.

There was also recourse to another, though limited, appeal, to establish an Educational Trust with wide terms of reference but intended primarily to assist parents with payment of fees and to provide scholarships. With a number of larger donations from educational and other trusts, as well as individuals, and two unexpected legacies, a total of over £100,000 was raised in a relatively short time. The Old Novocastrians also organised an appeal to establish scholarships named after E. R. Thomas and T. T. Anderson, to be administered as part of the general Scheme. In this way, the School was able to continue to provide for some boys from poorer homes as it had done for much of its history, of which direct grant was no more than one phase. Nine years after the end of direct grant, and three after the first intake under independence had left, there were few signs of any decline in standards, but many that the School was flourishing as never before. Speculation about possible waste of talent of boys who might have come but did not would be idle.

A further consequence of the abolition of direct grant was the need to revise the Scheme of Government. The main factor was that the strong representation from local authorities was no longer appropriate. Further, a reorganisation of local government was taking place at about the same time. A new Scheme was proposed to the Charity Commissioners, and approved on 26 September 1975. The main change was a reduction in the number of Governors nominated by local authorities from twelve to eight, with Newcastle reduced from ten to three, Northumberland County Council remaining with two, and additions of Durham County Council with one and the newly-established Borough of North Tyneside with two. The number of co-optative Governors was increased from four to eight, thus keeping the total constant at twenty-one. Other Governors continue to be nominated by the

Universities of Oxford, Cambridge and Durham (one each) and Newcastle upon Tyne (two). The opportunity was also taken to remove various anomalies, such as specifying the amount of the fees, the limitation of 'maintenance allowances' payable to boys to £10 a year, and prescribing a minimum of £150 a year to be spent on leaving exhibitions.

(iii) *Assisted Places*

The Education Act of 1980 provided, *inter alia*, for the award of Assisted Places at selected independent schools, and regulations for the Scheme to come into operation by September 1981 were laid before Parliament in November 1980. The main provisions were that schools which were accepted for participation agreements could award specified numbers of places each year to applicants selected according to their own normal procedures, to receive remission of fees according to parental income on a scale starting at the lower end with full remission, with rising parental contributions to a level at which full fees had to be paid. Separate quotas were to be fixed for admision at 11+, 13+ and 16+ (to sixth forms). Not less than 60% of places had to be filled by pupils from maintained schools, but a concession to the comprehensive lobby was that the number of places at 16+ was limited to five per school, with approval of the local authority needed for an award to a pupil from a maintained school. The income scale was subject to annual review, as was the amount of remission for individual pupils, according to changes in parental income as well as in the scale itself. The full cost of remission, including in appropriate cases such items as grants for uniforms, travel and meals, was met by the Department of Education and Science. As had been the case under direct grant, the fees charged to pupils under the Scheme had to be approved by the Department, and excluded certain items, such as provision for scholarship funds, which was reasonable enough, but allowed contributions for buildings, which had been largely excluded from direct grant fees.

Remission was limited to tuition and comparable fees, with exclusion of boarding charges. The Scheme was thus directed largely to day schools, though some boarding schools participated, not only for their day pupils but also for a limited number of boarders, using their own resources to provide scholarships where needed. Acceptance by the Department required a school to provide evidence of a good academic record over a broad curriculum as well as adequate general facilities and a range of other activities. The elaborate questionnaire which had to be completed included an item: 'Other non-educational activities'. The Headmaster was tempted to reply 'None', but instead listed a large number of so-called extra-curricular items which occupied a good deal of the 'free' time of most of the boys. There were also conditions about provision of information for parents, including details of curriculum, and publication of examination performances, which was required also for maintained schools under the 1980 Act. Not all schools which sought to enter the Scheme were accepted.

The Scheme aroused the instant hostility of the enemies of independent education, including the Labour Party, the Liberal Party, the Social Democratic Party, many Local Education Authorities, including Newcastle, Durham, Gateshead and North Tyneside, the teachers' unions, especially the National Union of Teachers, as well as most of what was now the 'educational establishment', largely indistinguishable from the 'comprehensive lobby', and including many of the staffs of training colleges, university departments and institutes, most of the education correspondents of the leading newspapers and television 'presenters' and 'commentators', with some headmasters of independent schools. The Scheme was roundly condemned and misrepresented. It was said to be restoration of the direct grant 'by the back door' and 'ignoring the local authorities', which was partly true, though there was no subterfuge. It was allegedly designed to help the 'wealthy', or at least the 'middle classes', and to reinforce 'privilege'. Mrs Shirley Williams regarded it as 'utterly divisive', being based 'on offering places to the most able children' (the logic is not clear). It was also said to 'pour money into the coffers' of the schools, and keep them in existence whereas otherwise they would presumably have to close. It would also further 'deprive' and 'damage' the maintained schools, presumably by reducing available funds and encouraging the 'creaming' and 'poaching' of their abler pupils. One education professor commented that it was designed to encourage 'some of the worst tendencies in British education', though without specifying what these were.

None of these reactions, as predictable as they were fallacious, would have mattered if it had not been for an announcement by the Labour Party that when they were returned to power they would forthwith abolish the Scheme, without any period of phasing out. It was to be expected that the SDP and the Liberal Party would advocate phasing out the scheme. This posed a dilemma for the schools, with the risk that if they entered the Scheme, within a few years they might be saddled with a moral commitment to maintain a substantial proportion of their pupils who could not pay the normal fees. Many local authorities, including those in the School's catchment area, resolved that they would do whatever they could, within the law, to frustrate the Scheme, and North Tyneside and Gateshead specifically ruled that in no circumstances would they approve the award of an Assisted Place to a pupil from one of their schools for transfer to the sixth form of an independent school.

The Governors, after considerable deliberation, decided that the risks must be accepted in the interests of once again providing wider opportunities to talented boys from poorer homes. In this they took into account that they had the capital of the Educational Trust as a last resort. The majority of former direct grant schools, including the other three in Newcastle which had opted for independence, decided likewise, and the total number entering participation agreements for 1981 was 229. The quotas for the RGS were 55 boys at 11+ and 13+ (in practice the former preponderant) and the maximum of 5 at 16+. They were equivalent to about 40 per cent of the total annual intake and were in line with many of the other major schools, though above the national average. The national figures were just under 4000 at 11+ and 13+ and 960 at 16+.

The Scheme proved attractive to parents, and for September 1981 the RGS had a significant increase in the total number of applications at 11+, above the level of the previous five years of post-direct grant. Parents were offered the choice of applying only for an Assisted Place or the alternative either of an Assisted Place if one were available, or payment of fees if one were not and the candidate reached the standard for admission. Both categories drew significant numbers of applications. Although the quota of 55 places was not filled until 1985, the successful candidates were of high quality, and most came from relatively poor homes. There were no applications at 16+, and this seems to have been partly from lack of knowledge of the Scheme and partly from the hostile attitude of local authorities, which did little to help parents. Indeed, as far as candidates for assisted places at 11+ were concerned, local education authorities tried to discourage Heads of maintained primary schools from providing reports on candidates. These efforts had little effect, for most Heads were more concerned with their pupils' interests than with the ideology of opposition to independent education. As a result of efforts by the School, in 1982 there were more applications for sixth-form entry. In two cases, the local authorities refused approval, entirely on grounds of their original decision not to participate. Fortunately, the School was able to provide bursaries for the two boys on the same terms as Assisted Places. Moreover, the School joined with others in similar case to make representations to the Secretary of State, which resulted in removal of this power from the local authorities from September 1983. There has since been a particularly marked increase in applications at 16+, no doubt largely as a result of the growing inadequacy of sixth forms in comprehensives, and in some cases their replacement by sixth form colleges. Thus in 1983 the School wished to award 10 Assisted Places to 16+ candidates, but was limited to five. The other five were awarded equivalent bursaries from other sources. This has become a regular feature.

In other ways, the experience has been typical of the national picture, with a widening of the opportunities for talented children, and a school population drawn from a wide spectrum of 'social class' and parental income, but with no distinctions between them. The Public Schools Commission noted that the direct grant schools were markedly free of any internal 'class' or other distinctions between pupils, and that there was no kind of recognition that some pupils had free places whereas others had not. Indeed, it seemed somewhat surprised that pupils whose parents paid full fees did not receive any preferential treatment, which illustrates its failure to understand the character of the schools. The same is true of the Assisted Places Scheme; nobody other than those few who administer it even knows which pupils have Assisted Places, and nobody else wishes to know. As has long been the case, differences of 'class', income, 'ethnic' background, and all the other so-called 'divisive' characteristics of a certain brand of sociological theory, count for nothing; all that matters is the ability and aptitude of the individual pupil coupled with genuine effort to develop it and thereby contribute to the corporate life of the School.

Chapter VIII

SOME IMPRESSIONS OF THE SCHOOL IN THE TWENTIETH CENTURY

i) *THE RGS IN THE TWENTIES AND THIRTIES,* by *William Lough*

I entered the Junior School in September 1922 when I was eight. No doubt my parents had worried as to whether I would pass the entrance examination, but with two brothers at the School and my father having been there in the Rye Hill days, I had taken for granted that I would follow them. I had looked forward to wearing the school cap with its proud double badge and its coloured star which denoted your house. Living in Jesmond I was a Blue, but I often wished I were a Brown travelling on the electric train to Jesmond Station, or, better still, a Red coming from across the Tyne. Being a Blue seemed tame in comparison.

We juniors were taught on the ground floor of the main school. At prayers (not 'assembly') we sat in the front pews, patrolling prefects to left and right. 'Come to me after prayers' meant reporting to the sixth-form area behind the platform and being awarded lines or, if you were arithmetically advanced enough, a 'cube'. Stevens's invaluable *School Register* (1955) contains a list of past assistant masters, but does not mention mistresses. In J1 I was taught by Mrs Burns and in J2 by Mrs Akhurst, who later ran her own preparatory school in Osborne Road. I remember both as strict but kindly teachers. One of the subjects Mrs Burns taught us was nature study and I have not forgotten, nor failed to observe, her strict injunction: 'Never pick up a mouse by the tail!' After J2 I passed into male hands. My form master in J4 was 'Buggy' Little, whom we liked, although he was somewhat short-tempered, as befitted a colonel. It was not difficult, if he was in a good mood, to start him off on his war experiences. Form master of J6 and head of the Junior School was the formidable Rutty. Above his blackboard, printed in chalk on the wooden frame, was the legendary 'Non Angli, sed angeli' of Pope Gregory the Great. When displeased with us, Rutty would sweep up to the board and alter the inscription to 'Non angeli, sed Angli'. Later he would relent and reverse it. His standard imposition was the copying out of the 128 lines of Gray's 'Elegy in a Country

Churchyard', a punishment which no doubt enriched for life at
least some who suffered it. You could be high in Rutty's favour
one moment and in deep disgrace the next. How you stood in his
eyes was especially important on Friday afternoon, because then
he would read out the form order for the week, which we had to
copy into our 'form order book'. The book had then to be
presented to him for his written comment and handed in again on
Monday morning, signed by a parent. Sometimes you bore it home
proudly, at other times you sought mother's rather than father's
signature on Monday morning.

To a small boy most of the masters of course appeared old, and
indeed 'Bulldog' Stallworthy and 'Daddy' Laws were masters
whom my father remembered from his Rye Hill days. However
even masters like 'Dicky' Pye, 'Paddy' Lance, 'Bill' Brodie and
'Puppy' Johnson (who owed his nickname to his being 'Bulldog's'
assistant in the French department) seemed scarcely less venerable. One master who looked young, even to us, was 'Jimmy'
Herdman who taught us French in a lively way and whose dramatic
recitation of 'Le corbeau et le renard' is vivid in my memory. In
those days masters were mostly seen in gowns – some wore caps as
well – and that perhaps helped to make them seem older to us
small boys. The custom of wearing gowns in the classroom
declined during the twenties and, I think, ceased in the thirties.*
Some masters, notably H. N. ('Boiler') Smith, held out longer
against the changing fashion, but even Smith in the end abandoned
his gown and seemed in doing so to take on a new, more benign
persona. I am not certain that 'George' Burdon, whom I cannot
recall otherwise than in black suit and cap and gown, ever did
capitulate. Burdon was one of the few masters by whom I was
never taught and with whom I never came into contact.

Thomas inspired a special awe. In his presence one felt
somehow grubby and unworthy. I still picture him immaculate in
dark blue suit and white collar. Walking or standing he always
held his head high and, with his aquiline nose, bore an air of
distinction, indeed of nobility. His appearance on the platform at
prayers imposed immediate silence, and he had only to stand in
the middle of the hall at break for a hush to descend. He would
speak out forcefully against anything which he regarded as morally
wrong and any behaviour which might bring discredit on the
School. One occasion – I do not recall what form I was in then –
remains impressed on my memory. Thomas was addressing the

*It was revived in the 1950s (Editors' note).

chool after prayers and expressing his disgust at reports he had
ceived of smutty talk. He concluded his outburst by declaiming
a passionate tones Sir Galahad's 'My strength is as the strength of
n because my heart is pure', turned and strode off the platform,
aving us with that last word, 'pure', ringing unforgettably in our
ars. To set against that memory is another of a house tea at which
o my astonishment, or rather embarrassment, so incongruous
ith his Headmasterly dignity did it seem to me, he joined in the
nging of a popular song of the period which began: 'Chick, chick,
hick, chick, chicken, lay a little egg for me'. Thomas took care to
e seen constantly around the School, observing, chiding,
ncouraging. There was a period when he would exhort dawdlers
ith a sharp 'Vite! Vite!' Many will recall his personally led
ampaign to eradicate the dandelion. He took trouble to learn
oys' names. He evidently made a point of knowing at least one
act about every boy. A contemporary tells me that the fact
homas knew about him was that his mother was subject to
iverish headaches, and that he found it very embarrassing to be
ssociated in Thomas's mind with his mother's ailments. Thomas
ound time to do some teaching. I had him briefly for physics and
ater for chemistry. I was too overawed to be at ease with him as a
eacher. One very vivid memory is of a chemistry lesson in which
ie promised he would produce some ozone for us to smell. The
lemonstration appeared to succeed. He was holding a dish up to
iis nose and proclaiming: 'Ha! Just like Brighton!' when the
nixture exploded in his face and he rushed out of the laboratory,
eaving us horror-stricken and sure that he was blinded. However
ie soon returned, rubbing his face with some substance, and
issured us that he was unhurt, carrying off the incident with
idmirable aplomb. In the sixth form we had a regular weekly
period with Thomas which might be divinity or philosophy (holism
vas at one time an enthusiasm of his, following a visit to South
Africa on which he met Smuts), discussion of some topic of the
day, or talk by a visitor. He was fond of the Prophets – 'Hosea has
a message for every one of you', I remember him proclaiming –
and the Psalms. Sometimes he set us passages to be learned by
heart.

I have a clear memory of the ceremony in 1923 at which the
memorial organ was unveiled. I can still picture the drawing aside
of the Union Jack to reveal the carved organ face with its solemn
inscription and recall the sound of that sad hymn 'O valiant
hearts'. Each boy received a copy of a commemorative volume

271

which contained the names of the dead together with
biographical note on each and in many cases details of th
circumstances of their death and tributes to them. I rememb
reading and re-reading my copy and, even as a small boy, having
sense of the utter horror and tragedy of that war. Each year th
Armistice Day ceremony would reawaken that feeling. Thoma
would lead the observance of the two minutes' silence – an
silence it was – the beginning and end of which were proclaime
by cannon and the end marked too by the sound of factory siren
The hymns were in keeping: 'O God our help in ages past'; an
Kipling's 'Recessional'. The words of the latter had not y
become unacceptable.

The organ was a splendid acquisition. The hall became visuall
and musically unthinkable without it. It lent dignity and solemnit
to prayers and doubtless helped many to learn to love wh
George Eliot called 'that strange blend of exultation and sadnes
which belongs to the cadence of a hymn'. For myself I can say th
the tunes and, for a great part, the words of the hymns we san
have remained with me throughout my life. Those we sang mos
frequently were the well known morning hymns. 'Christ whos
glory fills the sky', 'Forth in thy name O Lord I go', 'New ever
morning is the love' are the ones that come most readily to mind
The collection contained a number of Latin hymns, but there i
only one – *O gentes omnes undique* – which, I recollect, w
learned, and sang from time to time. Thomas had a fondness for
hymn by the former Headmaster of Rugby, Jex-Blake, whicl
enjoined us to be thankful 'for the thrill, the leap, the gladness o
our pulses flowing free' and once became quite angry because w
were singing it with such lack of conviction. I think we took neithe
to the sentiments nor to the tune. As a Welshman Thomas migh
have been expected to give us a lead, but at prayers he did no
obviously join in the singing.

Prayers were, of course, not attended by the quite considerabl
number of Jews in the School. The service was undenomination
in character. I remember, when a master, hearing it criticized a
not specifically enough Christian. There was muttering a
Thomas's habit of concluding his prayers with the words 'throug
Jesus Christ our *Leader*'. It is related that once Michael Roberts
when mildly reproved by Thomas for rarely attending prayers
retorted: 'Your prayers, Sir, are for atheists and agnostics. I am
Christian!' The story is not improbable. Thomas never resente
plain speaking and Roberts was certainly given to it.

Of course hall and platform are associated in my memory with
any occasions other than prayers. There were Lord Mayors'
sits with the pleasant anticipation of the traditional request for a
y's holiday. There were tediously long prize-givings with rare
yous moments, as when one local dignitary, pointing to the
rtly then Dean of Durham, told us: 'You'll have to eat a lot of
idding before you're as fat as the Dean there', or another
pressed the hope that we would 'all grow up into fine men and
omen'. School concerts, plays, like Simpson's memorable
gamemnon, house singing competitions – all took place in the
ll. Sometimes the whole School would be addressed by a
stinguished visitor. One such was the then famous Savoyard, Sir
enry Lytton, who sang to us and also confided that he had run
vay from school to get married. I remember wondering at the
ne what Thomas thought of that revelation. A visit which gave
e particular pleasure was that of the 'Intimate Opera' company,
om which I date my liking for opera.

In 1925 I passed into the 'Twos'. We from the Junior School now
und ourselves alongside and in competition with the 'scholarship
ys'. My tutor from now on was the amiably eccentric 'Paddy'
ance. His tutor's report on me invariably read 'conduct good' and
nnot have been very helpful to my parents. In my first term in
e 'Twos' fell the four hundredth anniversary celebrations. I
ppose it was fair to date the foundation of the School from the
gning of Horsley's will, though the handsomely bound little
tory of the Royal Grammar School' by Laws and Brodie, of
hich every boy received a copy, states firmly enough on the title
age 'founded by Thomas Horsley in 1545'. I have always
ssumed, perhaps wrongly, that the celebration in 1925 was part of
homas's ambitious plans to enhance the standing of the School
cally and nationally. Until I recently learned otherwise I had
ways attributed to Thomas the initiative in the re-erection at the
uthern gate of the School of the pillars which had stood at the
ntrance to the Virgin Mary Hospital. However Thomas must
rtainly have welcomed the step.

To revert to the anniversary celebration, the actual ceremony
vidently made much less impression on me than the 1923
remony, since my only recollection is the deplorable one that at
e necessarily boring rehearsal a paper dart of mine sailed out of
n upstairs classroom into the midst of proceedings in the hall,
ausing me to be summoned to Thomas's presence, luckily to
ceive nothing more than an admonition. No doubt I expected to

273

be caned, for Thomas did cane, but, I think, unwillingly and only
for serious offences. Rutty, as Head of the Junior School also
caned, but I do not think that other masters were authorized to do
so, though the PT master, Leblique, and his successor, Colonel
Robinson ('Potson'), used to inflict summary and (as I can testify)
painful punishment, the former with a cut-down billiard cue, the
latter with a rattan cane. Generally the power to award the much
disliked Saturday morning detention ('Saturday morning, 9.15
sharp!') was an adequate instrument in the hands of assistant
masters for dealing with unsatisfactory work or conduct, and
anyhow the masters with whom one dared take liberties were few.

The list of masters in the 1925 commemorative volume shows
how Thomas had already introduced new blood into his staff. Of
the men appointed some – Herdman, Theakstone, Anderson,
Dean, Boll, Meaken – were to join established figures like
Williams, Middlebrook, Smith, to form the backbone of the staff
for the next thirty years and more. Others – Bunn and Roberts
spring immediately to mind – were to move on but to leave a
strong mark on the School. If Thomas was seeking men who would
stir and stimulate, he found them in these two, who let in a blast
rather than a draught of fresh air and whose influence extended
beyond the class-room to the whole life of the School. They must
have been a trial to their staider colleagues for they often shocked
us by their unconventional ways. I remember enjoying English
with Bunn who had us out on the floor acting the ballad of 'The
Abbot of Canterbury' with borrowed (or commandeered?)
masters' gowns for costume. His history teaching was equally
lively, though in the Fours we bore him some grudge for the
collective disaster we suffered at the School Certificate
examination, which we attributed to his cavalier attitude to the
syllabus. I have a vivid memory of his musical appreciation periods
in the sixth, in particular the thrill of hearing for the first time 'The
Silver Swan' and a Palestrina mass. Neither he nor Roberts were
comfortable, patient teachers, prepared to go at the pace of the
slowest. I remember once asking Roberts in physics to go over
something again and getting the cold reply: 'I never produce the
same rabbit twice'. Both professed contempt for marks and exams.

Two memories of 1926 stand out in my mind. The first is of
prayers on the first day of the General Strike: Thomas looking
particularly grave and announcing that we were to sing that other
version of the National Anthem, 'God bless our native land'. The
other memory is of the shock on hearing that Leblique, feared for
his strictness yet liked, had killed himself.

1926 was the year of the first school camps. Bunn and Roberts, ho were already starting new societies, producing plays and enerally revolutionising life outside the classroom, were the riving force behind the enterprise, though it was the devotion and amina of 'Tucker' Anderson, Pallister, Watson and others which nsured that school camps became an established institution. homas gave strong support, seeing in them no doubt a means of roviding for the day-boy some experience of communal living, as ell as the challenge of hard physical effort and exposure to wind nd weather and, sometimes, to danger. For a boy like myself, rought up to believe that wet feet could lead to pneumonia, it was n experience at my first camp to see Roberts plunge into and cross a mountain stream and to be invited brusquely to follow im. That first camp was a harsh introduction, for we were flooded ut. From their modest beginnings at Dipton Mill the camps teadily increased in number and variety. The Stratford camps, hough not 'real camping' (the site was a permanent one), rovided a week by the river as well as a concentrated course of hakespeare at the new Festival Theatre. I have a special reason to emember the 1929 camp, because I was only saved from drowning n the Avon by the quick action of one of our party who was enerally looked upon as a 'black sheep'.

From the late twenties reading parties and journeys abroad as vell as camps became an integral part of school life. Herdman nd Theakstone took parties to France, and Theakstone smaller roups to Germany. The French parties stayed in schools, the ierman ones with families. Anatole was no believer in the simple fe and would never have been persuaded to camp. However the ourneys to Germany were made on the small, essentially cargo-arrying vessels of the Tyne-Tees Steam Shipping Company plying etween the Tyne and Rotterdam, Antwerp and Hamburg, and here was always a strong risk of seasickness, from which Anatole imself suffered horribly. I recall hearing his groans when being ressed by the steward to a 'nice 'am sandwich'. I was one of the roup which he took to Hanover in 1930. I recollect our asking him n that visit who this Hitler was, whose name and face we kept eeing on posters, and being told that he was a nine days' wonder nd not to be taken seriously. Mention of Herdman and heakstone brings to mind their numerous productions of French nd German plays during the thirties. They took over from gruff Puppy' Johnson, a demanding producer, as I found when I twice ad a part in a French play. I still smile to myself when I think of

275

the deft way in which once, just before the curtain rose, h
transformed a male chest into a female bosom by the simple mean
of crumpled newspaper.

Returning to 1927, that was also the year in which Milner joine
the staff simply as 'music master', I think, rather than with the titl
of 'director of music'. In the Junior School we had had 'singing
under 'Daddy' Smallwood, whom I remember as wearing a cap bu
not a gown, which I thought odd. It was thoroughly enjoyable t
sing the songs in the little blue book we used (words only), song
like "Twas Friday morn when we set sail', 'The jolly Arethusa'
'All through the night', but I do not recall that after the Junio
School we had any more music periods and I have always regrette
not having been given some basic musical training at that receptiv
age, just as I wish that 'drawing' had been more imaginativel
taught in my day. Anyway Milner's appointment marked th
beginning of a period in which music played an ever mor
important part in school life, more and more boys learne
instruments, the orchestras and choirs were created, the hous
singing competition was instituted and the school echoed in th
lunch hour and on Saturday mornings with 'noises, sounds an
sweet airs'. It is well known how enthusiastically Thomas wa
behind this expansion which he led from the front by taking up th
'cello. New masters were encouraged to follow his example, bu
perhaps did not always do so wholly willingly. At any rate there i
a story that at one school concert certain discordant sound
procured the release of two young masters from what the
regarded as an imposition.

Was it in 1926 also that 'Willy' Featherston ('Featherbed'
constructed his famous sand-yacht which he sailed at Druridg
Bay? I am not sure of the year, but I remember the wide currenc
which his 'fine day for boating' (Northumbrian vowels an
intonation) gained in the School for a time.

Games and sports played a larger part in the life of many of m
contemporaries than they did in mine. I enjoyed them in th
Junior School, especially cricket. The sound of the motor mower
the smell of the freshly cut grass, the impatient waiting for the en
of the lesson, the disappointment when it rained, are vivi
memories. After Junior School I seem to have lost interest. Whe
I was in the middle school we started using the Bento
playing-fields. What has stuck in my memory however is not th
games we played there but the journeys to and fro in the rattly an
smelly blue corporation buses of the time.

SOME IMPRESSIONS OF THE SCHOOL IN THE TWENTIETH CENTURY

I have dim memories of the visit of the King and Queen in 1928 to open the Tyne Bridge and the new Heaton Grammar School. I seem to remember our proceeding to Heaton in a kind of military operation under the command, appropriately, of 'Boiler' Smith and, perhaps erroneously, associate the occasion with the singing of Parry's 'Jerusalem'. Of 1929 my memories are stronger. It was the year of the North East Coast Exhibition which was held in what was then called 'Bull Park'. An attraction of the exhibition was a carillon from Belgium on which recitals were given at intervals during the day and I associate with that summer the somewhat melancholy strains of Beethoven's 'Minuet in G' which were constantly wafting over to the School. 1929 was also School Certificate year for my form. Shortly before the exam we attended a performance at the 'Royal' of our set play, *Twelfth Night*. What I chiefly remember of the evening is the struggle to concentrate on the play while my thoughts kept wandering to the road accident that lunchtime in which one of our form had been killed.

The early nineteen thirties were an exciting time to be at the School. It was a period of change and expansion. The houses were renamed in accordance, I suppose, with Thomas's insistence on the public school status of the RGS. Robert Davison, who was head boy in the year 1930–31, tells me that Thomas invited him to choose which of the four historic names his house, Green, should bear. He chose Eldon. In the same year the light blue blazer and cap with the new badge were introduced. I still think they were pleasing. I do not recall feeling humiliated by having to wear a cap and, unless I am deceiving myself, I believe that I was still wearing mine as a prefect. However there were some who would not conform, and I am told that Thomas later relaxed the rule for prefects. From a boy's point of view the capital event of the time was the opening of the swimming bath, yet another gift of Sir Arthur Sutherland. For all his munificence it cannot be said that Sutherland was popular with us boys. His interest in the School was felt to be somewhat proprietorial. A symptom of this feeling was the birth of the irreverent practice of introducing his name into the last verse of the School Song.

To this period too belonged the addition of the theatre with its well-found stage, and the transformation of the art room into the handsome panelled Plender Library. We sixth-formers were allowed to work there in our free periods and began to regard the room as our domain and to resent the intrusion of masters. I associate it especially with those discussions and arguments –

277

religious, philosophical, political – that too often diverted us from our set work but were doubtless part of our education. Nowadays the room looks different. At the south end there used to be a dais, also a door through which Thomas used sometimes to make a surprise and unwelcome entry. We had our prefects' meetings with him there. I recall one at which, having found that the greater freedom of speech and suggestion he had conceded to us was, inevitably, being abused, he burst out with: 'I'm tired of this damned democracy. *I* am the Headmaster!' Once the sixth form had to assemble there to be addressed by the great anthropologist, Sir James Frazer, author of *The Golden Bough*. The frail old man could however do no more than murmur an apology for disappointing us. I was deputed to escort his charming French wife who, when in the course of conversation I confessed that I had not yet been to France, embarrassed me considerably by her rejoinder: 'Eh bien, monsieur, tant pis pour la France!' The Plender Library was much used by the various school societies. It provided a dignified meeting-place for the Debating Society which flourished at that time thanks to such lively debaters as G. D. R. Davies and Lyall Wilkes. It was the latter, I think, who was responsible for the adoption of the custom of signifying assent and dissent by the cry of 'why aye!' and 'why no!' respectively, a custom which, I understand, has not survived.

What good fortune it was for the School when, in 1931, Miss Steven was appointed to take charge of catering. My memory of the pre-Steven days is of eating a sandwich lunch in a rather bleak dining hall. Under Miss Steven's management lunch, an excellent hot meal served in a refurbished dining hall, became a significant social occasion in the life of the School. The numbers staying for lunch grew to the point where three sittings became necessary. 'Ma' believed firmly in good order and discipline. She was no respecter of persons. Once at tea I heard Thomas venture the jocular remark that he had already seen the cake figure as pudding, only to receive 'Ma''s crushing rebuke: 'Eat it up and don't grouse!' With her in command behind the scenes functions such as house teas and the Toast List became very pleasurable occasions. She had no doubt of her importance and walked with a queenly tread, but under a brusque manner she hid the kindest of hearts. Mention of 'Ma' reminds me that there were others of the non-teaching staff who at various times were important in our daily life. There was the caretaker, Innerd, first of the dynasty, constantly on the prowl, so it seemed, to catch us small boys in ome misdemeanour. Perhaps the bark of Challons, school ecretary. 'the Major', was worse than his bite, but it is the fierce ark that I remember. His successor was the gentler Padgham, a amiliar figure to us all because for years he had come round lasses in first period to take the names of absentees. Later, as a naster, I learned to respect him as the hardworking servant of a by o means easy master.

The hopes placed in the North East Coast Exhibition of 1929 vere vain, for that same year came the Wall Street crash and the eginning of the world economic crisis. And so it was that a period n which the School was flourishing as never before coincided with a deteriorating national and international situation. The growing ikelihood of another war was a horrifying prospect. Many of us in he sixth were strongly moved by the anti-war books of the late wenties and early thirties: 'All quiet . . .', 'Journey's End' (of which I recall a fine School production), the war poetry of Owen and Sassoon. Nor could we believe that the League of Nations and he succession of disarmament conferences could fail. In 1932, with Thomas's blessing, a letter went from the sixth form to the Prime Minister, appealing to him to support disarmament, 'to remove the black cloud hanging over our lives'. Inevitably there were 'pacifists' and 'militarists' in those days. Many of us would nave nothing to do with the OTC 'Join the Corps and become a corpse' was a crude slogan of the period. By the time I left school he 'black cloud' was still blacker, for Hitler was already in power.

Thomas was never too busy to talk to Old Boys. To call on him at School was to be invited to lunch at his high table. Those of us who, encouraged by him, had sought and secured a place at Oxford or Cambridge remember his unfailing attendance at our O.N. dinners. It may not be generally known that he often put some welcome pocket money in the way of old boys 'down for the vac' by engaging them to assist the regular staff towards the end of term. The remuneration, I recall, was £1 a day – a not ungenerous sum in those days. It was on such an occasion that he invited me to join the staff. I was very ready to serve under him and to learn my job under Anatole, and proud to become the colleague of men like 'Sammy' Middlebrook. As a master I found that Thomas trusted you and was always ready to advise and encourage you. I appreciated too that he did not hold your mistakes against you. Once I was in charge of an inter-school cross-country event and, because of my inadequate arrangements for the finish, the race ended in chaos and recriminations. To my surprise and relief he

279

dismissed the matter as of no importance, thinking no doubt that I had learned my lesson.

Looking back I am sure Thomas must have intended my first term as a master to be a probationary one. I found myself required to take the Autumn 'retakes' in four subjects. Once I walked out on them in despair, to find them thereafter more docile. Otherwise my recollections of the classroom over the next three years are somewhat dim. Stronger are the memories of school camps – for I was soon conscripted by 'Tucker' Anderson – of climbing and walking trips to the Alps and the Jura under the unforgettable leadership of Michael Roberts, of struggles to master the flute at least to the point of being judged fit to join the orchestra. Throughout those years however the international situation was growing ever more threatening as Hitler's intentions were revealed. There were at times political tensions in the common room which Anatole would try to relieve with an appropriate Russian proverb, or his: 'It's all the fault of those bloody foreigners!'

Thomas was interested by the way in which the Nazi movement had captured the mass of German youth and he accepted an invitation to visit one of the special schools for training future leaders. He asked me to accompany him and I joined him in Berlin in the Easter holidays of 1938. He was of course treated as an important visitor. The moment of that visit which I treasure came when one of the two officials briefing him explained that of course they did not insist that pupils should be tall, blond and blue-eyed. 'No, it wouldn't be wise, would it?' he said, looking hard at the two short, dark men and treating them to his characteristic 'ha-ha'. He told me after the war how horrified he had been when I had pointed out to him a newly posted announcement that two men had been executed with the axe that very morning for treason.

Later that year came the Czech crisis and the threat of immediate war. I remember listening appalled to Hitler's brutal address to the German people, to hear which I had invited our German *assistant* to my home. That the threat of war was real was brought home by the chilling sight of the sandbagged School hall, a sight I can never forget. Somehow the shock of that crisis braced us for the events of the following year and we accepted calmly the evacuation to Penrith. I like to believe that in the early days there I was of some help to 'Tucker' in his search for billets and in the running of 'Sandath'. At the end of that first term at Penrith, in company with other young masters, I departed for other scenes.

(ii) *THE WAR-TIME EVACUATION, by Donald Shipley*

In the five years of its evacuation the RGS experienced a new form of school life, a discontinuity in its long history and a potential for good and ill both for itself and for its temporary home. Its experience was almost unique, for over the whole country only 14% of the children who were expected to be evacuated stayed more than a few months, and the RGS was one of the rare schools that stayed on as a unit. Personal impressions of what it was like have been recorded by George Pallister in his 'Evacuation', published in 1979. In contrast with what were regarded as 'golden years for the School' in the 1930s, with their regular routine of work and play, predictable achievements and firm discipline under the ever-present authority of the Headmaster, evacuation meant makeshift, unsettled conditions and the decentralization of control: it was recognized as a 'crisis' for the School. For some boys it was a baffling, even worrying, absence of regulation and routine guidance, but new freedoms gave other boys an appealing libertarian opportunity for self-fulfilment and self-discipline. Could it be that during evacuation the School perhaps acquired its own liberal momentum for change to add to the general slackening of authoritarian discipline in the years immediately after the war?

Amid the growing tension in Europe the government had long been taking advice about the dangers of air raids and the effects of bombing on cities, and judging by events in Spain and China they expected sudden massive destruction and mass exodus to the country in panic. Sir John Anderson's committee was formulating final plans for the evacuation of schoolchildren, which had been under consideration for several years. Parents, teachers and others had submitted their opinions, many opposed to the suggestion, and in the end it was decided that the scheme should be voluntary. As a direct grant school the RGS and its Governors as yet felt free to make their own arrangements for evacuation and had already responded energetically to government circulars on the subject of air raid precautions when, for instance, a wall of sandbags was built in the hall as 'an air raid shelter' in the 1938 crisis and T. T. Anderson had searched the north of England for a suitable country house to accommodate the School in an emergency. Such a realistic view of a possible outbreak of war was far from common at that time in Britain.

Early in 1939 the government announced details of its scheme, designating danger, neutral and reception areas and requiring parents in danger areas to make their choice. RGS was in the danger area which extended from Newcastle to Wallsend and Tynemouth on the north side of the river, and from Whickham Gateshead and Felling to Hebburn, Jarrow and South Shields on the south side. In February the House Committee had advised that in their opinion the Governors would 'incur grave responsibility if they attempted to carry on the School in some place outside the danger zone', because the School had 'no funds available out of which the cost of doing this could be defrayed and parents might not be willing to be parted from their sons or pay the increased fees' for boarding. The Governors referred the matter back for further consideration and in March the Headmaster announced that the School would join the government's scheme: no schools in the danger area would remain open if war came. In April he was co-operating, like other headteachers, with the local authority 'in making the arrangements for the evacuation when ordered by the government on the occasion of an emergency'.

The government gave local authorities the responsibility and powers to make the necessary plans. The Town Clerk, John Atkinson, became the Evacuation Officer, but later Thomas Walling, the Director of Education, was made Schools Evacuation Officer. In the spring term of 1939 Walling assigned schools to the reception areas and worked out the details with, for instance, the London and North Eastern Railway Company for the massive movement of over 30,000 children away from the danger area in a single day, and the schools were told of the arrangements that had been made. Headteachers were required to ascertain parents' wishes at meetings to be held between 27 April and 5 May and E. R. Thomas met parents on 4 May when they expressed their confidence in the scheme. The School was allocated to Penrith: for Walling envisaged that poorer schools were, if possible, to be sent to nearer destinations and senior schools to the more remote parts. He also tried to match each school with a similar school in the reception area, so that similar facilities could be shared, and Penrith's Queen Elizabeth Grammar School together with two maintained schools were to receive the RGS.

These arrangements, then, were made on behalf of all schools by Thomas Walling. One thing that E. R. Thomas was able to do in preparation which perhaps other Headmasters may not have done was to make close and repeated contact with the receiving schools, Penrith Urban District Council, Church authorities and other institutions, to arrange accommodation for administration and teaching over and above what was to be provided under the scheme, some of it in extra rooms which had to be rented. He also met the Billeting Officer, Mr Huntley, who was the Clerk to the Council, for, in addition to providing for the continued education of evacuees, the local authority in the reception area was required to list accommodation in private households for them. During the summer months homes were found for boys, masters and masters' wives, so that when on 1 September Poland was invaded and schools were closed, children were taken to safety with their teachers and settled in their billets.

The School and the town seem to have been ideal partners. Penrith, a country town of about 9000 inhabitants, on the edge of the Lake District, had most of the amenities a city-dweller would appreciate. It also had a long history, its own ancient Grammar School, a lively community with active leaders and traditional values, many of its members prosperous and church-going; a society anxious to help and to contribute to the war effort. Other schools were not so fortunate. There were exceptions, of course, in Penrith: Mr Huntley had a major task to persuade householders voluntarily to take in evacuees, and there were cases of householders preferring to make more lucrative arrangements with unofficial evacuees. Over the country, even where compulsory orders had been made, some householders were taken to court before they accepted anyone; and there were unhappy billets which had to be changed in the first few days when parents visited their sons by arrangement with the Headmaster.

The other partner, the School, was, for its part, well equipped for the ordeal. It had earned a national reputation before the war for its academic record and for its advanced and enlightened ideas and practice of education. The emphasis that was put on pastoral care and leisure activities contributed much to its ability to withstand the pressures of uprooting and severance from home. The tutor system brought continuous supervision by a 'School Father' and guidance throughout the boy's changing world of school. Camps, clubs for sports and hobbies, arts and science societies, encouraged active participation and leadership among the boys in the company of a team of masters dedicated to the School, whose interests reflected and were reflected in the range of its activities. Prefects took much responsibility for general discipline and were mature young men, among the most distinguished in academic work and games, a valuable support.

'Evacuation, which started as an administrative problem,

became instead a multitude of problems in human relationships', and the Government's scheme has since been criticized for concentrating almost wholly on the administrative arrangements to the neglect of human nature. However, a warm welcome was awaiting the RGS at the railway station, for the Penrith authorities had arranged for the School to be met on arrival with emergency rations, a meal, escorts, cars and supervisors. But anxieties still remained: for children, some of whom found leaving home a terrifying experience, exposed to physical, moral and psychological dangers; for parents, facing the splitting up of families, with men, too, going away to war; for the School, improvising facilities for care and education; for hosts and hostesses, opening their homes to strangers; for staff, uprooted indefinitely from their homes; for Penrith, meeting its own problems of war and blackout, with men away, adjustments in employment, shortages and the influx not only of the RGS but of other Newcastle children, too. So despite the excellent arrangements made by Atkinson, Walling and Huntley, and the work of E. R. Thomas during the past seventeen years which had prepared the School to 'stand on its own feet', as time went on in Penrith strains built up which gave rise to the human problems. It is not difficult to imagine the impact on a small household of active, sturdy-spirited members of the RGS: small households, too, could not always offer the comforts many boys had enjoyed at home. *Lancet* reported that 'enuresis (bed-wetting) proved to be one of the major menaces to the comfortable disposition of evacuated children', and it happened at Penrith. Cases of indiscipline arose. In the town, too, shopkeepers were suspected of giving favoured treatment to their own customers at the expense of the visitors over goods in short supply.

Elsewhere problems of this kind seemed insurmountable and it is a commonplace that evacuation brought to light facts which revolutionized the study of sociology. Surveys were made and in Cambridge, for example, lack of information about individuals, of social workers to tackle problems and of facilities for parental consultation were identified and deplored. The RGS was fortunate in having useful resources of pastoral care: the tutor system, parents' conferences, experience of camps and long-established concern for the individual were adapted to provide some remedial treatment, however amateur, and masters' wives and the ladies of Penrith did important work as voluntary helpers. Parents attending a meeting in the first few days thought the weekly maintenance allowance payable to householders inadequate and agreed to supplement it with an additional 5s which, though resented by other schools in the area, greatly eased the School's acute problems of billets, much aggravated from time to time by the arrival of unofficial evacuees who offered higher payment.

The provision of hostels, running counter to the government's initial preference for private billets, was perhaps one of the most significant features of the RGS evacuation. Conditions in the hostels varied from the spartan to the moderately comfortable; the usual furnishings – camp-beds or double-bunks, trestle tables and sometimes not even any floor-covering – were far from luxurious. Yet in spite of hard winters, hostels were very healthy and so popular with boys and parents that there were waiting lists for transfer from billets, though it was recognized that for some a billet was preferable. It was difficult at times to find enough suitable assistant masters to become wardens, and in 1942 the Headmaster himself took over Roundthorn for a time. There were other problems. Loyalty to the hostel cut across the House system and prevented the fullest integration into the School. By 1943 the *Novo* reported that leisure hours, particularly in hostels, were almost wholly occupied with trivialities, but masters and boys were convinced, and still are, that there were enormous gains in independence, self-sufficiency and self-maintained discipline from the communal life in hostels.

As time went on, new strains built up. Staff and senior boys were called up, societies were less active, the *Novo* itself attracted fewer contributions. The salaries of the staff were eventually increased to meet out-of-pocket expenses but complaints brought the response from Newcastle that 'there was a war on' and from Penrith 'that some of the Governors do not realise the very great difficulties under which we have been working'. The *Novo* was soon reporting the first fatal casualties among Old Boys.

Teaching was at the beginning of the war a reserved occupation for men above the age of 25; later, from 1 August 1940 the age was raised to 30. Replacements for staff were hard to find. There were some appointments of men but the main help came from ladies, of whom seven are recorded in addition to those teaching music. A list of staff at Penrith shows the Headmaster and a total of forty men assistants, but only 24 were there permanently. 11 men served in the forces, others went to do scientific research or other work. Prefects were allocated to tutor sets to interest themselves in individual members, reinforcing the efforts of tutors, and other senior boys were called upon and urged 'to help younger boys along'.

Above all, perhaps three features distinguish the RGS evacuation from others that did not last. The strong sense of purpose alongside frank discussion of difficulties is well illustrated in the *Novo*. The continuity of examination success was largely made possible by the wise provision of extra accommodation which enabled a full day of nine lessons to be timetabled instead of the half-day schooling of the double-shift system. But most important was the enormous effort made to occupy the minds, bodies and interests of the boys. This last need was recognized in a Board of Education Circular issued late in August 1939, which recommended a strict daily routine, the exploitation of interests offered by the locality and the provision of leisure activities. Where children immediately began to return home, a school could not have had time to initiate such a programme, but the Circular reads almost as a blueprint for life at the RGS both pre-war and during evacuation, for leisure activities supervised by masters with appropriate skills and experience ranged immediately from mountaineering and bird-watching to drama, music, games and cadet training: studies appeared in the *Novo* of the origins of Queen Elizabeth Grammar School, the receipt of its Charter in 1564 and its history; of the uses of the Beacon to give news of the Scots and the Spanish Armada; of the plague in Penrith and the guns Cromwell brought to the town. Boys and masters took part in local productions in Penrith Playhouse, contributed to the town's war effort and gave help on, at times, up to 35 farms, with 300 involved lifting close on 1000 tons of the early potato crop and bringing in the harvest. An allotment, obtained from the Council, was cleared, cultivated and extended in area by 1942 to an acre of land.

The language of fact scarcely conveys the spirit of RGS evacuation which showed from the start when the Headmaster called for the School Song to be sung at the first assembly in Penrith and for tutors to fill the long hours of leisure each day in the fortnight before term opened with outings and expeditions into the countryside, while men with cars returned to Jesmond to fetch books and equipment additional to the bulk items carried by lorry, and others set up what was available to turn temporary accommodation into workable class-rooms and laboratories. Games and societies were soon in full swing and as much as possible school life was shared with the community as it had been at home: musical evenings, chamber concerts and an unofficial dance band gave entertainment; gym displays, sports days and team games attracted spectators. Men and senior boys served with local men in the LDV (Home Guard); the JTC band often paraded through the streets; the blue blazers were everywhere; dignitaries of Penrith UDC, the Lord Mayor and Sheriff of Newcastle and the Chairman of Governors came. Patriotic slogans, topical debates, thoughtful articles and HM Forces Letters in the *Novo* kept the war in mind but seemingly everyone from Headmaster down enjoyed skating on the lake in the hard winters. Above all, perhaps, the figure of Tucker Anderson endlessly on his round of upset billets embodied that spirit rising to the countless demands of the emergency, resulting in close friendships and lasting relationships in many happy billets, and many memories of a fresh strenuous open-air life enhanced by the evident immediacy of achievement that came with daily knowledge of tension survived and crisis surmounted: aptly described as the School's longest and most successful camp.

Letters from parents to tutors expressing appreciation for the interest being taken in their sons' welfare reveal that boys were very happy and benefiting from their experience. Other parents wrote of their own and their sons' problems arising from conditions they experienced and regretfully took their boys home. Despite its efforts the School was unable to maintain the number on roll. In the summer of 1939, an extra fifty boys left the School, no doubt to avoid being evacuated. By December 1939, after a term in Penrith, another 179 had left, many evidently for the same reason. Already in the November the government had been forced to re-open schools in danger areas to accommodate children who had rejected evacuation. The mood is illustrated by letters and a leading article in the *Evening Chronicle* during the Christmas vacation: RGS parents while admitting the great administrative success wanted the Chairman of Governors to hold a meeting to ascertain whether a majority supported evacuation or would prefer to take what appeared only a slight risk at home provided air raid shelters were built on the School field, in order to avoid the sacrifice of money, moral training and family life. The School stayed on but the loss of pupils continued, alongside a similar loss of recruits, whose numbers fell from the normal annual intake of 120 down, for example, to 63.

There was much distress in these circumstances and many were deprived of the education they desired at RGS. Nevertheless it must be said that the immediate effect on the School was to ease some of its difficulties: those who stayed were clearly the more successful survivors and the departure of unhappy evacuees brought relief, albeit unwelcome. In the long term on the other hand, with the roll down almost to 500 in December 1942, it is not surprising that deficits accumulated over the next four years to a total of £4860 in March 1945, which the Finance Committee of the Governors attributed each year to 'a substantial decrease in the fees and Board of Education grant consequent upon the reduction in the number of boys attending the School'. Increase in numbers in Penrith was prevented by the difficulty of finding billets and replacements for teaching staff.

Members of staff were deeply concerned for their own and the School's future and early in 1942 had suggested that a Junior School should be opened in Newcastle or Gosforth to aid recruitment, but the House Committee did not favour the idea and the Governors decided against it. At the same time, too, the Headmaster asked the Governors to protest against the Ministry of Health's 'unjust attitude towards members of the School living in neutral areas': the School 'was evacuated as an entity' and the refusal to pay billeting allowances except for those in danger zones 'impaired the School's comprehensive and democratic re- cruitment'. Repeated complaints were rejected by the Ministry: it would, of course, be difficult to justify payments on grounds of hardship except for the boys who were at the School in 1939 and the same rule held against payment of lodging allowances to staff appointed at Penrith.

In 1943 the *Novo* reported that 'the momentum which carried the School forward after evacuation was now palpably declining'. The main compulsion to stay in Penrith was lacking, for the danger to life hardly materialized on Tyneside after the raids between July 1940 and December 1941, in which nearly 400 people were killed and Manors Goods Station was destroyed, but later a suggestion to end evacuation was rejected by Sir Arthur Sutherland because there had been fourteen casualties in a recent raid. Masters with property in the North East, some of whom had already had their homes requisitioned, were impatient, and in the autumn of 1943 a staff meeting showed a majority in favour of returning. The House Committee reported in November that the Regional Commissioner had agreed to vacate the School premises in June 1944, and the reopening in Jesmond was planned for the

September. At this time the Ministry of Health also announced the end of its scheme, and in December Newcastle brought home its last 475 surviving evacuees. The war in Europe went on until 8 May 1945.

Judgement has been made on the national evacuation that the fears that motivated it were much exaggerated and with hindsight the upheavals and expense were not necessary. Of the 1½ million evacuated at the start 900,000 were back home by 8 January 1940, and in March 1944 only 181,000 were still away from home. However, evacuation has ever since been regarded by RGS as a highlight: in the Headmaster's report, 'probably the most memorable event in all its long history'. Some people chose not to take part; for many who did it was a harrowing experience. Yet many have since acknowledged that it was a most valuable educational experience for life and many enjoyed it; and at the 'Reunion 40 Years On' held in 1979 at Penrith, large numbers of Old Boys, hosts, hostesses and their families met once more and proved the warmth of the relationships that were forged in those difficult times. The services of E. R. Thomas were recognized in the New Year Honours List of 1941 when he was awarded the O.B.E. Old Boys have constantly expressed their gratitude and admiration for Tucker Anderson and all the others who served them and the School with self-sacrificing devotion and concern. Their contributions were unstinted and indispensable to creating and maintaining that remarkable spirit and united effort which carried the School through. Its members survived a rare test of character and have a proud place in its tradition. The Finance Committee expressed, on 11 July 1944, their hope that 'with the return of the School to Newcastle and the substantial increase in the number of boys which may be expected, the financial position will improve'. 220 boys, double the normal intake, were admitted to the School in September and at the end of the financial year there was an excess of income over expenditure of £3086 12s 3d. But the Headmaster reported to the Governors that having nearly one third of the boys new to the School at the beginning of the term would 'present many problems calling for careful consideration'.

(iii) *THE SCHOOL IN THE 1950s, by Anthony Tuck*

In the history of the nation the nineteen fifties has acquired a poor reputation amongst decades, as an era of dullness between post-war austerity and the optimistic, expansive, swinging sixties. At RGS the decade happened to coincide with the headmastership of

O. W. Mitchell, a distinctive and in some respects controversial period in the School's history which contrasted not only, of course, with the war-time experiences of the School but also with the period of office of his successor, W. D. Haden. My own career at the School (1948–59) was almost exactly co-terminous with Mitchell's, and it also coincided with the final years of service at the School of the men who had 'formed the backbone of the staff' over the previous thirty years: Middlebrook, who was Second Master from H. N. Smith's death in 1952 until retirement in 1958; Anderson, who was Head of the Junior School until he retired in 1957, the Theakstone brothers, Akhurst, Herdman, Boll and Meaken. The continuity of service by so many members of staff was almost certainly one reason for the School's rapid return to normal after its war-time difficulties, and by 1948 parents who entered their sons for the School evidently regarded it as firmly re-established and enjoying its pre-war reputation.

E. R. Thomas had still been Headmaster when I took the entrance exam for the Junior School in the spring of 1948, and even to a child of seven newly entering the School in the following autumn the sense of reverence and awe which he had inspired was still discernible. But young children in particular live for the present and the immediate future, and I have no recollection that the School dwelt on or felt nostalgia for the past. Although it was only four years since the School had returned from Penrith to Newcastle the experience had little meaning for those who had been too young to share it and to understand why it had been necessary, though of course many of the boys who were at the end of their school careers when mine was just beginning must have had vivid personal recollections of Penrith, and of the Headmaster and staff who had guided the School through that difficult period.

Post-war austerity, and in particular the recurrent fuel shortages of the late 1940s, had a much more immediate impact, not least when Mr Mitchell asked all those who could do so to go home for lunch rather than burden the School kitchens with the task of catering for them. So marked a change in school policy, with its implications for social and leisure activities, can only have arisen from dire necessity, and fortunately did not last long. Children growing up in post-war Newcastle, however, were in one respect much more fortunate than their contemporaries in such cities as Hull, Coventry, Plymouth, and above all London. Newcastle had suffered comparatively little bomb damage, and both the centre of the city and the immediate surroundings of the RGS survived almost intact. The site of the bombed-out Eslington Hotel opposite the School was but a small reminder of the effects of war, while the School buildings themselves, though requisitioned, had scarcely suffered at all. This too must have made the resumption of normal routine after the evacuation much easier.

A child's memory, however, is selective, over-simplified and self-centred, and a child of eight or nine has little understanding either of events in the outside world or of the character and dynamic of an institution. The most vividly recalled occasions when the outside world impinged on the routine of the School were not necessarily those of the greatest significance. The death of King George VI was announced to us at a sombre assembly on the afternoon of 6 February 1952, confirming rumours which had been sweeping the School that morning and which had originated with those who had heard the news on the radio before setting out for school. But an event of much greater significance for the world, the Korean War, which was at its height in the autumn and winter of 1950–51, made little impact on the younger boys. For the older ones it was no doubt a different matter, since National Service might entail participation in the war. But if they felt any sense of foreboding it did not communicate itself to the lower forms of the School, and I have no recollection of hearing that any former pupil of the RGS had been killed in Korea.

As we grew up, so the adult world, or more particularly the world of the teenager (a new word in the 1950s) made itself felt, though at first in a limited and muted form. The teddy-boy cult, which was mainly a working-class phenomenon, scarcely impinged at all on the School, though the 'Tony Curtis' hairstyle occasionally made its appearance, together with the crew-cut, and there were those who claimed to have bought drape suits, though such garb never made its appearance in the School. The RGS's entry into the new world of youth culture took place in spectacular fashion in 1957 when a group from the sixth form entered the local heats of a national skiffle contest. These heats were held at the now-demolished Empire Variety Theatre, and were decided on the length and volume of the applause given to each group. It was no difficult task to organise an enormous audience for the RGS contestants and thus to ensure their probably undeserved survival to the last heat, where victory would have ensured their appearance against national competition. Unfortunately they failed at this hurdle, either because others had got round to packing the audience, or because the judges now based their decision on other criteria than applause. The behaviour of the audience earned some strong condemnation by the local press, but the Headmaster took the view that the promoters of the event got what they asked for. Jazz and skiffle made more of an impact on the School than the rock and roll craze (again, perhaps, a reflection of the social composition of the School), and the enthusiasm for the jazz revival of the late fifties produced some memorable arguments with Jack Wolstenholme on the merits or otherwise of music based on improvisation.

The Suez episode of November 1956, however, provided those of us who had entered the School in the late 1940s and early 1950s with our first significant political memory, and for the first time public affairs became for us a topic of serious discussion at school. Opinion amongst both the boys and the staff was bitterly divided, mirroring the division in the nation at large, though I recall that the majority sense amongst the fifth- and sixth-formers was that the whole operation was a mistake. This view brought fierce argument with some members of staff and with the Headmaster. Lesson time was spent discussing the rights and wrongs of the action, and there was an undercurrent of fear that a much wider conflict might result. It also had a long-term effect on the political opinions of that generation: few of them were voters in the 1959 general election, for the age of majority was still 21, but all of them had the vote in 1964, and the sense of outrage and dismay at what had happened in 1956 had its effect in the ballot box then and not at the time of Macmillan's triumph in 1959.

For some, of course, the brief war of November 1956 had a more immediate and personal significance. The prospect of military service loomed over all those who had been born before 1940, and although it might be postponed by university entrance it could not be avoided, and, in the opinion of most, it was better got out of the way before going to university. But the decision to abolish conscription was taken some years before the last generation of recruits were called up, and those of us born after the crucial date never had seriously come to terms with the prospect of military service. Few of us regretted this, and most of us were positively glad. In the stories that came back from our elders, no doubt exaggerated in the telling, it appeared a pitiful waste of time, truly, in the old cliché, 90 per cent boredom and 10 per cent terror – especially if one was unlucky enough to be sent to Cyprus.

The distinction between those who did National Service and

those who did not has proved to be one of the most significant and enduring of boundaries between the generations. For National Service linked those who did it with the whole generation of their elders who had served in the Second World War and in subsequent campaigns, whereas those of us born since 1940 have no experience whatever of military service unless we have specifically sought it: we are the first generation since the nineteenth century of whom that is true. On the other hand the impending abolition of conscription did not appear to have much effect on the school CCF. In keeping with the voluntarist tradition of the School the CCF had never been compulsory, and boys who had no prospect of National Service and no interest in a career in the regular forces still valued the training and discipline that it offered, though alternative activities such as the Outward Bound Schools, which were supposed to inculcate the same qualities, became more popular in the late 1950s.

In the history of the School as a community, the period is given unity by the personality of Oliver Mitchell. Mr Mitchell left behind at Owen's School Islington, his previous post, an impression of greatness,* but at RGS his reputation was not to be so clear cut, and in the later years of his headmastership he incurred criticism both within and outside the School, particularly over his handling of disciplinary problems. He was a man who defied categorisation, but whose principal characteristics were kindliness and sympathy towards the individual boy. His respect and concern for the individual, and especially for those boys who were in any kind of trouble or difficulty, made him admirably suited to inherit a school such as RGS with a liberal and individualistic tradition, which had been nurtured by E. R. Thomas but which almost certainly antedated his period of office as Headmaster.† It was often said of Mr Mitchell that he was ahead of his time, but this too is an oversimplification. Had he continued in office in the 1960s his liberal and tolerant approach, which was often criticised in the 1950s, might have muted some of the clashes which arose from the rebelliousness of the 1960s generation, but his concern for the individual, and his great kindness and humanity, were timeless qualities that arose from his own experience and his own philosophy of life rather than as a response to any fashion of the time.

*See above, p. 220.

†Sir Arthur Sutherland observed in his Memoirs that the School was 'rather casually run' in the 1880s!

Some of the changes Mr Mitchell introduced, which now seem trivial or superficial, gave the misleading impression at the time that he was trying to bring the RGS closer to the public school tradition, whereas one of the more significant features of RGS in the later 1950s was the strong collective feeling that it was not a public school and should not ape the manners and traditions of such a school. Schoolboys are apt to fasten on to the trivia of institutional life and endow them with much more significance than they possess, but we did not wholly welcome or appreciate such innovations as the use of *The Public School Hymn Book* in morning assembly instead of *Songs of Praise*; the establishment of Founder's Day, with a service in Jesmond Parish Church, was an instant tradition especially difficult to understand when the early history of the School was shrouded in obscurity; while the public controversy in which Mr Mitchell engaged about the literary merits of the School Song placed him, in the eyes of many, in the invidious position of defending the indefensible. The encouragement of House spirit, too, was a forlorn hope. In a day school, and in particular one with such a strong voluntarist tradition as RGS, House competition in sport or anything else was a frail plant, and the allocation of boys to Houses in accordance with the district in which they lived led to substantial inequalities in the number of boys in each House. As recruitment from some of the older residential areas such as Jesmond and Benwell declined, so Horsley House found itself last in virtually every competition, outpaced by those Houses which recruited from such expanding areas as Gosforth, the coast, and south Northumberland. In a period of rapid social change and family mobility such a basis for a House system was bound to weaken the credibility and viability of the system, and in the end be replaced by a different system of allocation.

If in these comparatively minor matters Mr Mitchell did not gauge the mood of the School, in many other ways he very clearly did. In some of his staff appointments he chose young men with distinctive personalities who established a strong social *rapport* with the sixth form, in and out of school, which was of great value in terms of informal education and perhaps created in sixth-formers' minds a standard of interest in and involvement in pupils' work and general social and intellectual development which led to some disappointments when these same sixth-formers went on to Oxford or Cambridge. Outside the class-room some of these members of staff were creative in ways which aroused the interest and respect of the sixth form. William Thornton was a regular contributor to *Punch* and in 1962 published a novel, *Possit*, which was described at the time as 'the "Lucky Jim" of the provincial grammar school'.* Anthony Tomkins was that rarity in the 1950s, a schoolmaster with a Ph.D., while in sport John Elders, who was soon to become coach to the England team, brought a much more professional approach to Rugby Football training. These young members of staff took an independent critical line which was stimulating and impressive to sixth-formers, though they made even more difficult the notion of conformity to a particular mode of behaviour and thought which was in any case widely thought to be undesirable at RGS.

In his approach to the curriculum, Mr Mitchell showed his unique and unpredictable combination of tradition, freedom and innovation. The re-establishment of the teaching of Greek in the middle school was an important and brave step, but it had the undesirable consequence of allowing some boys to abandon all science except mathematics after only two years in the School. The result was that a small but significant minority of boys left school almost entirely ignorant of the experimental sciences. This may have been one reason amongst many for Mr Mitchell's advocacy in the later 1950s of a broader education and his establishment of General Studies as a formal part of the curriculum.

The re-establishment of Greek was successful and Classics grew in strength in the late 1950s and early 1960s. At the time, however, fifth- and sixth-formers perceived English, history, modern languages, and the experimental sciences as strong subjects in the School, and their judgement was vindicated by the number of open awards in these subjects won at Oxford and Cambridge in the late 1950s. But there were also some surprising features of the curriculum: there was no teaching of the life sciences, except to a small number of sixth-formers for whom a degree in medicine at King's College was the eventual goal; mathematics was not as strong as it was to become under Frank Budden in the 1960s; and the teaching of art occupied a very modest place in the timetable. Religious education was scarcely conducted at all, and there was considerable feeling that it need not be taken seriously. Although Mr Mitchell himself was a sincere and committed Christian, the ethos of the RGS in the 1950s remained strongly secular. This was another respect, perhaps, in which RGS differed sharply from both public boarding schools and some independent day schools,

*Review in the *Newcastle Journal*.

and the innovation of the Founder's Day service in Jesmond Parish Church made little spiritual impact.

Outside the formal bounds of the curriculum the life of the school continued to flourish as it had done before the war under E. R. Thomas. Orchestral and chamber music concerts were of a high standard, and under the energetic leadership of Jack Wolstenholme some, such as the performance of *Hiawatha's Wedding Feast*, were on an almost heroic scale. Music in the School was very broadly based, with the second and third orchestras acting as enthusiastic nurseries, and the public performance of chamber music was encouraged even amongst boys in the middle school, though the nerve-wracking nature of such performances was sometimes only too apparent. On the other hand for those who lacked the talent, or the enthusiasm, for instrumental or choral work the ordinary teaching of music left something to be desired, and it was possible to reach the fifth form with only the slenderest grasp of the fundamentals of musical theory.

Drama, too, was encouraged early in one's school career. The fourth-form play was an opportunity for young tyros to gain their first experience of Shakespearian acting before an audience; the Linguists' plays in French and German represented achievement in the manipulation of foreign languages which some universities would probably have envied; and the XXI Club showed itself capable, over the years, of tackling the whole range of English drama from Shakespeare to T. S. Eliot and Christopher Fry. Indeed, the interest in contemporary drama, both for reading and performance, was one of the more stimulating aspects of the teaching of English at the school in the second half of the 1950s. But drama at the RGS in the 1950s reached its height with John Duncan's production of *Dr Faustus* in 1958. John Duncan himself played the title role, and Richard Napper designed a set even more outstanding than his set for *The Importance of Being Earnest* two years earlier, which had received a round of applause in its own right. John Duncan went on to produce an outstanding *Tamburlaine* for OUDS, and then to take part in the production of TW3 for the BBC, providing an RGS link with the satire boom of the mid 1960s.

Sport, of course, played an important part in the life of many of the boys at RGS. In the Junior School boys played soccer, and when they transferred to the Senior School they expressed some dismay at having to take up Rugby. This was scarcely surprising, since the early 1950s saw Newcastle United at the height of its

296

fame, and the idea of emulating Jackie Milburn seemed much more appealing than playing a game which enjoyed much less prestige and popular support on Tyneside and which few local schools played. Indeed, the most serious opposition was found as far away as the West Riding, Edinburgh and Glasgow. Some of the minority sports were played to a high standard. The School's tennis players were seldom seen, but they were highly successful in the competitions for the Glanvill Cup and the Youll Cup, earning from the *Times* correspondent in 1958 the somewhat dubious compliment 'Dark Horses of the North'. In 1958, too, three former pupils gained blues at Oxford and Cambridge for boxing, described by Mr Mitchell, in a significant phrase, as 'the cleanest English sport in the world' but already the subject of some controversy at school. At the fifth-form stage some boys took up rowing on the filthy river Tyne, and were transported to the boathouse above the old Scotswood Bridge in buses provided, appropriately enough, by Messrs Galley. Crews entered the regattas on the Wear, at Talkin Tarn, at Dumfries, and elsewhere, but they also engaged in more casual feats such as rowing to the High Level Bridge or seeing just how far up the Derwent it was possible to go without running aground. Rowing on the Tyne had its hazards: falling in meant an immediate visit to the RVI, and shipping on the river above Newcastle was more extensive then than it is now, presenting the risk of being run down by such vessels as the two CEGB barges *Bobby Shaftoe* and *Hexhamshire Lass* which plied to and from the Stella power stations taking ash to be dumped out at sea.

Yet sport did not occupy an overwhelmingly dominant place in the School's concerns. The achievements of the first XV or the first XI were matters for public congratulation, but Mr Mitchell ensured that outstanding musical and dramatic performances, even those of lower forms and lesser orchestras, received their due share of public compliments. Although the Head Boy was often, though not invariably, a distinguished member of the first XV, sporting prowess was never a necessary condition for appointment as a prefect, and, by the sixth form, games could be avoided if one wished to do so. Both David Layton and John Elders preferred willing enthusiasts on the Rugby field to an army of incompetent conscripts, and for the second and third year sixth the pressure of academic work was always an acceptable reason for non-participation. Indeed, few members of staff were more genuinely pleased at the academic successes of the athletically incompetent than Bill Tunstall, head of PE from 1958 onwards, who congratulated award winners with the lines from Goldsmith's *Deserted Village* (much out of fashion in the English department):

> And still they gazed, and still the wonder grew,
> That one small head could carry all he knew.

For most boys, of course, academic work had become their central concern by the time they reached the fifth form, and there was some feeling that academic success provided the main purpose and justification for being at such a school. This view appeared at its crudest in the hostility towards the Junior School shown by some boys and some members of staff. They argued that entry at seven was obviously much less rigorously selective than entry at eleven; that entry was governed by the depth of the parent's purse; and that in spite of these limitations transfer to the Senior School at eleven was virtually automatic. Such 'meritocratic' views were not uncommon in the late 1950s, but they made for a degree of self-confidence tinged with arrogance which was sometimes abruptly checked by exposure to tougher competition at the ancient universities. Mr Mitchell vigorously repudiated such views: he believed that the School should not be rigorously selective, that a wide range of ability and talent was beneficial to the School community, and that the School should not seek to deprive the other grammar schools in the city of all their talent. Such principles, however sensible they seem in retrospect, were often lost on those who could not be dissuaded from the apparently simple meritocratic argument. It is interesting to note that similar arguments to those used by Mr Mitchell in the 1950s are now being used to oppose a move which is in one sense another form of academic creaming, the admission of girls to the sixth forms of independent boys' schools.

Yet the concern for academic success did not lead to an undue stress on academic achievement for its own sake. Few of us in the second half of the 1950s took more than three or four 'O' levels, and some subjects which were taken to fourth- or fifth-form level and then dropped were never examined at all – in my own case, Greek, geography and German. The advantage of such a system was that fifth-formers who did not take, say, 'O' level English or history could pursue a broader syllabus than the constraints of the exam would have allowed, exploring the modern novel with William Thornton, ancient history with Middlebrook, or New

298

Testament Greek instead of Xenophon's *Anabasis*. But the idea of by-passing at 'O' level subjects to be taken at 'A' level aroused misgivings at the time, produced one or two spectacular casualties, and was abandoned in the time of Mr Mitchell's successor. On the other hand, it did serve to inculcate the view, which had great value in a highly selective academic institution, that there was much more to education than passing exams and that the accumulation of examination passes for their own sake had little merit.

For the most senior boys, of course, private study was as important a part of the curriculum as formal teaching, and for boys attempting to work on their own the physical constraints of the School were obvious and irksome. The School had survived the war unscathed, but by the mid 1950s had reached a size of over 800, at which point the pressures on accommodation became almost intolerable, and the major building programme of 1956 did not really solve the most pressing problem, accommodation for the sixth form. Mr Mitchell was very sympathetic to the sixth form's difficulties: all sorts of expedients were tried, but they could not disguise the fact that the School was overcrowded. It is not surprising, therefore, that the Lit. and Phil. became the extension of the RGS when work was in mind, and such cafés as the News Theatre in Pilgrim Street and that quintessential expression of the character of the late 50s, the El Caramba Café in Clayton Park Square, with its Espresso steam coffee machine and LP record player, became the venues for social gatherings. Though unofficial, this removal from the School premises was accepted both by the Headmaster and by most of the staff. For the scientists, lab accommodation was probably much more satisfactory, and had indeed been improved by the 1955 extensions; but for boys on the arts side even the Plender Library was unsatisfactory, since it was pressed into use from time to time as a class-room, and in any case the Lit. and Phil.'s resources were, of course, incomparably richer. Several years later the School lost part of its playing field when the central motorway was built, and then the opportunity for the expansion and reorganisation of accommodation was grasped in a much bolder and more far-sighted manner than seemed possible in the 1950s.

The School in the 1950s had a rich and varied internal life, bearing out the truth of Dr Thomas's observation many years earlier that it was a most unusual boy who could not find his hobby or interest well catered for at school. Yet the School did not expand the boys' wider horizons quite as fully as it might have done. School camps, of course, were as popular as they had been before the war and still occupied a central position in the School's philosophy. For younger boys in particular they often provided the first opportunity to get away from home and family for a connected period, and they gave rise to the memorable discovery that masters could be human. The harvest camps ceased when mechanisation took over from human labour, but for fifth- and sixth- formers the History camps, held in conditions of relative comfort, allowed boys to visit such far-flung outposts as Shrewsbury, Canterbury and, most memorably, Norwich where, in circumstances reminiscent of *The Happiest Days of Your Life*, accommodation was provided in the buildings of the Norwich Girls' High School. However, apart from the Norway tours, which ended in 1956, the school did not try to organise trips abroad: a suggestion that the History camp should be held in Paris was turned down flat, perhaps for fear that history would fail to compete with Paris's other attractions. It is not clear why visits abroad did not take place in the late 1950s, but it may be that the race week camps in reality occupied too dominant a position. Their success, and the aura surrounding them, distracted attention from the horizons that widened so dramatically in Europe from the mid 1950s onwards. If there was any failure of imagination, or perhaps too firm a devotion to the traditions established between the wars, it lay here.

By 1959 the RGS very much bore the stamp of Mr Mitchell's personality. In many matters he showed flair, judgement and imagination; and even on the controversial question of by-passing examination subjects at 'O' level he stood by his judgement and loyally sought to implement the guiding principles laid down when the GCE was established. But his touch seemed less sure on disciplinary matters, and the harsher judgements that were made about his regime stressed, perhaps unduly, the indiscipline that many felt had developed in the School. Traditionally in boys' public schools the masters left discipline to the Headmaster and the prefects. The RGS was no exception, but even so the School was run on a loose rein. E. R. Thomas could show an autocratic firmness, for example in keeping the School at Penrith against the wishes of many parents and staff; but his own philosophy endowed him with a respect for the individual conscience and a tolerance of blunt speaking which militated against the imposition of a rigid disciplinary code within the School. Mr Mitchell's concern for the

300

ndividual was no less deep seated, and he found no difficulty in ccommodating himself to the liberal tradition at RGS. But in the ate 1950s there was some feeling, both inside and outside the chool, that liberty was degenerating into licence, and that disorder and petty vandalism were rife. Mr Mitchell exhorted the taff to tighten up on discipline, but the staff believed that they did not always receive the support which they needed from the Headmaster, and whereas both sides accepted the liberal tradition at the School and sought to work within it, there was a general recognition that to do so involved more strain and wear and tear on both Headmaster and staff than they would suffer if a rigid disciplinary code was enforced.

Both sides had good grounds for their concern, in my own recollection. There undoubtedly was some slackness amongst the taff about turning up on time for classes and noting who was absent; while the staff believed that the Headmaster viewed some offences with undue leniency. By virtue of his position the Headmaster had to bear more than his fair share of the blame for the problem. As his successor was to discover, it was far from easy to impose a rigid code of behaviour where none had existed before, when many of the staff were unwilling to co-operate, and at a time when parental and other outside pressures for discipline and conformity were becoming much less powerful. By working with the grain of the School rather than against it Mr Mitchell avoided fundamental and prolonged conflict over the discipline of the School, at the price of much criticism and some unfavourable publicity. Boys of 14 or 15 might mistake liberalism and individualism for weakness, but in the long run such an approach was more valuable and more profoundly influential than a regimental system imposed from above. The institutional values implied by a liberal approach to discipline were unusual in the 1950s, as many of us discovered when we compared notes with our contemporaries from other schools, but they made it easier for the RGS to come to terms with much more fundamental rejection of discipline and authority displayed by the generation of the 1960s.

(iv) *THE 1960s – SOME PERSONAL IMPRESSIONS,*
by Roger Hennessey

Any era is a candidate for the time-worn catchphrase 'an age of change'. However, historians will possibly perceive the 1960s as a definite watershed in our society and economy; one distinctly felt this to be the case at the time, on both sides of the iron railings in

Eskdale Terrace. I arrived at the RGS in September 1962 as one of a quartet of new masters and was specifically charged with the business of setting up an Economics Department, itself a harbinger of curricular change. I was just in time to see the last of the old order, both at the RGS and in Newcastle upon Tyne itself. The School and the city which I left over a decade later were both changed radically, although retaining important elements of continuity.

My own career at the RGS started two years after W. D. Haden became Headmaster. What he intended to be School policy and how his intentions were perceived may not always have coincided but certainly staff common-room talk was that he felt it necessary both to reduce and to sharpen the annual recruitment of pupils. The ability to judge optimum sizes and time-scales is a rare one amongst administrators and, happily for the RGS, Mr Haden had this quality. So it was that the combined roll of Senior and Junior Schools, which stood at 1030 in 1960. fell to 874 in 1964. The purges having been completed, rolls rose once again to 997 in 1972, at the end of Mr Haden's regime. One controversial by-product of these demographic shifts was the establishment of a group of 'flyers' or pupils of unusual academic ability. This experiment encountered considerable scepticism and hostility from important sections of the staff and it was not sustained although the coincidence of the now-mature 'flyers' in their last year with a normal crop of 'Oxbridge' scholars put the RGS at the top of the much coveted Oxford and Cambridge scholarships stakes in one year, the year that a new edition of Sampson's *Anatomy of Britain* was composed, thus recording the fact and irritating the RGS's various rivals.

If the movement of total rolls was in part the result of the Headmaster's conscious policy, the increase in the number of pupils staying on into the sixth form was much more the result of external influences, although the fact that the School could respond to this increase in demand was to the credit of the Governors and the Headmaster. Whilst a notionally-calculated fifth form (taking this group to be one fifth of the Senior School below the sixth form) fell to 33.5% of the sixth form in 1964, it was 44% of a large sixth in 1972. Folklore had it that leaving at the end of the fifth year was fairly normal at one time; very possibly it was (this would have been before my time) but certainly it was fairly exceptional by the late 1960s. Why was there this secular shift? Probably for two closely-related reasons. First, our society has for

302

a long time been characterised by 'credentialism', or the need for people to qualify formally and professionally for increasing numbers of places and posts. Secondly, government became well aware of the swelling demand for more refined and extensive education and it decided to expand the higher education system of the country first in the university sector after the Robbins Report in 1963, and later in the polytechnics. These changes affected the RGS directly and quickly. The sixth form grew from its 'low' of 182 in 1964 to 259 in 1972, and eventually required more facilities – a modernised curriculum, social accommodation, library space etc. The Headmaster and his staff had to become acquainted with the mysteries of 'UCCA'.* Dozens of sixth-form students who would once have entered commerce or industry directly from the school now had to suffer the tensions of interviews, conditional offers and the arrival of 'A' level results looming over the summer holidays. The result of these changes was that the RGS more than met the challenges of the Robbins era.

A profoundly important influence upon the RGS in the 1960s was the 'teenage revolution', which probably had its roots in the economic changes of the 1950s and 1960s: the long training inherent in credentialism, modern technology, increasing productivity, relatively high wages for the young and their great mobility. For the first time in its history the RGS had to face a far more mature and autonomous pupilariat, but one which inherited a long tradition of independent-mindedness. There were many issues and problems thrown up by accelerating 'teenism', for example farouche styles of dress which took school uniform to the margin of acceptability and occasionally beyond it. One favourite way of testing the taboos of bourgeois society was the adoption of extremely long hair lengths. In more subtle ways traditional forms of culture which the RGS hallowed and transmitted had to face new rivals, notably in the fields of literature and music. The teenage 'problematic', as sociologists might have put it, is now very familiar and older generations have learnt to adjust, as have the young, although the situation is not and can never be an easy or stable one. In the 1960s it was entirely new in the forms it took and it says much for the Headmaster and his deputies, George Dean and then Colin Nichols, that they 'knew where to stop' in this as in other things. Later generations may not know the heart of the problem, for so little was recorded at the time. Suffice it to

*The Universities' Central Council on Admissions, established in 1961 (Editors' note).

say that the Headmaster had to steer a course between the optimistic left on the staff and a doom-laden right (fearful of anarchy and original sin) whilst keeping a community of 800 audacious boys on an even keel. It struck me on joining the RGS and never ceased to intrigue me, how much order was kept with so few sanctions; still less with the ending of corporal punishment in the 1960's. Nevertheless, the two standpoints remained and the sagacious L. Meaken once summed up the problem by quoting the dictum that 'whilst some said all boys were bad, others said there was some good in every boy'. The more positive line on human nature was essentially the RGS one and I hope that it remains so.

The last of the secular changes to press upon the RGS in the 1960s and one which was to bring about fundamental alterations in its status (but after the departure of Mr Haden) was the increasing 'politicisation' of education. At the start of the 1960s the position of the RGS was generally taken for granted as one of the direct grant grammar schools on Tyneside, but as the decade wore on the very existence of selective schools became itself a political issue, they became, like so much else, another 'problematic'. One by one the local authorities of the North East converted their secondary schools into comprehensives and abandoned selection at 11+. Towards the end of Mr Haden's regime the political pressures grew: Newcastle upon Tyne was developing its own comprehensive school system, the Donnison Report* questioned the direct grant system itself and although this was shelved during the Conservative government of Edward Heath (1970–74), the RGS became an independent school when the direct grant system was phased out. Whilst changes thus came to a head after the 1960s, the Headmaster and staff were increasingly aware during the 1960s that they were working within a system which was itself a cause of political division and discussion. I know of no evidence that these changes interfered in any way with the quality of education offered by the RGS but they were an increasing presence in school life.

Against a background of great changes, all kinds of everyday incidents and episodes tend to fall into place and to make sense. The great sea-changes of the 1960s are less daunting when seen in context, and yet those changes were so deep that Newcastle upon Tyne in the early 1960s seems twenty-five years later a city set on another planet at another time. The Newcastle to which I moved

*First and Second Reports of the Public Schools Commission, 1968 and 1970 (Editors' note).

n 1962 was an exotic city to a southerner. It swarmed with yellow electric trolleybuses from Denton Square to Wallsend Boundary, and lessons in the Plender Library might halt while a mineral train started to tackle Jesmond Bank. RGS itself was in grounds that ran past a shady 'pinfold' or paddock to the Great North Road, innocent of motorways or fly-overs. Two narrow toeholds on the old way of doing things occurred in that initial academic year at RGS. My first Speech Day (Autumn 1962) was the last to be held in the great hall at RGS, with parents, pupils and a sprinkling of O.N.s squeezed into what was a close family occasion. The speaker was Lord Howick of Glendale, scion of a proconsular family. His address, which exhorted boys to 'go out' and help administer and develop the Commonwealth, sounded stirring but it was distinctly dated by the early 1960s and I remember it raised not a few eyebrows. Still, it was listened to with respect and its memory suggests how far we have progressed since, to the world of OPEC, Zimbabwe and micro-chips. Subsequently we held all such meetings in the City Hall, a change which never seemed to 'gell', in that the place seemed both physically and functionally remote from the *genius loci* of the RGS. Perhaps time has healed this lesion. At least more people were accommodated under the new arrangements.

My first year also marked the passing of the old Durham GCE board. This was a friendly and local affair, whose examination dates left something of a vacancy in upper-sixth life at the end of the summer term. The strategy was to fill the vacuum with various mind-improving and broadening activities. I was volunteered into taking a party down to the 1200 foot level at Weetslade pit, north of Gosforth and long since closed. Greater sacrifice did a southerner never make, I thought, as I crawled along seams bubbling with fire-damp, a mighty cutter roaring ahead of me and wry comments from various sixth-formers to the rear. As I remember, one of them later stated in the *Novo* that I had appeared chic, or fetching, in my pitman's gear – a fair average piece of RGS putting-down, just in case I felt too noble.

Even in 1962, the tempests of change were distinctly marked. Mr Haden had decreed that boys were to remain 'on site' in the lunch hour. Ingenious minds were ever at work, like the Spanish officials of old, to 'obey, but not comply'. A trip into town on the pillion of Bill Cuthbertson's 'Martha' (a vintage motor-bike decked out in army khaki) usually revealed a few sixth-formers scuttling into the shades of such long-forgotten nooks as Lambert's Leap, or Marianople Street.

A powerful magnet keeping boys within bounds was the superb cuisine of Mrs Teunon* and her staff. There were no fewer than three lunchtime sittings, all taking place in what later became the library and sixth-form areas. It was a point of honour at the table run, variously, by Alan Mitchell, Joe McDonald and myself to be finished and cleared up first – I used to urge the sixth-formers that 'eating is a physical, not a social function', a philistine and erroneous observation with which they agreed wolfishly.

After the opening of the new dining hall in 1968, much of the catering area became a social milieu for the sixth form. Mr Haden decided to take advantage of the change and recast the organisation of the sixth, Howard Burchell and I taking responsibility for the upper science and arts sixth respectively. The upper sixth area was painted in a rather limp light grey, much beloved of interior decorators in those days. The upper sixth treated this with scant respect, and grubbiness multiplied by the 'vandal cube law' until the sixth-form committee rose to the occasion and repainted it 'voluntarily' in hot tangerine one half term. More memorable was Dickie's magnificent art deco sunburst round the sixth-form clock, all the more splendid for being some two or three years in advance of the 1930s cult. The existence of a semi-autonomous sixth form in its south-wing satrapy enabled morning assembly to be more accurately attuned to the needs and tastes of senior and junior boys. Twice a week the sixth held its own assembly, and we ran a long gamut of experiments with various readings. I cannot say whether Ian McGill's readings from Nietzsche accorded with the spirit of the Education Act 1944 and its requirements regarding acts of worship, but, like Howard Burchell's description of the moral dilemmas of J. Robert Oppenheimer, it was good, thought-provoking material which started arguments, as it was intended to.

Another mid-sixties modification in corporate assemblies was the rationalisation of sixth-form lectures. In my early RGS days I recall addresses to the whole School, such as that of the Bishop of the Arctic, engagingly titled 'Archibald the Arctic', a mode of address which went down a treat amongst the pupils. Mr Haden asked me to organise a course of talks for the sixth, and this developed into two per term (per stratum of the sixth) thinning out in the summer. Alas the exigencies of the timetable meant that these lectures tended to coincide with the same lessons, and this usually seemed to imply double science practicals. I was always

*Mrs Teunon succeeded Miss Steven as catering officer in 1956 (Editors' note).

:eply grateful to Ken Macdonald and Bill Brydon that they went
ong with this irritant with such little fuss. The lectures were
a eclectic offering – humanism; Catholicism (from a Jesuit);
anagement science; gynaecology and astronomy to name but a
w. The latter was given by Professor Curtis FRS, a Governor of
e School. During his address the wobbly and inadequate screen
 Room M (the 1950s lecture theatre) fell on the erudite professor
: bore an image of the great nebula in Andromeda at the time)
us maintaining the jinx-tradition of Room M. During the talk
 another Governor, Professor Scothorne, a water-hammer
:veloped in Charles George's laboratory, so that the speaker was
gularly interrupted by machine-gun rappings. One significant
cident during a sixth-form lecture spoke volumes about the
GS. Our district Inspector of Taxes was initiating the sixth into
e mysteries of the Finance Act. One boy asked a technical
1estion, and the Inspector replied by quoting a large passage of
1reaucratic prose verbatim. He was clapped, even cheered, to a
an by the sixth form who could always be relied upon to admire
e expertise of technique; the sphere of knowledge was less
1portant than the sheer mastery of a skill.

The modernisation of the *Novo* in the late 1960s was brought
)out less by chance than by the impact of new technology and
stes. No one could hope to equal, let alone emulate, the
istained accuracy and literary rigour of the *Novo* under Maurice
)obinson and his editors. Mindful of this, I took over general
versight of the Thunderer of Jesmond after it had a short
terregnum under Raymond Bratt. Once again, I was just in at
1e end of an Old Order. The magazine was letterpress-printed by
a old-established Gateshead firm. I knew the burdensome joy of
1stling through sheafs of galley-proofs, arguing to the small hours
ith the editors about punctuation, literary freedom etc., and
.cing the termly inquisition from a common room which had
:come used to total accuracy and impeccable style from Maurice
)obinson. But, by 1969, the great inflation was selecting at least its
:cond gear and *Novo* printed the Gutenberg way was proving
ver more expensive. New generations of RGS boys complained
: the dreariness of mere words in an audio-visual world.
.ccordingly, we moved into a world of phototypesetting, offset-
tho and a far higher ratio of graphic to literary work. Various
xperiments were tried: 'Kasimir' the all-knowing RGS gossip-
)lumn; strip-cartoons; daring poetry etc., all against a traditional
ackground of school rapportage. We even offset costs by taking

307

on advertising and selling off old copper blocks when world coppe
prices hit an all-time high – fruit of having an alert economic
sixth. I found that mathematicians were incomparably accurate a
proof-reading; whilst the literary editors took excellent care o
commissioning or writing creative work and acting as final court o
appeal over grammatical disputes. Most heartening of all was th
enthusiastic support Maurice Robinson gave the whole enterprise
I approached him obliquely after some of the more *outré* number
appeared, but need not have worried for he was ever enthusiasti
at the notion of people writing and enjoying the business, eve
unto the scurrilous Kasimir.

There are other and very considerable tracts of RGS life lef
virtually untouched by my personal survey. For one thing
although the author of *Newcastle Royal Grammar School Cricke
Club 1861–1979* notes that the 'Celtic spirit may have caused E. R
Thomas to incline towards rugby rather than cricket', I have t
confess that the Celtic spirit can move in other and mysteriou
ways and has inclined this particular vessel for its powers to suffe
a lifelong, highly un-Anglo-Saxon and virtually total dis
enchantment with sport. And yet, no one could live and work i
RGS and not note some distinct and revealing elements of th
sporting life which would tell him a great deal about the essence o
the school. Broadly speaking there were three such elements. Firs
was a noticeable spirit of voluntarism about RGS sport. Althoug
there was an irreducible minimum of compulsory games,
considerable part of the School's sporting enterprise rested or
purely free choice. This seemed to sustain immense enterprise, fo
example a highly successful Rugby club whose first XV lost onl
three school matches in the late 1960s (it was unbeaten in 1969–7
scoring 379 points against 75) and producing an Oxford Blue i
Alan Douglas. Cricket also touched high registers in 1960s
although my own contribution to it was confined to being *Nov
reporter for the 'R. W. Wilkinson Benefit Match', a facetious titl
for the farewell match of a fellow historian on the staff. On th
more serious side, RGS cricket started the decade in the glow o
such reputations as those Brodrick (who went up to Cambridg
and obtained a Blue in 1961) and J. S. Wilkinson, one of a selec
group of bowlers who saw off Boycott in their time. The year 196
was something of an *annus mirabilis* for RGS sport, the only yea
when the first XI was unbeaten, matching the achievements of th
Rugby XV.

A second feature of RGS sport was its sheer variety, and thi owed much to its third feature, the long hours of patient organisation put in by a generation of schoolmaster-sportsmen which can have had few rivals. John Elders' reputation was international, but even the marginal non-sportsmen in the common room realised how much cricket and boxing owed to Donald Meaken, rowing to Joe Liddell, boxing *and* rowing to Bill Cuthbertson, tennis to Colin Dales and swimming to Bill Tunstall and Geoff Knowles. Every Friday, late leavers from the School ground could see the school's CCF (itself sub-divided into Army and Royal Navy sections) smartly performing its evolutions under the watchful eyes of Messrs Luke and Gibson, or Sgt. Major O'Brien.

Some other features of RGS life have also been done quite inadequate service by my *tour d'horizon* of the 1960s. For example, RGS music was a strong and vigorous growth. Under Jack Wolstenholme's leadership it sustained no fewer than three orchestras and coped competently with a very wide repertoire. For example, in the months of November and December 1968 there were concerts offered by the First and Third Orchestras and by the Chamber Orchestra with music by Handel, Corelli, Ravel, Mozart, Beethoven and Schubert as well as compositions and arrangements by Mr Strange of the RGS music department. I attended far too few of these concerts, although the ones I did go to were delightful and memorable, in starkly direct contrast to the extraordinarily feeble choral traditions of morning assembly, another feature of RGS life which was problematic in those days. The RGS music tradition like much of its sport rested on voluntarism; so also did the cluster of clubs and societies which could cater for a wide range of tastes – transport, war-games, model railways, blues, golf, history, etc., a not unusual collection but covering a wider spectrum than is normally the case; for example there was a very large Christian Union, so large that it contained its own sub-divisions; there was also the enigmatic *Logoi* for free-thinkers and supporters of alternatives. There flowered briefly but luxuriantly each year a crop of summer camps arranged to cater for different year groups at different locations. The speed with which these camps were organised, manned, pitched and struck was admirable. My association with the Tucker Anderson tradition of camps was entirely vicarious, as Editor of the *Novo*, in which capacity I became an armchair expert on the Ryedale, Eskdale and Wensleydale sites. As with RGS sport, the camps were a feature of School life which one knew instinctively

309

offered some of the fundamental keys to understanding the essence of the school as a community.

One must beware in school histories, whether official or anecdotal, of harping unduly on excellence. The 'everyday situation' which the mass of us experience is not often lived at the cutting edge of excellence. Most pupils at the RGS were, by the nature of the entrance selection system, of above average ability. Nevertheless, within the RGS they spread out along our own normal distribution curve and, as statistics suggest, 'most people are average' in a given group. I draw attention to this set of platitudes in order to put one part of the record straight, for it was often said by critics of the RGS that the School only cared about high-flyers. This accusation was mischievous and without foundation. I know full well that the greater portion of professional discussion in the common room was about the problems and difficulties of pupils who struggled in one way or another – their interests were attended to with great seriousness and at no time treated as of secondary importance in the way implied by the anti-RGS myth-makers.

I noted at the beginning of my survey that in spite of the confusion of the 1960s some things endured. For example, there was an unchanging pool of School life in that dark end of the corridor near the Masters' cloakroom beside the caretaker's Aladdin's cave with its stock of unusual keys and great items of woodwork undergoing repair. Here, in 1972 as in 1962, I used to hear boys attempting to get 'off games' of a Wednesday. I could hear masterpieces, the weirdest baroque creations of the malingerer's art, but nothing that could out-fox John Elders.

Another unchanging feature of RGS, and possibly one of the most valuable creations of Tyneside was (for want of a better word) 'Geordism', a kind of rough and kindly radicalism. Geordie absolutely never learned to tug forelock or doff cap to the gentry, for he was, and I hope still is, nature's own democrat. On the other hand he was virtually never trendy or facetiously insolent in the way of parlour rebels; it was very much man-to-man as equals. A last RGS memory sums it up. It was the first lesson of term with a lower sixth and I was setting about taming high spirits before getting down to the grind. One sixth-former spoke out in medium-broad Jarrovian: 'Mr. Hennessey, great heavens man, you've shrunk.' No one, but no one, is proof against that kind of treatment.

Chapter IX

DEBTS TO THE PAST AND
PROSPECTS FOR THE FUTURE

The Royal Grammar School is a complex institution which has become what it is by organic growth over the decades. There is no such thing as a bird's-eye view of its history with which this volume could end.

An aerial view of its present geographical context may however be illuminating. Rarely can the choice of a school's site have been so formative, even if it partly illustrates the irony of unintended consequence: whereas the transfer to Jesmond in 1906 was conceived as a matter of surburban migration, it later acquired different significance as some of the main focuses of the city's life shifted towards Eskdale Terrace. Adjacent now (as can be seen in plate VII) are the impressive structures of a university and a polytechnic, and between the two within a few minutes' walk of the School stands the Civic Centre itself, self-confident embodiment of the expansionist mood of the 1960s. Viewed from the air the divisive swathe of the urban motorway of the 1970s may seem to cast doubt on this cosy picture, but by throwing the School into a vehicular cul-de-sac it has given us the rare luxury of a near-central site which is yet relatively untouched by city centre problems. Certainly we feel ourselves to be central both in location and in sentiment and in these senses to 'belong' to the city of Newcastle.

There was never much chance that the Royal Grammar School on this site would be a neighbourhood school as normally conceived. Flanked on the south-west by the city's central precincts, it is further insulated from housing to the north-west by the unique phenomenon of the Town Moor. To the north and east there are residential areas but their links with the School are less than might be expected: local residents may indeed be less certain about the credentials and even the whereabouts of the Royal Grammar School than others living miles away. For increasingly this has become a school of regional catchment.

311

The trend has been hastened by developments in public transport. A recent survey of daily travel habits within the School showed that, whereas only one boy in 20 walked or cycled from home each day, over 60% were carried for all or part of their journey by Metro, that remarkable creation of the 1980s. Those with nostalgic memories of earlier times may not readily warm to the clinical efficiency of Jesmond Metro Station by contrast with its character-laden predecessor now ingeniously converted to a pub, but for ease of travel from the east, whether north or south of the Tyne, or from Durham or Hexham with connections at the Central Station, we are curiously fortunate. Admittedly the behaviour of boys on crowded public transport remains a time-honoured focus of complaint, some of which is justified, but if human nature remains unregenerate the new pattern of schoolboy commuting amounts for us to a revolution in convenience. This is one reason for the even spread of the present school population over all parts of the conurbation and into many outlying areas beyond: 30% live within the boundaries of Newcastle, while the rest are equally divided between counties north and south of the Tyne.

Fifty years ago – as can be clearly seen from the accompanying maps – there was a much heavier concentration north of the river, and this pattern of recruitment continued strongly into the 1950s and 1960s. In part it reflected the workings of the scheme of fee-subsidy then in operation, for under the direct grant system some free places were conditional on local authority approval. Our links were strong with Newcastle and became even stronger with Northumberland, but they were more tenuous to the south since the authorities there chose to make no use of the system. The withdrawal of direct grant by a Socialist Government in the mid-1970s and its replacement first by our own limited offer of Bursaries, then by the Assisted Places Scheme of a Conservative Government, have brought to light a powerful interest in the Royal Grammar School in counties south of the river whose populations were earlier debarred from or unaware of the benefits of schemes of fee-subvention. Local authorities no longer control our flow of applicants in any way. The decision lies firmly with a boy's parents, who choose according to their circumstances and pay according to their means. In this way the politics of fee assistance have combined with the logistics of public transport systems to make this School a truly regional centre.

Despite the distances of daily travel for many it is noteworthy that never in the twentieth century has the School sought to emulate the Boarding School tradition by detachment of boys from their parents, if we may exclude the special circumstances of the war-time evacuation to Penrith. Even the limited expedient of a single boarding house has been rigorously and rightly avoided – the bane of many regionally orientated day schools, committed as they often are to the unhappy compromise of classes on a Saturday morning. Family contact is integral to the School's philosophy. Daily commuting by the boys is matched by periodic attendance by their parents, though the pattern of their support for School events is distinctive and somewhat idiosyncratic – strong for half a century in the areas of music and drama, fitful in the various arenas of sport.

The annual event with the strongest pull on parents is undoubtedly the year-group Conference, an index perhaps of parental priorities. Their primary purpose in attending is to discuss the progress and problems of their sons, checking that they are properly fulfilling themselves in pursuit of their often high-flying ambitions. All will be looking for fifth-form results which allow entry to the sixth form, and the majority will regard this in turn as a ladder into higher education. For although direct entry to a career reasserts some appeal in an era of elusive job-prospects, the fact is that year by year all but a few of the upper sixth aim for university or polytechnic, while a speciality in Oxford and Cambridge entry has been developed for those who aspire to it, giving an undoubted edge to the school's reputation. Such an 'academic' emphasis is of course expected of a grammar school, but at least the Royal Grammar School is relatively free of the snobberies which define the academic in terms of the theoretical by disparaging contrast with the applied and the practical: art for example flourishes at all levels and there have been strong moves into curricular technology and micro-electronics. Yet the School is big enough to combine all this with a continuing pattern of scholarship in the more traditional disciplines. The reputation it covets is for many-sided achievement.

Curriculum in secondary schools is a vexed educational issue and it would be wrong to give too bland an account of Royal Grammar School solutions. Even in our selective context, where every pupil can manage a rigorous programme, there is a limit to the number of areas of study which can be crowded into the timetable, and in the years of general education to the age of 16 we notice the inbuilt instability of any system which lists some subjects as 'common core' for all and others as available options: consensus

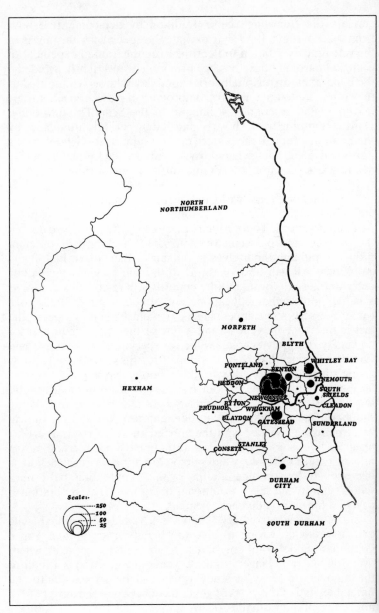

Areas of Residence of RGS Boys, 1934–35.

314

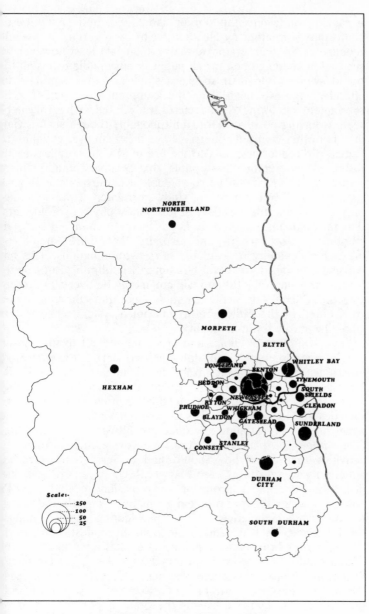

NORTH
NORTHUMBERLAND

MORPETH

BLYTH

PONTELAND
BENTON
WHITLEY BAY
HEDDON
TINEMOUTH
HEXHAM
RYTON
NEWCASTLE
SOUTH
SHIELDS
PRUDHOE
WHICKHAM
CLEADON
BLAYDON
GATESHEAD
SUNDERLAND
CONSETT
STANLEY

DURHAM
CITY

SOUTH DURHAM

Scale:-
250
100
50
25

Areas of Residence of RGS Boys, 1984–85.

315

is lacking on where the border should lie, and any imposed conformity – whether by Headmaster or by government – would redefine rather than eradicate the problem. At least however we succeed in keeping open for all pupils in our middle forms all the broad avenues into later specialist study and thus capitalise on an advantage we have over the comprehensive school. The subsequent narrowing of the focus of study in the sixth form can be seen as having positive merit, unfashionable though such a view may be: other civilised countries have the seemingly enlightened system of broader curricula to the age of 18, but they less easily foster in their senior school pupils that positive commitment to serious study which can be so valuable a feature of the English sixth form. Commitment to study correlates with choice of programme, and the corollary of this philosophy is twofold – first that the sixth form should be large (as the maintained sector is painfully rediscovering) and secondly that there should be maximum flexibility of available subject-combinations. This has become a hallmark of Royal Grammar School policy: in a sixth-form year-group of 150 there will commonly be over 50 different trios of 'A' level subjects under study – not quite the 'negotiated curriculum' of the radical reformers but a system which caters whole-heartedly for individuality.

This promotion of choice and of a commitment to the chosen option extends emphatically into the extracurricular, where we inherit a formidable legacy from the Headmastership of E. R Thomas in the 1920s and 1930s. Blending the cult of individuality with a strong sense of the communal bond provided by clubs and societies and shared activities such as orchestras and camps, he never tired of proclaiming or pioneering this aspect of school life. 'The attempt is made', he wrote, 'to provide such diversity of activities that every boy should find at least one which he voluntarily adopts during each year of his school career.' Such has been the subsequent profusion of provision in the School's voluntary sector that the problem for many now is not the search for one congenial activiy but the bewildering choice amongst several, especially if we add in the great diversification of sport The breadth of this educational vision evokes a warm response: parents and boys may well opt initially for the Royal Grammar School as a centre of academic learning, of examination success and lofty career aspiration, but in the years of passage through it they commonly learn to savour the other important modes of self-fulfilment which it has on offer. The ever-changing panorama

316

of such extra-curricular pursuits is summarised and projected in publications which are important to the School's sense of identity. The *School Year*, compiled each autumn for the annual gathering of boys, parents, staff and Governors at Prizegiving, and the termly school magazine, the *Novo*, wrestle with constrictions of space and cost to do justice to it all. There is indeed a presentational problem amidst such proliferation: over twenty individual sports now enjoy their seasonal ebb and flow; half a dozen concerts or dramatic productions now punctuate each termly programme; traditional features such as mid-summer camps, the Combined Cadet Force or the Debating Society, all of which have maintained an enthusiastic following for more than half a century, now jostle in the calendar with modish ski-parties, rejuvenated language exchanges, and sprightly new clubs ranging from computing to bee-keeping, which will similarly stand the test of time or prove to be splendidly ephemeral. This welter of non-prescribed activity is a curious and special feature of the twentieth century history of the School, a function of its expanding size and seemingly irrepressible vitality.

The multi-faceted complexity of Royal Grammar School life – academic and extra-curricular – can at times be uncomfortable, and beneath our brave facade lies many a half-resolved problem for Headmaster, staff or boys. The Headmaster's dilemma is related to the sheer size of the School, twice as large now as it was intended to be at the time of transfer to Eskdale Terrace. Spurts of building in the 1930s, 1950s and 1970s have catered adequately for rising numbers and blossoming activities (gymnasium, art room, theatre, music school, laboratories and workshops), but the problem remains of structure and organisation. There is a tenacious assumption that we remain one family community, where everything is the concern of everybody and the Headmaster is invited to take a pastoral though not patronising interest in detail on every front. He may profoundly wish to maintain that role, but there is a tension between this fine ideal and the inevitable logic of more decentralised management in the face of greater numbers, new complexities and heightened expectations. The problem has been eased in recent decades by the much greater autonomy of our Junior School, which in separate new premises offers all that is best in primary and preparatory traditions under the management of its own Headmaster. One should record too the marked increases in Bursarial and secretarial staff which offer invaluable support and make our former regimes seem quaintly old-fashioned. Yet in the educational organisation of our Senior School we cling to a 'squashed-pyramid' management structure in which only the Headmaster and Second Master are substantially free of teaching commitments and even they make their forays into the classroom.

Some of the strains fall squarely on their colleagues, many of whom shoulder the burdens of delegated administration in conjunction with their full or nearly full teaching programme as well as their share of pastoral responsibility. The fusion of diverse roles is welcomed, the job-satisfactions are great, but the resultant physical and emotional drain on staff is severely taxing. Even our class-sizes do not offer the respite common in schools of the private sector, since the far-sighted or money-conscious designers of our main buildings provided amply large classrooms and our policy is to fill them in the lower and middle reaches of the School while in the sixth form our departments rarely enjoy the easing provided by low student demand. All this together with the widespread determination to share wholeheartedly in the School's extra-curricular enterprise – at the expense of evenings, weekends or stretches of the holiday period – creates in our staff common room a special atmosphere of dedicated idealism, a buoyancy deriving from a strongly felt unity of purpose, but an undoubted admixture of stress and strain.

Nor does the School's posture on matters of discipline provide the kind of artificial comfort to harassed staff which might be looked for – if not necessarily found – in a 'tough' regime. There are delicate and controversial questions in this area, not only about the principle of whether a school in our tradition could be successfully managed in an uncompromising disciplinary style, but about the interpretation of the relevant facts of our history. My own surmise is that the genius of the Royal Grammar School has for half a century been the cultivation of certain liberal values even if superficial appearances have sometimes suggested otherwise: respect for individuality has been generally preferred to repression, and consensus to conflict or imposed control. This is in part a luxury which any selective school can and should afford, in part a reflection of the traditions of our locality, but more specifically it is a legacy of attitudes inherited from influential individuals in the School's past. Beyond doubt one prevalent strand in the School today is a good-humoured tolerance of eccentricities of all kinds, including some behavioural deviance. The challenge therein is to define and monitor the acceptable

318

limits of our liberalism and to devise a proper response to the minority who take unreasonable advantage of the freedoms offered and threaten to wreck our delicate conventions. A structure of good order is indeed a precondition of all else.

For boys the problems which offset the sheer enjoyment of school life are similarly related to its complexity. They may have tiring journeys to and from home each weekday and may be drawn additionally into weekend School activities, while simultaneously trying to savour family life and neighbourhood friendships; in their studies they must either work hard to satisfy the high expectations of parents and teachers, or suffer the anxieties and tensions of failing to; additionally they will come under subtle and direct pressure to choose from a bewildering array of voluntary pursuits, feeling perhaps inadequate if they don't, yet exposed to another range of pressures and demands if they do; more generally they must hold their own in a bustling community which seems to reward the high-spirited but may dub them arrogant or cheeky. If they are not sharp-witted, resourceful and resilient on arrival, they will find it useful to develop these qualities over the years. Wealth, status and social background matter much less. The School is thus unashamedly meritocratic, prizing the upward thrust of individual initiative – a restless and in a sense classless community. Visitors who expect a toffee-nosed decorum are surprised not to find it. Yet the pressures upon boys do not end there, for they are further urged to be tolerant and considerate in their relationships, which for many is the biggest challenge of all. If the climate of the Royal Grammar School is thus extremely bracing, it must be added that most boys quite evidently thrive on it. Education by exhilaration might almost be our motto.

It is difficult to stand back from this educational ferment and view the School in broader perspective. At very least it is a notable establishment whose regional catchment carries its reputation to all parts of the North East. But do we go further and aspire to a kind of national standing? Are we recognised as one of the great and famous English schools, and if not ought we to be? Institutional pride might coax us into that kind of self-esteem and there is year by year a trickle of tempting evidence, as we reach the national finals of this or that competitive event or uncover evidence that our academic results are second to none in the country. Yet there are limits to the legitimate aspirations of the Newcastle Royal Grammar School to such national status, and doubts as to whether we should even wish it.

The first mild corrective is to ask how many nationally famous individuals this School has produced. The answer is 'not many', though that may say something about the curiosities of received routes to fame. A second and related point is to analyse the geographical distribution of former members of the School: if membership of our Old Novocastrians Association may be taken as a guide (and its brisk trade in information extends to all parts of the world), it is noteworthy that a clear majority live in Newcastle or its region. Even of those who nowadays choose a remoter university for their degree course a high proportion still seek a return to the North East during their subsequent career. Comparison with the clientele of the traditional British boarding school will point the contrast. The latter, being rooted in the moneyed classes but un-rooted in a given locality, are doubly disposed to seek to make their mark on the national scene, whereas the products of a school with a historic commitment to fee subsidy, anchored in a remote northern province, are likely to have more limited horizons. They will seek social mobility only within the narrow limits of routine ambition and geographical mobility only insofar as regional sentiment will allow it. Many Old Novocastrians will of course move on to the national stage, reaching the upper echelons of their profession, but more characteristically they are content to make their mark as good citizens in the area of their childhood and education. In this they frequently retain an affection and respect for the RGS as the *alma mater* of their schooldays. The School thus fosters and focuses a legitimate local pride.

If a future Labour Government were to outlaw the Royal Grammar School along with other fee-paying schools, there would be consternation in the most unlikely sectors of Newcastle and its area. Senior Socialist councillors, a succession of whom have visited the School as Lord Mayor on their first day of office, would certainly question the wisdom of such a step in relation to a school whose corporate presence and institutional stature they had personally savoured. Local teachers and headteachers, whose paymasters have at times urged a policy of non-cooperation, would widely regret the passing of an educational pace-setter whose benefits to many a pupil they had personally witnessed – sometimes within their own families. In any case this cataclysmic view of the future seems scarcely to ring true. There are grounds to hope that the Assisted Places Scheme may anchor itself in widespread public esteem as an element in a less monolithic and a less dogmatic concept of educational provision, where pluralism and parental choice have some part to play and where the excellence of certain independent schools is not marked 'reserved for the wealthy'. If battle-lines there have to be, they are as likely to be drawn between competing systems within the maintained sector itself. In the resultant instability it may be regarded as good that certain schools in the security of their independence can continue calmly to do business and keep alight the torch of a particular ideal.

The independent sector is a kind of barometer with which the nature of the country's mainstream provision of schools can be gauged. When that provision consisted of grammar and secondary modern schools with all the apparent pains of discriminatory selection, the independent schools were often presented and gratefully accepted as models of the intellectually 'comprehensive' community. With the progressive embodiment of that comprehensive ideal in our state provision, a concern about the education of the gifted child has reasserted itself and independent schools with experience in that field are accorded a degree of public sympathy and respect. Furthermore, as expenditure cuts force some local schools back upon the bare central core of educational provision, there is an inevitable interest in any institution which offers still a broader vision and a notion that good education may essentially reside in the voluntary extra. That widely shared ideal is no doubt one of the inspirations behind the new consensus in favour of 'profile reporting', implying as this must the provision of ample and varied opportunities for the student's profile to emerge, but times are not auspicious for the general realisation of this fine concept. If an independent school offers a convincing model, burnished bright as at the Royal Grammar School through decades of inspired initiative and determined continuity, it may be viewed by others with a mixture of admiration, wistfulness and envy. It would be sad if it fuelled the ardour of the abolitionists.

One curious result of Socialist threats has been a new and somewhat artificial solidarity amongst independent schools both nationally and locally. The 1980s have seen unprecedented little gatherings of the headteachers of all such schools on Tyneside, their friendly rivalries submerged, their heterogeneity suddenly acquiring virtue amidst the campaigning for free parental choice. Dame Allan's School for Boys deserves particular mention not only as an alternative local provider of secondary education in the grammar school tradition but for the implicit or potential challenge it presents to the pattern of boys-only education, its sister school for girls being housed on the same campus. Where does the Royal Grammar School stand in this connection? Its Governors have probably never addressed themselves to the question of coeducation and certainly they have never been under economic pressure to do so, but when at the turn of the century they opted for the Eskdale Terrace site they no doubt saw advantage in its contiguity with the Central Newcastle High School and the Church High School, Jesmond's two established schools for girls. With the unfreezing of attitudes in subsequent decades the wisdom of this strategy has become abundantly clear. Many of the social benefits of a mixed school have been available through shared extra-curricular activity and manifold less organised forms of association, while the well-documented snags of coeducation are conveniently side-stepped: if, for example, boys and girls were taught together on Eskdale Terrace, there would be every danger of sex-stereotyping in the roles they played and every likelihood that fewer girls would study sciences and fewer boys languages in the sixth form. One can say and believe all this without denying the obvious fact that the boys-only education of the Royal Grammar School is a historical accident and in some sense an anachronism. Its preservation is perhaps as unnatural as its overthrow would be unnecessary.

Change is no stranger to the Royal Grammar School scene, as the chapters of this volume make abundantly clear. In a sequence of mostly tentative, pragmatic steps the School has adjusted itself to the mood and needs of the time, constantly responding, occasionally pioneering. Yet in such transitions it lives always with the traces of its own history through the uncanny tenacity of earlier practices and philosophies. They may be superseded but are not often wholly suppressed. This is evident in quite tangible aspects of school organisation: we have a curriculum which is both 'traditional' and 'modern'; we have a pastoral system which blends the time-honoured role of tutor with the more recent innovations of form-supervisor and year-group head. In the realm of more generalised ideas there is the same instinctive preference to preserve rather than discard, the effect being that each new generation inherits a richer blend of guiding principles than the last – not always too comfortable in their coexistence. Determinedly we espouse the virtues of disciplined orderliness *and* untrammelled individuality, the philosophies of competitive thrust *and* compassionate concern, the ideals of dedicated academic study *and* eager involvement in extra-curricular distraction. In defiance of logic we seek the best of both worlds.

Zealous readers of this history will be able now to annotate and extend this list of Royal Grammar School themes. They constitute such a fruitful flux of ideas that the School is at very least saved from all risk of dullness or stolidity. At worst it could suffer a mild crisis of identity. At best it is flexible enough to meet effectively whatever educational challenges the future may bring.

APPENDIX I

The Old Books of the School Library

1. Akenside, M.: The pleasures of the imagination, London 1744.
2. [Another copy]
3. Akenside, M.: Poems, London 1772, 4to.
4. The same, 8vo.
5. Akenside, M.: The poems, Dublin 1772.
6. Aristophanes: Comoediae undecim, Basileae 1532.
7. Aristotle: De rhetorica libri tres, Londini 1696.
8. Athenaeus: Deipnosophistarum libri xv, [Heidelberg] 1597.
9. Basil, St.: Opera omnia, Parisiis 1638, 3 vols.
10. Bell, W.: A new compendious grammar of the Greek tongue, London 1776.
11. Bible, Hebrew: [The Pentateuch, with commentaries, Genoa 5378 (=1618)].
12. Bible, Greek: Vetus testamentum, Oxonii 1720.
13. Bible, Greek: Novum . . . testamentum. Coloniae Allobrogum 1620.
14. Bourne, H.: The History of Newcastle, Newcastle 1736.
15. Brand, J.: The History and Antiquities of . . . Newcastle, London 1789, 2 vols.
16. [Another copy]
17. Budaeus, G.: Commentarii linguae Graecae, Basileae 1556.
18. Budaeus, G. & al.: Dictionarium Graeco-Latinum, post correctiones G. Budaei [etc], Basileae 1584.
19. Caesar: Commentarii, Glasguae 1750.
20. Carleton, G.: The life of Mr. Bernard Gilpin, London 1629.
21. Casaubon, I.: Animadversionum in Athenaei Dipnosophistas libri xv, Lugduni 1600.
22. Cellarius, C.: Geographia antiqua, Londini 1786.
23. Chrysostom, St John: [Works in Greek], Etonae 1610, 8 vols.
24. Cicero: Opera omnia, Parisiis 1565–6, 4 vols.
25. Cicero: Epistolarum libri xvi ad . . . Atticum, Amstelaedami 1684, 2 vols.
26. Cicero: Orationes, Amstelodami 1685, 4 vols of 6.
27. Clement, St of Alexandria: Opera, Lutetiae 1629.
28. Clement, F.: Ciceronis . . . latinae elegantiae instrumentum adverbiale, Londini 1582.
29. Demosthenes: Orationes de republica duodecim, Londini 1775, 1 vol. of 2.
30. Dionysius: Orbis descriptio, Oxoniae 1697.
31. Elstob, E.: The rudiments of grammar for the English-Saxon tongue, London 1715.
32. Erasmus, D.: Adagiorum chiliades, Francofurti 1599.
33. Erasmus, D.: Adagiorum chiliades, Hanoviae 1617.
34. Eusebius: Ecclesiasticae historiae libri decem, Moguntiae 1672.
35. Festus and Flaccus: De verborum significatione libri xx, Amstelodami 1699.
36. Greek Anthology: Collectanea Graeca, Edinburgi 1789, 2 vols of 3.
37. Hesychius: Lexicon, Lugduni Batavorum 1746, 2 vols.
38. Homer: Odyssea, Cantabrigiae 1711.
39. Horace: Poemata omnia, Venetiis 1519.
40. Horace: Q. Horatius Flaccus, Antverpiae 1608.
41. Hornius, G.: A full and exact description of the earth, Amsterdam 1700.
42. Hutchinson, W.: A view of Northumberland, Newcastle 1778, 2 vols.
43. Hutchinson, W.: The History and Antiquities of . . . Durham, Newcastle 1785, 3 vols.
44. Johnson, J.: The riches of gospel grace, Warrington 1776, 1 vol. of 2.

APPENDIX I

45. Junius, H.: Lexicon graecolatinum, Basileae 1548.
46. Juvenal: Satyrae, Basileae 1551.
47. Juvenal: Satyrarum libri v, Hanoviae 1603.
48. Juvenal: Satyrae, Ultrajecti 1685.
49. Keith, T.: A key to the complete practical arithmetician, London 1790.
50. Labb, P.: Eruditae pronuntiationis catholici indices, Londini 1771.
51. Livy: Libri omnes superstites, Francofurti ad Moenum 1628.
52. Lucian: Opera, Salmurii 1619, 1 vol. of 2.
53. Lucian: Opera, Amstelodami 1687, 2 vols.
54. March, J. and Welwood, J.: A vindication of the present great revolution in England, London 1689.
55. Martial: Epigrammatum libri xv, Lutetiae Parisiorum 1617.
56. Martinius, M.: Lexicon philologicum, Bremae 1623.
57. Moll, H.: Atlas geographus, London 1711–17, 2 vols of 5.
58. Munton, A.: Several sermons, Newcastle 1756.
59. [Another copy]
60. Nazianzen, St Gregory: Opera, Parisiis 1630, 2 vols.
61. Newcastle General Magazine, Newcastle 1753.
62. Ovid: Opera, Francofurti 1601, 3 vols.
63. Pagninus, S.: Thesaurus linguae sanctae, Lugduni 1529.
64. Panvinius, O.: Antiquitatum Veronensium libri octo, Verona 1647.
65. Parliament: Two ordinances . . . for the maintenance of some preaching ministers in the cities of Yorke [etc], 26 Decemb. 1643, London 1645.
66. Parliament: The curtaine drawne, or, the Parliament exposed to view, London 1659.
67. Parliament: Several proceedings in Parliament from . . . 7 of February, to . . . 14 day of February, 1649, London 1649.
68. Perottus, N.: Cornucopiae Latinae linguae, Basileae 1536.
69. Pliny: Epistolae, Florentiae 1515.
70. Plutarch: Opera, Geneva 1572, 5 vols.
71. Politianus, A.: Opera, Basileae 1553.
72. Polus, M.: Synopsis criticorum, Londini 1669–71, 5 vols.
73. Portlock, W. H.: A new . . . collection of . . . voyages and travels, London 1794, 2 vols.
74. Rosinus, J.: Antiquitatum Romanarum corpus, Lutetiae Parisiorum 1613.
75. Sallust: Opera, Amstelodami 1690.
76. Sallust: Quae extant, Cantabrigiae 1710.
77. Salmon, N.: Stemmata Latinitatis, London 1796, 1 vol. of 2.
78. Sanctius, F.: Minerva, Franquerae 1693.
79. Sophocles: The tragedies, translated . . . by George Adams. London 1724, 1 vol. of 2.
80. Stephanus, H.: Thesaurus Graecae linguae, Geneva 1573, 1 vol. of 5.
81. Story, J.: An introduction to English grammar, Newcastle 1778.
82. Suetonius: C. Suetonius Tranquillus, Lugduni Batavorum 1656.
83. Suidas: [Lexicon Graecum], Coloniae Allobrogum 1619, 1 vol. of 2.
84. Tacitus: Opera, Antwerpiae 1627.
85. Tacitus: Opera, Parisiis 1776, 6 vols of 7.
86. Terence: Comoediae sex, Londini 1749.
87. Thucydides: De bello Peloponnesiaco libri octo, Francofurti 1594.
88. Virgil: Bucolica et georgica, Madrid 1608.
89. Virgil: Bucolica, georgica et liber Aeneidos, Leyden 1645.
90. Virgil: Opera, Venetiis 1624.
91. Vossius, G. J.: Etymologicon linguae Latinae, Amstelodami 1695.
92. Warden, J.: A collection from the Spectator [etc], Newcastle 1752.

APPENDIX I

)3.   Warden, J.: A collection from the Spectator [etc], Newcastle 1761.
)4.   Warner, F.: A system of divinity, London 1767.
)5.   Xenophon: De Cyri institutione libri octo, Oxonii 1727.
)6.   Xenophon: Opera, n.p. [   ] 1581.
)7.   Young, E.: The complaint, London 1743.
)8.   Zuingerus, T.: Theatrum humanae vitae, Basileae 1586, 4 vols.

Although there are only 98 works printed before 1800 in the School Library at present, the collection is disproportionately interesting both historically and bibliographically. It represents not so much a collection of textbooks for lower forms, as a scholarly library for upper forms and for the masters – thus it includes no grammars, the basic material of the School's activity. The one exception to this is a remarkable survival, No. 27, which is a broadsheet guide to the adverbs in Cicero, published in 1582. This is thought to be unique, and in view of its ephemeral nature may well be a relic of the Elizabethan school.

Only three items can be securely located in the Library before the Civil War, all by virtue of a most distinctive and unusual feature. They are Nos. 55 and 83, and a detached binding which cannot now be assigned to any work. Inserted into the leather of the front cover of each item there is a paper slip overlaid with a transparent horn cover, recording its donor. No. 83 reads 'Ex dono Thomae Liddle Armigeri, as usum scholae Neopurgensis apud Anglos Boreales. Jun. 12. 1620', No. 55 'Scholae Novicastri me dedit Lionellus Maddison, Eques Auratus, 1633', and the detached binding 'Ex dono Guielmi Hall, Alexandri Davison'. The donors had all been, or were to be, mayors of the town, but the books do not seem to have been presented (as one might have expected) on the occasion of their election. It is probable that this curious way of recording the donor's name was a common characteristic of books in the Library before the Civil War, and that subsequent rebinding (particularly in 1699, as we shall see) has obliterated the evidence.

Many of the books in the School's Library were apparently destroyed during the siege of 1644, and George Ritschel persuaded the Common Council to spend some money between 1651 and 1655 to replace them. But not until the death of Amor Oxley in 1669 do we have any information about what books the School possessed. In his will Oxley left fourteen books to the School, 'forasmuch as the free school in Newcastle lost its library when the town was stormed and plundered by the Scotish army, and I then lost my own library.' The books are listed in a schedule, and included Nos 8, 9, 17, 18, 23, 24, 27, 52, 60, 63, 70, 96. Only two works seem to have disappeared subsequently (the poems of Homer, published by Henri Estienne, and the works of St Gregory of Nyssa). The list contains a high proportion of patristic literature, in line with Oxley's theological interests; one at least of them (No. 60) had been left to Oxley by his close friend and religious confidant, Edward Rochester.

Oxley's successor, Richard Garthwaite, is known to have made only one addition to the collection – No. 72, to the publication of which he had been a subscriber, and which includes some manuscript notes about his subscription. But the Library was transformed shortly after Garthwaite's death, by Thomas Rudd. He was greatly interested in books and manuscripts, and later became librarian to the Dean and Chapter of Durham, producing the first full catalogue of their manuscripts. He was appointed Headmaster of the School in 1699, and immediately set about organising its Library. He went through it during 1699 and 1700, writing 'Liber scholae publicae Novocastrensis MDCXCIX' or 'MDCC' on each title-page, and often a short note on the character and quality of the edition. In addition, he arranged the rebinding of many volumes in a uniform pattern of suede leather with blind-tooled decoration, while in 1699 a friend of his from Durham, a lawyer named Henry Lambton, gave at least three recently-published books to augment the collection – Nos 7, 53 and 78. On 20 March 1700 Rudd persuaded the Common Council to buy another eight recent works for the School, of which Nos 25, 26 and 91 survive. (The others were Cicero's *De Officiis,* Callimachus, Theocritus, Ludovicus Lucius's *Dictionarium* and the *Etymologicum Magnum.*) The following contain a date in Rudd's hand on the title-page or were rebound by him: 7, 8, 11, 13, 21, 24, 26, 27, 30, 32, 35, 41, 53, 56, 62, 71, 87, 88, 98. Thus some thirty-four works still in the Library were definitely there by 1700.

The vicissitudes which books in the Library could suffer at this time is illustrated by a note in No. 9, from Oxley's bequest. 'This book of the free school in Newcastle was taken as a pledge more than twenty years ago by the Reverend Robert Thomlinson; now it is returned to the School Library as agreed, . . . June 23 1732' (my translation from the Latin). Thomlinson was of course the great bibliophile founder of the large library annexed to St Nicholas's; in 1715 he was appointed Master of the Hospital. It is possible that other books from the School found their way into Thomlinson's collection, which is now housed in the Newcastle Central Library.

The general decline of the School during much of the eighteenth century is reflected in the small and miscellaneous collection of books which were probably acquired then (some eighteenth-century works, like the substantial group of Akenside's works, were of course acquired later when the School became interested in its old boys). Even Hugh Moises, although a famous and effective Master, seems not to have made any notable additions to the Library of the School. The one major development in his time was that in July 1762 an organisation named The Associates of Doctor Bray 'sent down from London a valuable Lending Library, to be kept at the Grammar School, for the Benefit of young Students of Divinity there', as part of a national scheme to create parochial libraries; this presumably became merged with Thomlinson's Library, though its actual fate is unknown. At all events, it would not have been part of the School Library proper.

Some of the gaps which had developed in the collection by the end of the century were, however, filled by Moises's successor, his nephew Edward Moises. Between 1787 and 1790 he gave a number of books to the School, of which Nos 6, 22, 38, 40, 50, 76, 79, 86 and 95 still survive. Nos 38 and 79 seem to have been bought by Moises in his last year as an undergraduate at Cambridge, in 1783. These purchases represent the last occasion on which sixteenth- or seventeenth-century printed books were bought for the School's working Library, although at intervals ever since individual donations of interesting or valuable works have been made to the School (a modern example would be Lord Runciman's gift of No. 39). Other items which are known to have come to the School since 1800 include the following: Nos 1, 3, 4, 15, 19, 31, 64, 75, 85. The most spectacular volume in the collection probably came to it in this way: it is No. 84, Justus Lipsius's great edition of Tacitus published by the Plantin press. It is bound in calf decorated with a pattern of gold fleurs-de-lis and crowned 'L's, with in the centre three shields, one bearing the Arms of France, the second those of Navarre, and the third a crowned 'L'. On its title-page is the inscription, 'E Libris Regiae Bibliothecae Galliae, 1632.' It is clear that this volume was bound for the royal library of France under Louis XIII, whose court was deeply interested in the political lessons of Tacitus and Lipsius, though how the book made its way to Newcastle is a mystery. It is perhaps an appropriate reasure for the School of a town which inscribed a quotation from Tacitus above its gate in 1649.

The collection had become very neglected by the end of the nineteenth century, such that when Laws wrote his history in 1925 he could identify only a small proportion of Oxley's bequest. In 1931, when Lord Plender paid for the fitting up of a new School Library, he also paid for the rebinding of some of the old books, but they were not catalogued, nor were all the volumes which needed repair unearthed from their various hiding-places round the school. In 1954 and attempt at a proper catalogue was made by a pupil, Ian Jamieson, but not until 1963/4 were all the volumes assembled in one place and catalogued accurately. At the same time a second programme of rebinding and repair was embarked on. Since 1964 the collection has remained in the School Library.

APPENDIX II

*The Headmasters of the Royal Grammar School**

c.1560–1584	John Gray.
1584–1594	Humphrey Gray.
1594–1599	Francis Burrowes.
	Cuthbert Ogle.
1599–1602	William Allanson.
1602–1612	Francis Burrowes.
1612–1623	Robert Fowberry, M.A.
1623–1629	Edward Wigham, M.A.
1630–1635	Thomas Gibson, M.A.
1635–1645	Amor Oxley, M.A.
1645–1648	Nicholas Augar, M.A.
1648–1657	George Ritschell, M.A.
1657–1662	John Newman.
1662–1669	Amor Oxley, M.A.
1669–1690	Richard Garthwaite, M.A.
1690–1699	John Cotteral, M.A.
1699–1709	Thomas Rudd, M.A.
1710–1715	James Jurin, M.A., F.R.S.
1715–1738	Edmund Lodge, M.A.
1738–1749	Richard Dawes, M.A.
1749–1787	Hugh Moises, M.A.
1787–1828	Edward Moises, M.A.
1828–1834	George Ferris Mortimer, M.A.
1834–1847	John A. Wood, M.A.
1847–1871	James Snape, D.D.
1873–1883	Brian Christopherson, M.A.
1883–1912	S. C. Logan, M.A.
1912–1921	John Talbot, M.A., B.Sc.
1922–1948	E. R. Thomas, O.B.E., D.C.L., M.A., M.Sc.
1948–1960	O. W. Mitchell, M.A.
1960–1972	W. D. Haden, M.A.
1972–	A. S. Cox, M.A.

*This list departs from the traditional list in a number of respects. For more detailed discussion of the Headmasters between 1560 and 1662, see Chapter I.

NOTES

Chapter 1

1. See John Brand, *The History and Antiquities of the Town and County of Newcastle upon Tyne*, i (London 1789), pp. 307–8 and 312 n.2.
2. *Registers of Bishops Tunstall and Pilkington*, ed. G. Hinde (Surtees Society, vol. clxi, 1952), p. 30; Brand, *Newcastle*, i, p.78.
3. The mid-sixteenth-century figure is based upon the muster rolls of 1539 and 1547, printed in Richard Welford, *History of Newcastle and Gateshead*, iii (Newcastle 1887), pp. 174–94 and 244. The seventeenth-century figure is based on the Hearth Tax of 1665, details of which are printed in Roger Howell, Jr., *Newcastle upon Tyne and the Puritan Revolution* (Oxford 1967), pp. 350–2. These original figures need to be multiplied to produce an overall estimate. For the muster rolls, I have used the estimated proportion of men aged between 16 and 60 (the musterable population) in 1545 to be found in E. A. Wrigley and R. S. Schofield, *The Population History of England 1541–1871* (London 1981), Table A3.1, p. 528. For the Hearth Tax, I have used the multiplier suggested by ibid. pp. 571–12. These two calculations produce remarkably similar results when set against the overall increase in England's population over the period, figures for which are from Wrigley and Schofield's Table A3.1, p. 528.
4. The figures for freemen come from Howell, *Puritan Revolution*, p. 353. They are compared with an estimate of the males aged 25–40 within the town each decade based on the national figures in Wrigley and Schofield, *Population History*, Table A3.1, divided by 430×2. For the other towns, see Peter Clark and Paul Slack, *English Towns in Transition 1500–1700* (Oxford 1976), p. 115.
5. See the discussion in Howell, *Puritan Revolution*, pp. 35ff.
6. See R. A. Houston, *Aspects of Society in Scotland and North East England c.1550–c.1750*, unpublished Ph.D Thesis, University of Cambridge 1981; D. Cressy, "Social Status and Literacy in North East England 1560–1630", *Local Population Studies*, xxi (1978), pp. 19–23.
7. *Injunctions and other Ecclesiastical Proceedings of Bishop Barnes*, ed. J. Raine (Surtees Society, vol xxi, 1850), pp. 42–3.
8. This estimate is based on Wrigley and Schofield's national figures, *Population History*, Table A3.1.
9. These calculations are based on the figures in Lawrence Stone, "The Educational Revolution in England 1560–1640", *Past and Present*, xxviii (1964), p. 51, compared with the overall population trends for the age-group in Wrigley and Schofield, *Population History*, Table A3.1.
10. A. R. Laws, *Schola Novocastrensis*, i (Newcastle 1925), pp. 89–90; Howell, *Puritan Revolution*, p. 328 n.3.
11. Laws, *Schola Novocastrensis*, p. 68.
12. J. Selden, *Opera Omnia*, iii (London 1726), col. 2016.
13. Richard Welford, *History of Newcastle and Gateshead*, ii (London 1887), pp. 259–60.
14. According to John Foxe, *The Acts and Monuments*, ed. Josiah Pratt, vii (London 1877), p. 407, Nicholas Ridley "learned his grammar with great dexterity in Newcastle, and was removed from thence to the university of Cambridge." He graduated B.A. in 1522. He was helped through school and university by his uncle Robert Ridley, who also enjoyed a distinguished career at Cambridge, as an early humanist. Another Northumbrian of the same type

was George Folbery, B.A. 1515, late Master of Pembroke (Nicholas Ridley's college). All three may well have been at the Newcastle school. For their careers, see the D.N.B., A. R. Emden, *A Biographical Register of the University of Cambridge* (Cambridge 1963), p. 480, and John Venn and J. A. Venn, *Alumni Cantabrigienses Part I to 1751*, ii (Cambridge 1924), p. 154. An example of a student at Louvain is "Thomas Brandelinghe de Novo Castro, Anglus" who matriculated there on 19 August 1523 *(Matricule de l'Université de Louvain*, ed. A. Schillings, iii (Louvain 1958), p. 701).

15. The agreement is printed in Brand, *Newcastle*, i, p. 86. The original is MS 8/1/50 of the Tyne and Wear Archives.

16. See J. M. W. Bean, *The Decline of English Feudalism 1215–1540* (Manchester 1968), pp. 286ff.

17. R. F. Tuck, "The Origins of the Royal Grammar School Newcastle upon Tyne", *Archaeologia Aeliana (A.A.)* 4th series xlvi (1968), p. 231.

18. Ibid. pp. 240–1, though the suggestion there that he was at Queens' should be emended, for that John Gray was Vicar of Foxton by 1552, and would never have subsequently become a schoolmaster. John Gray of Clare is much more likely. See Venn, *Alumni Cantabrigienses Part I*, ii, p. 251.

19. Laws, *Schola Novocastrensis*, i, p. 30.

20. See Keith Wrightson, *English Society 1580–1680* (London 1982), p. 34.

21. At Pontefract in 1583 the Master received £20, the usher £5 7s. 2d. (The Victoria History of the County of York, ed. W. Page, i (London 1912), p. 437). At Wakefield in 1607 the Master received £26 13s. 4d., the usher £12 (ibid. p. 443). At Doncaster the town paid their Master £10 and their usher £5 in 1581/2 (ibid. p. 447), while at Pocklington in 1599 the Master was supposed to receive £25–30 and the usher £10 (ibid. p. 465). The Doncaster figure may, like Newcastle, represent only a component, as unlike the others it was not an endowed school.

22. Tuck, *The Origins*, p. 232.

23. Ibid. p. 262.

24. Ibid. p. 239.

25. For Raimes, see Venn, *Alumni*, iii, p. 416 ("Rames"). For Bullock, see the D.N.B. There, his origins are thought to be obscure; but in 1552 "Georgius Bullocus, Novicastrensis, Anglus" matriculated at Louvain University, at a time when George Bullock of St John's is known to have gone into exile. He returned under Mary and became Master, fleeing to Louvain again under Elizabeth. "Dominus Georgius Bullocq, Anglus, magister noster" entered the University in 1568. The two Bullocks may well have been the same man. Schillings, *Matricule* iv, pp. 463 and 744.

26. See the D.N.B. article on Pilkington.

27. The records of part of this campaign are in the Cause Papers of the Consistory Court of the Archbishops of York, at the Borthwick Institute of the University of York, CP G.1305. (The court heard appeals within the Province.) Other papers, once at Durham, are in the interleaved volume of Bourne's *History* owned by the Newcastle Society of Antiquaries; see J. R. Boyle, "Christopher Hunter's copy of Bourne's History of Newcastle", *AA* N.S. xv (1829) pp. 177–78.

28. H.M.C. Cecil MSS, Part I, p. 311.

29. Welford, *History*, ii, p. 378.

30. Schillings, *Matricule*, iv, p. 710; Brand, *Newcastle* i, p. 589.

31. The Crown presentations are in *Calendar of Patent Rolls, Elizabeth I* ii 1560–63, p. 479, and iii 1563–66, p. 92. Brand, *Newcastle* i, p. 428, records that "one Cuthbert Bewicke" procured the presentation, and mentions the

town's grant of presentation of the Magdalene Hospital in 1569. The similar grant for St Mary's is mentioned in the Ewbank papers; see Tuck, *Origins*, p. 232. For the testimony of leading merchants on Raimes's behalf, see the papers at the Borthwick Institue mentioned above n. 27. The Bishop's final dispossession is recorded in A. M. Oliver, *Early Deeds relating to Newcastle upon Tyne,* Surtees Society cxxxvii (1924), p. 7.

2. W. K. Boyd ed., *Calendar of State Papers relating to Scotland,* iii (Edinburgh 1903), pp. 28 and 34.
3. Tuck, *Origins*, p. 242.
4. Ibid. p. 233.
5. Ibid. p. 233.
5. Laws, *Schola Novocastrensis*, i, pp. 37–39.
7. *Calendar of Patent Rolls, Elizabeth I* vii 1575–78, p. 433.
8. This appears from Henry Anderson's remark later that the town spent "great sums in procuring a new charter to make the town capable" of the grand lease. H.M.C. *Calendar of the Manuscripts of the Marquis of Salisbury*, iv (1892), p. 209.
9. Welford, *History*, iii, p. 18.
0. Brand, *Newcastle*, ii, p. 184.
1. See the will of Robert Lambe, Welford, *History* iii, p. 32.
2. H.M.C. *Salisbury MSS* iv, p. 209.
3. Brand, *Newcastle*, ii, p. 269.
4. H.M.C. *Salisbury MSS* iv, p. 209.
5. This story may be seen in the following entries of the *Acts of the Privy Council of England* N.S. xxv, pp. 31–2, 219, 381; xxvi, pp. 27, 512; xxvii, p. 311; xxviii, pp. 225, 311, 317, 627; xxix, pp. 181, 199, 295 and 358 (which was the record of the committee's decision).
6. Brand, *Newcastle*, ii, pp. 270–71.
7. *Acts of the Privy Council* N.S. xxx, pp. 427–28.
8. Welford, *History*, iii, p.186.
9. Laws, *Schola Novocastrensis* i, p. 38.
0. Welford, *History*, iii, p. 114 (transcript of Lansdowne MS 81 f. 41).
1. See Clare Cross, *The Puritan Earl* (London 1966).
2. Welford, *History* iii, p. 114.
3. Laws, *Schola Novocastrensis*, i, p. 43.
4. Tuck, *Origins*, pp. 251–53.
5. N.C.A. Chamberlains' Accounts.
6. Tuck, *Origins*, p. 256, Joseph Foster, *Alumni Oxonienses 1500–1714*, ii (London 1892), p. 475.
7. Foster, ibid.
8. Tuck, *Origins*, p. 233.
9. Ibid.
0. Laws, *Schola Novocastrensis*, i, p. 45.
1. Brand, *Newcastle*, ii, pp. 622–23.
2. Tuck, *Origins*, p. 254.
3. Ibid, pp. 255–56.
4. Laws, *Schola Novocastrensis*, i, p. 44; J. Piele, *Biographical Register of Christ's College 1505–1905*, i (Cambridge 1910), p. 225.
5. Brand, *Newcastle*, ii, pp. 188–9, 273–5.
6. Laws, *Schola Novocastrensis*, i, p. 44; J. Hodgson, *A History of Northumberland Part II*, i (Newcastle 1827), p. 297.
7. Tuck, *Origins*, p. 262.
8. Brand, *Newcastle*, i, p. 588ff.

NOTES

69. Tuck, *Origins*, pp. 264–65.
70. See the engraving opposite p. 80, Laws, *Schola Novocastrensis*, i.
71. Tuck, *Origins*, pp. 263–64.
72. Venn, *Alumni Cantabrigienses Part I* ii, p. 153; J. Lawson, *A Town Grammar School through Six Centuries* (Oxford 1963), p. 69; *Northumberland County History*, xiv, pp. 221–23.
73. Laws, *Schola Novocastrensis*, i, p. 66.
74. Ibid, pp. 62ff.
75. Ibid, p. 66.
76. W. Gray, *Chorographia* (London 1649), p. 25.
77. Welford, *History* iii, pp. 246–47.
78. Tuck, *Origins*, pp. 266–67; Welford, *History*, iii, pp. 251–52.
79. Brand, *Newcastle* i, pp. 83–84; W. H. Knowles, "The Hospital of St. Mary the Virgin, Newcastle-upon-Tyne", *A.A.* N.S. xv (1892), p. 206.
80. His successor (brother of Amor Oxley) was inducted 14 October 1622, *Northumberland County History*, xii, p. 431.
81. Howell, *Puritan Revolution*, pp. 53ff.
82. He appears in Fowberry's will (see above n. 77), and may be the Mr Gray mentioned as teaching in the School between Fowberry and Wigham. See Laws, *Schola Novocastrensis*, i, p. 76.
83. J. Walker, *An Attempt towards Recovering an Account of the Numbers and Sufferings of the Clergy of the Church of England . . . in the Late Times of the Grand Rebellion* (London 1714), p. 252.
84. Ibid.
85. See his life in the D.N.B.
86. J. E. Prescott, "The Grammar School of Carlisle", *Trans. of the Cumberland and Westmorland Antiq. and Archaeol. Soc.* N.S. xvi (1915–16), pp. 1–28; D. M. Smith, *Guide to Bishops' Registers of England and Wales* (London, Royal Historical Society, 1981), pp. 258–59.
87. Piele, *Christ's College*, i, p. 437; *Admissions to the College of St John the Evangelist*, i (Cambridge 1882), p. 14.
88. *Admissions to St John's*, pp. 5, 8.
89. Laws, *Schola Novocastrensis*, i, p. 77.
90. Piele, *Christ's College*, i, pp. 225, 305.
91. *Northumberland County History* xiv, p. 322; Laws, *Schola Novocastrensis*, i, p. 86.
92. Ibid. p. 88; Piele, *Christ's College* i, p. 410.
93. Howell, *Puritan Revolution*, p. 92.
94. Piele, *Christ's College*, i, p. 305.
95. Ibid. pp. 376, 410, 427 and 429.
96. Ibid. p. 322.
97. Ibid. p. 421.
98. See "Admissiones Sociorum" in T. Baker, *History of the College of St John the Evangelist*, i (Cambridge 1869), pp. 285ff.
99. Venn, *Alumni Cantabrigienses Part I* i, p. 257; *Admissions to St John's*, i, pp. 15, 164, 169 and 170.
100. M. Hope Dodds, ed., *Extracts from the Newcastle upon Tyne Council Minute Book 1639–1656*, (Newcastle 1920), p. 14; R. Surtees, *The History and Antiquities of the County Palatine of Durham*, i.2 (London 1816), pp. 119–20.
101. Laws, *Schola Novocastrensis*, p. 87; Howell, *Puritan Revolution*, i, p. 323.
102. A. G. Matthews, *Walker Revised* (Oxford 1948), p. 290.
103. Hope Dodds, *Minute Book*, p. 42.

NOTES

04. M. McDonnell, *The Registers of St Paul's School 1509–1748* (n.p. 1977), pp. 120–21; J. Watney, "The Mercers' School", *Transactions of the London and Middlesex Archaeological Society* N.S. i (1904), pp. 125–27.

05. Laws, *Schola Novocastrensis*, i, p. 96.

06. Howell, *Puritan Revolution*, p. 323; Laws, *Schola Novocastrensis*, i, p. 104.

07. Hope Dodds, *Minute Book*, p. 85.

08. Howell, *Puritan Revolution*, pp. 218ff.

09. Brand, *Newcastle*, i, p. 48. (The quotation is from Tacitus, *Agricola* 3).

10. See C. Webster, *The Great Instauration* (London 1975).

11. Ibid. p. 297; Surtees, *Durham*, iii, p. 417.

12. Hope Dodds, *Minute Book*, p. 85; H.M.C. *Report on Manuscripts in Various Collections* i (1901), pp. 15–16.

13. Webster, *Instauration*, pp. 105–6; D.N.B. s.n. Woodward.

14. Howell, *Puritan Revolution*, pp. 324–25; V.C.H. Surrey ii p. 180 (though for correct name, see Venn, *Alumni Cantabrigienses Part I* i. p. 571).

15. Howell, *Puritan Revolution*, pp. 325ff.

16. R. F. Young, *A Bohemian Philosopher at Oxford in the 17th Century* (London 1924); Howell, *Puritan Revolution*, p. 327 n.3.

17. Ibid. p. 328; Laws, *Schola Novocastrensis*, i, p. 103.

18. T. H. Rowland, "Curriculum of the Royal Grammar School, Newcastle-on-Tyne", *(Durham) Research Review* iii (1952), pp. 35–40; Laws, *Schola Novocastrensis*, i, p. 103. The late date is confirmed by Keith Thomas's observation that provisions against "barring-out" in northern England tend to be late seventeenth-century. K. V. Thomas, "Rule and Misrule in the Schools of Early Modern England", *University of Reading Stenton Lecture* 9, (Reading 1976), p. 27 and n.112.

19. See the instructions for the First Form, Rowland, *Curriculum* p. 37.

120. Thomas, *Rule and Misrule, passim*.

121. Webster, *Instauration*, p. 239.

122. Laws, *Schola Novocastrensis*, i, p. 105.

123. Ibid. pp. 112, 118.

124. Howell, *Puritan Revolution*, i, p. 211.

125. Laws, *Schola Novocastrensis*, pp. 91, 113. See Hope Dodds, *Minute Book*, p. 218 for an earlier payment of arrears to Oxley.

126. Laws, *Schola Novocastrensis*, i, pp. 119, 125.

127. Piele, *Christ's College*, ii p. 4.

128. Laws, *Schola Novocastrensis*, i, pp. 124–25.

129. Ibid pp. 128, 131; Howell, *Puritan Revolution*, pp. 111, 219, 268.

130. (W. H. D. Longstaffe, ed.), *Memoirs of the Life of Mr. Ambrose Barnes*, Surtees Society, i, 1 (1866), pp. 409, 403.

131. Laws, *Schola Novocastrensis*, i, p. 130.

132. Tuck, *Origins*, p. 269.

133. Laws, *Schola Novocastrensis*, i, p. 131.

134. Ibid. pp. 131–32.

135. R.G., *A censure* sig. B1.

136. Ibid. sig. B2v.

137. Ibid. sig. G1.

138. See M. W. Flinn ed., *The Law Book of the Crowley Ironworks*, SS 167 (1952), esp. p. xiv.

139. Laws, *Schola Novocastrensis*, i, p. 132.

140. Ibid. p. 131.

141. See H. C. Darby ed., *A New Historical Geography of England* (Cambridge 1973), p. 361.

142. Laws, *Schola Novocastrensis*, i, p. 143.

NOTES

Chapter II

1. F. J. G. Robinson, *Trends in Education in Northern England during the Eighteenth Century: A Biographical Study*, unpublished Ph.D. Thesis, University of Newcastle upon Tyne 1972, vol. I p. 130.
2. In 1817 the Common Council allowed the use of the grammar school premises for St John's Sunday School which continued there till its move to newly-built buildings in nearby Rosemary Lane in 1825. Newcastle Common Council Book (CCB) (1799–1810), 13.12.1817 (Tyne and Wear Archives).
3. *Letters of Spencer Cowper, Dean of Durham* (Surtees Society, vol. clxv, 1950), p. 102.
4. The King v. Archbishop of York (1795), Term Reports, vol. vi, p. 490.
5. N. Carlisle, *A Concise Description of the Endowed Grammar Schools in England and Wales*, two volumes, 1818; *Reports of the Commissions to Inquire Concerning Charities* (CCR), 32 reports in 38 volumes, Sessional Papers 1819–40.
6. William Woodman Papers, Society of Antiquaries of Newcastle upon Tyne (Northumberland County Record Office).
7. Newcastle Chamberlains' Accounts, May 1710 (Tyne and Wear Archives).
8. CCB (1699–1718), 28.7.1710.
9. Ibid. 26.3.1700; Newcastle Journal, 23 December 1758.
10. CCB (1718–43), 11.7.1737.
11. Ibid. 26.9.1737. The various payments to Lodge were subject to deductions if he voluntarily accepted other paid employment.
12. CCB (1743–66), 14.1.1765.
13. E. Mackenzie, *A Descriptive and Historical Account of the Town and County of Newcastle upon Tyne, including the Borough of Gateshead*, ii, (Newcastle 1827), pp. 434–6; CCB (1785–99), 6.10.1794.
14. Brand, *Newcastle*, i, p. 104; Carlisle, *Concise Description*, ii, p. 255; but vide CCR 23, 1830, p. 388, "There is no property now known to belong to the grammar school, and we are assured that the corporation are not possessed of any lands which could have been derived from the will of Thomas Horsley".
15. Quoted in E. Hughes, *North Country Life in the Eighteenth Century: the North East, 1700–1750* (Oxford 1952), pp. 342–3; CCB (1699–1718), 15.12.1714.
16. CCB (1824–35), 23.12.1828. An advert did appear in the Newcastle Journal for 26 April 1746 but this was to announce the arrival of a teacher of writing and arithmetic apparently for the Free Writing School, though he was referred to as "usher in the Free School of Newcastle-upon-Tyne".
17. CCB (1743–66), 26.6.1749. Nicholls was possibly Frank Nicholls a physician who at the time lectured in anatomy at Oxford or, more likely, Dr John Nicoll (Nichols) headmaster of Westminster School, 1733–53.
18. CCB (1699–1718), 28.7.1710. At Hexham Grammar School candidates could submit Latin and English verse. Thomas Hudson who was a successful candidate in 1742 wrote, "These Verses, Sir, to me belong,
   "I hope your favour for my song,
   "& for your health shall be my pray'r,
   "God save King George and Mister May'r".
   Lockhart MSS. (Northumberland County Record Office).
19. CCB (1718–43), 26.9.1737.

NOTES

20. CCB (1766–85), 20.9.1781. Brand published his history in 1789. He was resident secretary of the Society of Antiquaries in London from 1797 to his death in 1806.
21. Newcastle Chamberlains' Accounts, 1709–10.
22. Quoted in H. Twiss, *Life of Lord Chancellor Eldon* (London 1844), p. 34.
23. CCB (1817–24), 23.12.1822.
24. CCB (1766–85), 16.12.1778.
25. Brand to Ralph Beilby, 5 April 1784, in *Archaeologia Aeliana* 3rd series xiv (1917), p. 5.
26. Carlisle, *Concise Description* ii, p. 255.
27. CCB (1718–43), 26.9.1737. The masters' houses were originally the dormitory of the hospital.
28. Brand, *Newcastle*, ii, footnote x, p. 95. Jurin had carried out a successful series of public lectures, had taken private pupils and had published an edition of Varenius's Geography.
29. Newcastle General Magazine, February 1754, p. 108; ibid., February 1758, p. 110.
30. CCB (1743–66), 10.1.1749.
31. CCB (1718–43), 30.9.1736.
32. Dawes to John Taylor (St John's College, Cambridge) 1744?, in Emmanuel College Magazine, vol. v no. 2, 1894.
33. CCB (1743–66), 26.6.1749.
34. Randall MS 11 (Durham Dean and Chapter Library). The antiquarian Thomas Randall who was headmaster at Durham School (1761–8) most certainly was acquainted with Dawes.
35. Quoted in J. Brewster, *A Memoir of the late Reverend Hugh Moises, M.A., Headmaster of the Royal Grammar School Newcastle upon Tyne*, 1823, p. 20.
36. CCB (1743–66), 20.1.1752.
37. Newcastle Journal, 6 August 1774.
38. 1 James I, c. IV.
39. Durham Diocese Subscription Book XIV 5 (1731–59), (Durham Dean and Chapter Library). Munton subscribed at the same time as curate of St Andrew's Newcastle.
40. Quoted in J. Murray (ed.), *The Autobiographies of Edward Gibbon*, 2nd edit. (London 1897), p. 51.
41. G. Chapman, *A Treatise on Education*, 3rd edit. (London 1784), p. 47.
42. CCB (1718–43), 11.7.1737; Brewster, *Moises*, p. 21; CCB (1743–61), 24.4.1761; Newcastle Journal, 19 May 1764. Hugh Moises is supposed to have raised the numbers to 133 scholars, but no date for this is given by J. Bruce in his *A Memoir of Charles Hutton* (London 1823), p. 10.
43. Robinson, Thesis, i, p. 17.
44. Brewster, *Moises*, pp. 24–5.
45. Ibid. pp. 24–5.
46. Quoted in W. Clark Russell, *Collingwood* (London 1891), p. 6.
47. Brewster, *Moises*, p. 24.
48. CCB (1699–1718), 5.5.1712. In 1720 William Wilkinson was awarded the £5, although he did not go directly from the grammar school to Christ's College Cambridge.
49. CCB (1766–85), 18.6.1778. Rather oddly, the order of Common Council refers to a vacancy having occurred.
50. Brand, *Newcastle*, footnote x, p. 91.
51. Bruce, *Hutton*, p. 10.
52. Newcastle Chronicle, 18 April 1767.
53. J. Baillie, *An Impartial History of Newcastle and its Vicinity* (Newcastle upon Tyne 1801), pp. 285–7. Baillie himself had been the proprietor of private

academies in Newcastle and Sunderland.

54. List of Pupils of Rev. William Turner's School in Newcastle, B–4–35 (Chetham's Library, Manchester). Turner charged five guineas for day pupil studying the classics. At the grammar school during the same period terms fo sons of non-freemen were four guineas for Latin, Greek and Hebrew; on guinea for mathematics and natural philosophy; half a guinea entrance fee.
55. Newcastle Courant, 3 January 1747.
56. Ibid. 20 June 1795.
57. D. Defoe, *Compleat English Gentleman* (c. 1728–9), edit. K. Bulbrin, (London 1890), p. 127.
58. *Outlines of the Plan of Education adopted in the Royal Grammar School Newcastle upon Tyne, A.D. 1793.*
59. Quoted in Twiss, *Eldon*, p. 35.
60. Carlisle, *Concise Description* ii, p. 278; p. 260.
61. Brand, *Newcastle*, i, p. 669.
62. Carlisle, *Concise Description* ii, p. 238.
63. Twiss, *Eldon*, p. 39.
64. CCB (1699–1718), 7.10.1700.
65. Newcastle Courant, 24 November 1711; 5 March 1712. The venue was mos probably the grammar school.
66. Ibid. 1 July 1749.
67. Brewster, *Moises*, p. 28.
68. V. Knox, *Liberal Education or a Practical Treatise on the Methods o Acquiring Useful and Public Learning*, 5th edit (London 1783), p. 280.
69. *The Newcastle Freeman's Pocket Companion by a Burgess* (J. Clark (Newcastle 1808) p. 85. The following year R. L. Edgeworth published hi *Essays in Professional Education* which argued that "the value of all education must ultimately be decided by its utility". This was part of a lively debate mainly on university education, which was carried on in the quarterlies. T utilitarians like Edgeworth, the classics was patently a useless form of study.
70. W. H. Yate, *To the Mayor, Aldermen, and Common Council of the Town an County of Newcastle upon Tyne*, 1812, p. 3.
71. J. Clark, *Newcastle Remembrancer and Freeman's Pocket Companion*, 1817 p. 93.
72. CCB (1810–17), 2.10.1817.
73. Brewster, *Moises*, pp. 26–31.
74. B. Green, *Some Account of the Hospital of St Mary the Virgin in Newcastl. upon Tyne* (Newcastle 1845).
75. CCB (1817–24), 14.1.1823.
76. Carlisle, *Concise Description*, ii, p. 259.
77. Samuel Johnson, *Life of Addison*, quoted in Carlisle, *Concise Description* ii p. 631.
78. Brewster, *Moises*, p. 26; Twiss, *Eldon*, p. 38. Tradition has it that the tabl which still stands on the platform in the school hall was used as a floggin table.
79. CCB (1817–24), 30.9.1824.
80. Calendar of Petitions to Common Council (1786–99), p. 2 (Tyne and Wea Archives). Hugh Moises was shortly to resign as headmaster but he retaine the mastership of the Hospital till his death in 1806 when Edward Moise succeeded him. The interesting point about the petition is that the boy "conceived themselves to be part of a body corporate together with th Master of the said hospital". Among other things, this illustrates the clos connection between the School and the Hospital.
81. CCB (1785–99), 22.3.1787. The use of the Spital Croft as a boys' playgroun

NOTES

had been granted by the Common Council in December 1755, the ground being sub-let to a tenant.

82. Twiss, *Eldon*, p. 40.

NOTES

Chapter III

1. Mackenzie, *Newcastle*, i, pp. 429–31, 440–41; Newcastle Common Council Book (CCB) (1824–31), 19.1.1829 (Tyne and Wear Archives); ibid. (1831–35), 3.7.1834; *Proceedings of the Newcastle Town Council*, 14.1.1846, p. 92 (published annually in Newcastle; hereafter cited as *Procs. Newcastle Council*).
2. Mackenzie, *Newcastle*, ii, pp. 432–43.
3. Schools Inquiry Commission, v, part 2, p. 752, no. 16,306.
4. *Procs. Newcastle Council*, 5.5.1847, p. 172.
5. RGS Archives, Governors' Scrap Book, p. 43.
6. Laws, *Schola Novocastrensis*, ii, p. 162.
7. CCB (1817–24), 23.12.1822.
8. Ibid. 14.1.1823.
9. CCB (1824–31), 19.1.1829.
10. Ibid. 23.12.1828, 19.1.1829.
11. W. Parson and W. White, *History, Directory and Gazetteer of Durham and Northumberland*, i (1827), pp. lxxv-vi (the figures probably refer to 1826; cf. Mackenzie, *Newcastle*, ii, p. 442; RGS Archives, Snape Papers, p. 13.
12. CCB (1831–35), 3.7.1834.
13. Newcastle Central Library, Local History Collections (LHC), Local Tracts, vol. 48 item 5a (Report of the Committee on Schools, Charities and Hospitals presented at a Council meeting held October 24, 1838), p. 2.
14. Schools Inquiry Commission, v, part 2, p. 751, no. 16,297
15. Mackenzie, *Newcastle*, ii, p. 437; R. S. Watson, *The History of the Literary and Philosophical Society of Newcastle-upon-Tyne (1793–1896)* (London 1897), p. 107.
16. Mackenzie, *Newcastle*, ii, pp. 431, 441; CCB (1817–24), 14.1.1823 (note the absence of direct or implied criticism of Moises).
17. CCB (1817–24), 14.1.1823.
18. CCB (1824–31), 19.1.1829.
19. Durham, Dean and Chapter Library, 'Durham Diocese Book' s.a. 1793; Fordyce *Local Records*, ii (1857), p. 244.
20. CCB (1831–35), 19.7.1833.
21. RGS Archives, Snape Papers, p. 67.
22. CCB (1831–35), 3.7.1834.
23. Newcastle Central Library, LHC Local Tracts, vol. 48, item 5a.
24. RGS Archives, Snape Papers, p. 14.
25. Schools Inquiry Commission, v, part 2, p. 752, no. 16,306.
26. *Procs. Newcastle Council*, 14.1.1846, p. 92. (see also *Procs. Newcastle Council*, 2.12.1845, p. 136 and 1.2.1843, p. 144).
27. *Procs. Newcastle Council*, 1.2.1843, p. 144.
28. *Procs. Newcastle Council*, 14.1.1846, p. 92.
29. The materials relating to the Bruces are collected in J. B. Williamson, *Memorials of John Bruce* (Newcastle 1903), Gainsford Bruce, *Life and Letters of John Collingwood Bruce* (London 1905); see also D. P. Leinster-Mackay in *Durham and Newcastle Universities Research Review*, ix. no. 44 (1980), pp 85–90.
30. Schools Inquiry Commission, viii (1868), p. 286 (the first of the unnamed private schools is Bruce's).
31. Bruce, *Life and Letters of John Collingwood Bruce*, p. 7.

NOTES

32. Schools Inquiry Commission, viii, p. 319.
33. RGS Archives, Snape Papers, p. 4.
34. Bruce, *Life and Letters of John Collingwood Bruce*, pp. 53–54; Schools Inquiry Commission, v, part 2, pp. 749–50.
35. Newcastle Central Library, LHC 'Bruce's Academy', item 1; *Procs. Newcastle Council*, 7.7.1836, p. 158; Schools Inquiry Commission, viii (1868), p. 286.
36. Watson, *History of the Literary and Philosophical Soc.*, pp. 261–64; *Procs. Newcastle Council*, 6.6.1855, p. 158; ibid. 12.12.1855, p. 26. Schools Inquiry Commission, i, 137.
37. Bruce, *Life and Letters of John Collingwood Bruce*, p. 74.
38. Newcastle Chamberlains' Accounts, 1829–30, 1830–31, 1831–32, 1832–33, 1833–34 (Tyne and Wear Archives 543/184–188); *First Report of the Finance Committee* (1836), p. 12; *Abstracts of the Accounts of the Mayor . . . of the Borough of Newcastle upon Tyne* 1836–37, p. 14; 1837–38, p. 14; 1838–39, p. 13; 1839–40, p. 14; 1840–41, p. 15.
39. N. McCord, *North East England, An Economic and Social History* (London 1979), p. 74; B. Keith-Lucas, *English Local Government in the 19th and 20th Centuries* (London 1977), pp. 13–14..
40. N. McCord, 'The Making of Modern Newcastle', *Archaeologia Aeliana*, 5th series, xi (1981), p. 339.
41. *Procs. Newcastle Council,* 7.7.1836, p. 2.
42. *Procs. Newcastle Council,* 9.1.1839, pp. 1–2.
43. 5–6 William IV, c. 76, sect. 92; *First Report of the Finance Committee* (1836), p. 3.
44. This paragraph is based on Newcastle Chamberlains' Accounts between 1829 and 1834 (Tyne and Wear Archives 543/184–188) and on the printed *Abstracts of the Chamberlain's Accounts* between 1831 and 1835; after 1835 the accounts were published annually under the title *Abstracts of the Accounts of the Mayor . . . of the Borough of Newcastle upon Tyne* (hereafter cited as *Abstracts of Accounts*).
45. Laws, *Schola Novocastrensis*, ii, p. 131, 147–48 (J. Angus), 154.
46. Bruce, *Life and Letters of John Collingwood Bruce*, p. 62.
47. *Procs. Newcastle Council*, 6.6.1855, p. 160.
48. Schools Inquiry Commission, v, part 2, p. 752, no. 16,306; ibid. xix, p. 119.
49. Schools Inquiry Commission, viii, p. 282.
50. Bruce, *Life and Letters of John Collingwood Bruce*, p. 7; Schools Inquiry Commission, ii, p. 749, nos. 16,300–16,304.
51. Carlisle, *Concise Description*, ii (1818), p. 255; Newcastle Central Library, LHC Local Tracts D2, no. 13, pp. 3–5; Gateshead Observer, 11.11.1837.
52. *Procs. Newcastle Council*, 1.2.1843, pp. 143–45; ibid. 1844, pp. xvii–xix, 60–63; J. C. Bruce, *A Handbook to Newcastle-on-Tyne* (Newcastle 1863), p. 43; John Latimer, *Local Records* (1832–57) (1857), p. 182.
53. R. J. Charlton, 'The Streets of Newcastle' (n.d.), p. 220 (copy in Newcastle Central Library, LHC N536C); *Procs. Newcastle Council*, 11.1.1843, pp. 96–97.
54. M. A. Richardson, *Descriptive Companion through Newcastle upon Tyne and Gateshead* (Newcastle 1838), pp. 280–81.
55. RGS Archives, Snape Papers, p. 15.
56. RGS Archives, Snape Papers, p. 14; Schools Committee Minute Book, i, pp. 253, 288 (Tyne and Wear Archives 589/488).
57. RGS Archives, Snape Papers, p. 48 and 'Sources', i, p. 72; iv, p. 4; Schools Inquiry Commission, xix, p. 121.
58. Schools Inquiry Commission, viii, p. 288.
59. See below pp. 107–10, 117.

NOTES

60. Schools Inquiry Commission, v, part 2, p. 754, no. 16,337.
61. *Procs. Newcastle Council*, 3.7.1861, p. 339.
62. Schools Inquiry Commission, xix, p. 124.
63. *Procs. Newcastle Council*, 6.6.1855, pp. 157–59 *passim*.
64. Newcastle Central Library, LHC 'Facts and Scraps', viii (1862–65), p. 802.
65. Schools Inquiry Commission, xix, p. 119.
66. Newcastle Weekly Chronicle, 18 March 1871; RGS Archives, Snape Papers, p. 88.
67. Newcastle Daily Chronicle, 8 November 1880; RGS Archives, Snape Papers, p. 19.
68. RGS Archives, Governors' Scrap Book, pp. 174–175.
69. RGS Archives, Snape Papers, pp. 66–68; Bruce, *Life and Letters of John Collingwood Bruce*, p. 187.
70. James Snape, *The Corporation of Newcastle and the Rev. Dr. Snape: Letters and Documents on the Circumstances of his Case* (Newcastle 1877), p. 6.
71. Newcastle Central Library, LHC 'Facts and Scraps', viii (1862–65), p. 802.
72. Schools Inquiry Commission, xix, p. 120.
73. *Procs. Newcastle Council* 3.4.1839, pp. 3–8; ibid. 2.4.1845, pp. 241–48; 9–10 Vict. c. 42.
74. Watson, *History of the Literary and Philosophical Soc.*, pp. 261–65; *Procs. Newcastle Council*, 2.5.1855, pp. 135–136 ibid. 15.8.1855, pp. 174–75.
75. *Procs. Newcastle Council*, 6.6.1855, pp. 156–63; ibid. 12.12.1855, pp. 22–30; ibid. 6.2.1856, pp. 75–81; RGS Archives, *Scheme for the Application of the Surplus Income of the Hospital of St Mary the Virgin . . . Newcastle . . . Approved by the Court of Chancery by Order Dated 1st May 1858*.
76. See below p. 117.
77. Schools Committee Minute Book i (1862–78), p. 375 (Tyne and Wear Archives 589/488); RGS Archives, Governors' Scrap Book, *passim*.
78. Schools Inquiry Commission, i, p. 447.
79. Schools Inquiry Commission, v, part 2, p. 757, no. 16,367.
80. *Procs. Newcastle Council*, 7.5.1873, p. 350.
81. Schools Inquiry Commission, xix, p. 119–124; there is useful information in Newcastle Central Library, LHC 'Facts and Scraps', viii (1862–65), p. 802.
82. See below pp. 111–13.
83. *The Builder*, xix (1861), pp. 548–49, 570; Schools Committee Minute Book, i (1862–78), pp. 17, 22, 144, 194 (Tyne and Wear Archives 589/488).
84. RGS Archives, 'Sources', i, p. 82 (Letter of G. H. Glendinning, 7.2.1928, p. 2).
85. *Illustrated London News*, xlviii, no. 1,374 (9.6.1866).
86. John Oxberry, 'The Royal Free Grammar School, Newcastle upon Tyne: Miscellaneous Notes', pp. 6–7, in Newcastle Central Library, LHC L373 N536R no. 34782; Newcastle Daily Journal 23–24 May, 1866.
87. Newcastle Central Library, LHC Local Tracts D48, no. 26.
88. *Procs. Newcastle Council*, 7.3.1877, p. 246.
89. Schools Committee Minute Book, i (1862–78), pp. 281, 294 (Tyne and Wear Archives 589/488).
90. ibid. p. 288.
91. ibid. pp. 283–84, 288, 294.
92. *Register of the Royal Grammar School Newcastle upon Tyne 1545–1954*, ed. B. D. Stevens (Newcastle 1955), p. 162; RGS Archives, Governors' Scrap Book, p. 39.
93. *Procs. Newcastle Council*, 11.7.1866, p. 240; ibid. 5.8.1868, p. 376: *Abstracts of Accounts*, 1877–78, p. 75.

NOTES

94. Schools Inquiry Commission, xix, p. 123; Stevens, *Register, passim*.
95. *Procs. Newcastle Council*, 20.11.1872, p. 27; RGS Archives, 'Sources', iii, p. 333 and School List, 1881; Newcastle Central Library, LHC Local Tracts, vol. 28, no. 26, p. 3.
96. Snape, *The Corporation*, pp. 11, 37.
97. Schools Committee Minute Book, i (1862–78), pp. 329, 331 (Tyne and Wear Archives 589/488).
98. RGS Archives, Snape Papers, pp. 17–18.
99. Schools Committee Minute Book, i (1862–78), p. 337 (Tyne and Wear Archives 589/488); Snape, *The Corporation, passim*.
00. This paragraph is based on Schools Committee Minute Book, i (1862–78) and ii (1878–88) (Tyne and Wear Archives 589/488–489) and on the *Abstract of Accounts*.
01. Schools Committee Minute Book, i (1862–78), p. 406 (Tyne and Wear Archives 589/488); Newcastle Central Library, LHC Local Tracts, vol. 28, no. 26, p. 3; RGS Archives, Snape Papers, p. 79.
02. *Procs. Newcastle Council*, 9.11.1870, p. 12; ibid. 11.1.1871, p. 127.
03. Based on *Abstract of Accounts*.
04. *Procs. Newcastle Council*, 7.2.1877, p. 158; ibid. 25.1.1882, pp. 98, 100; cf. R. Anchor Thompson, *A Defence at Law of an Educational Charity and of the Rights of the Poor in the Same* (1879), p. 5 (Tyne and Wear Archives 604/136; Public Record Office, ED 27/3766).
05. *Procs. Newcastle Council*, 7.7.1877, p. 158–59; see above p.106.
06. *Procs. Newcastle Council*, 4.4.1873, p. 365; ibid. 7.5.1873, p. 350; ibid. 7.2.1877, p. 158.
07. Schools Committee Minute Book, i (1862–78), p. 484 (Tyne and Wear Archives 589/488).
08. RGS Archives, Governors' Scrap Book, accounts *passim* and the 1888 Statute and Scheme.
09. Thompson, *Defence at Law*, pp. 8–9.
10. Ibid. pp. 29–41.
11. Draft of a Scheme for the Virgin Mary Hospital and the Grammar School, referred by the Corporation to the Charity Commissioners, October 1883 (dated 1885), Tyne and Wear Archives 604/566 (see 604/567–8 for later drafts of the 1888 Scheme).

NOTES

Chapter IV

1. *Lit. and Phil. Society Transactions*, vol. 268, pp. 25–7.
2. *Newcastle upon Tyne Council Records 1887–88*, p. 443.
3. RGS Governors' Minutes 12 November 1888. *Novo*, vol. iii, no. 2 1888.
4. *Novo*, vol. i, no. 1 1888.
5. Virgin Mary Hospital (hereafter VMH) Trust Minute Book, vol. i, 28 Oct. 1887; 14 Dec. 1887; 5 March 1889.
6. *Novo*, vol. i, 1885; vol. iii, no. 2, 1888; vol. xii, 1897.
7. RGS Archives: A. S. Bibby, 'The RGS 70 Years Ago'.
8. RGS Governors' Minutes 10 March 1890
9. Public Record Office ED.27/3767.
10. *Novo*, vol. vi 1891.
11. *Newcastle City Council Reports 1890–91*, 16 Dec. 1890 pp. 355–61.
12. RGS Governors' Minutes 13 July 1891; 22 Jan. 1892.
13. RGS Governors' Minutes 11 April 1892.
14. RGS Archives; Governors' Scrapbook: Headmaster's report 18 Feb. 1895.
15. RGS Governors' Minutes 15 July 1895; Letter to clerk from R. S. Watson 30 Dec. 1895, 10 Feb. 1896; 27 Feb. 1896.
16. RGS Archives, Governors' Scrapbook 1896: Headmaster's report.
17. Newcastle Daily Chronicle 2 Feb 1897.
18. *Newcastle City Council Minutes* 1896–97 pp. 328–34 29 April 1897; letter to the Council 4 May 1897.
19. RGS Archives, Governors' Scrapbook: Headmaster's annual report 14 Feb. 1898.
20. Sir J. Fitch, *Report on the Technical Education in the City* (Newcastle 1897) pp. 6–7, 32–35; See also below, p. 134.
21. RGS Governors' Minutes 23 Dec. 1898; Newcastle Journal 16 Dec. 1898; Newcastle Daily Chronicle 22 Dec. 1898; Daily Leader 24 Dec. 1898.
22. VMH Trust Minute Book, vol. ii 14 Dec. 1898; 21 Feb. 1899; 28 Feb. 1899; 12 April 1899.
23. *Newcastle City Council Minutes 1899–1900* pp. 315–23 4 March 1900.
24. RGS Archives, Report of Board of Education Inspection 25–27 March 1903.
25. A. Acland, *Studies in Secondary Education* (London 1892); R. B. Haldane, *Autobiography* (London 1929) pp. 97–98; The Times 2, 21 Oct. 1896; see also M. J. Wilkinson, *Educational Controversies in British Politics 1895–1914*, unpublished Ph.D. Thesis, University of Newcastle upon Tyne 1978, chapter II.
26. *Bryce Report* (1895), vol. ii, pp. 2–32; vol. iii, Appendix 5, p. 556; vol. iv, Appendix 3B; vol. v, pp. 57–61; Memorandum by A. F. Leach, Assistant Charity Commissioner, on the History of Endowed Schools; Memorandum of John Bidgood, p. 393.
27. Article by J. G. Fitch in *Encyclopaedia Britannica*, vol. xxvii, 1902, p. 676.
28. Education (England and Wales) Act, 1902.
29. Public Record Office ED,35/2020.
30. Ibid.
31. RGS Governors' Minutes 27 March 1903.
32. B. Webb, *Our Partnership* (London 1948), p. 169.
33. *Newcastle Education Committee* Minutes vol. i, 1903–4.
34. Tyne and Wear Archives, Minutes of Newcastle Higher Education Sub-Committee, vol. i, 1903–4.

NOTES

35. M. E. Sadler, *Report on Secondary and Higher Education in Newcastle upon Tyne*, (Newcastle upon Tyne 1905), pp. 3–4, 11–15, 49–51, 78; G. A. N. Lowndes, *The Silent Social Revolution* (Oxford 1937), p. 107.
36. Sadler, *Report*, p. 51.
37. Public Record Office, ED.35/2020.
38. Ibid; VMH Trust Minute Book, vol. ii, 10 Nov. 1903.
39. Newcastle Journal 3 July 1903; 4 July 1903.
40. *Report of the Board of Education*, 1905–6 pp. 44–46.
41. ibid. 1903–4 pp. 45–47; 1905–6 p. 46.
42. Tyne and Wear Archives, Education Department, Correspondence files Box 10611.
43. S. Middlebrook, *Newcastle upon Tyne: Its Growth and Achievement* (Newcastle 1950), p. 250.
44. Public Record Office, ED.35/2020.
45. VMH Trust Minute Book, vol. ii, March–August 1906; University of Newcastle upon Tyne Archives, Trevelyan Papers, CPT 14; RGS Governors' Minutes 18 June 1906; 10 Sept. 1906; 17 Dec. 1906.
46. RGS Archives, News Cuttings; North Mail 3 Apr. 1906; 18 Jan. 1907; Newcastle Daily Chronicle 17 Jan. 1907.
47. *Novo*, vol. xxi 1906–7; vol. xxiii 1909; vol. xxv 1911.
48. *Report of the Board of Education* 1905–6 p. 59; RGS Archives, Report of Board of Education Second Inspection 9–11 Apr. 1907.
49. Public Record Office, ED.24/256.
50. Public Record Office, ED.24/267.
51. *Hansard* 4th series, vol. 171, cols 102–121.
52. *Report of the Board of Education* 1906–7, pp. 10–11; 1907–8 pp. 47–55; Public Record Office, ED.12/122.
53. RGS Governors' Minutes 8 July 1907; 21 Oct. 1907; 23 Dec. 1907; Public Record Office, ED,35/2020.
54. Public Record Office, ED.35/2021; RGS Governors'Minutes 15 June 1908.
55. Public Record Office, ED.35/2021.
56. Ibid; RGS Governors' Minutes 12 Oct. 1908; 3 May 1909.
57. RGS Governors' Minutes 13 Sep. 1909; Public Record Office, ED.35/2021; Newcastle Daily Journal 14 Sep. 1909; North Mail 22 Dec. 1909; Tyne and Wear Archives, Higher Education Minutes vol. II 26 Oct. 1909.
58. Public Record Office, ED.35/2021.
59. VMH Trust Minute Book, vol. ii, 23 Nov. 1908; 29 April 1909; 17 May 1909.
60. RGS Governors' Minutes 13 Dec. 1909; 15 June 1910; Public Record Office, ED.35/2021; Tyne and Wear Archives, Education Department: Correspondence files, box 10665.
61. *Hansard* 5th series, vol. 16 col. 2465; RGS Governors' Minutes 17 Oct. 1910.
62. The circular was written by the Board of Education's chief Inspector for elementary schools, Edmund Holmes. Both Runciman and Morant had left the Board by December 1911.
63. VMH Trust Minute Book, vol. iii, 18 July 1910; 28 Oct. 1910; 24 Feb. 1911; RGS Governors' Minutes 24 July 1911; Public Record Office, ED.35/2021, 2022.
64. VMH Trust Minute Book, vol. iii, 27 Apr. 1911; 18 Sep. 1911; RGS Governors' Minutes 28 Apr. 1911; 17 July 1911.
65. RGS Archives, Report of Board of Education Third Inspection, 12–15 Mar. 1912; Public Record Office, ED.35/2021.
66. RGS Governors' Minutes 15 Apr. 1912.
67. Ibid., 30 Apr. 1912.
68. Public Record Office, ED.35/2021; *Report of the Board of Education* 1907–8 pp. 47, 55; 1911–12 pp. 5–6, 12–13.

69. *Novo*, vol. xxiv, 1910; vol. xxv, no. 1, 1911; vol. xxvii, 1912; RGS Governors' Minutes 15 July 1912.
70. Ibid., 16 Sep. 1912.
71. Ibid., 20 Oct. 1913.
72. Public Record Office, ED.27/8249; ED.35/2023; VMH Trust Minute Book, vol. iii, 29 Jan. 1913; 5 June 1913; RGS Governors' Minutes 19 Jan. 1913.
73. Public Record Office, ED.35/2023; CAB.37/117/90; Nuffield College Oxford, Gainford Papers; RGS Governors' Minutes 18 May 1914.
74. Northern Echo 6 Mar. 1914; RGS Archives, Revised Scheme of Government 4 July 1914; Public Record Office., ED.35/2023; ED.27/8249; North Mail 27 July 1917; Newcastle Daily Chronicle 21 July 1917; VMH Trust Minute Book, vol. iv, 1914–20.
75. *Novo*, vol. xxvii, no. 2 1913.
76. RGS Archives, News Cuttings, Prize Days, 17 Dec. 1915, 8 Dec. 1921; RGS Governors' Minutes 11 May 1920; *Novo* vol. xxxii July 1918.
77. RGS Governors' Minutes 7 July 1917.
78. Public Record Office, ED.35/2021.
79. *Report of Board of Education*, 1919–20; 1924; Lowndes, *Silent Social Revolution*, pp. 113–15; R. H. Tawney, *Secondary Education For All* (London 1922).
80. RGS Governors' Minutes 10 July 1917; 11 Feb. 1918; 10 Feb 1919; 16 May 1919; 11 May 1920; 14 Feb. 1921; 23 May 1921; Public Record Office. ED.12/196, 199; *Report of Consultative Committee on Examinations in Secondary Schools* (Cmd 6004) 1911; *Report of Departmental Committee on Scales of Salaries in Secondary Schools* (Cmd 9140) 1918; Lowndes, *Silent Social Revolution*. p. 134.
81. *Hansard*, 5th series, vol. 104 col. 341; The Times 10 Aug. 1918; RGS Governors' Minutes 11 May 1920; J. A. Pease, 'A National System of Education for England and Wales,' *Contemporary Review* cxi (1917) pp. 137–144; *Education 1900–1950: Report of the Ministry of Education* (Cmd 8244) 1950, pp. 246–48.
82. Above, pp.168–69.
83. Public Record Office, ED.35/2021.
84. RGS Archives, News Cuttings, 22, 24 Feb. 1921.
85. Public Record Office, ED.12/196.
86. *Hansard* 5th series, vol. 104, col. 342; Sadler, *Report*, p. 50; Tawney, *Secondary Education For All*.
87. Nuffield College Oxford, Gainford Papers 72A; *Report of the Board of Education* 1905–6, p. 47.

NOTES

Chapter V

1. RGS Archives, Speech Day Programme 1923, p. 2; 1926, p. 3; 1927, p. 3; 1928, p. 3.
2. Sir Arthur recalled his career in *Tynesider*, as told to and written by Leonard Johnstone, (Northumberland Press; Gateshead, 1974).
3. Newcastle Central Library, pamphlet by O. Thompson, clerk to the VMH Trustees, on the financial aspects of the Hospital, 1964, p. 5.
4. Tyne and Wear Archives, VMH Trust Minute Book, 1921–28, p. 106.
5. This discussion is based on VMH Trust Minute Book, 1921–28, pp. 111–226; Public Record Office, ED. 27/8249; Thompson, pamphlet pp. 6–7; St Mary's Hospital (Newcastle upon Tyne) Act 1927, 17 & 18 Geo. 5 Ch. xcviii.
6. RGS Archives, Cash Book no. 6.
7. VMH Trust Minute Book, 1928–33, pp. 26, 72, 104, 150, 222; Minute Book, 1933–38, pp. 2, 58, 106, 144, 202; RGS Governors' Minutes 10 July 1934; 9 July 1935; 14 July 1936; 15 June 1937.
8. VMH Trust Minute Book, 1933–38, pp. 194, 220; 1938–44 p. 39; Public Record Office, ED. 27/9619; RGS Archives, E. R. Thomas letters file 2.
9. Public Record Office, ED. 27/9619.
10. VMH Trust Minute Book, 1944–48, pp. 22, 32, 36, 43; see below, p. 264.
11. Thompson, pamphlet, p. 8.
12. This discussion is based on Board of Education Regulations for Secondary Schools, published in *Statutory Rules and Orders* 1922–35. For the grant income to RGS in 1939 see RGS Governors' Minutes 11 July 1939.
13. J. A. Partington. *The History of the System of Direct Grants to Secondary Schools*, unpublished M.Ed. Thesis, University of Durham 1967, pp. 111–15.
14. See above, p. 153.
15. Public Record Office, ED. 35/5664.
16. Public Record Office, ED. 35/5664.
17. RGS Archives, Cash Books nos 6 & 7; RGS Governors' Minutes 10 July 1934.
18. RGS Archives, E.R. Thomas letters, file 2; Board of Education circular 1259; Partington, Thesis, p. 111.
19. See above, pp. 163–64.
20. *Novo,* February 1920, p. 13.
21. *Proceedings of the University of Newcastle upon Tyne Philosophical Society* vol. i no. 1 (1964), pp. 1–17; no. 14 (1968), pp. 170–77.
22. *Novo,* July 1922 p. 1.
23. RGS Archives, Report of Inspection 1926, p. 4.
24. RGS Archives, Report of Inspection 1936, p. 2.
25. RGS Archives, Speech Day Programme, 1923 p. 3.
26. RGS Archives, Speech Day Programme, 1927 p. 3.
27. Letter from Ioan Thomas (E. R. Thomas's son) to A. S. Cox, 19 June 1985.
28. RGS Archives, Speech Day Programme 1928: typewritten text of Headmaster's speech enclosed with printed programme.
29. These figures are based on an analysis of examination results printed in Speech Day Programmes.
30. RGS Archives, Report of Inspection 1936, pp. 6, 23.
31. See above, pp. 115–16.
32. See above, p. 174.
33. Public Record Office, ED. 35/5664.

347

34. These figures are based on an analysis of entries in the *Staff Registers*, RGS Archives.
35. Max Black, *The Nature of Mathematics* (London 1933).
36. S. Bowie, 'An Application of American Army Intelligence Tests', *British Journal of Psychology* vol. xiii (1920–21), pp. 389–97.
37. For much of what follows, see *A Portrait of Michael Roberts*, ed. T. W. Eason and R. Hamilton, (Chelsea, published by the College of S. Mark and S. John, 1949), especially chapter ii 'The Schoolmaster', by M. F. Cunliffe.
38. See below, Chapter VIII.
39. See below, pp. 200–1.
40. Quoted in *Michael Roberts*, pp. 36–37.
41. RGS Archives, E. R. Thomas letters file 2.
42. Public Record Office, ED. 35/5664.
43. Letters from Ioan Thomas to A. S. Cox, 19 June 1985.
44. See, for example, RGS Archives, Speech Day Programme 1935, p. 17.
45. Ibid.
46. Ibid., 1930 p. 7.
47. RGS Archives, Report of Inspection 1936 p. 21.
48. RGS Archives, Report of Inspection 1926 pp. 14–15.
49. Public Record Office, ED. 109/4709: Inspectors' Report for Music, 16 March 1927.
50. *Novo*, December 1928, p. 103.
51. RGS Archives, Report of Inspection 1936, p. 18.
52. *The Listener*, 14 November 1934, pp. 828–29.
53. RGS Archives, Speech Day Programme 1933, p. 22.
54. See especially G. Pallister, 'Camps and Mountains', in *Michael Roberts*, pp. 22-32; *Novo*, December 1950, pp. 41–68.
55. *Listener*, p. 829.
56. RGS Archives, Cash Book no. 5.
57. *Novo*, June 1923, pp. 39–40.
58. RGS Archives, Cash Book no. 6.
59. RGS Archives, Speech Day Programme 1930, p. 3; *Novo*, March 1931, pp. 20–21.
60. *Novo*, July 1930.
61. RGS Archives, Cash Book no. 7.
62. RGS Archives, Report of Inspection 1936, p. 4.
63. A. M. Sutherland, *Industry – Thrift – Ambition*, speech in appreciation of the Presentation of the Honorary Freedom of the City of Newcastle upon Tyne July 3rd 1936, p. 9.
64. See below, pp. 225–26.
65. RGS Governors' Minutes 15 July 1937, 12 October 1937, 8 February 1938, 12 July 1938, 11 October 1938.
66. A detailed account of this period in the School's history is given below by Donald Shipley. The subjects treated here are those that seem most relevant to the earlier part of this chapter.
67. See below, p. 281.
68. RGS Archives, E. R. Thomas letters, file 6.
69. RGS Governors' Minutes, February 1939.
70. RGS Archives, E. R. Thomas letters, file 6.
71. This discussion is based on an analysis of the correspondence in RGS Archives, E. R. Thomas letters, file 6.
72. RGS Governors' Minutes July 1940.

NOTES

73. This discussion is based on an analysis of the correspondence in RGS Archives, E. R. Thomas letters, file 6.
74. *Novo*, December 1925, pp. 91–93.
75. Laws, *Schola Novocastrensis*, i; Volume ii appeared in 1932.
76. A. R. Laws and J. B. Brodie, *The Story of the Royal Grammar School*, published by the School, (1924).
77. RGS Archives, Speech Day Programme 1924, p. 3.
78. *Novo*, December 1930, title page.
79. *Novo*, December 1930, p. 166; March 1931, p. 3.
80. RGS Archives, Report of Inspection 1926, p. 7. Information about recruitment derived from Report of Inspection 1926, p. 4; 1936 p. 24; Stevens, *Register*, passim.
81. RGS Archives, Speech Day Programme 1925, p. 5.
82. RGS Archives, Speech Day Programme 1929, p. 7; 1935, p. 22.
83. RGS Archives, E. R. Thomas letters, file 6.

NOTES

Chapter VI

1. *Abolition of Tuition Fees in Grant-Aided Secondary Schools: Special Report of the Committee on Public Schools*, (London 1943), p. 4.
2. Partington, Thesis, p. 121.
3. RGS Governors' Minutes 1943.
4. *Special Report of the Committee on Public Schools*, p. 12.
5. *The Public Schools and the General Educational System*, (London 1944).
6. Partington, Thesis, p. 124; *Hansard* 5th series vol. 396 cols. 222–223.
7. RGS Governors' Minutes 1945.
8. Primary and Secondary Schools Grant Regulations 1945, S.R.O. 636/1945.
9. RGS Governors' Minutes 1945, 1946.
10. Appendices to RGS Governors' Minutes for November each year include audited accounts for the previous financial year.
11. Education (Miscellaneous Provisions) Act 1953, Section 6(2)(a).
12. Minutes of special Governors' Meeting 18 November 1947, where an application to increase fees from £42 and £46 to £47 and £50 was approved.
13. RGS Governors' Minutes 1951, 1954, 1956, 1960.
14. RGS Governors' Minutes: meeting of Finance Committee 4 November 1954.
15. RGS Governors' Minutes 1955, 1958, 1960.
16. RGS Governors' Minutes 1958, 1959.
17. RGS Governors' Minutes: Accounts for 1948 and 1960.
18. RGS Governors' Minutes 1948.
19. Information derived from *Who's Who*, *Oxford University Gazette*, and contributions to *Novo* by S. Middlebrook and G. S. Dean.
20. R. A. Dare, *A History of Owen's School* (Wallington 1963).
21. The term 'multilateral' is used in the *Report of the Consultative Committee of the Board of Education on Secondary Education* (the Spens Report), (London 1938), though the Report does not recommend that such schools should be established.
22. Ministry of Education, Pamphlet 19, 1951.
23. See plate XII.
24. Stevens, *Register*, published in 1955.
25. These phrases are taken from the Headmaster's Reports in Speech Day Programmes, RGS Archives.
26. This may well be a sentiment E. R. Thomas had also expressed.
27. RGS Archives, Speech Day Programme 1958, Headmaster's Report. These Reports are an eloquent exposition of the progress of Mr Mitchell's thought and aspirations for the School.
28. Stevens, *Register*; RGS Governors' Minutes, 1948–60.
29. RGS Governors' Minutes, meeting of special sub-committee 13 December 1949.
30. RGS Archives, File of correspondence connected with the equipment of the new building 1955-56.
31. RGS Governors' Minutes, 14 July 1954.
32. RGS Governors' Minutes, 11 July 1951.
33. See below, p. 329.
34. See below, p. 253.
35. RGS Archives, Report by HM Inspectors 1956.
36. RGS Governors' Minutes, Report of House Committee to Governors, 6 November 1958.

NOTES

37. See below, p. 255.
38. S. Middlebrook, *Newcastle upon Tyne: Its Growth and Achievement*, (Newcastle 1950).
39. Published by the Royal Grammar School in 1974.
40. *Novo*, March and December 1956.
41. RGS Governors' Minutes, July 1955: Report of the School Medical Officer.
42. Much of the information about the curriculum is based on the Report by HM Inspectors 1956.
43. See above, p. 189.
44. *Report of the Secondary School Examinations Council*, (London 1947); Ministry of Education Circular 168, April 1948.
45. Ibid.
46. The age limit was relaxed with effect from 1953: Ministry of Education Circular 251, April 1952.
47. RGS Archives, Speech Day Programmes 1950, 1951, 1952: Headmaster's Reports.
48. *Novo*, December 1955.
49. *Novo*, July 1953: unfortunately no copy of the film is known to be extant.
50. *Novo*, December 1954. The first service was held on 5 November 1954.
51. RGS Governors' Minutes, 26 March 1957.
52. *Novo*, January 1964.
53. Information derived from lists given in Speech Day Programmes, RGS Archives.
54. RGS Governors' Minutes 22 July 1955.
55. Mackenzie, p. 425.
56. All the tables of examination results, State Scholarships and LEA awards are calculated from lists in Speech Day Programmes, RGS Archives, and the figures must be regarded as approximate.
57. The Examining Boards were not permitted to award distinctions at 'A' level until 1953: *Report of Secondary School Examinations Council*, April 1953.
58. Information about extra-curricular activities is derived entirely from *Novo*, 1945–60.
59. *Novo*, April 1960.

INDEX

INDEX

Edinburgh, City, 40
Edinburgh University, 57, 187, 192
Education, Board of, See Board of
  Education
Education, Ministry of, See Ministry of
  Education
Ehrlich, Dr. H., 116
Elders, J., 230, 295, 297, 309, 310
Eldon, Lord, See Scott, John
Ellis, Dr. E., 230
Erasmus, Desiderius, 31, 60
Ewbank, H., 15, 16, 18
Exclusion Crisis, 36

Fagin, H., 165
Faustus, Doctor, Plate XX
Featherston, W., 276
Fenwick, J., 25
Ferne, J., 49
Fife, Sir John, 71, 92
Fisher, H.A.L., 173
Fitch, Sir Joshua, 133
Fleming Committee, 213, 214
Fletcher, Prof. G.B.A., 218
Fowberry, R., 19, 20, 22, 330
Fraser, Sir James, 278
Fremingham School, 103

Gandy, H., 219
Gardiner, D., 19
Gardiner, R., 19
Garnett, Prof., 127
Garthwaite, R., 35, 36, 37, 327
Gateshead, 11, 59, 62, 131, 139, 144,
  192, 193, 282, 307
Gateshead Education Authority, 266,
  267
George VI, 291
George, C., 307
Gibson, D., 24
Gibson, T., 22, 23, 330
Giessen University, 97
Gilpin, A., 33, 34
Glasgow University, 86
Goodhard, Dr. A.L., 238
Gottingen University, 192
Gower, R., 35, 36
Grammar Schools, Decline of, 39-40,
  42, 60-64, 72, 73
Grantham, Mrs. V., 219, 226
Gray, F., 22, 26
Gray, H., 11, 19, 330
Gray, J., 10, 11, 330
Gray, R., 34, 35

Gray, W., 20
Gregson, T.L., 96, 106
Grey, Earl, 162
Grey, William Lord, of Wark, 23, 26
Gudge, M., 28
Gurney, (?), 143

Haden, W.D., 290, 299, 301-10 *passim,*
  330
Hadow, Dr., 162, 170
Haileybury School, 175, 187
Haldane, R.B., 138, 152
Hall, N., 26, 28, 34
Hall, Dr. Wilfred, 218
Hall, W., 48, 55
Hammond, J.L., 84, 86, 96, 97, 105,
  106, 107, 111
Harrison, R., 58
Harrow School, 165, 238
Hart Vicarage, 79
Hartburn, 17, 21
Hartlib, S., 28, 29, 30, 31, 35
Hartlib, S., the younger, 30
Hartwell Exhibitions, 55
Harvey, E.G., 219
Hastings, Henry, Earl of Huntingdon,
  14, 15
Haydon Bridge Grammar School, 51, 62
Headlam, T., 77
Headmasters' Conference, 166, 175
Health, Ministry of, See Ministry of
  Health
Heath, Edward, Prime Minister, 304
Herdman, J.A., 270, 275, 290
Heworth, 50
Hexham, 33, 200, 312
Hexham Grammar School, 42, 47
High Court of Justice, 117
Hitler, Adolf, 275, 280
Hobbs, Thomas, 52
Holden, W., 52
Horsley, T., 7, 8, 210, 223, 273
Houghton-le-Spring Grammar School,
  57, 59
Howell, A., 219
Howick, Lord, 305
Hull Grammar School, 19, 60, 124, 165
Hunter-Blair, Dr. P., 218
Huntley, Mr., 283, 284
Hutton, Dr. C., 58, 59

Illinois University, 192
Industrial Fund, The, 226
Innerd, W., 278

354

INDEX

Inspectorate of Schools, His/Her
 Majesty's, 35-38, 147, 148, 153, 154,
 156, 160, 165, 208, 216
Isle of Man, King William's College,
 220, 229
James VI and I, 17
James, Dr. E., 238
Jamieson, I., 329
Johns, R., 19
Johnson, A.E., 270, 275
Johnson, J., 33
Jurin, James, 43, 45, 48, 49, 50, 51, 63,
 330, Plate IX

Kenyon, Lord Chief Justice, 42
Kirby Lonsdale School, 35
Kirby Stephen Grammar School, 42
Knowles, G.F., 309
Knox, Vicesimus, 63
Korean War, 291
Krisopp-Read, W.H., 219

Labour Party, 174, 253, 266, 267
Lamb, H., 55
Lambert, Sir Arthur, 186, 204, 218
Lambton, H., 328
Lance, P., 270, 273
Latham, Mr., 121
Laws, A.R., 6, 7, 71, 126, 192, 210, 223,
 251, 270, 273
Layton, Prof. D., 229, 297
Leblique, L.B., 274
Leech, Dr. J.W., 186
Leeds Grammar School Case, The,
 64-65
Lemington Adult School, 199
Leipzig University, 57
Leyden University, 57
Liberal Party, 266, 267
Libraries, 20, 65
Licensing of Schoolmasters, 52
Liddell, J., 309
Liddle, T., 327
Lilburne, J., 22, 23, Plate VIII
Little, A.W., 269
Liverpool College, 112, 132
Locke, John, 52, 68
Lodge, Edmund, 44, 45, 48, 49, 50, 51,
 55, 56, 57, 329
Lodge, Edmund, the younger, 55
Logan, S.C., 91, 123, 124, 125, 126, 128,
 129, 131, 132, 133, 134, 152, 156, 157,
 158, 159, 161, 163, 164-65, 175, 187,
 330, Chapter IV *passim*, Plates III,
 XIII

London, 13, 26, 28, 29, 30, 41, 65, 98,
 107, 119, 142, 203, 290, 327
London, Schools
 Chelsea, College of St. Mark and St.
  John, 194
 City of London School, 80
 Hackney School, 45
 Hammersmith Godolphin School, 106
 Hammersmith Latymer Upper
  School, 132
 Islington Owen's School, 220-21, 293
 Kensington Proprietary School, 80
 Mercers' School, 27, 194
 St. Paul's School, 27
 Southwark St. Saviour's School, 29
 University, 192, 193
 University College London, 87
Longley, Sir Henry, 139
Losh, J., 83
Louvain University, 6, 10
Lowes, J., 79, 81
Luke, G., 309
Lumsden, E., 24, 25
Lunn, Sir George, 162, 169, 171, 186,
 195, 196, 204
Lusmore, C.R., 126
Lyon, P.H.B., 238
Lytton, Sir Henry, 273

McDonald, J., 306
MacDonald, K., 307
MacDonald, Ramsay, Prime Minister,
 195
MacKail, Mr., 157
Mackenzie, E., 71, 77
Macmillan, Harold, Prime Minister, 292
Maddison, L., 327
Manchester Grammar School, 44, 54,
 57, 68, 118, 157, 238, 242
Manners, M., 44, 56, 59
Markham, L., 218
Marris, Sir William, 186
Martin, P.M., 238
Matthew, Bishop Toby, of Durham, 15,
 17
Meaken, D., 290, 309
Meaken, L., 304
Metcal, J., 36
Middlebrook, S., 221, 229, 230, 279,
 290, 298, Plate XII
Military Academies, 111
Milner, A.F., 199, 200, 229, 276
Ministry of Education, 214, 215, 216,
 217, 223, 233, 245

INDEX

INDEX

Plender, William Lord, 175, 202-03, 227, 329

Ponteland, 21

Privy Council, 13, 14, 15, 21

Pye, R., 270

Raimes, J., 9, 10, 11, 26

Rand, S., 29

Ravensworth, Earl of, 106

Regulations for Secondary Schools (1907), 165

Revolution, of 1688, 36

Richardson, T.M., 123, 128, 132, 134, 145, 149, 158, 162

Ridley, M., 6

Ridley, Viscount, 219

Riots in schools, 32

Ritschel, Georg, 30, 32, 33, 36, 327, 330

Robbins Report, 303

Roberts, W.E. (Michael), 188, 193-95, 200-01, 229, 272, 274, 275, 280

Robinson, A.C.H., 274

Robinson, M.G., 193, 307, 308

Robson, Gladys, 219

Robson, R.E., 218

Rothbury Grammar School, 67

Rowland, T.H., 31

Rowmaine, R., 23, 24

Royal College of Physicians, 51

Royal Commissions

Bryce Commission, 138-39, 143

Charity Commission, 42, 104, 111, 119, 120, 121, 123, 126, 127, 134, 135, 139, 140, 141, 145, 147, 181, 182, 183, 264

Endowed Schools Commission, 111, 118

Public Schools Commission, 258-60, 261, 262, 268

Schools Inquiry Commission (Taunton), 76, 84, 92, 93, 111, 133, 139

Royal Grammar School

Age of admittance, 62, 67, 124, 225, 267

Age of leaving, 67, 112, 113, 124, 130, 141, 144, 153, 163, 189

Appeals, 254, 255, 256, 257, 264

Arms, Coat of, 210

Assisted Places Scheme, 263, 265-68, 312, 320

Association Football, 125

Boarding, 48, 93, 107, 110, 146, 313

Branch School, The, 132-33, 135, 137, 141, 144, 164

Royal Grammar School (cont.)

Bursarship, 219, 317

Camps, 194, 200-01, 229, 237, 247, 275, 280, 287, 300, 309, 317

Charlotte Square, RGS at, 96, 99, 107, 110, 115

Classes, size of, 5, 318

Clerk to Governers, 219

Clubs, See Extra-curricular Activiti

Combined Cadet Force, 221, 226, 2 247, 293, 309, 317

Corporal punishment, 32, 68, 274

Criticism of school, 66, 310

Curriculum, 31, 32, 60-64, 73, 74, 7 76, 81, 94, 103, 112, 140, 147, 148, 163, 224, 230-31, 235, 246, 252, 295 299, 302, 313, 316, 322

Daily routine, 32, 67, 105, 152, 286

Debts, 116-19, 147, 156, 174, 254

Decline, 43-44, 68, 70, 71, 72, 98

Direct Grant Status, 179, 184, 214, 228, 254, 256, 257-65, 304, 312

Disciplinary problems, 293, 300-01, 303-04

Drama, 200, 227, 249, 275, 277, 29

Endowments, 45, 80, 90, 102, 103, 104, 111, 114, 117, 119, 123, 128, 1 168, 183, 184, 217

Enrolment, 53, 54, 63, 71, 72, 74, 7 76, 79, 81, 96, 97, 107, 113, 118, 12 130, 131, 133, 135, 148, 153, 154, 1 161, 166, 172, 175, 179, 211, 224-25 252, 262, 267, 268, 287-88, 289, 299 302, 303, 317

Eskdale Terrace, RGS at, 146-47, 170, 257, 277, 311, Plates IV, V, VI Building developments at, 150-51 201-05, 225-27, 252-57

Evacuation in wartime, 178, 184, 18 205-09, 212, 213, 280, 313

Examinations, 85, 103, 203, 286

Entrance, 154, 164, 172, 217, 228 267, 269

GCE, 178, 231-35, 242-46, 298-99 300, 303

Higher School Certificate, 189, 19 211, 232-33, 235, 242-44

School Certificate, 232-33, 235, 24 244, 274

University Locals, 86, 111, 114, 1

Exclusion Crisis, 36

Extra-curricular activities, 125, 152, 197, 198, 236, 249, 252, 266, 275, 28 286-87, 309, 316, 318, 323

INDEX

359

INDEX

INDEX